Intelligence and Intelligence A

This book tracks post-9/11 developments in national security and policing intelligence and their relevance to new emerging areas of intelligence practice such as corrections, biosecurity, private industry and regulatory environments. Developments are explored thematically in three broad parts:

- Applying intelligence
- Understanding structures
- Developing a discipline

Issues explored include: understanding intelligence models; the strategic management challenges of intelligence; intelligence capacity building; and the ethical dimensions of intelligence practice. Using case studies collected from wide-ranging interviews with leaders, managers and intelligence practitioners from a range of practice areas in Australia, Canada, New Zealand, the UK and the USA, *Intelligence and Intelligence Analysis* identifies examples of good practice across countries and agencies that may be relevant to other settings.

Uniquely bringing together significant theoretical and practical developments in a sample of traditional and emerging areas of intelligence, this book provides readers with a more holistic and inter-disciplinary perspective on the evolving intelligence field across several different practice contexts.

This book will be relevant to a broad audience including intelligence practitioners and managers working across all fields of intelligence (national security, policing, private industry and emerging areas). The book will also be useful for intelligence researchers as well as students taking courses in policing and intelligence analysis.

Patrick F. Walsh is a senior lecturer (criminal intelligence) at the Australian Graduate School of Policing, Charles Sturt University, Australia; a Board member of the Australian Institute of Professional Intelligence Officers (AIPIO); and managing editor of the *AIPIO Journal*.

Intelligence and Intelligence Analysis

Patrick F. Walsh

Routledge
Taylor & Francis Group

LONDON AND NEW YORK

First published 2011
by Routledge
2 Park Square, Milton Park, Abingdon, Oxon, OX14 4RN

Simultaneously published in the USA and Canada
by Routledge
711 Third Avenue, New York, NY 10017

Routledge is an imprint of the Taylor & Francis Group, an informa business

British Library Cataloguing in Publication Data
A catalogue record for this book is available from the British Library

Library of Congress Cataloging in Publication Data
Walsh, Patrick F.
Intelligence and intelligence analysis / Patrick F. Walsh.
p. cm.
Includes bibliographical references and index.
1. Intelligence service. 2. Biosecurity. 3. National security.
4. Terrorism–Prevention. I. Title.
JF1525.I6.W385 2011
327.12–dc22
2010048177

ISBN: 978–1–84392–738–9 (hbk)
ISBN: 978–1–84392–739–6 (pbk)
ISBN: 978–0–203–81593–9 (ebk)

Typeset in Times New Roman
by Keystroke, Station Road, Codsall, Wolverhampton

Printed and bound in Great Britain by
CPI Antony Rowe, Chippenham, Wiltshire

In loving memory of Craig Glenroy Patterson, 29/10/66–15/9/08

Ja, du weisst es, teur Seele,
Das ich fern von dir mich quale.

Contents

Illustrations

Foreword

Whether you are a student of intelligence or practising intelligence as a civilian, or a member of a defence force, police organization or law enforcement body, you will find *Intelligence and Intelligence Analysis* to be an excellent contemporary examination of intelligence practice. The author, Patrick F. Walsh, is an experienced practitioner in the field of intelligence, having worked in national security as well as transnational and organized crime agencies. He is now an accomplished academic making a valuable contribution to the knowledge and practice of intelligence.

At the time of the Global Financial Crisis in 2008, I asked many business leaders both in Australia and overseas how the crisis came upon us so quickly. How, I asked, with all the sophistication of environmental scanning and budget forecasting models employed by developed economies, did this happen without anyone seeing it? In a world where every developed nation typically has financial regulatory agencies, treasury departments and even access to the expertise of the World Bank and the International Monetary Fund, the Global Financial Crisis impacted almost without warning.

So if the best minds in the world cannot see these things coming, how do the rest of us establish an *intelligence discipline* that will predict crime and crime trends? In a period where terms such as *petabytes* (a thousand terabytes) and *exabytes* (a thousand petabytes) are becoming commonplace, we have to adopt practices and systems that will examine the data, make sense of them and give leaders an opportunity to make the right decision. This book examines current models and systems of the intelligence process and explores future models such as *competitive analytics*.

I have always regarded the role of intelligence as similar to that of the market researcher. There needs to be someone who can say with a degree of certainty and confidence where to place resources to maximize impact. Ideally, this would be done to improve efficiency and reduce costs as well as have a lasting impact, such as the dismantling of an organized crime syndicate.

Intelligence and Intelligence Analysis provides a critical examination of the development of the discipline of intelligence in a variety of professions from national security agencies to police to corrections. The author compares the developments in five countries: Australia, Canada, New Zealand, the United States of America and the United Kingdom. The book takes into account a variety of government inquiries including the 9/11 Commission Report, the US Senate Committee on the Judiciary Concerning Detainee Interrogation Techniques, the Clarke Inquiry conducted in Australia in 2008, the O'Connor Commission in Canada in 2006 and the Intelligence and Security Committee report into the London terrorist attacks in 2005.

In the past decade, many commentators have criticized intelligence collection techniques but there are few bodies of work that address the *ethical considerations* arising out of intelligence collection techniques and intelligence reporting. This book examines the efficacy of reform legislation governing intelligence collection and dissemination as well as the tension between professional and objective systems of intelligence analysis and political expediency.

Just as globalization brought with it transnational crime and new national security threats, so will developments in technology and the *connected* world of today bring with it a whole new suite of problems to be defined and solved. Issues of culture, education, intelligence sharing and speed of delivery will need to be addressed.

Intelligence and Intelligence Analysis discusses the evolution of the practice of intelligence from discipline to profession and in between. Importantly, it recommends education as the pinnacle to improved performance, provided there are clear standards and monitoring practices in place.

The book looks at some of the committees formed by governments to ensure better intelligence outcomes such as the National Intelligence Co-ordination Committee in Australia, the Intelligence Assessments Committee in Canada and the Office of the Director of National Intelligence in the USA. It examines improvements to the skill level of intelligence personnel by looking at education and career structure and, finally, the book looks at the important area of intelligence research.

Where criticism has been levelled at intelligence agencies in the past, much of it has been about using outdated structures and systems to collect, analyse and share the intelligence product. *Intelligence and Intelligence Analysis* concludes by recommending a research strategy that will seek to continuously improve the discipline and direction of the intelligence role, including consensus on definitions of intelligence and analysis.

After all, the market research strategies adopted in the private sector over the same period have adapted to a whole new set of practices aimed at maximizing profits and reducing costs. Why should policing and national security be any different?

This book offers considerable potential for a better understanding and practice of intelligence for the newcomer to the role as well as experienced practitioners. It is a compendium of past practices and theories, commissions of inquiry, government policies and legislation from five nations, and ideas about how to improve intelligence performance. It is essential reading for anyone who practises in the discipline of intelligence.

Mick Keelty, APM
Former Commissioner of the Australian Federal Police

Preface

This book started with an interest in understanding how intelligence and intelligence analysis practice is changing in a *post-post-9/11* world. After the initial flurry of intelligence reforms post 9/11 in Australia, Canada, New Zealand, the UK and the USA, intelligence practice in these countries is now being shaped by a security environment that is yet to be fully understood. However, we know enough about the security environment to suggest that its global, national and local manifestations are more networked than perhaps at any time in modern history. What are the implications of this for intelligence and intelligence analysis? The large, historic and backdrop issues of war and peace between nations remain critical, yet intelligence as a service to decision-makers needs to adapt more widely to an ever increasing suite of threats by 'global outlaws' emerging at different levels of the security environment. The growing complexity of the security environment, where the boundaries of foreign, military, domestic, policing and national security intelligence are becoming blurred, suggests that a more holistic understanding of 'intelligence' is required. This book is a small step in that direction.

In summary, the objective is to bring together in the one volume 'traditional areas' of intelligence practice (national security and policing) and 'emerging' practice areas. In part this approach is to address what I argue is a siloing of intelligence studies. There is an increasing body of works being published about intelligence, but they generally focus on national security or policing issues rather than attempting to bring these together in order to provide a greater synthesis of what intelligence practice is becoming ten years on from 9/11.

While there will always be boundaries between different intelligence practice contexts such as national security, policing and emerging areas, the common thread will be how intelligence is applied and whether it constitutes good practice. The complexity of the security environment and the increasing need for different practice contexts to work in more fused ways suggest that no practice area holds the monopoly on good ideas; and so a more holistic and inter-disciplinary understanding of intelligence practice will benefit all practitioners.

In addition to arguing for a holistic approach to intelligence and intelligence analysis, this book seeks to address three major questions: (1) what is intelligence?; (2) what makes intelligence practice effective?; and (3) is there a discipline of intelligence? All three of these questions are interconnected and seem to me at least to be important foundations to keep in mind for understanding how intelligence can help decision-makers make better sense out of a complex and often bewildering security environment.

This book is aimed at a broad audience: intelligence executives, managers, analysts, researchers, academics and students. The emphasis is on practitioner insights on a range of themes. I wanted the book to be more than anything a reflection on what practitioners are doing and how that may improve intelligence practice as well as contributing to the three central questions of the book listed above. I am particularly mindful to produce a work that critiqued practice, but above all highlighted positive examples of good practice. My own view is that there has been enough 'negative press' about various intelligence agencies in recent years, and it is now time to investigate where good practice is occurring and disseminate the lessons learnt from these examples more widely.

Acknowledgements

This work would not have been possible without the support and contribution of a number of people. For most of the interviews conducted for the book I have been able to acknowledge people's contributions throughout the text. There are some contributors who provided me with valuable insights, but did not wish their comments to be attributed and I have respected these requests. In either case, I am extremely grateful for everyone's contribution. I found people were generally frank, open and honest with their insights and I think the book is richer for these.

There are some people and organizations I particularly want to thank for being so generous with their support and time. First, I wish to thank Glen. Thanks mate for everything! Thanks also to Julio for playing the role of 'mentor' even though it was sometimes like being at boot camp. A very big thanks to my friend Victoria Herrington for her support during this project. I am particularly indebted to Dr Robert Fahlman (RCMP), Mark Evans OBE (New Zealand Police), the FBI, NYPD, LAPD and Department of Homeland Security.

I am also very grateful to my employer, Charles Sturt University in Australia, for providing me with special studies program leave in 2009 to do much of the research for the book. I would also like to thank Susan Dunsmore, Maggie Lindsey-Jones and the team at Keystroke for their invaluable assistance. Lastly, I wish to thank Brian Willan for 'signing me up' originally and the Routledge team for their professionalism and patience.

List of abbreviations

ABIN	Australian Biosecurity Intelligence Network
ACC	Australian Crime Commission
ACID	Australian Criminal Intelligence Database
ACIIS	Automated Criminal Intelligence Information System
ACLU	American Civil Liberties Union
ACPO	Associations of Chief Policing Officers
AFP	Australian Federal Police
AIPIO	Australian Institute of Professional Intelligence Officers
AIS	Analytic Integrity and Standards
AMCOS	Auckland Metro Crime and Operational Support Group
APEC	Asia-Pacific Economic Cooperation
APPSC	Australasian Police Professional Standards Council
AQTF	Australian Qualifications Training Framework
AQUIS	Australian Quarantine Inspection Service
ARF	ASEAN Regional Forum
ASIC	Australian Securities Investments Commission
ASIO	Australian Security Intelligence Organisation
ASIS	Australian Secret Intelligence Service
ATO	Australian Taxation Office
AUSTRAC	Australian Transaction Reports and Analysis Centre
BJA	Bureau of Justice Administration
BOM	Board of Management
BWC	Biological and Toxin Weapons Convention
CACP	Canadian Association of Chiefs of Police
CAD	computer-aided dispatch
CAP	Career Analyst Program
CASIS	Canadian Association for Security Intelligence Studies
CBRN	chemical, biological, radiological and nuclear
CCI	Critical Command Information
CCIM	Canadian Criminal Intelligence Model
CCIS	Canadian Criminal Intelligence System
CCS	Civil Contingencies Secretariat
CDC	Centers for Disease Control and Prevention

CHF	Canadian Hunger Foundation
CHIS	covert human intelligence sources
CIA	Central Intelligence Agency
CII	correctional intelligence initiative
CIROC	Canadian Integrated Response to Organized Crime
CISC	Criminal Intelligence Service of Canada
CLER	Commonwealth Law Enforcement Arrangements Review
COBR	Cabinet Office Briefing Rooms
CRIME	Consolidated Records Intelligence Mining Environment
CSC	Correctional Service Canada
CSE	Communications Security Establishment
CSIS	Canadian Security Intelligence Service
CTAG	Combined Threat Assessment Group
DCI	Director of Central Intelligence
DEA	Drug Enforcement Agency
DEFRA	Department for Environment, Food and Rural Affairs
D Geo Int	Directorate of Geospatial Intelligence
DGIA	Defence Geographic and Imagery Intelligence
DHS	Department of Homeland Security
DIA	Defense Intelligence Agency
DIGO	Defence Imagery and Geospatial Organisation
DIO	Defence Intelligence Organisation
DIS	Defence Intelligence Staff
DMIs	District Managers: Intelligence
DNI	Director of National Intelligence
DOJ	Department of Justice
DSD	Defence Signals Directorate
ECCC	Extraordinary Chambers in the Courts of Cambodia
ECPA	Electronic Communications Privacy Act
EPIC	Electronic Privacy Information Center
FBI	Federal Bureau of Investigation
FIG	Field Intelligence Group
FISA	Foreign Intelligence Surveillance Act
FISC	Foreign Intelligence Surveillance Court
GCHQ	Government Communications Headquarters
GCSB	Government Communications Security Bureau
GDP	gross domestic product
GIS	geographic information systems
GIWG	Global Intelligence Working Group
GNP	gross national product
GPHIN	Global Public Health Intelligence Network
HDI	Human Development Index
HIDTAs	High Intensity Drug Trafficking Areas
HMIC	Her Majesty's Inspectorate of Constabulary
HPA	Health Protection Agency

HSIE	Health Security Intelligence Enterprise
HSPD	Homeland Security Presidential Directives
HSTA	Homeland Security Threat Assessment
IACA	International Association of Crime Analysts
IACP	International Association of Chiefs of Police
IALEIA	International Association for Law Enforcement Intelligence Analysts
IARPA	Intelligence Advanced Research Project Activity
IAS	Intelligence Assessment Secretariat
ICE	Immigration Customs Enforcement
ICSR	International Centre for the Study of Radicalisation and Political Violence
ICTY	International Criminal Tribunal for the former Yugoslavia
IGIS	Inspector General for Intelligence and Security
IIEA	International Intelligence Ethics Association
ILM	Integrated Lifetime Management Programme
INR	Bureau of Intelligence and Research
IPCC	Independent Police Complaints Commission
IRTPA	Intelligence Reform and Terrorism Prevention Act
ISC	Intelligence and Security Committee
ISE	Information Sharing Environment
ITAC	Integrated Threat Assessment Centre
JCLEC	Jakarta Centre for Law Enforcement Cooperation
JIC	Joint Intelligence Committee
JIS	Jam'iyyat Ul-Islam Is-Saheed (or the Assembly of Authentic Islam)
JRIC	Joint Regional Intelligence Center
JTAC	Joint Terrorism Analysis Centre
JTTF	Joint Terrorism Task Force
KDD	knowledge discovery and dissemination
LAPD	Los Angeles Police Department
LASD	Los Angeles Sheriff's Department
LCIP	Leadership in Criminal Intelligence Program
LEIT	Law Enforcement Intelligence Training Committee
MAFBNZ	Ministry of Agriculture and Fisheries Biosecurity New Zealand
MCA	Military Commissions Act
NAB	National Assessments Bureau
NATO	North Atlantic Treaty Organization
NBACC	National Biodefense Analysis and Countermeasures Center
NBIS	National Biosurveillance Integration System
NCA	National Crime Authority
NCIS	National Criminal Intelligence Service
NCPE	National Centre for Policing Excellence
NCTC	National Counterterrorism Center
NCTR	National Criminal Target Report
NEC	National Executive Committee
NGA	National Geospatial Intelligence Agency

NGO	non-governmental organization
NIC	National Intelligence Centre
NICC	National Intelligence Coordination Committee
NIM	National Intelligence Model
NIO	National Intelligence Office
NIU	National Intelligence University
NJTTF	National Joint Terrorism Task Force
NOMS	National Offender Management Service
NPIA	National Policing Improvement Agency
NRO	National Reconnaissance Office
NSA	National Security Agency
NSIC	National Strategic Intelligence Course
NSIP	National Security and International Policy Group
NSLs	National Security Letters
NSW	New South Wales
NTAC	National Threat Assessment Centre
NVQ	National Vocational Qualification
NYPD	New York Police Department
NZ	New Zealand
NZIIP	New Zealand Institute of Intelligence Professionals
NZP	New Zealand Police
NZSIS	New Zealand Security Intelligence Service
OCIJ	Office of the Co-Investigating Judges
OCP	Office of the Co-Prosecutor
OCTA	Organised Crime Threat Assessment
ODNI	Office of the Director of National Intelligence
OECD	Organisation for Economic Cooperation and Development
OFCANZ	Organised Financial Crime Agency of New Zealand
ONA	Office of National Assessments
OSJ	Operation Safe Jails
OSP	Office of Special Plans
PDG	Policing Development Group
PDIP	Professional Development in Intelligence Programme
PESTELO	Political, Economic, Social, Technological, Environmental, Legislative and Organizational
PIERS	Prevention, Intelligence, Enforcement, Reassurance and Support
PIF	Pacific Island Forum
PNG	Papua New Guinea
PNHQ	Police National Headquarters
PRS	Priority Rating System
PSI	Proliferation Security Initiative
PTCCC	Pacific Transnational Crime Coordination Centre
PTCN	Pacific Transnational Crime Network
RAHS	Risk Assessment and Horizon Scanning Programme
RAMSI	Regional Assistance Mission to Solomon Islands

RAT	Routine Activity Theory
RCMP	Royal Canadian Mounted Police
RFI	Request for Information
RFP	Request for Proposal
RGC	Royal Government of Cambodia
RISS	Regional Information Sharing Systems
ROIC	Regional Operations Intelligence Center
RSIP	Royal Solomon Islands Police Force
RTCC	Real Time Crime Center
SARA	Scan, Analyse, Respond, and Assess
SAR	suspicious activity reporting
SARS	severe acute respiratory syndrome
SCCA	Society of Certified Criminal Analysts
SCNS	Secretaries Committee on National Security
SET	Strategic Execution Team
SIPRNet	Secret Internet Protocol Router Network
SIRC	Security Intelligence Review Committee
SMS	Strategic Management System
SNA	social network analysis
SOCA	Serious Organised Crime Agency
SSCI	Senate Select Committee on Intelligence
STARS	Strategic Targeting and Resource Selection
SWOT	Strengths, Weaknesses, Opportunities and Threats
T&CG	tasking and coordination group
TCU	Transnational Crime Unit
TEW	Terrorism Early Warning
TRAM	Target Risk Assessment Methodology
UN	United Nations
UNDP	United Nations Development Program
USAMRIID	United States Army Medical Research Institute of Infectious Diseases
VPD	Vancouver Police Department
VPIM	Victoria Police Intelligence Model
WHO	World Health Organization
WMD	weapons of mass destruction

Introduction

Intelligence practice, as it is traditionally understood in areas of policing, security and defence, has undergone significant changes in the past decade. The post-9/11 surge – both in investment and interest in all issues regarding intelligence – is changing how scholars, practitioners and the community view intelligence in novel ways. Despite this great focus on 'intelligence', there are still many unanswered questions about intelligence and intelligence analysis in the current 'post-post-9/11' environment.

A healthy discussion persists among academics, practitioners and commentators about the role of intelligence and intelligence analysis. Despite this, we seem no closer to identifying what intelligence means more broadly now, a decade on from 9/11. Presuming that future discussion will clarify what intelligence is now in an increasingly complex security environment, there are also other fundamental questions to be answered. One of these is: *what makes intelligence practice effective?* Another important issue that needs addressing is *the extent to which intelligence is a discipline* and *what the implications of this would be for intelligence practice.* An increasingly complex security environment defined more by 'global outlaws' than conflict between states suggests there ought to be some urgency by scholars and practitioners in responding to such questions. There are no easy answers to these questions. One of the complicating factors in finding answers is that the intelligence field is as fragmented as some of the intelligence communities that will be discussed in this book. While the extent of fragmentation across intelligence communities varies, it has resulted in a limited opportunity for practitioners in different areas of intelligence to learn from each other. The relative siloing of intelligence into 'policing', 'national security' or 'private sector' intelligence, has also produced a similar fragmentation of intelligence scholarship. Scholars tend to work in one field such as policing, rather than across one or more fields. This has also resulted in less cross-fertilization of ideas, knowledge and theory building within the broader intelligence field. At the same time, the fluid security environment has resulted in different understandings between scholars and practitioners on what 'security' is, which obviously impacts on how they approach their work. And a broader security environment has also brought in other newer intelligence players. In this book, I refer to these 'newer players' as areas of emerging intelligence practice. The entry of these into the security environment also adds to this fragmentation and siloing of intelligence knowledge and practice.

The fragmentation of practice and lack of theory *within* and *across* different fields of intelligence, most importantly, have contributed to missed opportunities for the integration of intelligence knowledge into tactical, operational and strategic decision-making. Since 9/11, while a greater body of research is now available on several features, such as 'intelligence failure' (Zegart 2007) and accountability issues (Gill and Phythian 2006), a more evidence-based approach to intelligence across all its practice contexts is needed in order to assess how good intelligence practice can be better integrated into decision-making.

The three questions posed in the Preface – (1) what is intelligence?; (2) what makes intelligence practice effective?; and (3) is there a discipline of intelligence? – are the subject of this book. These questions are addressed by taking a holistic perspective to intelligence – one that will examine both the traditional and emerging practice boundaries of intelligence practice. While national security or policing intelligence officers review their own literature to address such questions *for them*, these answers will be richer and more informed by looking outside their domain to other practice areas of intelligence, particularly in attempting to answer the question 'what does good practice look like?' Given the fragmented nature of the intelligence field, this book's main contribution is to survey significant theoretical and practical developments in a sample of traditional and emerging areas of intelligence in the one volume rather than separately. The aim is to provide readers with a holistic perspective on the evolving intelligence field across several different practice contexts. This will allow practitioners in one field to learn about good practice examples and theoretical developments in other contexts. For example, there are numerous examples of how risk management, analytical tools, and even models such as intelligence-led policing as practised in one area are also relevant in others. Yet 'good practice' in one area is not necessarily being adopted elsewhere due to siloing of practice environments and lack of cross-disciplinary connections.

Using case studies collected by interviewing leaders, managers and intelligence practitioners from a range of practice areas in Australia, Canada, New Zealand, the UK and the USA, I have identified examples of good practice, which I hope will help encourage a greater cross-fertilization of ideas throughout the field, and also progress the theory and practice of intelligence. The case studies range across many themes in the book, including emerging intelligence practice, capacity building, implementing frameworks and management issues. I have taken care not to unduly extrapolate from any of these case studies, but the book is richer for the insights from practitioners. Their insights contribute to building evidence of what constitutes the good practice that academics and practitioners need to build further on.

The three critical questions above are challenging and, given the dynamic nature of the security environment, answering them is a bit like trying to shoot at a fast moving target. The difficulty in achieving this is compounded by taking a more holistic view of intelligence rather than just focusing on national security or policing contexts. I argue the security environment and decision-makers' responses to it are in many respects making what were always artificial boundaries between practice contexts even less meaningless in the future. However the future security environment unfolds, intelligence will play a role, and these three questions will remain central to our understanding of what intelligence is and how to improve it.

The structure of the book

The chapters are organized according to three broad themes: *applying intelligence, understanding structures* and *developing a discipline*, each with its own Part. This structure, and the collection of relevant chapters in each Part, are designed to address different aspects of the three central questions discussed earlier. The individual chapters are laid out in the following manner. In Part I ('Applying intelligence'), Chapter 1 ('Traditional intelligence practice') traces the origins and functions of intelligence practice in the national security and policing intelligence contexts. I refer to these contexts as 'traditional intelligence practice' as historically they have been the oldest and commonly used forms of intelligence practice, excluding military intelligence. The aim of the review is to place the 'newer applications' of intelligence, discussed in Chapters 2 and 3 into historical context. Chapter 1 will also show how developments in national security and policing in Australia, Canada, New Zealand, the UK and the USA have shaped our understanding of what intelligence is over time in other areas. In particular, the chapter's survey of developments in national security and policing will demonstrate how a 'culture of secrecy' has defined much of traditional intelligence practice. This has created contradictions at times between the need to share sensitive information in a timely way, and an inability to do so due to closed systems. The chapter concludes by suggesting that a similar 'culture of secrecy' and several other doctrinal components have been adopted by practitioners in emerging areas of intelligence practice.

Chapter 2 ('Emerging intelligence practice areas') describes using two case studies (corrections and biosecurity), to demonstrate where and how intelligence methods are being used in newer practice areas; including the private sector, health, customs and corrections. Case study material from Australia, Canada, New Zealand, the UK and the USA will help illustrate how 'cultures of secrecy' and other doctrinal influences from national security and policing, are helping to shape the frameworks and processes of intelligence in emerging areas. The chapter concludes with a summary of the current key challenges confronting intelligence practice in these areas, including, as noted earlier, the current fragmentation between emerging and traditional practice areas. Finally, Chapter 3 ('Intelligence and capacity building') examines how intelligence practice is being applied in vulnerable and fragile states. Discussion is based on two interesting case studies, the Australian Federal Police's (AFP) Pacific Transnational Crime Network (PTCN) and the UN Assistance to the Khmer Rouge Trials in Cambodia. The aim in this chapter is to examine what intelligence means in capacity building contexts, and how to build more effective, sustainable and 'democratic' intelligence systems in fragile states. These questions are increasingly important in the current security environment defined by transnational security threats. For many Western nations, capacity building projects that involve intelligence are an extension of their domestic intelligence capabilities. Therefore, in addition to understanding how such projects are being implemented in recipient countries, it is important to assess how projects enhance the intelligence capabilities of donor countries.

Part II ('Understanding structures') consists of three chapters – again aimed at addressing aspects of the three broad questions posed above. The focus is shifted away from how and in which contexts intelligence has been applied to exploring intelligence as a system of processes and functions that occur in broader structures or frameworks. Chapter 4 ('Intelligence models and frameworks') defines the core components of an intelligence framework. In addition, drawing on interviews and secondary sources, the chapter explores five current intelligence frameworks in Australia, Canada, New Zealand, the UK and the USA to illustrate how frameworks are being implemented, and whether they demonstrate elements of good practice or not. This chapter argues that there has been little reflection by practitioners and researchers on what makes effective and adaptable intelligence frameworks and this needs to change if intelligence agencies are to adapt to the evolving security environment. Chapter 5 ('Building better intelligence frameworks') extends many of the themes in Chapter 4. Using a summary of the key similarities and differences identified between the case studies discussed in Chapter 4 as a foundation, this chapter will provide a deeper theoretical consideration of the components within intelligence frameworks. In particular, case study discussions in Chapter 5 will be used to address three central questions. First, what are the key strengths and weaknesses in the frameworks? Second, to what extent can either the components and/or frameworks be exported to different agencies and contexts? Third (and largely depending on the answers to the two other questions), how can we use this greater understanding of intelligence frameworks and components in different contexts in order to build better practice and promote the growth of theorizing in intelligence?

Chapter 5 concludes by developing a model of what makes an effective intelligence framework, arguing that good practice may be difficult to pin down, but in most cases it will be the result of a combination of sound core intelligence processes and key enabling activities. Chapter 6 ('Intelligence leadership and management') underscores the importance of focused and sustainable leadership in building sound intelligence components and key enabling activities. A case is made that of all the key enabling activities, 'intelligence governance' is the most crucial for leaders to deal with and therefore represents the greatest challenge. The chapter also suggests that the increasingly complex security environment makes the role of intelligence leaders and managers even more pivotal in the future. But leaders and managers will need to create 'better value' from intelligence for decision-makers. Chapter 6 argues that their mastery of a range of issues will be pivotal to whether their organizations can adapt successfully and be seen as effective and valuable by their political masters and the public.

Part III ('Developing a discipline') consists of four chapters, each contributing, albeit in different ways, to addressing the three central questions of this book. Each chapter discusses a range of themes which are relevant to the fundamental questions of what intelligence is, what is good practice, and whether intelligence is a separate 'discipline' of knowledge. Chapter 7 ('Ethics and legislation') addresses the recent ethical debates about intelligence practice, particularly in the national security and policing intelligence contexts. It explains how the post-9/11 security environment has reinforced many of the long-standing ethical dilemmas of intelligence practice. The ethical dimensions of intelligence practice are illustrated using recent examples such as the coercive use of intelligence, involving torture, attempts by political leaders to politicize intelligence and the wikileaks affair. Chapter 7 argues that there needs to be more meeting of minds between theorists and practitioners on how intelligence practice can be informed ethically. The chapter also examines recent reforms and implementation of new accountability and legislative responses to counter-terrorism and organized crime over the last decade, and how they too are driving more ethical and effective practice.

Chapter 8 ('Analytical innovations') draws on analytical themes discussed in earlier chapters. The focus is on highlighting the cognitive, inter-disciplinary and technological innovative dimensions of analysis. Chapter 8 argues that it is the 'inter-disciplinary' origins of intelligence analysis that have not fully been taken advantage of and this has impacted on our understanding of 'what constitutes an intelligence discipline'. Moving forward, it will be the inter-disciplinary nature of intelligence analysis, in addition to some specific technological innovations, where future improvements in the field can potentially be made.

Chapter 9 ('Intelligence education and professionalism') maps recent key developments in intelligence education. It traces the rise, for example, of university course offerings in intelligence across Australia, Canada, New Zealand, the UK and the USA, and in the number of 'industry courses' being offered by intelligence agencies themselves. The chapter argues that much of this growth is welcome. However, it has frequently resulted in ad hoc course development, which may not result in better intelligence training or equip students with the appropriate mix of graduate attributes or competencies required for specific roles. The chapter concludes with a discussion of some key themes of 'intelligence professionalism' including attracting and retaining staff, creating career pathways and continuing professional development.

Chapter 10 ('Research and theory building') uses many of the key themes raised earlier (particularly by Chapter 5) to develop a research strategy for intelligence. The strategy includes examples from areas where current research has made progress to others which remain largely unexplored. The research strategy is not prescriptive or complete. Its main objective is to stimulate greater debate among researchers and academics on the importance of a strategic approach to intelligence research. The second half of the chapter describes current theoretical developments in the intelligence field and explores the extent to which they are linked to research or informed by other fields such as cognitive and social psychology, management and other disciplines. The chapter also identifies a number of factors which are currently inhibiting theorizing in the field.

The final chapter ('Conclusion') draws together key themes throughout the book and the implications for the future development of intelligence and intelligence analysis more broadly across different practice contexts.

Part I

Applying intelligence

1 Traditional intelligence practice

Introduction

This chapter traces the origins and functions of intelligence practice in the 'traditional' environments of national security and policing. It has two aims: first, it will provide a brief overview of how intelligence historically has been applied in Australia, Canada, New Zealand, the UK and the USA. This overview provides a broad thematic discussion of major historical milestones, which have been important in shaping the development of traditional intelligence practice. This discussion sets the scene for further in-depth development of themes, concepts and issues raised in the three Parts of the book (Applying intelligence, Understanding structures and Developing a discipline). Second, the chapter will argue, based on the origins of traditional intelligence practice, that a set of common characteristics has developed, which help to delineate the uniqueness of 'intelligence' from related activities such as research, analysis and information management. I have called these three characteristics an evolving *intelligence tradition.*

While others may argue for a different set of characteristics – even a long list – it is clear from the historical review in this chapter that these characteristics represent at the very least how intelligence has been viewed in the past. This intelligence tradition will continue to shape how traditional approaches to intelligence are applied, but is also relevant to defining understanding how new intelligence structures, processes and methods are being used in emerging areas of intelligence practice discussed in Chapter 2.

The origins and functions of traditional intelligence practice

National security intelligence practice

Defining 'intelligence' in a generic sense, let alone national security intelligence, is contentious, different perspectives are included or excluded depending on the view of the scholar or practitioner. I will not engage in these debates here, and national security intelligence is defined as intelligence collected, analysed and disseminated for decision-makers in the support of the security of the state.

By 'security of the state', I mean not just the prevention or prosecution of wars *between* states, but also security of individuals *within and between* states. The definition draws on the human security agenda, which gained momentum in the mid-1990s (Hampson *et al.* 2002). The *Human Security Report* (HSC 2005) includes the security of people within states from political violence (terrorism, civil war, state collapse), economic vulnerabilities and even disease and natural disasters. This inclusive definition of security is more accurate in tracing how national security intelligence has evolved and responded since the end of the Second World War from a preoccupation with fighting or preventing wars between states to currently supporting a broader human security agenda.

In addition to defining national security intelligence, it is also equally difficult to plot its origins. Intelligence historian David Kahn suggests that the Ancient Egyptians used 'codes' on the walls of their monuments (1996: 71–73), and most students of intelligence will be familiar with the work of fourth-century BC Chinese general Sun Tzu, *The Art of War*. Sun Tzu used a network of spies to gain information about the military capabilities and intentions of enemies (Sun Tzu 2002). The focus here is the broad developments within national security intelligence from the end of the Second World War up to the present, as it was not until this period that we saw the emergence of national civilian intelligence operations with global reach.

Table 1.1 provides a summary of the origins and functions of the major national security intelligence communities of Australia, Canada, New Zealand, the UK and the USA. Broadly, the functions of many agencies across each country are similar. For example, in Table 1.1 it is clear that the UK MI6 and the Central Intelligence Agency (CIA) are involved in the collection of foreign intelligence, and each country has a dedicated sigint collection agency (sigint is a general term for the process of collecting intelligence from intercepted electromagnetic waves, usually referred to as signals). There are of course, several differences between and even within the national security intelligence communities of the countries listed in Table 1.1. Historically, variations have emerged as a result of different organizational structures, political cultures, legal systems and bureaucratic styles, existing in each of these countries.

The historical significance of many of these factors has been well documented, particularly relating to the US and UK communities, in a growing number of volumes on the history of various intelligence agencies. Christopher Andrew's book, *The Defence of the Realm: The Authorised History of MI5* (2009) is a good recent example. However, despite each intelligence agency in Australia, Canada, New Zealand, the UK and the USA following its own historical path, their origins and functions were also shaped by some similar events from the end of the Second World War, through the Cold War and up to the present. The events from 1945 to the present day did help define mutual interests and common values between the intelligence communities of these countries. Mutual interests and broadly similar liberal democratic outlooks also resulted in commonalities developing both within and between intelligence agencies in structure, priority setting and accountability processes.

A detailed discussion of all historical events that have impacted the origins and functions of all national security agencies in each country is beyond the scope of this book. In the USA alone, there are 17 agencies officially designated as part of its national security intelligence community and an entire book could easily be devoted to them alone. Instead, subsequent chapters will examine a selection of thematic changes (e.g. organizational restructure, analytical innovations and legislative reform) in the national security intelligence agencies of the five democratic countries chosen as the subject of this study and how these help us understand the evolution of national security and other practice contexts for intelligence. However, in order to provide some context for this discussion, it is important first to understand the broad historical catalysts for change in national security intelligence agencies from the end of the Second World War to the present.

From post Second World War to post Cold War

Wartime intelligence cooperation between the five allies (Australia, Canada, New Zealand, the UK and the USA), particularly between America and the UK, set the stage for common approaches and cooperation during the Cold War period. Wartime technological advancements such as signals intelligence (sigint), overhead imagery and counter-intelligence also produced greater modernization, specialization and cooperation between the national security intelligence communities in the five countries. These intelligence arrangements became even more formalized in the Cold War period, starting with the 1946 UK/USA Communications Intelligence Agreement, where the five countries agreed to share their sigint collection efforts with each other. This agreement stipulated that the following sigint agencies would share their intelligence: the National Security Agency (the USA), Government Communications Headquarters (the UK), Communications Security Establishment (Canada), the Government Communications Security Bureau (New Zealand) and the Defence Signals Directorate (Australia).

The UK/USA Communications Intelligence Agreement led to some geographical specialization between each country's sigint collection agency. The agreement has been tested through the years, most notably in 1985, when the USA restricted its sigint supply to New Zealand after that country banned nuclear-powered vessels from its ports. The agreement also provided the basis for closer cooperation in other areas of intelligence practice, including humint (human intelligence) and sharing intelligence products. The desire by the USA in particular, but also the other four UK/USA Agreement countries, to contain Soviet interests globally became the central focus for all of their national security intelligence agencies. At the conclusion of the Second World War and the early stages of the Cold War, other non-state actor security interests were largely subservient to or viewed through the prism of the broader Soviet threat. The dominant application of national security intelligence efforts in the latter half of the twentieth century up to the end of the Cold War in 1991, focused on expensive technical intelligence gained from satellite reconnaissance and sigint. The height of the Cold War was more than anything a 'sigint war' between the USA and the Soviet Union. The successful

Table 1.1 Origins and functions of select national security agencies

Types of intelligence	The UK	The USA	Australia	Canada	New Zealand
Signals Intelligence	Government Communications Headquarters (GCHQ) *Est.: 1919*	National Security Agency (NSA) *Est.: 1952*	Defence Signals Directorate (DSD) *Est.: 1947*	Communications Security Establishment Canada (CSE) *Est.: 1946*	Government Communications Security Bureau (GCSB) *Est.: 1977*
Foreign Intelligence (humint*)	Secret Intelligence Service (MI6) *Est.: 1909*	Central Intelligence Agency (CIA) *Est.: 1947*	Australian Secret Intelligence Service (ASIS) *Est.: 1952*	No specific foreign intelligence agency, but CSE provides some foreign intelligence collection via its sigint capabilities.	New Zealand Security Intelligence Service (NZSIS) *Est.: 1956*
Domestic Intelligence	Security Service (MI5) *Est.: 1909*	1. Federal Bureau of Investigation (FBI) *Est.: 1908* 2. Department of Homeland Security (DHS) – *Office of Intelligence and Analysis Est.: 2003*	Australian Security Intelligence Organisation (ASIO) *Est.: 1949*	Canadian Security Intelligence Service (CSIS) *Est.: 1984*	NZSIS
Intelligence Assessment	1. Joint Intelligence Committee (JIC) 2. Joint Terrorism Analysis Centre (JTAC) *Est.: 2003*	1. Office of the Director of National Intelligence (ODNI) *Est.: 2005* 2. CIA *Est.: 1947* 3. Bureau of Intelligence and Research (INR) *Est.: 1946* 4. National Counterterrorism	1. Office of National Assessments (ONA) *Est.: 1977* 2. National Threat Assessment Centre (NTAC) *Est.: 2004*	1. Intelligence Assessment Secretariat (IAS) 2. Integrated Threat Assessment Centre (ITAC) *Est.: 2004*	1. National Assessments Bureau (NAB) *Renamed March 2010 (formerly the External Assessments Bureau)* 2. Combined Threat Assessment Group (CTAG) *Est.: 2004*

	UK	USA	Australia	Canada	New Zealand
		Center (NCTC) *Est.: 2004*			
Military Intelligence	1. Defence Intelligence Staff (DIS) *Est.: 1964*	Defense Intelligence Agency (DIA) *Est.: 1961*	Defence Intelligence Organisation (DIO) *Est.: 1990*	Department of National Defence/Canadian Forces – Director of General Intelligence Production	Directorate of Defence Intelligence and Security *Est.: 1998*
Imagery Intelligence	Defence Geographic and Imagery Intelligence (DGIA) *Est.: 2000*	1. National Reconnaissance Office (NRO) *Est.: 1960* 2. National Geospatial Intelligence Agency (NGA) *Est.: 2003 (prior to 2003 formerly the National Imagery and Mapping Agency (NIMA))*	Defence Imagery and Geospatial Organisation (DIGO) *Est.: 2000*	Directorate of Geospatial Intelligence (D Geo Int)	NZDF Geospatial Intelligence Organisation *Est.: 2008 (prior to 2008 formerly the Joint Geospatial Support Facility)*
Agencies with national policing/law enforcement functions	Metropolitan Police *Est.: 1829*	FBI DHS	Australian Federal Police (AFP) *Est.: 1979*	Royal Canadian Mounted Police (RCMP) *Est.: 1920 (formerly the North-West Mounted Police (Est.: 1873))*	NZ Police *Est.: 1886*
Organized Crime	Serious Organised Crime Agency (SOCA) *Est.: 2006*	FBI	Australian Crime Commission (ACC) *Est.: 2003*	Criminal Intelligence Service Canada (CISC) *Est.: 1970*	Organised Financial Crime Agency of New Zealand (OFCANZ) *Est.: 2008*

* Intelligence collected by humans either through covert means (e.g. espionage) or through official channels (e.g. diplomatic liaison).

prosecution of this war relied on sigint collection agencies having strict control over the knowledge relating to their collection capabilities and which aspects of Soviet capabilities they were targeting. The absolute secrecy adopted by sigint collection agencies contributed significantly to a developing culture of secrecy within national security intelligence agencies during the Cold War and up to the present.

While significant sums were invested in UK/USA Agreement countries' intelligence agencies, these agencies were not able to predict the collapse of the Soviet Union, the country which had been their key threat from 1945 to 1991. The mixed track record of many agencies during the Cold War, and the emergence of a fluid security environment – no longer defined by US–Soviet rivalry – raised questions from some academics, commentators and politicians about the future relevance of such agencies (e.g. Gill 1996a; Draper 1997). Additionally, the incoming first Bush Administration – using the rhetoric of a 'peace dividend' derived from defeating the Soviet Union – was focused on maximizing any savings that could be made from defence and intelligence budgetary allocations. In the 1990s, the Bush and Clinton Administrations, along with Congress, decreased intelligence budgets. For example, during the 1990s, the CIA's budget declined by 18 per cent, which resulted in a 16 per cent reduction in its workforce during this decade (Tenet 2002). Similarly, in 1996, the UK Treasury initiated cuts, which led to a reduction in MI6 staffing levels to about 2150 (Dorril 2001: 780). The collapse of the bipolar security structure of the USA and the Soviet Union revealed a greater diversity of threats, such as international terrorism and drug trafficking, which national security intelligence agencies had always monitored, however, during the height of the Cold War they were not seen as existential threats to the state.

Hence, the first half of the 1990s could be typified as a time of adaptation by national security intelligence agencies to an evolving and less certain security environment. Agency heads were starting to show an increased awareness of, if not complete understanding of, myriad transnational security threats, which progressively began to define the new security environment. On 2 February 1993, R. James Woolsey commented to the Senate Select Committee on Intelligence (SSCI), just before he was confirmed as Director, Central Intelligence, that the security environment was changing. Woolsey, who served as Director of the CIA from 1993 to 1995, described both the complexity of the new security environment and the need for intelligence in the following colorful way: 'We have slain a large dragon by defeating the Soviet Union, but we live now in a jungle filled with a bewildering variety of poisonous snakes, and in many ways the dragon was easier to keep track of' (Woolsey, quoted on Center for Intelligence Studies website). The statement reflected the difficulty that agencies such as the CIA were having in adjusting their collected and analytical assets from a single large and enduring target (the Soviet Union) to a multitudinous number of smaller and more fluid targets. For national security intelligence agencies, efforts to recalibrate intelligence collection assets were made more difficult as policy-makers failed to provide them consistently with a clearly articulated list of their priorities. For example, under the first Clinton Administration, despite some efforts to remedy the collection and analytical priorities framework, terrorism remained a 'Tier 3' (lowest priority issue) (FAS 1995). Despite several Islamist terrorist plots and attacks against US interests from 1993 up to 9/11, including Al Qaeda's October 2000 assault on the US warship *USS Cole* in Yemen, the Bush Administration still had rogue states and their weapons of mass destruction (WMD) as its highest priority (Taylor and Goldman 2004: 425). However, there is no doubt by the end of the 1990s, Australian, Canadian, New Zealand, UK and US intelligence agencies had all developed a sophisticated understanding of the transnational national terrorist threats, particularly of the Al Qaeda 'brand'.

9/11, accountability and the commodification of intelligence

However, the events of 9/11, the first mass casualty terrorist attack on US soil, represented a 'wake-up call' for the US intelligence community. They also had strategic significance for the intelligence communities of Australia, Canada, New Zealand and the UK. Additional events after 9/11 including the nature of intelligence supplied to political leaders about the presence of WMD in Iraq in 2003, the Bali bombings (in October 2002) and the London bombings (in July 2005), also resulted in significant internal reflection for the US, UK and Australian intelligence agencies on their collection and analytical capabilities against such threats. For Canada, the 'wake-up' call for their national security intelligence agencies was not 9/11, but an event nearly two years earlier on the US-Canadian border. When interviewed on 26 August 2009, two senior Canadian Security Intelligence Service (CSIS) officers suggested that the foiled December 1999 attempt by Canadian-Algerian Ahmed Ressam to blow up Los Angeles International Airport became the major catalyst for a greater shift in focus by their agency from counter-intelligence to counter-terrorism. The underlying concern for CSIS officers was that Canada could be a base for attacks against its major trading partner, the USA.

The two significant inquiries after 9/11 – the House and Senate Intelligence Committee's Joint Inquiry (2002) and the 9/11 Commission Report (2004) – produced a series of findings about deficiencies within the US intelligence community, particularly the CIA and the Federal Bureau of Investigation (FBI). Reported deficiencies were numerous, ranging from human error, problems with analysis, collection and information sharing. In many respects, the deficiencies identified reflected earlier issues already noted in at least 14 major studies on intelligence reform from 1995 to 2002 (Zegart 2007: 199–200). The outcomes of the post-9/11 era inquiries have been a great deal of introspection by academics and practitioners about how fit for purpose and accountable national security intelligence agencies are (e.g. Hitz and Weiss 2004; Zegart 2007). The discourse of 'intelligence failure' has become popular again long after Richard Betts' seminal study of the subject in 1978 (Betts 1978). Chapter 6 will explore 'intelligence failure' and 'intelligence reform' more closely and how managers can use the 'lessons learnt' from recent inquiries to promote better practice and organizational adaptability. However, the post-9/11 inquiries in the USA, the UK and Australia were different from earlier ones in two major respects.

First, as discussed further in Chapter 4, key recommendations from these inquiries have resulted, in many cases, in major structural changes to intelligence communities not seen for decades. In particular, changes in the USA include the creation of the Department of Homeland Security (DHS) and the Office of the Director for National Intelligence (ODNI). Second, the post-9/11 inquiries have become much more public and politicized processes than their predecessors. The public, politicians and the media engaged actively in the flurry of post-9/11 inquiries, frequently expressing their frustration over what they perceive as a series of 'intelligence failures', including 9/11, Iraq, the London bombings and the Bali bombings. Governments have become aware of a lack of public confidence in some national security intelligence agencies and as part of their review and reform processes have pushed these agencies to provide more public insight into their roles and the accountability mechanisms governing them, where possible. Recommendation 23 of the Flood Report (a study of Australia's intelligence community), illustrated the point by suggesting that an unclassified brochure should be published describing the role of each agency (Flood 2004: 185). The other factor influencing the extent to which national security intelligence has become a 'public commodity' has been the more proactive approach being taken by these agencies towards counter-terrorism since 9/11. New counter-terrorism laws and enhanced investigative powers, hastily drafted after 9/11, have meant, in the words of one former CIA officer Charles Cogan, that agencies are not just passive recipients of intelligence but active 'hunters' as well (quoted in Gill and Phythian 2006: 76). As discussed in Chapter 10, the urgency in attempting to prevent the next terrorist attack and a more aggressive approach to intelligence collection and operational activity have resulted in a number of ethical and legal dilemmas for national security intelligence agencies, which has ensured they stay in the public spotlight. This is unlikely to change in the near future as national security intelligence agencies seek to balance secrecy, including their use of proactive intelligence collection, and targeting with greater legislative, political, judicial and public scrutiny.

In summary, the origins and functions of the UK and US national security intelligence agencies have developed partly organically and by design. Their development has been driven by the changing nature of the security environment in particular (from focusing on the Soviet Empire to chasing global outlaws such as transnational terrorists), and their ability to adapt to it. Change has also been driven internally by management via a diverse array of bureaucratic initiatives (see Chapter 6) and externally through political, legal and parliamentary oversight mechanisms (see Chapter 7). Increasingly, the contemporary security environment has also resulted in the blurring of boundaries between national security and other intelligence disciplines (policing and private sector). Attempting to 'join the dots' of myriad new threats in this complex environment questions the validity of historical and Cold War parameters of what national security, foreign, military or domestic intelligence are.

While greater cooperation between national security agencies under the UK/USA Agreement has facilitated even closer working relations in the post-Cold War period, even now in the post-9/11 world of 'need to share' information, many of these agencies remain bound by their own traditions. The cultures of secrecy forged during the Cold War have not disappeared and this means that not all intelligence can be shared automatically or promptly even with friends outside the UK/USA Agreement, such as in NATO (Clough 2004: 608). Other customs, norms, technological practices, which have long been the hallmark of many of their secret surveillance and covert operations, remain.

For the foreseeable future it's unlikely that the first two aspects of what I refer to as the evolving intelligence tradition – *the culture of secrecy* and detailed knowledge of *secret surveillance techniques* – will be challenged completely by governments or commentators. However, since 9/11, national security agencies have become increasingly public and political commodities and in that sense some of the 'mystery gloss' has been rubbed off. In many respects, now they are becoming just like other bureaucratic agencies, where the public and their political masters are increasingly interested in seeing if their operations are ethical, legal and value for money.

Policing intelligence

In contrast to the small number of agencies which comprise the national security intelligence communities of the UK/USA Agreement countries, the number of policing agencies in each country, with the exception of New Zealand, is generally larger. New Zealand has only one policing agency, while the UK, the USA, Canada and Australia have several agencies with differences in jurisdictional responsibilities. For example, the USA has approximately 18,000 and Canada has 380 policing agencies. Examining the origins and functions of all their intelligence capabilities is therefore not possible in this volume. Instead, the focus will be on the key thematic and historical factors which have shaped the development and origins of policing intelligence in Australasia (Australia and New Zealand for brevity will be discussed in the same section), Canada, the UK and the USA. Given the limited space, discussion will also centre on specific agencies due to the relative impact they have had in their country on policing intelligence developments, and to highlighting specific themes for closer study in subsequent chapters. For example, it is difficult not to talk about the origins and functions of US policing intelligence without examining the FBI, or similarly developments in the UK without looking at the Metropolitan Police. There are also other agencies which could be discussed here including those which have some policing powers or others with more enforcement or regulatory functions (for example, revenue, immigration, customs), but discussion here is restricted to traditional policing agencies.

UK developments

Grieve provides a comprehensive summary of historical developments in UK policing intelligence. He suggests that 'Intelligence as a discipline had been known to UK public policing, as early as 1805, and with the Metropolitan Police its earliest connections were also with military intelligence.' The link with military intelligence resulted in the early use by the police of informants and surveillance to support investigations (Grieve 2009: 30–46). Historically, UK policing intelligence derived from a combination of external and internal factors. Leadership and the managerial reform initiatives of chief constables and commissioners have obviously been an important internal factor. The increased uptake in technology from the 1960s onwards has also transformed all aspects of policing, including intelligence. Technology has allowed greater specialization within policing intelligence in areas such as crime analysis – a topic discussed in greater detail in Chapter 8.

The external factors arguably are more important in understanding the development of UK policing intelligence, and the role of a series of oversight measures and institutions has been particularly relevant in shaping intelligence capabilities. Since the 1970s, government and formal professional oversight initiatives have culminated in the creation of a more formalized, structured and legislated approach to policing intelligence in the UK compared to most other agencies in Australia, Canada, New Zealand and the USA.

Collectively, a number of oversight bodies, including the role of the UK Home Office, Her Majesty's Inspectorate of Constabulary (HMIC) and the Associations of Chief Policing Officers (ACPO), and the National Policing Improvement Agency (NPIA) have achieved a lot more influence on the development of UK policing intelligence capabilities than their counterparts in other countries discussed in this section. The HMIC is an independent advisor on UK police services and carries out regular inspections relating to their overall efficiency and effectiveness. In recent years it has completed a series of thematic inspections relevant to intelligence practice (HMIC 1997, 2000, 2005). The HMIC 1997 report, *Policing with Intelligence*, was particularly important in promoting proactive intelligence approaches into UK policing. ACPO is an independent professional body made up of the senior executives of the police services of England, Wales and Northern Ireland. It works with other stakeholders such as the HMIC, the Home Office and the Association of Police Authorities to promote leadership and the development of better doctrine across various policing areas. ACPO has also been active in the promotion of better policing intelligence in the UK through a series of reports known as the Baumber Report (ACPO 1975), the Pearce Report (ACPO 1978) and the Ratcliffe Report (ACPO 1986). The Baumber Report was influential in shaping modern UK policing intelligence in recommending standardized approaches for setting up force intelligence units across each of the 43 (English and Welsh) forces. The Pearce and Ratcliffe Reports looked at the establishment of regional criminal intelligence offices and field intelligence officers respectively. We will come back to a more detailed discussion of these reports in Chapter 6 in the context of how they are useful in helping managers and leaders focus on creating appropriate organization structures for policing intelligence today. The NPIA has a reforming role and works with the ACPO, the Home Office and individual forces to develop skills, professionalism, doctrine and capabilities in various policing areas. It has been very active in providing resources and training for policing agencies to enhance their compliance to the National Intelligence Model (NIM) – developed in 2000 to promote a common approach to intelligence across all English and Welsh forces.

Another important external driver impacting on the development of UK policing intelligence was the emergence in the 1990s of a 'New Public Management' ethos that was focused on maximizing cost efficiencies and effectiveness across the public sector. At this time there was growing political pressure for police to demonstrate the use of their limited resources more effectively. The 1993 Audit Commission report *Helping with Enquiries: Tackling Crime Effectively* underlined growing concerns within the government that police agencies needed to make better and more proactive use of their resources. This report, together with *Policing with Intelligence* (HMIC 1997), was critical to the evolution of intelligence-led policing approaches within UK policing. I will not dwell on the intelligence-led policing approach here as it will be discussed in more detail in the context of discussion of the NIM in Chapter 4. Ratcliffe (2008) also provides a comprehensive discussion of the development of intelligence-led policing in the UK for those wishing further detail. Suffice it to say, it is an approach that has generated discussion, particularly on agreeing on a single acceptable definition. Ratcliffe's discussion of intelligence-led policing suggests that the emphasis is on using intelligence proactively to target the main or serious offenders or crime problem areas in order to detect, or disrupt their activity (ibid.: 72–73).

Finally, the changing security environment has also been important in influencing the development of UK policing intelligence capabilities. Greater specialization within UK policing intelligence came early with the evolving security threat posed by Irish Republican terrorism. For example, the Metropolitan Police had developed a Special Branch in 1883 to deal with it and increasingly from the 1960s onwards all forces had developed their own special branches (Gill and Phythian 2006: 43). Early on these branches coordinated their activities with MI5 priorities and acquired intelligence using similar surveillance techniques to those used by national security agencies. This close relationship between police and security services fostered better working relations and mutual understanding of each other's work which was important when 9/11 and the 7/7 2005 bombings on London's transport networks occurred. The increasingly complex security environment of global terrorist networks, drug trafficking and people smuggling has also resulted in the emergence of new organizations and bureaucratic arrangements such as the Serious Organised Crime Agency (SOCA) in 2005 and the Joint Terrorism Analysis Centre (JTAC) in 2003. We will discuss these initiatives more fully in Chapter 4.

However, more importantly, the increasingly complex security environment and a growing reliance in UK policing on intelligence-led policing approaches have also resulted in a greater emphasis on proactive applications of intelligence aimed first to *disrupt* threats then build a case for prosecution (Innes and Sheptycki 2004). This is a break with the past, where the emphasis was reacting to a crime, and using intelligence retrospectively to build a chain of evidence for prosecution. Since 9/11, the shift in UK policing emphasis from prosecution to disruption is due to a combination of factors, including government pressure, limited resources and new legal frameworks that allow more proactive and interventionist approaches to intelligence collection. However, as we shall see in Chapter 7, the move towards proactive intelligence collection and operations has not been without their ethical, legal and social ramifications in the UK and elsewhere. In the UK over the past decade, various mechanisms have been introduced to control how policing intelligence is practised, such as the Regulation of Investigative Power Act 2000 (UK) and the introduction of a Surveillance Commissioner. Yet despite these, ethical, legal, social and operational implications are emerging with the shift towards more proactive and disruptive intelligence operations, particularly in the organized crime and counter-terrorism context (Innes and Sheptycki 2004: 22). The Independent Police Complaints Commission (IPCC) inquiry (the Stockwell Inquiry) into the shooting of the Brazilian Jean Charles de Menezes in July 2005 also underscored some of the adverse implications of a more proactive intelligence approach in a fast moving counter-terrorism operation (IPCC 2007).

Several challenges remain for UK policing intelligence and these are shared to a greater or lesser degree by policing agencies elsewhere. These challenges will be explored thematically in subsequent chapters, but include among others: cultural attitudes within some agencies about the role of intelligence in strategic and operational decision-making, better coordination and integration of intelligence databases with police information management systems, stronger strategic intelligence capabilities and assessing how the NIM may need to be adapted to future policing requirements.

Canadian developments

Most of Canada's older police forces appeared in the 1830s and 1840s, and in contrast to the UK, the origins of Canadian policing intelligence was shaped by the need early on to deal with huge distances between provinces and even some towns. Given there are 380 Canadian policing agencies, a thematic discussion of the origins and functions of Canadian policing intelligence is provided. Instead, I will restrict discussion here to the Royal Canadian Mounted Police (RCMP), which emerged from an earlier incarnation called the North-West Mounted Police, established in 1873. While the RCMP is not representative of all Canadian agencies, its national reach and close involvement with all policing intelligence developments in Canada provide insight into general policing intelligence trends in Canada. Particular trends relevant to the development of policing intelligence in Canada include changes to intelligence models, management, legislation and education issues.

Early specialization in Canadian policing was the catalyst for the gradual development of an intelligence capability in Canadian agencies. For example, as early as 1900, detective squads began to emerge and their further specialization in the 1950s and 1960s (e.g. vice and homicide squads) were important early markers in the development of policing intelligence in Canada (Hamilton 2006: 63). Another important developmental milestone in the 1960s in Canada was the country's early response to a growing organized crime problem, which was emerging in some of its large multi-ethnic cities such as Toronto and Vancouver. The creation of the Criminal Intelligence Service of Canada (CISC) in 1970 with a central bureau in Ottawa and nine provincial ones was an early attempt to provide a clearing house for sharing intelligence and analysis of organized crime across Canadian policing agencies (CISC 2009).

An early win for CISC was its creation in 1976 of the Automated Criminal Intelligence Information System (ACIIS), which allowed the gathering and sharing of intelligence across Canada's criminal intelligence community. A new criminal intelligence sharing platform is currently being conceived to replace the ACIIS platform (see Chapter 4). CISC is used by over 380 agencies at federal, provincial and municipal levels of policing. It has played an important role in the policing intelligence architecture of Canadian policing, particularly in developing a national threat picture and strategic intelligence analysis. From the early 1960s and up to the 1990s, other policing and analytical models such as community policing and crime mapping were also influential in the developing intelligence capability in Canadian agencies. In particular, the early application of community policing in dealing with organized crime across Canada was useful for building up intelligence collection and analysis.

Hamilton suggests that the growing diversity of Canada's criminal environment, particularly from the early 1960s to the present, made community policing strategies appealing for policing intelligence. He notes:

> Besides the traditional mafia, outlaw bike gangs and the Franco-Montreal underworld, new exceptionally violent players had appeared on the scene: new Chinese Triads, the Russian Mafiya, Haitians in Montreal, the Jamaican Posses in Ontario, violent Sikhs in the aftermath of the Babbar Khalsa insurgency, and the newly arriving Tamil Tiger supporters from Sri Lanka gave Canada a lot of experience in community policing initiatives.
>
> (Hamilton 2006: 70)

Community policing initiatives were also used by the RCMP in a 1985 terrorist investigation, where most of the suspects were from the Punjabi community in British Columbia (Deukmedjian and de Lint 2007). A second major theme in the historical development of Canadian policing intelligence is *accountability*. The 1981 McDonald Commission is arguably the most important example of how accountability has played an important role in shaping the origins and functions of Canadian policing intelligence. A full summary of the Commission's findings can be found in the study by the McDonald Commission (McDonald 1981b: 513–514). But the key recommendation of the Commission was for a new legal and organizational structure for Canadian national security intelligence, which would remove this responsibility from the RCMP and give it to a new civilian security intelligence agency, the CSIS in 1984. Until 1984, the RCMP's Security Service had been responsible for investigating threats to national security. With this responsibility now shifting to CSIS, the CSIS Act 1984, which created the new agency, was also important to policing intelligence in defining how CSIS would enter into joint activities with Canadian police forces. Cooperation and coordination, however, between the intelligence activities of CSIS and the RCMP were not optimal in the early years following the creation of CSIS.

This lack of cooperation became apparent following an official review of Canadian security and policing responses to an Air India bombing incident in 1985, when British Columbia-based Sikh radicals put two bombs on flights connecting to other Air India flights. The review by the Security Intelligence Review Committee (O'Connor 2006: 48) did highlight some patch protecting and suboptimal coordination of investigative efforts between it and the RCMP. However, increasingly in the 1990s, as the threats posed by transnational crime and terrorism grew, CSIS and policing agencies, particularly the RCMP, gradually became used to working with each other more effectively, and efforts have been made to forge greater understanding between the two agencies' operational methodologies. In 2009, one senior CSIS officer advised that a joint management team between the two agencies has been established to better coordinate their intelligence-led operational activity. There have also been more recent political and judicial reviews since the 1980s, such as the Arrar Commission, which have also focused on aspects of policing intelligence practice in Canada. The significance of some of these more recent reviews and their legislative impacts on policing intelligence in Canada will be discussed further in Chapter 7.

In summary, the origins and functions of Canadian policing intelligence have been driven broadly by similar themes found in other countries. Greater specialization in policing and intelligence methodologies has been important as have the early development of national coordinated responses to policing intelligence, with the creation of CISC. However, there have also been events unique to Canada that explain the development of policing intelligence there. The creation of a new national security intelligence agency out of a national policing agency is one interesting example. This common heritage between Canada's policing and security intelligence agencies has fostered the cross-fertilization of methodologies with CSIS and RCMP officers moving back and forth between the two agencies. In addition to promoting common understanding, it also helped foster the development and innovation of other more recent intelligence models such as intelligence-led policing (Hamilton 2006: 51).

Finally, another important factor driving review and reform in Canadian policing intelligence has been the willingness, at least periodically, by policing executives to experiment with new ideas or sponsor change. For example, Deukmedjian (2006) argues that it was the failure of community policing strategies that was a key driver for the RCMP adopting an intelligence-led policing response instead in December 2000. Chapter 4 provides a detailed discussion of current innovations in Canadian policing intelligence, including recent work being done within the RCMP and the CISC to develop a Canadian Criminal Intelligence Model (CCIM).

US policing intelligence developments

As discussed earlier, the large number of federal, state and local policing agencies in the USA, approximately 18,000, has resulted historically in a fragmented response to policing and policing intelligence (Ratcliffe 2008: 24). There are many historical reasons for this fragmentation. The political culture of the USA is one factor, where there has been a natural suspicion since independence of power being concentrated in one or two authorities. The gradual but unplanned settlement of large parts of the USA, particularly its central and western areas as late as the nineteenth century, also contributed to the fragmented state of US policing today. Whatever the causes for this fragmented response to policing, it remains the single most important feature in not only understanding the historical origins of US policing, but also what has been possible and what is not possible in its practice. See Carter for a brief overview of US policing intelligence (Carter 2004: 21–36). The main point that emerges from even a cursory review of US policing history is that it is not possible to talk about policing intelligence in any discernible sense until the mid to late nineteenth century. As Jeffreys-Jones notes:

> The institutions of the relatively new republic were still being organized, across the country – indeed the US Congress only established the Department of Justice in July 1870. And the establishment of the FBI was not to be for another 38 years.
>
> (2007: 3)

A major historical factor in understanding US policing from its earliest period to the present is the role the US political culture has played in its development. In addition to suspicions over the concentration of power, race politics, anti-communism, an innate public suspicion of surveillance, and bureaucratic rivalries between security and policing agencies, have all played a role in how policing intelligence evolved in the USA. The Bolshevik Revolution in Russia was to play a significant role in shaping the political culture of the USA for generations, including the national level policing intelligence culture. J. Edgar Hoover, Director of the FBI from 1924 until his death in 1972, raised concerns by many in the community about the extensive misuse of his agency's intelligence capabilities against innocent US citizens, particularly during the McCarthy period. Historian Jeffreys-Jones summarizes this period well, arguing that the FBI was the creation of progressives in the 1870s, however, during the McCarthy period it was becoming repellent to liberals (ibid.: 11).

The net result of such abuses at federal and state policing agencies resulted in the closing down of many police departments, which had an impact on their ability later to develop effective criminal intelligence capabilities (Carter 2004: 26). The other noteworthy event, which shaped US political culture and the trajectory of US national policing intelligence, was the passing of the National Security Act of 1947. The National Security Act created the CIA. The CIA was meant to provide a centralized approach to intelligence and the director of the new agency would also be given control over all aspects of intelligence (military, sigint and the FBI). The Act was seen by Hoover as a wing-clipping for the FBI as his agency – now more formally constraining the Bureau to domestic intelligence gathering rather than abroad. Hoover held the CIA in little regard and this led frequently to intelligence hoarding or lack of cooperation between the two agencies. Relationships between the CIA and the FBI ebbed and flowed under different leaderships post-Hoover and this remained a problem up to 9/11 (Hulnick 2004). Leaving the organizational cultural issues between the CIA and the FBI aside, the unifying and coordinated objectives sought by the National Security Act for US intelligence arguably resulted in the opposite – a more fragmented approach to domestic and international security issues.

More recently, attempts have been made to address this fragmentation of policing intelligence with initiatives such as the Regional Information Sharing Systems (RISS) network, which is used as a formal method of passing criminal intelligence between agencies. In the post-9/11 environment, several initiatives have been implemented; partly to overcome the lack of coordination between the intelligence functions of US policing intelligence agencies, but also to promote better practice underpinned by intelligence-led policing approaches. One example is the National Criminal Intelligence Sharing Plan sponsored by US Chiefs of Police, aimed at promoting greater coordination and common practice approaches (GIWG 2003).

The post-9/11 intelligence field has also seen the growth of fusion centers where several agencies are embedded in the one location to share intelligence, and more recently initiatives such as suspicious activity reporting (SAR) system have developed to improve the proactive detection and sharing of intelligence particularly on terrorism. Fusion centers and SAR systems are still evolving and are works in progress and will be examined more fully in Chapter 4. In addition to new initiatives, the events of 9/11 at the federal policing level resulted in significant resources and powers being given to the FBI, and deeper structural changes to the broader US intelligence community with the creation of the DHS in March 2003. The DHS for the first couple of years of operation looked like an agency in search of a purpose, however, in our discussion on the strategic management of the intelligence function in Chapter 6, we will see how this agency could play an important role in promoting better policing intelligence capabilities across federal, state and local agencies. The perceived failure of key US intelligence agencies such as the FBI and the CIA to detect and disrupt the 9//11 attacks also resulted in the Bush Administration giving them more powers to collect intelligence proactively with less oversight than before.

The significance of changes to post-9/11 US intelligence legislation will be discussed more fully in Chapter 7. However, the signing into law by President Bush of the bill called the 'Uniting and Strengthening America by Providing Appropriate Tools Required to Intercept and Obstruct Terrorism' (the Patriot Act) was a significant reversal of previous reforms that were codified in the Foreign Intelligence Surveillance Act (FISA), passed in 1978 and designed to safeguard against the recurrence of surveillance abuses as happened in the Hoover period

(Bazan 2007). However, civil liberty, privacy concerns and public perception that the US intelligence community after the 9/11 reforms was still doing a bad job, continued to raise concerns about the extension of powers to policing intelligence agencies, particularly the FBI (Hulnick 2004). As discussed later in Chapter 7, the Obama Administration has reviewed the earlier legislation and guidelines issued by the former Bush Administration for intelligence collection by the CIA and the FBI. It is probably too soon to predict the results of these reviews and their impact on policing intelligence more broadly in the USA.

In summary, the origins and functions of US policing intelligence were driven by a combination of factors. Again there are some themes familiar to other countries discussed in this Part. The greater uptake of technology and specialization in policing and intelligence methodologies has been important. However, there is also a combination of other events more unique to the USA that explains the development of policing intelligence there. For example, the large number of police services and the fragmented response to policing at the federal, state and local levels make the implementation of truly national approaches to intelligence practice like the UK NIM difficult. The significant and ongoing reform of policing intelligence post 9/11, particularly at the federal and regional levels, has seen the adoption of initiatives to better promote coordination and more proactive intelligence strategies between agencies. However, new initiatives need to be balanced against the US public's natural suspicion of police powers and the will of politicians and management to see the reforms through.

Australasian policing intelligence

In comparison to the fragmented US policing intelligence response, Australia with its eight police forces and New Zealand with one national police force, might imply, due to the smaller size of each policing community, a more unified and common historical approach to policing intelligence in Australasia. However, the history and origins of policing intelligence in both countries suggest that even within the one agency, the New Zealand Police (NZP), there have been diverse approaches to policing intelligence from early days. Rivalries and distrust between different area commands of the NZP and between Australia's federal policing agency – the AFP – and its state policing counterparts resulted historically in different and uncoordinated approaches to intelligence. The origins and functions of Australasian policing intelligence are partly the result of factors seen elsewhere in the UK, Canada and the USA, but also reflect other unique historical 'local' influences. Again, Australasian policing intelligence practice has been influenced by the use of technology, the uptake of new policing models (e.g. community policing and problem-orientated policing) and responding to new public managerialism ideas. All of these have been important in shaping the development of Australasian policing, but given they have already been discussed, I will focus on those issues that have been unique to shaping policing intelligence capability in both Australia and New Zealand.

The first different characteristic that defined the policing intelligence of Australasia was the relative geographic isolation of Australia and New Zealand, which meant that external threats were few and internal ones were not complex. There was some early development of intelligence capabilities, for example. Finnane argues that in the case of Australia, most Australian police forces from 1880 to 1930 underwent refinements in their organizational structures. This refinement included the development of specialist roles including the increased capacity for intelligence, surveillance and forensic work (Finnane 1994: 31).

However, the isolation of Australia and New Zealand resulted in what Rogers refers to as a 'benign threat environment leading up to the end of the Second World War and some would argue three decades after it' (Rogers 2009: 14), which did not encourage the development of more sophisticated thinking about and application of intelligence in Australasian policing agencies. In other words, neither Australia nor New Zealand policing agencies were confronted with either the suite or complexity of terrorism, nationalist, organized crime and communist threats experienced by their UK and US policing counterparts. A similar trend emerged within New Zealand policing. In the beginning there was more than one police force in New Zealand, though earlier versions were regional or local in focus, and intelligence practice was rudimentary. The unification into one policing agency in 1886 resulted in greater rationalization of resources and also the ability for improvement in various policing specializations including intelligence.

However, in the 1970s, the changing threat environment overseas started to impact on the Australasian region and the introduction of illicit drugs and increased migration changed the nature of both countries as their criminal markets became more connected to global trends. In addition to a greater connection to global drug markets, Australia and New Zealand policing agencies became more concerned about terrorist attacks offshore. For Australia, Rogers argues that the attack by the Black September faction on the Israeli contingent at the Munich Olympics on 7 September 1972, and the detonation of an explosive device outside the Hilton Hotel in Sydney on 13 February 1978, during a Commonwealth Heads of Government Meeting, sharply refocused the attention of the federal and state level policing on their counter-terrorism capabilities.

After the 1978 Hilton Hotel bombing, two influential inquiries were initiated by the Australian federal government at the time: the Marks Inquiry, which reviewed current Commonwealth Law Enforcement arrangements (Marks 1978), and the first of what was to be two reviews by Justice Hope, which looked at Australia's protective security arrangements, particularly the relationships between the police services and the national security intelligence community (Hope 1979). Both the Marks and Hope inquiries were important early catalysts in building up the intelligence functions of Australian policing agencies. The Marks Inquiry was significant as it led to the establishment of the AFP in 1979. In just 30 years, the AFP's broad mission now includes a growing number of national and international issues such as counter-terrorism and organized crime to an even more diverse role of activities today including peacekeeping, high tech crime, money laundering and most recently war crime investigations. For the past decade, the AFP's role in peacekeeping has been particularly interesting and Chapter 3 will focus in part on how it has been involved in building intelligence capacity in fragile South Pacific states.

In Australia, the 1980s and the 1990s saw several other independent reviews, which were not necessarily focused primarily on policing intelligence, but also impacted on how it was practised. There is insufficient space to provide full coverage on all of them. However, the federal government's review (the Costigan Commission in 1984) and the NSW state-based review (the Wood Royal Commission in 1997) were arguably the most important ones during this time. The Costigan Commission's review of corruption associated with maritime unions resulted in the creation of a federal organized crime body, the National Crime Authority (NCA), in 1984. The NCA was given strong coercive powers to collect intelligence and evidence to deal with organized crime. Although the NCA was abolished in 2003, and replaced by the Australian Crime Commission (ACC), the ACC has kept these coercive powers (see Chapter 7 for a discussion of these coercive powers). The ACC has recently developed a new approach to intelligence and I will come back to this in Chapter 4 as part of a broader discussion on new intelligence frameworks. The Wood Royal Commission in 1996 and 1997 into police corruption within the NSW Police also resulted in some internal restructuring of its intelligence capability (Wood 1997; Walsh 2005). Some of this reorganization resulted in an integrated crime management model, which was advocated by the UK intelligence-led policing model (the NIM) as a best practice approach.

However, in Australia, the 1980s and 1990s continued to underline problems with the ways agencies conceptualized and used intelligence. In 1993, the Australian Government extensively reviewed via the Commonwealth Law Enforcement Arrangements Review (CLER) all aspects of Commonwealth (federal) law enforcement agencies' operations, including the performance of their intelligence functions. In particular, the report underlined a number of problems associated with intelligence practice, including tasking, coordination, analysis, collection and information management systems. The vulnerabilities detailed in the report relating to police information management systems worked against effective and proactive intelligence collection and analysis, which is meant to underpin contemporary intelligence-led policing practice (CLER 1984).

Many of the challenges to effective policing intelligence identified in the CLER Report almost two decades ago still exist. Subsequent chapters will address many of the challenges identified in further detail, but there also has been progress in some areas of policing intelligence practice in Australia. The growing threat from Sunni Islamic extremism, in particular the Al Qaeda 'brand', and other emerging transnational threats in the late 1990s such as maritime illegal immigration have resulted in further development of Australian policing intelligence capabilities. Additionally, in Australia in the late 1990s, there was growing evidence of the rhetoric of a 'whole of government approach' to policing and security issues being matched with reality. The AFP and other law enforcement agencies working in a tightly coordinated way with Australian national security agencies over maritime people smuggling from the late 1990s is a good example of a 'whole of government approach' in practice. Another example of a growing coordinated and integrated approach to intelligence between federal, state policing and security agencies was the model used for intelligence support for the 2000 Olympic Games in Sydney. While multi-agency fused responses to large events are common now, in 2000 this response was unique and represented an effective way for national security and federal law enforcement agencies to coordinate their intelligence support to NSW Police who were providing security at Olympic venues in Sydney. The multi-agency police and security agency model adopted for the 2000 Olympic Games was also another important example of how normative change and new habits of cooperation and coordination could provide a template for further joint federal-state policing intelligence strategic and operational planning.

The late 1990s was also a period in Australian and NZ policing, when the influence of UK intelligence-led policing approaches started to be visible in the reform initiatives of local policing intelligence models. Chapter 4 will focus further on how UK policing intelligence approaches have impacted on the development of intelligence structures and processes in Australasia, the USA and Canada. Suffice it to say, the extent to which UK intelligence-led policing approaches have been adopted in Australian policing agencies has been uneven. In a study completed in 2005 of four Australian policing agencies (ACC, AFP, NSW Police and Victoria Police), it was clear that both at strategic and operational levels, further integration of intelligence policing strategies was required for intelligence to reach its potential of providing proactive support to decision-makers (Walsh 2005). The Ratcliffe review of NZP intelligence in 2002 also identified some of the same problems, and barriers to an effective intelligence-led policing approach in that agency, including variations in structure between intelligence units, poor data sets and a lack of integration of intelligence into decision-making processes (Ratcliffe 2002). The current reform agenda of NZP which will be discussed in Chapter 4 is addressing these and other deficiencies.

The events of 9/11 and subsequent policy initiatives in both Australia and New Zealand to broaden traditional approaches to national security to include other issues, such as organized crime, have also resulted in further specialization in policing intelligence capabilities of both countries. In addition to new counter-terrorism measures, which will be discussed further in Chapter 6, there have been recent attempts in Australia to bring the organized crime work done by the ACC further into the centre of national security policy-making circles. In New Zealand the recent creation in March 2009 of the National Intelligence Centre for New Zealand and the establishment in July 2008 of a specialized organized crime body, the Organised Financial Crime Agency of New Zealand (OFCANZ), resulted in greater policing intelligence capabilities for New Zealand and stronger coordination with its national security intelligence community. In summary, the strategic management, policy reform environment of security and policing intelligence has been very active in both Australia and New Zealand. However, unlike the USA, in both countries, there has not been a comprehensive attempt to restructure national policing and security arrangements. Similar to developments discussed earlier with UK, Canadian and US policing, the post-9/11 environment in Australia and New Zealand has also resulted in the amendment or drafting of new laws, particularly counter-terrorism legislation. The impact of this new legislation on intelligence practice will be discussed further in Chapter 7.

An evolving intelligence tradition?

Based on the historical development and application of intelligence in the traditional (conventional) environments of national security and policing discussed earlier, this last section explores whether it is possible to talk about an evolving *intelligence tradition*. Tradition is defined broadly here as a set of beliefs, customs, practices, principles and accumulated experience handed down from earlier generations of intelligence practitioners that inform contemporary practice. The discussion above of national security and policing intelligence suggests that to some extent a broad tradition made up of similar language, norms, cultures and approaches has emerged. The characteristics of this tradition discussed here not only help explain the historical development of intelligence. Articulating broad components of an intelligence tradition also assists in delineating the uniqueness of intelligence from other fields (e.g. psychology, criminology, strategic studies or economics), which, as will be discussed in Chapter 10, is important to progressing intelligence-related research and theory building. Additionally, a basic conceptual understanding of an intelligence tradition is also helpful in understanding how intelligence is being applied in new environments.

There are three characteristics which describe the intelligence tradition: *the security environment, secrecy* and *surveillance*. However, I expect some readers would, depending on how they define intelligence, argue for a greater or lesser number of characteristics. Just what intelligence is or is not remains contested among academics and practitioners. For example, one senior national security officer interviewed for this book suggested that much of policing intelligence was not really intelligence as it was not secretly obtained or privileged information. This comment suggests a narrow view both of what secret information is and therefore what constitutes intelligence. Other perspectives, such as Ratcliffe's 3-I model (Ratcliffe 2008) are helpful in explaining what intelligence does (interpret the environment, inform decision-making, impact on the environment). However, what I am proposing by introducing this phrase 'intelligence tradition' is to distil down into only a few characteristics what is meant by the *business* of intelligence. However incomplete this list of three characteristics may be, at the very least, these characteristics have been fundamental to defining historically what intelligence is, compared to other similar activities, such as research, data analysis, information collation and report writing.

The security environment

The first characteristic that traditional approaches to intelligence have in common is the security environment. This environment may be different in some ways or similar in others, but the *raison d'être* for all intelligence is to provide decision-making support for those whose responsibility it is to manage a security environment. At its most fundamental level, intelligence is about supporting decision-makers to risk manage their operating environments. As seen earlier, managing the risks in the security environment could involve understanding a range of risks and threats related to terrorism, criminal gangs or reducing fraud occurrences within a business. The intelligence function must not only interpret the security environment, but given resources are limited, the analysis it provides must make it easier for decision-makers to set priorities for dealing with the suite of risks that exist. The decision-makers' priorities hence become the intelligence function's collection and analytical priorities. However, through the generation of new intelligence systems and processes, autonomous from formal tasking and coordination mechanisms, the intelligence function is able to recalibrate decision-makers' priorities, or better still warn about an emerging risk that the decision-maker has no knowledge of. Since 1945, in all types of national security intelligence agencies, we have seen the development of more formal intelligence collection and priority systems, partly driven by external political tasking, but also internally as part of agency management processes. Chapter 4 will examine these developments in the context of discussing contemporary intelligence frameworks more broadly.

Secrecy

Secrecy is the second but most important defining characteristic of this tradition. In earlier discussion about the origins of national security intelligence agencies, the very existence of many of them was kept secret from the public for decades. The history of MI6 is a good example of this preoccupation with secrecy; its existence was only officially admitted by UK PM John Major to the House of Commons on 6 May 1992 (Dorril 2001: 758). Historically, though not always in reality, intelligence has been defined by the ability to collect sensitive information without the target's knowledge. Secret intelligence collection is obviously important in order to provide decision-makers with forewarning about a target or a threat and its possible intentions. While the historical development of national security and policing intelligence shows an increasing reliance on open sources of intelligence, publicly available information sources on their own are not intelligence, and are not always sufficient to provide insights about a threat. The requirement to control secret information sources and collection methodologies has created by necessity a 'culture of secrecy' and this has become an important characteristic of the 'intelligence tradition'. The desire to collect secret information resulted in the development of closed information systems, and a 'culture of secrecy', where the 'need to know' principle governed distribution. However, the 'culture of secrecy' also resulted almost in a contradiction between sharing information with decision-makers or other stakeholders quickly, and closed information systems and practices protecting the information.

It would be incorrect, however, to suggest that closed secret information systems have prevented any sharing of tightly controlled information. As Herman notes, prior to 9/11 and its mantra of 'need to know', the current international intelligence system had already evolved into what he refers to as 'a patchwork of bilateral and multilateral arrangements of all kinds and all degrees of intimacy'. Herman also suggests that information sharing arrangements were 'unusual in their secrecy, but in every other way they are not unlike other inter-governmental arrangements that have developed in other specialized areas of government' (1996: 204).

However, operational sensitivities, national interest and agency rivalries within intelligence communities very often meant that in reality not all information was shared even between 'friends'. Arguably, however, the changing security environment may pose the greatest challenge to the culture of secrecy, which defined the work of national security and policing agencies in the twentieth century. The necessity of global cooperation in responding to most transnational threats today, and the need for UK/USA Agreement agencies to collaborate in their intelligence activities with less traditional partners in Europe, the Middle East and elsewhere will challenge traditional notions of what should be kept secret and why. However, there is no doubt that the current scope and nature of transnational security threats have resulted in more flexible and arguably networked approaches requiring at least some of a cultural shift away from earlier hierarchical Cold War structures and attitudes of secrecy within contemporary intelligence agencies. At the very least, traditional intelligence agencies are having to adapt their cultures of secrecy in order to work more effectively with new tiers of government and non-government agencies, which are themselves increasingly becoming part of national intelligence communities.

Surveillance

The third characteristic of the intelligence tradition is surveillance, which includes a number of related and inter-dependent activities, such as tasking, coordination, covert collection, analysis and decision-making support. Gill and Phythian argue that surveillance is a core concept to national security intelligence as '[it] helps generate knowledge in conditions of secrecy that can inform the formation and implementation of security policy; this is essentially a subset of the more general surveillance that constitutes contemporary governance' (2006: 29).

Clearly the increased global threat from terrorism, particularly since 9/11, means that there has been increase in surveillance by national security and policing intelligence agencies. Gill and Phythian are also correct in extending their definition of surveillance beyond national security and policing contexts. Surveillance is a common characteristic of all intelligence contexts, including within the private sector and the newer applications of intelligence discussed in Chapter 2. In the private industry context, for example, surveillance has many applications. Companies do 'spy' on each other and companies and governments spy on each other. For example, the 2009 case of the arrested Rio Tinto mining executive, Stern Hu, accused by the Chinese Government of spying and stealing state secrets by attempting to bribe Chinese steel companies over their steel prices (O'Sullivan 2009), and the German news service Deutsche Welle (23 May 2009) reported in 2009 that the security department of Germany's largest bank, Deutsche Bank, had allegedly been spying on employees by putting bank managers under surveillance and also other people outside the financial institution. On a less dramatic level, private industry use business intelligence processes and technologies such as analytics to project future threats to their financial viability.

Surveillance need not necessarily be a technologically dominant activity, and, however applied (whether physical, technical or electronic), it has become the cornerstone for intelligence collection and analysis across the traditional areas of national security and policing intelligence. The potential real strength of any surveillance is to provide forewarning of a threat. The dramatic developments in technologies throughout the Cold War have facilitated greater volumes and more rapid collection of covert information than frequently can be analysed. For example, the US sigint agency – NSA – like other sigint agencies, is in a dilemma between what can be collected and analysed. Of course not everything that is collected should be analysed. Surveillance is only useful if the significance of the information is assessed quickly and given to the relevant decision-maker.

Since the 1970s, technology has again become partly the answer to large data sets, particularly those collected by electronic surveillance methods. New intelligence applications being developed in one area of intelligence are being taken up by other areas. Technological advancements in software used in the private and the military sectors are supporting better intelligence analysis across broader applications of traditional intelligence practice. There is now analytical software which can assist in generating hypotheses, collating data (both quantitative and qualitative), brain storming and data mining. Various cognitive analytical techniques such as alternative analysis used initially in military and national security intelligence are now being increasingly used in policing intelligence (see Chapter 8). Strategic analytical tools, first used in the private sector (particularly engineering and business), are now being used in national security and policing intelligence to assist in strategic or estimative intelligence.

In addition to a range of analytical software that supports analysis, other older analytical tools traditionally used in business intelligence are now being increasingly utilized in national security and policing contexts.

Conclusion

This chapter provided a brief summary of the origins and functions of traditional areas of intelligence practice across Australia, Canada, New Zealand, the UK and the USA. Each country has developed intelligence agencies which reflect their own unique political and cultural environments. A broad analysis, however, of several factors across each country, including politics, bureaucratic cultures and the evolution of their security environments, suggests that there are many similarities between the national security and policing intelligence applications in these countries.

From this analysis, I would argue that a basic set of three characteristics has evolved into an 'intelligence tradition', which helps explain what intelligence uniquely is in these environments. It is likely that this 'tradition' will remain important in defining intelligence in the traditional practice areas discussed in this chapter. In contrast, Chapter 2 will shift the focus from the traditional practice areas to how intelligence is being applied in newer areas. The focus will be on two emerging practice areas, the first, corrections, which have already used some intelligence capabilities in recent decades, the second, biosecurity, where the application of intelligence principles and processes are still emerging. Both Chapters 2 and 3 argue that intelligence scholars and practitioners have not yet adequately engaged in discussion about how intelligence can be usefully applied in a range of emerging areas, both to improve the collective response to problems in the security environment, but also to assist in the development of a discipline of intelligence.

2   Emerging intelligence practice areas

Introduction

This chapter moves the focus from how intelligence has been applied in the traditional environments of national security and policing to 'emerging practice areas'. The phrase, 'emerging practice areas', could potentially have a number of different meanings. The term 'emerging' is also somewhat subjective and relative, in that what is considered 'emerging' for one observer may be defined as 'matured' for another. Nevertheless, despite a lack of precision in the phrase 'emerging practice areas', it is useful to describe an increasingly large number of public and private sector agencies, which are now developing intelligence capabilities to better inform decision-making. Emerging intelligence practice areas can also include agencies where intelligence is not a new addition to business processes, but can describe an environment where intelligence is not yet well coordinated or integrated into decision-making. Hence, the focus here is on practice areas in agencies, where intelligence is either relatively new and/or its application to tactical, operational and strategic decision-making remains under-developed compared to the traditional intelligence practice areas discussed in Chapter 1.

In the public sector, there is an endless list of agencies, which could be considered as having emerging intelligence capabilities. These include agencies with border protection functions such as immigration and customs, but also others with compliance and regulatory mandates in areas such as taxation, social security, securities, superannuation and anti-money laundering. The list of public sector emerging practice areas could also be extended to include corrections, juvenile justice and child protection. Examples in the private sector could include intelligence capabilities currently being developed in many large multinational companies in a range of business sectors: finance, mining, building, consumer services, biopharmaceuticals and utilities.

The significance of current developments in many emerging intelligence practice areas is still not fully understood by those working in the traditional areas of national security and policing. I argue in this chapter that, given the increasingly complex security environment, a greater understanding by those working in the traditional intelligence areas is needed on how intelligence capabilities are developing in emerging practice areas. In the past decade in particular, countering sophisticated terrorism and organized crime has required national security and policing agencies to work more closely in extended intelligence networks. These networks have included the specialized capabilities of regulatory and compliance agencies, particularly those working in tracking money flows, social security, corrections and immigration. Additionally, the private sector has become linked increasingly with public sector intelligence networks through areas such as fraud, identity theft, aviation security and critical infrastructure protection. The net effect of the widening of the security agenda means traditional intelligence providers in policing and national security are by necessity becoming 'networked' with a range of public and private sector agencies with whom in the past they would have limited or no interaction at all.

However, despite current efforts in Australia, Canada, New Zealand, the UK and the USA to link with a range of agencies with emerging intelligence capabilities, little is known about the nature of intelligence practice in these non-traditional practice areas. This is a vulnerability for both practitioners and academics seeking better practice across the wider intelligence spectrum. In particular, there are three important questions about emerging intelligence practice areas that remain unanswered in the current research. First, how has the increasingly complex and expanding security environment impacted on the development of intelligence capabilities in emerging practice areas? Second, how has the interaction with traditional intelligence players working on a range of 'whole of government' or 'all hazard' security issues influenced the type of intelligence frameworks and systems adopted in emerging practice agencies? Third, to what extent are emerging intelligence capabilities in emerging areas good practice?

Given the increasing number of public and private sector agencies that are now developing intelligence capabilities, this chapter will examine these three questions by focusing on two emerging practice areas (corrections and biosecurity). Both these areas provide good illustrations of how intelligence capabilities are developing in non-traditional security areas. The existence of intelligence capabilities across the corrections sector is clearly not new, however, in many respects, 'corrections intelligence' conforms to the broader definition described earlier of an emerging intelligence practice area. While progress is being made, it is clear from the discussion below that intelligence practice in the corrections sectors of Australia, Canada, New Zealand, the UK and the USA is still developmental. In particular, the outputs of intelligence in the corrections sector have not yet been sufficiently integrated into decision-making. I have selected corrections as the first emerging practice area to study in this chapter as recent progress in developing intelligence capabilities still, in most cases, requires more consolidation in each country. Additionally, as noted below, it is important to identify where the challenges remain to improve correctional intelligence practice, given the increased importance of linking this kind of intelligence with that collected by policing agencies in areas such as organized crime and terrorism. In contrast, the second example of emerging intelligence practice areas – the use of intelligence in biosecurity – is still relatively new. The need, however, for the effective application of intelligence practices by health and national security authorities in these countries to monitor and respond to epidemics, and potential bioterrorism is becoming more relevant as countries develop broader definitions of national security and the knowledge of how health-related threat issues are inter-related.

The corrections environment

Unsurprisingly, the correctional environments in Australia, Canada, New Zealand, the UK and the USA differ in a number of ways. To some extent, the differences are similar to those discussed earlier in Chapter 1, in the context of their national security and policing agencies. For example, variations in each country's political cultures and criminal justice arrangements have resulted in different responses to corrections policy. In the USA, for example, the corrections sector consists of federal and state prisons, while in Australia responsibilities for prisons remain with state governments. For Australia, this means that people charged with federal offences such as terrorism are held in custody in state prisons. The history and variations between the corrections sector of each country are documented by Cavadino and Dignan (2006) and Weiss and South (1998). Relevant to the development of intelligence capabilities in corrections are changes in the security environment that required correctional facilities to either establish or enhance existing intelligence capabilities. Correctional managers are requiring more support from their intelligence staff, more than just the traditional role of helping to risk manage offenders posing threats to prison staff and other offenders.

The question is, what has caused corrections administrators and facility managers to recalibrate the expectations they have of their intelligence capabilities? It is beyond the scope of this chapter to provide a detailed account of all the changes in the security environment which have impacted on the development of intelligence capabilities in prisons. Instead, I will focus on two priority areas: gangs and terrorism.

Gangs

In the USA, since the early 1950s, there has been a steady increase in the numbers of gangs in major cities such as Los Angeles, Chicago, Cleveland, Denver and St Louis. It is clear that in most of these major US cities, county and state jails have had some semblance of gang intelligence units for decades. In this section, however, I will focus on how intelligence has been applied to the gang problem in the Los Angeles County jail system where the threat was recognized early. The perspectives here on gangs in the Los Angeles correctional environment draw on relevant literature, and also an interview I conducted in 2009 with Deputy Sheriff, Ramon Munoz, who works in the Operation Safe Jails (OSJ) Unit for the Los Angeles Sheriff's Department (LASD). In Los Angeles, a gang intelligence unit was informally in existence in 1986, although it was not officially recognized until 1990, when it became known as the OSJ unit. It is responsible for monitoring the activities of in-custody street gang members, prison gang members and other disruptive groups within the county jail system.

The OSJ unit was created initially to build a nexus between what was occurring on the street and who was 'calling the shots' from the county jail. This wealth of intelligence has been invaluable to detectives and the district attorneys prosecuting crime on the outside. Across the rest of California, and the USA, many county jails have followed the Los Angeles County OSJ approach. For example, the San Diego County Sheriff's Department and Las Vegas Sheriff's Department officials have been liaising with the LASD, and are now in the process of launching similar OSJ programmes using their existing gang intelligence operations units. The scope of the 'gang problem' in the US corrections system spurred the creation of intelligence activities such as the OSJ. Concerns about the growing threat of gangs have also driven change in the prison sectors of other countries.

On a different scale, in New Zealand, Prison Services National Intelligence Manager, Rick McKee suggests that dealing with gang members in custody was also one of the main drivers for prison services developing an intelligence capability. New Zealand Prison Services data suggest that 24.5 per cent of the prison population are gang members, though McKee estimates the actual number is likely to be some 10 per cent higher. Overall, this is a high number but he said it also reflects the criminal environment outside in the community (interview, 10 March 2010).

Concerns about gangs have been one driver for the development of more effective intelligence capabilities in UK prisons, but not necessarily the main one. Other factors have also been influential, including a growing focus by corrections security and intelligence officers on organized crime groups and radicalization. One senior officer from the UK National Offender Management Service (NOMS) has suggested that it was a convergence of both these issues and others, including violence, drugs and obviously escape risk, which has driven improvements in intelligence capabilities in UK prisons. In a 2008 workshop on gangs and drugs hosted by the Correctional Service Canada (CSC), a senior manager of the UK NOMS said the gangs 'were emerging but not significant' (Wheatley, cited in CSC 2008: 17). There is also little available research that provides sufficient evidence of the 'gang problem' in UK prisons – whether they are a continuum of street gangs or form in prisons is not clear (Wood and Adler 2001).

Similar to the UK situation, it is also unclear to what extent a perceived gang problem in prisons in Canada and Australia has been the major catalyst for recent enhancements in correctional intelligence capabilities. However, in the case of Canada, it is obvious from recent CSC reports that gangs, particularly outlaw motorcycle gangs and aboriginal groups, are an increasing concern generally to correctional facilities. A 2009 *CSC Research Plan* identifies gangs and organized crime as a major strategic research priority (CSC 2009: 19). The CSC's 2008 Annual Report also reports on improvements being made in the development of security intelligence networks to support security intelligence officers to deal with gangs inside Canadian correctional facilities (CSC 2008: 42). Whether a growing gang problem in the Australian correctional environment has driven improvements in intelligence capabilities is less certain. In Australia, gangs in general remain under-defined and under-researched.

Despite variations in how the threat from gangs is assessed across the different countries discussed above, the increasing imprisonment of gang members and the need to manage gangs that form inside prisons have resulted in the requirement to risk manage the prison environment to ensure the safety of both inmates and staff. The USA and particularly large cities such as Los Angeles have been using intelligence for some time to assist in risk managing the growing gang problem in Los Angeles County. The risk of gang-related violence and crime in this one county jail system is high. Deputy Sheriff Munoz in an interview described the risk posed by a diverse range of gangs to Los Angeles County in the following way:

> Los Angeles County is the gang capital of the world. LA County has over 120,000 documented gang members in its system. We have all sorts of drug cartels, organized mafias, street gangs, racist organizations, internationals and domestic terrorist groups living behind our bars. No other county in California or even the United States has the melting pot that Los Angeles has.
>
> (interview, 11 March 2010)

In response to the threat posed by gangs in custody and in the community, enhanced attempts to collect intelligence in the corrections sectors of Australia, Canada, New Zealand, the UK and the USA have been made, including criminal history checks and close liaison with policing agencies. This information has facilitated a greater understanding of gang activity and a more effective separation and management of rival gangs who may incite violence. For example, in the Los Angeles County jail system and in other US prisons, classification units frequently do the initial separation of violent inmates from the lower security level inmates. Many of these units also act as intelligence units. The interception of communication (telephone and letters), surveillance and, in some prisons, the collection of covert information from informants or undercover officers, have also produced greater strategic and operational knowledge about the risks posed by gangs in US prisons.

Like the USA, UK prisons also use interception of communications and covert human intelligence sources (CHIS). There has also been an increased emphasis in recent years in the UK prisons on working more closely with policing agencies in sharing intelligence. All UK prisons have an identified police secondee to assist in joint working, which includes sharing of intelligence and operational activity. There are also networks with other law enforcement agencies such as, for example, Special Branch and, increasingly, SOCA. While an increasing amount of intelligence is being collected in UK prisons and shared with external agencies, some correctional intelligence staff have suggested that police intelligence is still not routinely shared with prisons. Practitioners I talked to suggested this was particularly important when police intelligence related to prison safety and security.

In addition to the above-mentioned collection methodologies, Prison Services in New Zealand also use what McKee refers to as 'intelligence-led searches', trust account analysis and 'RAT chats' or Routine Activity Theory interviews (interview, 10 March 2010). Additionally, deputies working in Los Angeles County jails collect intelligence by deciphering 'KITES' or notes, messages and letters that prisoners write.

New Zealand prisons have also developed various analytical products which are orientated specifically around gangs and gang members. These include 'subject profiles' (used to identify and provide recommendations against targeting specific members' centre of gravity and critical vulnerabilities), 'knowledge profiles' (which describe a specific gang's organization, *modus operandi* and links) and 'problem profiles' (which describe the specific criminal behaviours attributed to gangs and responses to these). Similar intelligence products are produced in the UK, Canadian and Australian correctional agencies. In addition to the kinds of gang-related intelligence products mentioned already, Munoz from LASD also described other additional products that are interesting: including 'imagery analysis' on baseball cards and tattoo decryption (interview, 11 March 2010).

Terrorism

In addition to dealing with a growing gang problem in prisons, the intelligence capabilities of correctional facilities are also being challenged by managing individuals with radical Islamic views, or those who have become radicalized while in prison. The conversion of prisoners to Islam and other religions while in prison is not remarkable and many long-term prisoners do so, motivated by protection, redemption or seeking a sense of belonging (Hamm 2009). However, since 9/11, there has been greater policy and research attention on prison radicalization and its link to terrorism. Understanding the process of radicalization of Islamic jihadists in the community is difficult enough. It remains a greater challenge to accurately assess the nature of the links between conversion, radicalization and terrorism in prisons. This has been due to a combination of things including relatively low sentence rates for newly prescribed terrorist offences and a lack of focus on radicalization and terrorism by custodial facilities. It is also only recent that a more evidence-based research approach has been adopted in the US and UK prison systems to better understand the links between radicalization and terrorist activity (see e.g. RAND 2008; Spalek and El Hassan 2007; Hamm 2009). Hamm's two-year study of prison radicalization in US prisons provides some evidence of how charismatic jihadists, such as Kevin James, a 26-year-old Black Muslim from South Central Los Angeles, can adopt the beliefs and terrorist tactics of Al Qaeda. In 2005, the FBI foiled a plot organized by James' radical prison Islamic gang, Jam'iyyat Ul-Islam Is-Saheed (JIS) (or the Assembly of Authentic Islam), which involved using a newly converted and radicalized parolee to attack US military sites and synagogues in the Los Angeles area (Hamm 2009: 668).

In the UK and the USA, since 9/11 there have also been well-known cases of individuals who have become radicalized in prison, including Richard Reid, 'the shoe bomber', and Jose Padilla. In more recent years, the nature of the potential threat posed by terrorism within correctional environments within the UK and the USA, in particular, has changed due to the increased incarceration of radical Islamic jihadists convicted of new terrorist offences in these countries. With an increasing number of jihadists in custody, there are obviously concerns in the corrections sector that these individuals will radicalize and recruit other offenders to extremist Islamic groups. It is important, of course, not to view the issue of radicalization as an intelligence collection and analytical priority for all prisons. There is a concern, however, that for many correctional intelligence officers and other staff, the lack of experience in handling individuals charged with terrorism offences will make it difficult for them to assess the threat such individuals pose to radicalizing other inmates. In addition to a lack of exposure to terrorist offenders, lack of knowledge about the drivers for radicalization, or Islamic society in general, also makes it difficult for intelligence officers to assess indicators for radicalization or the planning of terrorist activity. At the Los Angeles County jail level, Deputy Sheriff Munoz suggested that few deputies are familiar with Islamic and jihadist issues for two reasons. First, county jail intelligence officers are not likely to have in their custody inmates convicted of terrorist offences. These offenders are likely to be sent to state or federal prisons. Second, in Los Angeles County those inmates converting to Islam, who subsequently become radicalized, are likely to do so in state prisons where they are sentenced for longer periods (1–20 plus years) (interview, 11 March 2010). However, it is possible that individuals could become radicalized in the county jail system, but there is little awareness by correctional intelligence officers or research being conducted on which indicators may show this is happening. Munoz in his interview suggested that there was evidence in Los Angeles that some gang members are converting to Islam in US jails. He noted that inmates are meshing traditional Islam, 'prison Islam' and Western Islam (Nation of Islam) all together, though it is less clear why they are converting.

This blurring of gang affiliations with radical Islamic identity at the county level will require US correctional officers to develop greater situational awareness of the motivations and signs that gang members are becoming radicalized by extremist Islamic philosophies, and disseminate this information to the FBI, state and county police. The weak link in our knowledge about the potential threat posed by terrorism may not come from those convicted of serious offences, who will serve life sentences, but those who become radicalized serving shorter periods, who are then released back into the community. There have already been examples of individuals becoming radicalized during shorter sentencing periods, such as Kevin Gardner, who converted to extremism during his stay at a young offenders institution in the UK in 2006–2007 (ICSR 2010: 27). What the literature shows is that gauging the extent of radicalization in prisons remains unclear. The International Centre for the Study of Radicalisation and Political Violence's (ICSR) study of radicalization in 15 countries, entitled *Prisons and Terrorism*, and Hamm's research noted earlier, are a step forward, but challenges remain in mapping the extent of radicalization and how to maximize the role of intelligence in monitoring such activity (ICSR 2010; Hamm 2009: 677).

Corrections intelligence capabilities

The above provides a sketch of how some correctional agencies have developed intelligence capabilities to deal with the threats of gangs and terrorism. It is not possible to generalize from these observations as they are not in any way a representative sample of all developments in corrections intelligence across all agencies in Australia, Canada, New Zealand, the UK and the USA. A detailed understanding of the correction intelligence capabilities is complicated by a number of factors. First, gaining access to agencies to discuss their capabilities even in a general sense is difficult. Second, based on the small number of interviews I conducted with correctional officers, understanding intelligence capabilities is also limited by different views held by them on what intelligence is. Third, variations in the development of capabilities across agencies in the one country, and the size of many corrections communities make it difficult to gain any comprehensive understanding of the entire corrections intelligence sector. However, what is clear is that for many corrections agencies both the experience of having to deal increasingly with gangs, and now offenders in custody for terrorist offences, have become catalysts for improving intelligence capabilities. Managing the gangs problem particularly in the US correctional system, but also in Canada and New Zealand, has resulted in the development of better information (case) management systems for recording data and intelligence, the development of more systematic collection processes and the movement to link 'intelligence products' more to strategic and operational decision-making.

Such actions, though important to improving intelligence collection, will not amount to much unless they can be met by equal progress in analytical capabilities within the corrections sector. Again it would be inaccurate to over-generalize this point, but based on discussions I had with correction intelligence managers in Australia, New Zealand, Canada and the USA, the pace of development in the corrections analytical cadre remains slow. It was clear from these interviews that although civilian intelligence officers are being recruited to work in the corrections environment, prison officers still largely take on the role of 'intelligence officers' as an 'add-on' rather than being employed solely to work on intelligence. This means that in many correctional facilities intelligence collection and analysis are part-time activities, particularly in regional correctional facilities. A part-time and non-professionalized approach to corrections intelligence has consequences for the strategic, operational and tactical awareness of risks and threats in the prison environment. Additionally, the lack of relevant or quality training for corrections intelligence officers remains an issue in many correctional environments, though improvements in training are being made in some agencies across the countries discussed in this chapter.

Despite current deficiencies in capabilities, as noted earlier, a more challenging security environment (including complex gang networks and radicalized groups) has required correctional departments and facilities to develop a more sophisticated, strategic and operational response to applying intelligence. Corrections intelligence capabilities will always have a critical role in managing prison safety, but there is a sense now developing among a widening number of practitioners that it has other uses, including better prediction of potential threats and informing strategic decision-making. The priority of gang-related crime and terrorism in the security and criminal justice systems of the countries discussed here has also resulted in either the development or strengthening of various strategic arrangements between correctional facilities and state and federal policing agencies in these countries. Such relationships have provided operational support to policing operations, and also given correctional intelligence officers additional information about persons of interest within their facilities, who may be involved in illicit activity within or outside jail. The development now of more 'joined-up' approaches in some correctional intelligence environments with policing counterparts will continue to influence the ways prison managers develop their ideas about how to structure intelligence capabilities and what role intelligence plays in their prisons.

For example, in the USA, many fusion centers have become increasingly engaged with correctional intelligence officers due to concerns over prison radicalization. Some fusion centers have correctional intelligence officers seconded to them, while others have liaison arrangements or memoranda of understanding for sharing information. The inclusion of correctional intelligence officers in fusion centers is still relatively new, and it remains unclear to what extent corrections information is becoming efficiently integrated into such centers' operational intelligence priorities. In other non-US jurisdictions there are additional examples of loose or informal arrangements, where correctional facilities are not necessarily fused with policing agencies, but have other liaison arrangements and memoranda of understanding that define how intelligence can be shared.

As noted earlier, in the UK, SOCA works with the prison sector on organized crime issues. Corrections and police relations are also governed in many countries by specific legislation and regulations requiring corrections and agencies to share information. New Zealand Prison Services Intelligence Manager, Rick McKee described various acts governing relationships between prisons and various other agencies, including police, health, welfare, customs, immigration and inland revenue in New Zealand. However, in some Australian jurisdictions and in New Zealand, the level and quality of liaison between correctional and police intelligence officers vary. Some correctional officers I have talked to in recent years are frustrated by what they view as a level of mistrust between their agencies and their policing counterparts. This frustration is focused on what the police are prepared to share with them in return for information provided to police. In interviews in 2009, one senior corrections intelligence officer suggested that police mistrust in sharing their intelligence with correctional colleagues is a legacy issue relating to police perceptions of poor protection of information and sub-standard information systems in the corrections sector. However, the need for a 'whole of government' response to terrorism, organized crime and gang issues will in time improve working relations, if not entirely extinguish the mistrust and organizational cultural attitudes each may have for the other.

The second question, posed at the start of the chapter, is to what extent inter-action with traditional intelligence players such as national security or policing agencies has influenced the development of intelligence frameworks and systems in the corrections environment? Unfortunately, there is no clear answer to this question, as there is little research relating to this and other related correctional intelligence practice issues in most of the countries reviewed. Correctional intelligence officers and managers, particularly in the USA, have been frequent contributors to professional publications on intelligence matters (Garzarelli 2004; Buring *et al.* 2007). More recently, growing concerns about gang violence and terrorism are generating more evidence-based research approaches to correctional intelligence issues (Hamm 2009), but the output is low compared to other corrections research on topics such as suicide, mental health and addiction issues (Shoham *et al.* 2007). There may be a number of reasons for a lack of research in the public domain. First, as noted earlier, intelligence research potentially involves the investigation of systems and processes which are sensitive. The inappropriate dissemination of research that identifies specific vulnerabilities in correctional intelligence processes could jeopardize the safe operation of the facility being examined. The second reason may be the politicized environment in which many prison departments operate. This can result in overly risk-adverse executives not wanting to be seen to be exposing any shortcomings in the public arena.

Despite the dearth of current evidence-based research on the applications of intelligence in the corrections sector, in each country there is evidence of cross-fertilization of ideas, perspectives about intelligence doctrine, models, systems and processes being 'imported' from policing and other agencies. For example, in the Australian state of New South Wales (NSW), the Department of Corrections seconded a senior NSW Police officer to enhance its 'Corrections Intelligence Group' in 2004. Similarly, in New Zealand, Corrections Intelligence Manager Rick McKee originally came from NZP and prior to that had military intelligence experience in the New Zealand Army. McKee brought over from policing how to align strategically corrections to New Zealand Police so that both could operate as closely as possible. He has also applied to New Zealand prisons what he refers to as a 'diluted' version of the UK NIM. The UK NIM and other intelligence frameworks will be discussed in greater detail in Chapter 4. Additionally, in the LASD OSJ programme, deputies have worked already in a custody environment for a few years, and most also bring skills such as different languages, military intelligence experience or have a specific intimate knowledge of a gang. Based on discussions with some key UK prison officials, it seems that very few of their intelligence staff (or officers working within security departments of prisons) come from police backgrounds. There does seem to be some cross-pollination in training with UK prison intelligence staff learning from the police at a strategic level. The UK prison national intelligence model draws on police structures (e.g. $5 \times 5 \times 5$ evaluation), although one officer advised that there were not strong parallels with the NIM, given the absence in the prison system of a strong level 2 structure (regional), as seen in the NIM for police. Despite a different approach to intelligence, the same officer suggested that there were broad similarities between the NIM and the prison national intelligence model, with the latter running monthly security meetings as a basis for tasking.

The answer to the third question raised earlier – the extent to which developments within corrections intelligence over the past decade in these countries represent good practice – again remains unclear. Interviews revealed some examples of good practice in some correctional environments in Australia, Canada, New Zealand, the UK and the USA. Further research is required to evaluate what constitutes good practice within and between these countries. What is clear from the interviews is that, for many correctional agencies, the development of comprehensive frameworks (that include effective collection and analytical capabilities), which in turn are integrated into decision-making across the sector, is uneven and in most cases a work in progress. Given the difficulty of doing intelligence research in the corrections sector, it may be some time until there is a greater willingness by agencies to trust researchers in evaluating aspects of practice. Research that is commissioned by correctional agencies may still come with heavy caveats, thereby reducing a broader scholarly understanding of effective corrections intelligence practice.

Notwithstanding the lack of publicly available evidence indicating where improvements are needed in corrections intelligence, some of the current barriers to better practice resemble those raised in debates (in the last decade) about the role of intelligence in policing. One common impediment in both intelligence contexts is the internal culture which undervalues intelligence. Managers need to demonstrate to the executive and other staff the *value* of intelligence. The National Manager for Intelligence for NZ Prisons identified cultural barriers as a major stumbling block, not just for the executive in his organization but also, ironically, for new intelligence staff in the correctional environment who were yet to be convinced of the need 'to do intelligence'. McKee summarizes well the dual challenges correctional intelligence managers face of creating the context and getting people to see the benefits of better intelligence practice, which may not be visible immediately:

> The hardest thing I have found, and what I think is the most important issue for intelligence (as people, processes and products), is the context or 'fit' of intelligence. Too many organizations like the sound of this 'intel thing' and simply bolt it on to what they already have and expect it to deliver results. This was like painting red an old car and expecting it to go faster. Intelligence works best when it has the right environment for it to work in. In corrections and in policing [in New Zealand] a few years ago, the environment was not quite right and much of my work is still less about intelligence and more about creating the context for it.
>
> (interview, 10 March 2010)

Beyond these challenges a more effective fusion is needed of corrections intelligence into policing intelligence in areas such as counter-terrorism and organized crime. The increasing number of individuals incarcerated for terrorism offences will require more systematic and formalized approaches to the collection and analysis of corrections intelligence which is in sync with external stakeholders' priorities. In the USA, efforts are being made by the corrections intelligence sector to be more integrated with external agencies on counter-terrorism and other crime issues.

For example, the FBI and the Bureau of Prisons have been working to link county corrections intelligence to federal task force arrangements such as the Joint Terrorism Task Force (JTTF). At the federal level, there are over 100 JTTFs which feed into a National Joint Terrorism Task Force (NJTTF). At the NJTTF, corrections intelligence related to terrorism from the local level can be assembled to provide a more accurate national picture of terrorism and radicalization in prisons. The NJTTF has also developed the correctional intelligence initiative (CII) to prevent potential acts of terrorism by offenders in US prisons.

The CII is led by a Bureau of Prisons secondee to the NJTTF. The CII monitors and counters radicalization and recruitment of offenders by extremist organizations and individuals. It is through the NJTTF network and other outreach programmes that Department of Justice Bureau of Prisons and the FBI outreach and engage with correctional intelligence officers at state prisons and county jails. However, despite these federal top-down arrangements, it is unclear the extent to which local information is linked up in real-time communication with federal agencies. Using Los Angeles County as an example, while the LASD is part of the local fusion center (the Joint Regional Intelligence Center (JRIC)), it is unclear the extent to which they are liaising on terrorist or gang-related issues with their fellow deputies in county jails. It is also not clear how federal intelligence collection priorities or the recent SAR initiative (discussed in Chapter 6) drives collection at the county jail level.

Given signs of radicalization in some US prisons, there needs to be a better understanding among correctional intelligence officers of radical religious and political philosophies including militant and jihadist Islam. As noted earlier, it is not clear the extent to which correctional intelligence officers have knowledge of the signs of radicalization once someone converts in jail. More effective training and awareness of indicators towards radicalization and violence need to occur at the county, state and federal level. An understanding of radicalization, jihadist Islam and building intelligence frameworks to provide early detection of these will also be important in Australia, Canada, New Zealand and the UK. A greater willingness by correctional departments to support research projects that can both evaluate intelligence officers' understanding of emerging threats and offer recommendations for improving practice generally are critical to enhancing how intelligence can support decision-making in this environment.

The biosecurity environment

Beyond the 'headlines' of counter-terrorism and organized crime, there are a range of other equally serious threats located on an ever broadening security agenda. Biosecurity-related issues are another good example of a series of threats that are found at the intersection of traditional interpretations of international and national security and the broader post-9/11 homeland security agenda.

The term 'biosecurity' is similar to 'intelligence' in that it too has different meanings depending on the audience. The current literature reflects the ambiguity and debate surrounding the term, and also impacts on how the range of issues that fall under this broad term are dealt with as far as national policy setting is concerned. In the USA, for example, the term biosecurity was originally meant to encompass activities that prevent the transmission of infectious diseases mainly in plants and animals, but more recently there has been a shift to include humans and public health. Baker provides a good survey of different definitional perspectives, arguing that it has been defined differently depending on whether it has been interpreted in terms of the pathway of attack, the source of the threat, the target or a combination of all three (Baker 2009: 122). Biosecurity has also been used interchangeably with biosafety. Both terms are obviously related, but biosafety does have a slightly different meaning which it is important to clarify here. Biosafety, according to the US Centers for Disease Control and Preventions' (CDC) *Biosafety in Microbiological and Biomedical Laboratories*, is '[the] discipline addressing the safe handling and containment of infectious micro-organisms and hazardous biological materials.' The CDC suggests that 'the principles of biosafety were first introduced in its 1984 first edition of *Biosafety in Microbiological and Biomedical Laboratories* and have carried through to the most current fifth edition' (CDC 2009: 1). These principles focus on the containment and risk assessment of harmful biological materials. In summary, biosafety is about containing and safe handling of infectious biological material in order to protect laboratory workers, the environment and the public from exposure to infectious micro-organisms that are handled and stored in the laboratory. It involves a risk assessment process to ensure appropriate safety equipment is utilized to prevent laboratory-based infections. The focus for biosafety is on the protection of the individual working with micro-organisms in the laboratory rather than the community.

In contrast to biosafety, 'biosecurity' is newer terminology, and first came into vogue in the past decade. The fifth edition (2009) of CDC's *Biosafety in Microbiological and Biomedical Laboratories* does not define biosecurity but states its objective is to 'prevent loss, theft or misuse of microorganisms, biological materials, and research-related information'. 'This is accomplished by limiting access to facilities, research materials and information' (CDC 2009: 105).

The CDC explanation of biosecurity is too narrowly focused on laboratories and their employees as the source of threats or those most likely impacted by them. Other definitions are also too narrow – focusing on either 'accidental contamination' or 'deliberate acts of bioterrorism', without considering other biocriminal activities (Ryan and Glarum 2008: 19). In simple terms, the aim of biosecurity is to protect dangerous biological materials from *accidental or intentional release into the community or environment*. In other words, inherent to biosecurity is protecting *populations* of humans, animals and plants, as well as the environment rather than just the individual dealing safely with dangerous micro-organisms in a laboratory. The spread of micro-organisms could be of course by accident via a global epidemic or intentionally via a criminal or terrorist act.

Another potential difference between biosafety and biosecurity, is the latter involves the intentional release of dangerous micro-organisms which constitutes a criminal act. Someone who avoids declaring prescribed food items at the border, or a terrorist group who intentionally releases dangerous micro-organisms as a weapon against humans, plants, animals or the environment, both pose a biosecurity threat. In either scenario, intentional or unintentional (e.g. in the case of an epidemic), biosecurity involves the prevention, detection, assessment and response to biohazards on a community, national and global scale.

The focus in this section is to assess how emerging intelligence approaches are being applied in the national security and health sectors to deal with a range of biosecurity threats. These threats include those that are intentional (from 'weaponizing' dangerous biological material – bacteria, viruses and toxins), and others that are unintentional from a diverse range of pathogens that threaten the food supply and the environment. Given limited space, I will not focus on how intelligence support is provided to detecting or assessing the threat of biological weapons from states or rogue nations. The issue of state-based biological weapons programmes has been dealt with extensively elsewhere, for example, Christopher *et al.* (1997) and Alibek (1999) who provide a brief history of biological warfare programmes between the two principal Cold War protagonists, the USA and the former Soviet Union. In short, though, the USA, the UK and the former Soviet Union did develop a series of biological weapon programmes, which were very effective particularly in the 1960s and 1970s. Most of these were progressively terminated in the USA and the UK, however, the Soviets kept up their manufacture of biological weapons until the late 1990s when they reportedly destroyed their stocks (Ryan and Glarum 2008: 13).

Throughout the Cold War, the 1972 Biological and Toxin Weapons Convention (BWC) became the principal international instrument to attempt – although many would argue unsuccessfully – to ban the production and proliferation of biological weapons. The BWC always struggled to provide (like relevant conventions for nuclear proliferation) a suitable verification mechanism to monitor the destruction of agents, toxins, weapons and biotechnology required to make biological weapons. In 2001, efforts to improve the BWC's inspection and verification process stalled (Koblentz 2009).

After the Gulf War and leading up to the invasion of Iraq in 2003, diplomatic and intelligence attention shifted from residual WMD proliferation concerns between the USA and the former Soviet Union to the intentions and capabilities of rogue states and non-state actors. Although it is easy to lump the threat posed from each WMD source (nuclear, chemical or biological) together in the same acronym, the nature of the threat each poses is not the same. In each case there are differences in the ease of their production, proliferation and detection by intelligence capabilities. The production of fissile material (uranium or plutonium), its enrichment beyond a certain weight and the sourcing of specialized production materials, such as gas centrifuges, have globally been more controlled between the five major nuclear powers (the USA, the UK, France, Russia and China). Leaving aside concerns about North Korean and Iranian nuclear proliferation, in contrast to producing biological weapons, the development of a nuclear bomb still remains technically more difficult. The enrichment of uranium beyond a certain quality and quantity more quickly focuses suspicions and inspections from outsiders than those weaponizing biological materials. In contrast, the production and transfer of micro-organisms and related biotechnology are an easier enterprise for states and non-state actors. Biological materials can be produced easily and cheaply in the normal context of bioresearch, and those with harmful intentions can cover their tracks by carrying out their activities covertly in a range of legal public or private laboratory sites.

The extent to which intelligence agencies are able to detect and disrupt biological weapons proliferation remains today just as challenging as it was during the Cold War. The transference of biotechnology from one state to another attracts less attention from authorities given the multi-use of biological substances and technology in pharmaceuticals and vaccine production. The establishment by the USA in 2003 of the Proliferation Security Initiative (PSI), which uses US and other like-minded countries' intelligence and military efforts to proactively counter WMD proliferation between rogue states and non-state actors, may be beneficial in reducing the threat of biological weapons proliferation. National security intelligence agencies may 'get lucky' at intercepting the odd ship, which is transporting suspicious biological material and biotechnology from or to a country of concern. But the probability of intercepting, for example, shipments of biological material from North Korea, which reportedly does have the ability to produce biological weapons (Gronvall *et al.* 2009: 437), is extremely low, given pathogens and the technology to weaponize them are already freely available in most countries. Additionally, only very small amounts of biological material may be required for a successful bio-attack somewhere – making it unlikely a ship will be 'packed to the rafters' with anthrax. The fact that biological materials and biotechnology are now also inherently linked to legitimate global research and trade questions the validity of traditional non-proliferation and counter-proliferation measures in biosecurity, such as the PSI.

Intercepting or detecting biological weapons relies of course on having actionable intelligence that can provide forewarning that a bioterror attack is being planned. However, the Director of the CIA, Leon Panetta, at his confirmation hearing underlined the difficulty for intelligence agencies in finding the 'tactical footprint' of any imminent operation involving biological weapons (Panetta, cited in O'Toole and Inglesby 2009: 2). Despite enhanced biosafety and security in public and commercial laboratories in many Western countries, very small amounts of micro-organisms can still be produced quickly and discreetly with legitimate dual use biotechnology in these environments. Alternatively, micro-organisms can be produced in countries where biosafety and biosecurity standards and export regulations are weaker (e.g. North Korea, Iran and Syria). In contrast to nuclear and chemical weapons of mass destruction, where intelligence may be in a better position to warn ahead of time of a weapons programme or an attack, conventional intelligence collection strategies may not prove overly helpful in interdicting biological weapons, particularly in circumstances which do not require sophisticated ballistic launch programmes.

This difficulty in detecting the tactical launch of a 'bioterror weapon' also makes it challenging to assess accurately, with any confidence, what threat level is posed from different kinds of bioterrorism. As noted earlier, since 9/11, several concerns have been raised about the growing threat from bioterrorism (e.g. Brower and Chalk 2003; Gursky *et al.* 2003; O'Toole and Inglesby 2003). Such concerns are warranted by a number of incidents pre and post 9/11, which demonstrate the motivation of some groups, if not yet their capability to use biological weapons. For example, in the 2007 memoirs of George Tenet, the former Director of the CIA (*At the Center of the Storm*), Tenet mentions two individuals who were instrumental in Al Qaeda's attempts to develop a biological weapons capability. In 1999, Al Qaeda's Deputy Ayman al-Zawahiri recruited a Pakistani veterinarian Rauf Ahmad to establish a small biological weapon lab in Khandahar, Afghanistan. Apparently Ahmad's efforts were short-lived and he quit the operation reportedly over not being paid enough. The second individual, Yazid Sufaat, was a US-educated Malaysian biologist. Sufaat had isolated anthrax in a building in Khandahar, but it had not yet been weaponized. Both Ahmad and Sufaat were later arrested trying to flee Afghanistan in 2001 (Tenet 2007: 278–279). In 2002, incoming US forces destroyed Al Qaeda's bioweapons laboratories in Afghanistan. Although the labs were pre-operational, they demonstrated the ability of terrorist groups to adapt operational planning to bioterror rather than conventional attacks such as improvised explosive devices. A second worrying incident involved anthrax spores found in the US mail system. This attack turned out to be the actions of what the FBI believed to be a mentally unstable scientist, Bruce Ivins, who was working at the US Army Medical Research Institute of Infectious Diseases (USAMRIID) in Fort Detrick, Maryland. Ivins later committed suicide before being charged officially by the FBI in August 2008 (Mackenzie 2009). Although the attack killed only five people, it underlined to officials in the early days after 9/11 the vulnerability of the USA to other bioterror attacks.

While in a general sense, the threat from a potential bioterror attack exists, there are diverse assessments between scientists and intelligence experts on the capabilities of some terrorists groups to produce and 'launch' bioterror weapons of sufficient magnitude to kill hundreds of thousands of people. As noted earlier, the generally widespread availability of biological material occurring naturally in most countries, accompanied by cheaper communications, transportation and biotechnology globally makes the accessibility of biological material easier for terrorists who wish to use them. But accessibility does not necessarily mean easier weaponizing. In 1994, many years before the 2001 anthrax mail scare, the well-resourced and organized Japanese cult Aum Shinrikyo secured anthrax, botulinum toxin and

Q fever. They tried to release potentially deadly clouds of these biological substances at least a dozen times but were unsuccessful. In one instance, they used anthrax spores from the roof of a building in Tokyo, but they deployed a harmless strain used in veterinarian vaccines which had no effect on their human targets (Broad 1998). In March 1995, they turned instead to sarin gas – spraying it in the Tokyo subway – killing 12 people and injuring several thousand others.

The Aum Shinrikyo case illustrates that different bacteria and viruses have varying requirements for their production, storage and weaponizing, and these conditions must be met in order to safely produce sufficient amounts of the harmful micro-organisms required. A terrorist group could decide, for instance, to produce anthrax but first needs to source it. They could attempt to extract it from contaminated ground soil in areas where anthrax is endemic to cattle, or it could be sourced by a 'lone wolf sympathizer' working inside a usually highly controlled laboratory environment, or from an overseas supplier in the Middle East or Africa.

The terrorists would then need the services of a well-trained microbiologist who could adeptly and safely cultivate it. Biological weapons production obviously cannot be done in the same manner and conditions used by a group of people sitting around a kitchen table making a simple fertilizer bomb. Without a safe laboratory environment, with all the appropriate ventilation and barrier protections, the terrorists would kill themselves first before having the opportunity to launch their planned attack. Perhaps a well-resourced group, with the appropriate number of skilled biologists and technicians could cultivate anthrax, but the bacteria also needs to be freeze-dried, and most likely then rehydrated into an aerosol form for weaponizing. Weaponizing bacteria requires a scientist with additional technical skills beyond merely growing the culture. In any case both of these skills are not likely to be found necessarily in all microbiologists. The successful launching and dispersal of the biological weapon containing the anthrax also depend on selecting a delivery system that would ensure maximum exposure if the goal was multi-casualties.

Delivery of the weapon to the target also relies on wind, time of day, weather and atmospheric conditions, and perhaps ideally a cloudy day, given anthrax may quickly degrade in the sun as strong ultraviolet rays can degrade the bacteria's DNA. The point of the anthrax example is not to downplay the possibility that a terrorist group could produce and weaponize such a dangerous micro-organism. Rather, its intention is to highlight that it is not helpful to either overplay or underplay any specific biological weapon scenarios, without further intelligence and scientific analysis of the specific biological agent and the group showing intent to use it. It is clear that an operational decision by a terrorist group to go down the biological rather than conventional explosive weapons route throws up a number of additional logistical hurdles before a successful attack is possible. The conditions that will both constrain and facilitate the operational use of biological weapons need to be understood more across different bio-agents. In summary, a more sophisticated analysis of the risks and threats posed by specific biological agents and the groups that may wish to use them needs to occur.

Regardless of the level of uncertainty over the likelihood and capabilities of specific terrorists groups to carry out some kind of bioterror attack, there is at least a political consensus by the Australian, Canadian, New Zealand, UK and US governments that the use of biological weapons in terrorist attacks remains a significant threat. For example, in the US ODNI public version of the *National Intelligence Strategy*, 'mission objective one' and 'two' articulate clearly the priority of WMD proliferation and countering violent extremists' use of such weapons (ODNI 2009a).

While the focus by those on bioterrorist threats has been on 'traditional' agents such as anthrax, smallpox and the plague, there is an almost endless list of harmful micro-organisms and toxins that could be used by terrorists. The attack may not of course be in the first instance against humans, but could result in the release of a toxin or invasive species (plants, pest and insects) to impact the food supply or environmental security. There is also a range of new potential types of bioterrorist threats such as terrorists possibly using new genomic data or 'DNA hacking' to exploit DNA sequence information (Carlson 2003; Hammond 2006). Scientists using synthetic genomics have been able to reassemble the polio virus, which disappeared naturally in the 1970s, and the extinct 1918 strain of the influenza virus which killed 20–40 million people globally. Biotechnological advancements will soon allow scientists to decode the DNA sequence of other microbes and even create new microbes. Such biotechnology has dual use applications for legitimate biomedical research, but could also be exploited by terrorist groups seeking to use a 'super-bug' that had been genetically engineered with no available vaccine to counter it.

In light of the earlier discussion of biosecurity's broader meaning than bioterror attacks, a number of unintentional threats which might still have an impact on human biological security are pertinent. Again, the potential list is extensive, but would include pandemics such as the severe acute respiratory syndrome (SARS) and H5N1 which have already posed threats to global health. Biosecurity threats also include viruses, bacterial and other epidemic or infectious diseases to animals such as foot and mouth disease, which occurred in UK cattle in 2001, and biological threats to plants and the environment, which have a direct or indirect impact on humans from both a health and economics perspective.

Under the broader interpretation of biosecurity discussed earlier, the ability of intelligence applied both in the health and security context to tactically assess the possibility of an imminent threat (intentional or unintentional) is unclear. It is not possible to 'lock out' all hazardous pathogens which are readily found in nature to combat terrorism or any other biosecurity threat. Terrorist groups have proved to be flexible in their operational methodologies and target selection. Global trade in food commodities (plants and animals) also poses significant quarantine risks to particular countries, but these risks in many cases cannot be totally contained given that nations rely on such trade for continued economic development. This wider interpretation of biosecurity also means that intelligence officials working across the national security, health, agricultural, fishery, quarantine and animal health areas contexts, need to plan for a range of threat scenarios that go beyond conventional traditional biosecurity threat scenarios, such as anthrax attacks from terrorists. Others need to be considered, that are a bit more 'left of centre', yet could be possibly even more devastating on a nation's food supply, biodiversity and economy than the classical intentional bioterror scenarios.

As noted earlier in our discussion of bioterrorism, unintentional epidemics can quickly become global pandemics, with little warning, and the role of tactical intelligence sources in detecting and containing 'disease hot spots' in human, animal and plant populations will remain a challenge. It will also not be easy to assess, at least at the start, whether an epidemic was an intentional act of a jihadist terrorist, a racial supremacist, a disgruntled former government employee or whether it is an unintentional health event. Biosurveillance will be crucial in detecting epidemiologically early tactical indicators of a disease outbreak, and also hopefully mapping the actions of any perpetrators. But it will remain extremely challenging, and frankly is unrealistic for domestic security and policing intelligence to provide sufficient tactical warning to disrupt or contain every biosecurity incident, particularly those which may have just become operationalized.

As noted earlier, the military development of offensive biological weapons in the UK, the USA and the former Soviet Union during the Cold War provided much of the initial focus by national security intelligence agencies on this threat type. During this period, the focus of agencies such as the CIA was on the production and export of biological weapons and biotechnology in the Soviet Union. However, estimating the USSR's biological weapons capability was always an inaccurate process for reasons discussed earlier (Gronvall *et al.* 2009: 437). The application of biological weapons in the military context also provided some of the earlier impetus for the development of research and analysis of biological security and public health issues in civilian laboratories that we see today. The work carried out, for example, by USAMRIID – the US military laboratory discussed above – in Maryland has the primary responsibility for providing US military personnel protection against biological threats in the battlefield. However, its research activities are dual use and also provide the non-military population with medical defences against potential biological weapons. This exchange of biomedical research between defence and civilian laboratories in the USA provided an early model for cooperation between other federal government agencies, such as traditional intelligence agencies like the FBI, and those working in health-related areas that work with 'intelligence' from an epidemiological perspective.

Since 9/11, the scale and intensity of cooperation between traditional intelligence agencies (national security and policing) and other non-traditional players (in this case, health, epidemiology, biomedicine), who in the past would not normally have had a seat at the national security table, have increased. In the biosecurity context, a number of influences have brought national security intelligence, the health and scientific communities together. As discussed earlier, the 2001 anthrax in the mail incident and other unintentional health threats such as the 2005 SARS outbreak and avian influenza all have national security implications. These incidents cannot be dealt with by health or security agencies alone. I would argue that global health issues have become more securitized as the result of these recent pandemics, and this has consequences for how health and intelligence agencies now interact (Enemark 2007: 1–25). Pandemics, of whatever cause, also underscore the need for traditional intelligence actors (national security and policing agencies), and emerging intelligence practice areas (epidemiologist and biomedical scientists), to combine skills and capabilities in order to more effectively deal with a number of threat issues across the full biosecurity continuum.

In a sense, the 2001 anthrax spores in the mail incident became an early test case for how traditional intelligence agencies and those who use intelligence principles in a health or scientific context could work together on a biosecurity incident. The 2001 anthrax investigation brought policing and health intelligence workers closer together, with the FBI conducting a criminal investigation and the CDC conducting an epidemiological investigation. Tumin argues that these investigations in the FBI and CDC produced large amounts of information, though both agencies lacked protocols for 'sharing what they knew and distributing it correctly' (2007: 3). The anthrax mail threat investigation exposed the normal investigative challenges that 'traditional' security and law enforcement agencies such as the FBI face, but it also highlighted coordination and information management issues between law enforcement, health authorities (such as the CDC) and the scientific community. In summary, while the 2001 anthrax investigation highlighted challenges between agencies with a national security and others with a health focus, it represented, if not by design, an experiment on how such diverse agencies could collaborate during a biosecurity investigation.

The central question remains, however, to what extent are the evolving post-9/11 biosecurity arrangements in Australia, Canada, New Zealand, the UK and the USA fostering more effective and collaborative intelligence initiatives between traditional national security intelligence, health and scientific agencies? If intelligence is to play a role in the detection, prevention, disruption and response to biosecurity threats, intentional or otherwise, to what extent are good intelligence methodologies being applied in this context?

In the last section of this chapter, I summarize some of the key policy developments in biosecurity for these countries as they relate to answering this question. After a brief survey of recent biosecurity policy changes in each country, I will suggest some ways that current biosecurity arrangements might be better supported by the application of more effective and formalized intelligence methods and processes.

Post-9/11 biosecurity policy arrangements

Space does not permit a detailed listing of all major biosecurity policy landmarks in Australia, Canada, New Zealand, the UK and the USA, so discussion will be restricted to how key policy developments have influenced attempts by traditional intelligence practitioners (policing and national security agencies) to connect with their counterparts in the biosecurity intelligence context. The discussion will show that each country has developed their own unique response to biosecurity issues, however, two broad commonalities are immediately apparent. First, as noted above, in all these countries, especially after 9/11, a broader view of what constitutes national security has emerged, and issues such as bioterrorism and pandemics have as a result become more securitized in the past decade. Second, in all these countries post 9/11, there has been a greater attempt to rationalize government responses to biosecurity. Governments have gone about this rationalization differently, and for the most part it is too soon to provide any definitive evaluation as to whether they contribute to effective biosecurity in these states. In general, reforms in the UK, the USA and Canada have resulted in multi-agency response to dealing with various biosecurity threats and risks. In contrast, the New Zealand and Australian response has been an amalgamation of a series of previous agencies, which had different responsibilities for biosecurity into supra-agencies such as 'Biosecurity New Zealand' and 'Biosecurity Australia'.

Australia and New Zealand biosecurity policy

A common strand in both countries is to have a single agency dealing with this issue – at least the animal and plant aspects of biosecurity. In Australia since the election of the Labor Government in 2007 there have been a series of major national security-related policy statements released. I will come back to these in Chapter 6, but arguably the most important of these was the Prime Minister's National Security Statement, released in 2008. The Statement was important in signifying an even greater 'whole of government' approach to national security – one which adopted an all hazards philosophy to security issues. A key deliverable from the Prime Minister's Statement was to have a broader national intelligence community than the usual traditional groups of agencies. An expanded intelligence community now includes others such as the AFP, the ACC and Customs and Border Protection. A widening of the national security community now allows a broader number of agencies to decide on nationally significant intelligence requirements for Australia via the new National Intelligence Coordination Committee (NICC) (see Chapter 6).

However, other than Customs, the significance of biosecurity issues has not been captured in any significant way in the wider NICC membership. For example, the Department of Health and Ageing and the Australian Quarantine Inspection Service (AQUIS, now part of the new supra-organization of Biosecurity Australia) are not members of the NICC. A quick way to remedy this would be to have a member of the peak national committee of expertise of biosecurity, the National Biosecurity Committee as a member of the NICC, and ensure Australia's domestic security intelligence agency, the Australian Security Intelligence Organisation (ASIO), is represented on the National Biosecurity Committee. ASIO, the Defence Intelligence Organisation (DIO) and AFP have some expertise on aspects of bioterrorism, however, these agencies cannot provide the relevant scientific and epidemiological analysis of various biothreats, and it this expertise which needs to be represented in senior forums such as the NICC. Current arrangements reduce the efficient decision-making about a range of biosecurity threats (terrorists and non-terrorist), which potentially impact on the economic, social, health, political and environment security of Australia.

There are two recent additional policy landmarks that may be influential in the longer term in the development of biosecurity arrangements in Australia, though the jury is out as to what impact they will have on how traditional intelligence agencies (national security and policing agencies), and those with 'intelligence-like functions' in health, veterinary medicine, quarantine and biosecurity research can work closer together on a commonly understood biosecurity agenda. The first policy initiative is the Beale Report, *One Biosecurity: A Working Partnership* released in September 2008, which reviewed Australia's quarantine and biosecurity arrangements. The government had commissioned the review over concerns about the levels of cooperation and fragmentation between federal and state agencies responsible for various biosecurity activities. The review occurred against the backdrop of a few disease outbreaks in animals such as the Hendra virus outbreak (1994–2008) and equine influenza in 2007.

The Hendra virus was particularly concerning as it can be transmitted from its host (bats) to horses and then humans. Hendra virus incidents underscored deficiencies in Australian biosecurity arrangements, and the need for more collaborative connections between various experts dealing with different stages of a biosecurity threat. In the Hendra virus case, there needed to be better coordination and integration of expertise between those working on the virus, including wildlife biologists, vets and human disease specialists (Prowse *et al.* 2009).

The Beale Report is noteworthy in advocating Australia move away from a traditional isolationist defensive quarantine approach that tolerates no risk to a more realistic one in the age of globalization, which promotes a risk management approach pre-border, border and post-border. Beale was also noteworthy in recommending the development in Australia of one supra-institution that would pull together disparate agencies responsible for biosecurity. The report, however, makes scant reference to the role of intelligence in promoting better risk management of biosecurity, and there is only one reference to a new national biosecurity authority needing to work collaboratively with other relevant portfolios including police and intelligence agencies.

The focus of the report is squarely on quarantine, animal and plant biosecurity issues. There is no attempt, other than a passing reference, to examine how these issues are related to human biosecurity and bioterrorism issues (Beale 2008: 158). The final biosecurity policy initiative relevant here was the 2010 publication of the Australian Government's *Counter-Terrorism White Paper: Securing Australia – Protecting Our Community*. However, surprisingly, this report has no specific section on bioterrorism; these threats are dealt with superficially together with other WMD categories (chemical, radiological and nuclear weapons) (Department of Prime Minister and Cabinet 2010).

It is not certain when the recommendations of the Beale Report will be implemented fully. At the time of writing many of the recommendations were still being considered as part of the government's budgetary process. There is little publicly available detail also from the human health policy side of biosecurity. The Australian Government's Department of Health and Ageing simply states in its annual reporting cycle that it is 'working with its counterpart, the Department of Agriculture, Fisheries and Forestry to ensure human biosecurity aspects are "modernised and integrated" within the new holistic biosecurity approach that underpins the Beale Review' (Department of Health and Ageing 2009: 222). While Australia has an effective quarantine approach, it is still not clear how the disparate policy initiatives discussed above will provide the country with the *one* national biosecurity approach, which can best risk manage a range of human, animal, plant and environment biosecurity threats. The current Biosecurity Services Group in Australia's Department of Agriculture, Fisheries and Forestry has a compliance and investigations area. There is also an area in the Department of Health and Ageing that deals with health security (particularly the regulation of sensitive biological agents that could be used for terrorist purposes). Though it is not at all clear whether both these areas have developed strong intelligence systems and processes that can assist in risk management decision-making for known or future threats across the entire biosecurity continuum. Recently the Australian Government funded an Australian Biosecurity Intelligence Network (ABIN) to enhance connectivity, information management and analysis between biosecurity agencies. However, the usefulness of the ABIN for sharing relevant time-sensitive biosecurity information among all stakeholders is unclear, given funding for this project is only for 18 months and the network mostly connects biosecurity scientists rather other stakeholders such as policy-makers.

Given the current arrangements, it also unclear whether the Department of Health and the Biosecurity Services Group have securitized their work and view their activities as having broader national security implications. Despite the recent rhetoric of a more all hazards approach to national security, the fractured policy response leaves one wondering whether the Australian intelligence community fully understands strategically and operationally the full range of biosecurity threats (intentional or otherwise) that could impact on the health and prosperity of Australia.

In 2003, the New Zealand Government went through a similar biosecurity review process to Australia which resulted in a new biosecurity strategy. Also, like Australia, the review resulted in the amalgamation of various agencies and functions into one new department, the Ministry of Agriculture and Fisheries Biosecurity New Zealand (MAFBNZ). The New Zealand biosecurity review, *Protect New Zealand: Biosecurity Strategy for New Zealand* (New Zealand Biosecurity Council 2003), was authored by the Biosecurity Council and identified in some respects similar capability vulnerabilities to those found in the Australian Beale Report. For example, the *Biosecurity Strategy for New Zealand* also referred to a fragmentation of biosecurity activities across several agencies, isolated silos of information and poor information sharing and systems (ibid.: 23). The report also highlighted that a more proactive approach was required in assessing threats and that current arrangements (in 2003), did not provide for strategic identification and management of risks. The report concluded that risk management had become increasingly reactive and this had escalated costs (ibid.: 23).

However, the strategy did not articulate how intelligence collection and analysis across New Zealand's biosecurity sector could create a better understanding of risks and threats at a tactical, operational and strategic level. The report was also very scant on how plant and animal biosecurity is linked or could be integrated better with the New Zealand Ministry of Health biosecurity responsibilities. Finally, although the report at the beginning clearly stated that its focus was not on bioterrorism, interestingly it did comment that 'conceptually bioterrorism is simply another vector for transmission of unwanted pest and species' (ibid.: 7). Given this comment, it would have been useful for the authors to come to a conclusion if they saw a role for Biosecurity New Zealand in preventing bioterrorism through the transmission of such pests and species and what that role may be. However, it is also clear since the implementation of the 2003 Strategy, the new department – MAFBNZ – has progressed some intelligence initiatives to assist in developing a more proactive targeted approach to risks and threats particularly at the border. For example, since 2007, MAFBNZ intelligence staff have been co-located with other law enforcement intelligence officers based at the NZ Customs Service National Targeting Centre. These officers have been learning from Customs intelligence colleagues how to better profile biosecurity risks, including passengers arriving at air and seaports. This joining of biosecurity intelligence officers with Customs has also promoted better information sharing between agencies (Horton and Airs 2009: 7). The New Zealand academic and scientific community members such as the New Zealand Centre for Biosecurity and Infectious Diseases have also been active in the investigation, diagnosis and management of outbreaks of suspected infectious diseases. This centre highlights the importance of research in generating intelligence gathering on emerging diseases or other unusual or suspicious disease events. But again it is uncertain what links exist between this work and the collection and analysis on bioterrorism or biocrime threats by New Zealand's traditional policing (NZP) and key national security intelligence agency the New Zealand Security Intelligence Service (NZSIS). While the New Zealand Ministry of Health has portfolio responsibility for managing human diseases and pandemics, it is uncertain whether the new National Intelligence Centre at NZ Police Head Quarters, or the NZSIS run multi-agency Combined Threat Assessment Centre (CTAG), includes seconded specialist analysts, who could provide human or animal assessments on bioterrorism and other biosecurity threat issues.

The vulnerability of island countries such as Australia and New Zealand to the introduction of an exotic pest animal or plant, whether it was a terrorist, criminal or unintentional act, could easily threaten unprotected environments or unprotected primary industries. The net effect of such a scenario may be less compared in the short term to a terrorist group dispersing anthrax spores on the Sydney subway, but could do more damage in the long term if it impacted on the environment of the agricultural production of both countries. One estimate by Biosecurity New Zealand suggested a foot and mouth attack in that country would result in a 4 per cent drop in gross domestic product (GDP) in the first three months of the outbreak. After one year, it estimated that the cumulative loss in nominal GDP would be around NZD 6 billion (New Zealand Biosecurity Council 2003: 36).

Unlike Australia and New Zealand, the remaining countries (the UK, Canada and the USA) discussed below have multi-agency approaches to managing risks across their biosecurity sectors. Additionally, in contrast to Australia and New Zealand, the three countries share borders with others and in the case of the UK, multiple borders via the European Union.

United Kingdom biosecurity policy changes

In the UK, there are a number of government agencies that play a role in the country's biosecurity response at the national and local levels. In relation to the bioterrorism aspects of biosecurity, the Home Office leads the UK Government response and has a chemical, biolocial, radiological and nuclear (CBRN) team, and terrorism protection unit (with scientific seconders) to deal with bioterrorism issues. Several bioterrorism-related initiatives have come out of the Home Office Counter-terrorism Strategy, particularly in research, science, technology in the detection and management of biological incidents. In addition, the MI5-run JTAC now includes medical intelligence staff (Royal Society 2009: 5). Since 9/11, there have been changes at the Cabinet Office, which have brought enhanced levels of intelligence and policy coordination on all national security issues, including bioterrorism. For example, the establishment in 2001 of the Civil Contingencies Secretariat (CCS), which reports to the Prime Minister via the security and intelligence coordinator, was set up to improve the resilience of the central UK Government across a range of national security issues, including bioterrorism. 'Resilience' has become the core guiding principle for UK national emergency and contingency planning and has been defined by the Cabinet Office as 'the ability at every relevant level to detect, prevent and, if necessary, to handle and recover from disruptive challenges' (Cabinet Office 2003: 1). In March 2010, the Cabinet Office released further 'concept of operations' documents on how it would coordinate a response to a national emergency through its 'briefing rooms'. The March 2010 document lists pandemics such as H1N1 (swine flu) as one national emergency category that the Cabinet Office Briefing Rooms (COBR) would respond to (Cabinet Office 2003: 7).

Post 9/11, there have been also significant changes in the public health response to biosecurity issues in the UK. While the Department of Health provides 'resilience' in the prevention, control and treatment of infectious diseases, the Health Protection Agency (HPA) was created in 2003 to provide a more integrated response to protecting public health. The HPA has been established with functions that are not too dissimilar to the US CDC. It includes a number of important centres (the Communicable Disease Surveillance Centre, the Centre for Infections and the Centre for Emergency Preparedness and Response), which together provide impor-tant expert advice, early warning, investigation and response to accidental or deliberate threats to public health. The HPA's diagnostic and epidemiological expertise involves the use of 'health intelligence' techniques, with the establish-ment in 2004 of a medical intelligence unit, but it is not revealed if MI5 or policing officers are also part of the Agency's investigative team.

There are other policy players in UK biosecurity that stretch across other areas such as the Department for Environment, Food and Rural Affairs (DEFRA), which provides policy advice and some investigative capacity for controlling and managing the outbreak of diseases in the food supply, the environment and agriculture. However, again it is not revealed how animal health monitoring by DEFRA is integrated into policy responses to human health by the Department of

Health or the HPA. A 2009 Royal Society policy document argued that it 'was currently unclear which government department has overall responsibility for infectious diseases of both humans and animals at a policy level, and that a clear national policy is essential to achieve greater integration' (Royal Society 2009: 3). This suggests that despite the recent progress in the UK described above, there is not a single coordinated approach to biosecurity threats across the plant, animal and human health continuum. The UK fragmented response across all sectors of biosecurity is also common in the USA.

US biosecurity policy changes

Both the UK and the USA share other similarities in biosecurity policy approaches. Since 9/11 each has created new national security and health security arrangements, increased funding for biosecurity research and even conducted joint exercises together such as 'TOPOFF 3'. However, both countries' policy prescriptions are different in other respects, reflecting differences in their political structure, geography, population and overall funding for bioterrorism and biosecurity issues. All these factors have impacted heavily on the ultimately different policy approaches between the UK and the USA (Jones 2005).

The US policy approach to biosecurity has evolved rapidly since 9/11. It is not germane to discussions here to describe in detail all the major changes in biosecurity policies since 2001. Instead in this section, I will describe briefly some of the legislative and presidential directives that have shaped current policy directions, and show how these initiatives have impacted on the relationship between traditional intelligence and emerging intelligence practice in health sectors. As noted in Chapter 1, almost immediately after the 9/11 attacks the Bush Administration created the DHS in 2002. The DHS mandate included becoming the lead agency for domestic management and coordination of federal operations to prepare for, respond to and recover from biological weapons attacks.

Following the establishment of the DHS, President Bush issued a number of Homeland Security Presidential Directives (HSPD), which further provided a policy 'blueprint' for biosecurity issues. Starting in 2002 with HSPD 4, *National Strategy to Combat Weapons of Mass Destruction* (DHS 2002), Bush outlined a strategy to combat WMD, although the document did not say much about biological threats or the broader suite of biosecurity threats. A later HSPD emphasized other aspects of biosecurity discussed earlier in this chapter. For example, HSPD 9, *Defense of United States Agriculture and Food*, (DHS 2004a), called for a national policy to defend the country's agriculture and food supply against accidental and intentional disease outbreaks.

While these earlier executive measures were important, HSPD 10, *Biosecurity for the 21st Century* (DHS 2004b), and HSPD 21, *Public Health and Medical Preparedness* (DHS 2007), arguably have resulted in the most comprehensive US Government efforts to counter bioterrorism and other biosecurity threats. HSPD 10 was critical in laying down the foundations of a national biodefence programme that included threat awareness, prevention and protection, surveillance and detection and response and recovery. HSPD 10 in particular resulted in the establishment of three major initiatives: (1) the Biowatch Program (a network of environmental sensors to detect bioweapons attacks against major US cities); (2) Project Bioshield (a programme to accelerate the acquisition of medical counter-measures against bioweapons); and (3) the establishment of the National Biosurveillance Integration System (NBIS) (aimed at integrating human, animal and plant health surveillance information with food and environmental monitoring system and threat and intelligence information in real time). Another important measure was the creation of the National Biodefense Analysis and Countermeasures Center (NBACC), which does lab analysis to identify scientific underpinnings for current and future biological threat agents at Fort Detrick, Maryland.

HSPD 10 acknowledged that intelligence had an important role in enabling all these aspects of the national biodefence programme. However, the unclassified version of this document, at least, lacked any general comments about how intelligence could prevent or *disrupt* biological threats. The focus was more on how intelligence could play a role in responding to threats (DHS 2004b: press release).

HSPD 21 is also important in understanding US biosecurity approaches, as it established a strategy for public health and medical preparedness. Unlike HSPD 10, the focus is less on bioterrorism and more on providing a national approach to preparing US citizens against all kinds of potentially catastrophic health events. A big part of the strategy is the development of a national biosurveillance programme in order to better maintain situational awareness during a major health event. The directive is ambitious in that it seeks to engage government agencies at federal, state and local levels with academia and the private sector to respond effectively to a range of health incidents. Of particular relevance for national security and health intelligence agencies working closer together, the directive called for a 'national health security strategy'. The lessons learnt from the anthrax spore attack in the US mail system in 2001 in getting agencies with more traditional policing and security intelligence roles to work with those in the health sector have been progressed through HSPD 21, and subsequent initiatives such as the National Responses Framework.

However, despite progress being made between federal, state, local security and health services and the development of initiatives such as the 'National Response Plan', some biosecurity specialists have commented that the USA 'does not yet have a concept of operations or clear biosurveillance objectives' for such a plan. O'Toole and Inglesby argue that a 'concept of operations' is still needed that would 'map out how different levels of government, and critical private sector actors would respond to a bio-attack or to other public health emergencies of national significance'. They argue that a concept of operations is important in order to avoid a 'BioKatrina' (2009: 28).

Other researchers have welcomed the renewed policy emphasis on biosecurity, particularly the more 'whole of government' approaches emphasized through broad strategic statements such as HSPD 21. Nuzzo suggests that some headway has been made in implementing biosurveillance systems across the country, but the systems' ability to provide real situational awareness during what she describes as catastrophic health events is uncertain, given there is no clear overarching national strategy for designing, testing, staffing, maintaining or funding such a system (Nuzzo 2009: 37). Nuzzo also suggests that:

> A workable concept of operations must underpin any effective national bio-surveillance system if multiple agencies and authorities in the federal government responsible for parts of biosecurity are able to develop an effective national surveillance capability. Such a capability needs to capture and coordinate not just public health emergency responses, but also must have a way to bring in the broader security agencies response to any national health crises.
>
> (ibid.: 37)

As noted earlier, the DHS at the federal level is at the centre of a range of bioterrorism and biosecurity initiatives. Given also the central role that the DHS is establishing in coordinating federal, state and local approaches to intelligence generally, it makes sense for it to take a leadership role in coordinating health and national security intelligence flows relating to biosecurity issues. However, it is clear from interviews conducted for this book in the USA that the DHS is still building its capacity to generate its own intelligence as well as act as broker for intelligence produced at regional and local levels. Therefore DHS's ability to effectively coordinate intelligence from local and state policing, health and emergency agencies in order to predict or provide accurate real-time situational awareness during a public health crisis intentional or otherwise remains questionable. This is not to suggest that DHS is not making further improvements in connecting national security and health intelligence at federal, regional and local levels. But there are challenges ahead that will impact on the USA and the abilities of other countries in building integrated nationally effective biosecurity responses which bring together the appropriate mix of national security, policing and health intelligence expertise at the appropriate time.

Canadian biosecurity policy responses

Canadian biosecurity policy developments, like the USA, have been a multi-agency approach, though in contrast the pace of reform has been more incremental since 9/11. In Canada, the most recent significant biosecurity policy landmark was the release in October 2003 of the *National Advisory Committee Inquiry on SARS and Public Health*. This government-commissioned inquiry followed the SARS epidemic earlier that year, which by August 2003 had resulted in 44 deaths in the Toronto area. The report detailed a range of systemic deficiencies in Canadian public health including in information systems and sharing (Health Canada 2003: 1). The key recommendation of the National Advisory Committee report was that Canada needed a new national public health authority. This recommendation was implemented in 2004 with the establishment of the Public Health Agency of Canada. Within this new department a specialized area called the Canadian Centre for Emergency Preparedness has the responsibility for centrally coordinating public health issues as they relate to disease outbreaks and health security-related matters such as bioterrorism. The Centre is broken down into additional sections, such as the Counter Terrorism Coordination and Health Information Networks which liaise with other stakeholders to raise awareness and provide early warning response surveillance to the health related aspects of WMD. The Centre also manages the Global Public Health Intelligence Network (GPHIN), which provides an early warning global surveillance website to disseminate real-time information to public health professionals worldwide on risk management, prevention, control and response measures. GPHIN was developed in 1998 by Health Canada in collaboration with the World Health Organization (WHO). It has extensive coverage in seven languages and its news reports comprise 40 per cent of WHO's verified diseases outbreaks (Hitchcock *et al.* 2007: 210).

Other more recent policy and legislative progress has been made in making the links between national security and biosecurity. In 2009, the Canadian Parliament passed the Human Pathogens and Toxins Act, which provides domestic oversight of pathogens and toxins including an inventory of who possesses them, and assessments on how safely they are being stored to prevent their deliberate or accidental release. And, additionally, from a policy perspective Canada's Chief Public Health Officer spoke of a 'one health' approach, which suggests a desire to connect the plant, animal and human dimensions of biosecurity.

Though this is encouraging rhetoric, it is not revealed how these connections are being forged from a policy perspective on the ground. It is not clear how Public Health Canada health intelligence networks are securitizing potential biosecurity threats, nor whether CSIS or the RCMP is using this information to respond and predict health threats, which may be deliberately released into the community. A glance at the membership list of the CSIS-run Integrated Threat Assessment Centre (ITAC) suggests that Public Health Canada is not a partner agency within the Centre. It is possible that Public Health Canada may provide input into health security-related threat assessments, but a more integrated and strategic relationship between national security and health intelligence issues could be achieved by an appropriately cleared health officer being embedded in the ITAC. Additionally, more strategic and proactive working relationships between the scientific, national security and health communities over biosecurity will be required in the future if the government wishes to articulate a common vision for biosecurity. The Council of Canadian Academies may be the appropriate body to draft such a vision for the government.

Towards a more effective biosecurity intelligence approach

Based on the discussion above of biosecurity policy developments in Australia, Canada, New Zealand, the UK and the USA, it is clear that each country has developed their own policy prescriptions to this issue. Despite some of the differences, three common themes in each country can be identified, which underline the current challenges each face in building effective biosecurity intelligence capabilities. In particular, each of the themes shows that both traditional intelligence practice (policing and national security) and health intelligence agencies could do more collaboratively to detect and respond to a range of biosecurity threats.

The first challenge is, how can governments get beyond their current fragmented approach to biosecurity? The USA and the UK have the most fragmented policy response with the creation of new agencies and coordinating bodies, however, even in Australia and New Zealand there are still multiple agencies across the biosecurity sector responsible for a range of plant, animal and human health threats. Much work has been done on reforming different parts of the biosecurity spectrum – plants, animals and humans – yet less on how to integrate these reforms more effectively to produce holistic biosecurity strategies. This remains a concern in all of the five countries examined, and the impact of this fragmented policy and intelligence space is evident in recent disease outbreaks, which were not identified early or crossed animals to humans, causing death. Recent epidemics such as the Hendra virus and avian influenza are examples of zoonotic diseases that can only be effectively dealt with if scientists and others working across different components of the biosecurity spectrum collaborate on mutually understood national biosecurity priorities. Some scientists and policy-makers in the biosecurity area have started talking about a 'one health' approach (Prowse *et al.* 2009) to biosecurity, yet as noted earlier it is still too early to know whether governments are moving beyond such rhetoric in practical terms. In general, there needs to be a much stronger link to establishing biosurveillance and biosecurity intelligence goals with the broader national security priorities, and this needs to be managed at the central national intelligence coordinating level. So in each country discussed, whether it occurs in the contexts of central coordinating mechanisms such as the ODNI in the USA or the Joint Intelligence Committee (JIC) in the UK, more consideration needs to be given at the senior executive intelligence coordinating level in governments to biosecurity threats. In an increasingly 'all hazards' approach to national security, central government intelligence coordinating bodies need to provide a clearer guidance to political decision-makers of what the key intelligence collection priorities are for *all* 'biosecurity intelligence' related issues not just bioterrorism. This will require individual members of the intelligence community, and intelligence priority setting committees to look across the entire biosecurity spectrum, and assess how threats in one area may be related in other areas. The setting of biosecurity intelligence collection priorities will also require an integrated approach to biosurveillance across different contexts, including some areas that may have previously not been thought of as relevant to national security, policing and defence, including environment, fish and wildlife, agribusiness, public health, biotechnology, clinical areas and related research.

The second challenge to building a more effective biosecurity intelligence approach relates to human resources. In short, there needs to be greater biological, epidemiological and health intelligence expertise in policing and national security intelligence agencies. The incorporation of additional specialists will provide policing and national security intelligence agencies with more focused threat assessment, collection and analytical efforts for the prevention, detection and investigation of bioterrorism and biocrimes. In particular, based on much of the existing literature (which is lacking in any sophistication or precision about the nature of various biothreats), there is a critical need to more accurately estimate the risk and threat posed by biothreats. A more integrated role by epidemiologists, biologists and other public health experts in national security intelligence analysis and investigation will help to increase the accuracy or current calibration of biosecurity threats. Scientists can do this by helping to combine scientific disease modelling, biotechnology and biomedicine together with policing intelligence methodologies such as target profiling of offenders, and other evidence of conspiracy to use biological agents for malicious intent. Challenging, yet necessary questions need to be asked about the likelihood and capability of the use of various dangerous biological agents by various individuals or groups. For example, are the key biosecurity threats more likely to come from human transmission, zoonotic transmission, or via the environment, and what more can be done to assess their likelihood and capability using an amalgamated health and national security intelligence approach?

This second challenge is particularly important given in most cases a sudden disease outbreak frequently cannot be identified as deliberate or accidental, and disease experts will, at least in the first instance, be in a better position to track and interpret the significance of any biosecurity threat than their policing or national security intelligence colleagues. Additionally, enhanced levels of biosecurity expertise embedded with national security and policing intelligence agencies will be increasingly important in developing a more strategic approach to intelligence in the biosecurity context. Epidemiological modelling and some of the assessment work of future biological threats being sponsored by the DHS in the National Biodefense Analysis and Countermeasures programme, will also be useful in the early identification of other unintentional biological threats to humans, animals, plants and the environment. Some of these may not be terrorist-based, but many threats will still pose a worrying risk to national security and well-being. In summary, it is in this strategic space, where a threat has not yet actualized or caused harm that security and health intelligence principles can best be put to use to prevent, disrupt or contain myriad biosecurity threats, rather than merely reacting to a disease outbreak.

While it is desirable to increase the biosecurity intelligence capabilities of policing and national security intelligence agencies, the third challenge to overcome is to recognize and resolve differences between biological scientists and analysts working in traditional security contexts.

In Chapter 1, I described how the 'culture of secrecy' has defined strongly national security intelligence and policing practice. In contrast, the scientist tradition is marked by open enquiry, collecting and disseminating evidence in an open forum. So a key challenge will be to manage the different cultures, assumptions, priorities and even language between biological scientists and their national security and policing counterparts working on biosecurity issues. As noted earlier, some of these organizational cultural issues were on display during the 2001 anthrax investigation in the USA between CDC officers and FBI investigators. Not all these differences of course need to be resolved or are resolvable, but at the very least there needs to be a greater appreciation of what traditional intelligence and biological or biosecurity intelligence can bring to the table, and how each of these skill sets can inform better decision-making. Part of resolving some of the differences will obviously rely on a greater mutual understanding of skill sets.

For example, national security and policing analysts working in the biosecurity sector need to have at least a basic understanding of epidemiological principles, including their critical role in providing early warning of suspicious disease outbreaks, and their ability to model the trajectory of diseases. Biological scientists working on suspicious outbreaks need to understand various sensitive methodologies (for example, target profiling, covert sources and data matching), that their analytical cadre use to collect and analyse information on targets which may be intentionally releasing biological hazardous material into the environment. And there also needs to be a greater appreciation between the two that in some respects both health intelligence and national security intelligence analysts also use similar methodologies (e.g. geo-spatial information systems and analytics), albeit for different outcomes. A greater understanding between science and security colleagues of how similar and different methodologies are applied in various contexts, hopefully will result in a better integration of health and security techniques – allowing in turn for an improvement in the intelligence and evidence produced in biosecurity cases.

The fourth challenge that is obvious from the policy overviews for each country discussed above is information and intelligence sharing. To some extent, the information and intelligence sharing problem is not having necessarily insufficient intelligence, but in many cases there are too many sources of biosecurity information across a number of different systems. The diverse data sets dealing with biosecurity issues reflect in all these countries (some to a greater or lesser degree) the fragmented response to the issues among public and private agencies. Ideally, a more common biosecurity intelligence network that can move information and intelligence around between national security and policing agencies, scientists, public health officials and responders is required. There is a clear need to improve current biosecurity intelligence architecture and information management in order to maximize surveillance efforts against biosecurity threats in order to avoid a catastrophic biosecurity incident – intentional or otherwise. Nuzzo makes this point for the USA, arguing there is a need for one surveillance system rather than the many sometimes interoperable ones that currently exist. As Nuzzo suggests, 'It seems that one agency needs to take the lead in promoting better health information systems that can efficiently link health care and public health information' (2009: 37). Of course privacy issues arise here, and Americans have never been great fans of having their personal information, particularly health-related information, on government databases. But there does seem to be need for a system that can quickly move clinically relevant information from treating the individual patient to passing it on to other agencies if it has either broader public health significance, or is nationally significant from a biosecurity perspective. In the case of the USA, the

Department of Health should take on this health intelligence/information coordination role. But to be effective from a broader biosecurity perspective, relevant health care information needs to be better linked into the DHS intelligence network too, and this raises additional legal and governance challenges of possibly sharing some national security relevant information with scientists and clinicians in order to achieve better overall collection and analysis against a biosecurity threat.

In addition to developing national biosecurity intelligence and information networks that can allow real-time sharing of national security, policing and health intelligence, this system needs to promote better information sharing at the local levels. Again this is a challenge in any of the countries discussed above, given the large number of community, county, city, state and regional health departments, hospitals, public and private laboratories that may have useful information which could be swept up in any national biosecurity intelligence network. Again there are enormous challenges involved in just identifying what are the current platforms for data and information sharing and what are the legal, regulatory, liability issues relating to sharing of health data, criminal history information and top secret data (Tumin 2007: 10). One DHS-sponsored initiative to better integrate public health and community health interests into the broader Homeland Security information and intelligence sharing framework is the Health Security Intelligence Enterprise (HSIE), though this system is yet to become a fully developed framework to share health security information.

In the short to medium term though, perhaps in the case of the USA a more useful way to improve connectivity between those working on biosecurity in traditional intelligence agencies and those working on intelligence in the health or biology sector would be to maximize the latter's participation in the over 70 fusion centers established across the country – to better integrate counter-terrorism intelligence between federal, state and local authorities. Similar to the policing and national security agencies represented in fusion centers, health specialists can reach back into their own agencies and laboratories to source information which is directly relevant to assessing biosecurity threats.

Health authorities are in a position to more rapidly access and share information about suspicious disease outbreaks with their policing and national security intelligence partners, and this local information could more quickly be disseminated by DHS federally. Health experts could also contribute biosecurity expertise to any ongoing investigations generated from intelligence coming into the fusion center. Conversely the fusion center could prove to be an excellent structure to share relevant intelligence about various threat actors of concern to local health authorities, who will have a role in their containment or responding to them. In my visit to the Los Angeles fusion center (JRIC), it was pleasing to find that there is a registered nurse from the Los Angeles County Department of Public Health, and an analyst writing on a range of health security-related topics. In the case of Los Angeles too, the County Department of Public Health and the Los Angeles Field Office of the FBI have also established a technical advisory group to jointly share and analyse information that would allow the early detection and investigation of a WMD threat (Diamond and Kim 2010: 221). But it is not clear how other fusion centers have included health specialists to work across biosecurity issues that are relevant to their national security and policing counterparts in these fusion centers. There is also the question of whether the health specialist staff seconded to a fusion center are the most appropriate people to provide the necessary expertise to their policing and national security counterparts. What kind of mix of health expertise might be appropriate, epidemiologists, registered nurses, physicians, biologists and why? We have seen from the discussion above that other countries have also tried other ways to 'fuse' biosecurity intelligence and information such as in the JTAC and the medical intelligence unit in the HPA, but it is not clear to what extent the work on collection, analysis and investigations supports across the spectrum of biosecurity issues other than bioterrorism.

Conclusion

In conclusion, this chapter has focused on two emerging intelligence practice areas – one in the corrections and the other in the health context. Although the 'business' of corrections and biosecurity operate in very different environments, both reflect how intelligence capabilities are developing in non-traditional intelligence practice areas. In each sector there are significant challenges to the effective application of intelligence to inform decision-making. In corrections, there still remain in each of these countries concerns over the resourcing of intelligence functions to ensure adequate collection and analysis of threats at the operational, let alone at the strategic intelligence support level, for decision-makers. In many correctional environments, a fully developed intelligence framework is still not part, either by design or due to funding, of the core business. The growing concern in many prisons of increasing organized crime being conducted by offenders in prisons, and a greater need to understand levels of radicalization within prisons present complex challenges for the corrections environment. Such challenges will require the application of well-designed and well-run corrections intelligence programmes. Similarly, the biosecurity context, as discussed earlier, presents four key challenges for intelligence practice – some of these relate to definitional issues while others are more technical. At the definitional level, there is still an unresolved issue in many countries of what constitutes 'biosecurity'. This lack of certainty has clouded the policy response to biosecurity, and therefore which issues should be given priority and why. Not having a common policy understanding of what biosecurity is across the health and national security spectrums has also resulted in a fragmented intelligence response to the suite of potential threats. On a more specialized level, our discussion of policy developments above demonstrates that there are significant opportunities for national security agencies, policing and scientists to collaborate much more on biosecurity issues and investigations by using their specific approaches to intelligence. This is not to suggest, however, that such cooperation does not occur, merely that it needs to be more frequent and formalized in many cases.

To a large extent, the challenges identified in the corrections and biosecurity environments rest on the ability of political decision-makers and the executive leadership of the agencies concerned to understand more clearly how intelligence can *enable* their decisions, and help predict new evolving threats in these emerging intelligence contexts. This in turn will rely on corrections and biosecurity agencies building holistic approaches to intelligence, and embedding them in their overall organizational structures, rather than seeing intelligence as just a tool to be used periodically.

An effective intelligence system can only work if it is part of the real-time decision-making environment, where intelligence assessments are integrated into other information feeds decision-makers are receiving. The current rhetoric in many countries about 'homeland security approaches', 'national resilience' or 'all hazards approaches' suggests that policy-makers have in mind the inclusion of some of these emerging practice intelligence areas into a broader response to contemporary security issues. The rhetoric is noble in practice. However, the traditional intelligence practice areas of national security and policing, with their own distinct 'intelligence traditions' (including long-held cultures of secrecy) will find it challenging to work with emerging practice areas which do not share this same 'tradition' and have new intelligence frameworks that are yet to fully reach their potential. But in the two examples discussed in this chapter, it is obvious there are increasingly more threat issues emerging in the security environment, which are of common concern for traditional intelligence players and emerging practice areas. It is therefore in the interest of maximizing our impact on various threats in the security environment, that academics and practitioners expand their normally narrow focus on just national security or policing intelligence to evaluate what is being done in emerging practice areas. There needs to be far more attention than there has been to date on how activity in emerging practice areas can be used in a more integrated way to improve overall the ability of all decision-makers to make a positive impact on the security environment. The other important reality is that emerging intelligence practice areas are shaking the boundaries of our previous understandings of what intelligence is all about in the post-9/11 environment and what we need to do to improve it.

3 Intelligence and capacity building

Introduction

In this last chapter of Part I, the focus moves from the local and national applications of intelligence (both in traditional and emerging practice contexts), to examine how intelligence frameworks and processes are being implemented as part of broader capacity building in fragile states and regions. In a sense, part of the 'story' of national security and policing intelligence developments discussed in Australia, Canada, New Zealand, the UK and the USA also includes their involvement overseas in building local intelligence capabilities in fragile states. Overseas development in intelligence has been motivated by a number of factors, including of course such 'assistance' being an extension of the donor country's own collection and analytical capabilities. This was particularly the case during the Cold War where both the US-led and Soviet-led blocs were trying to garner support and interest in various parts of the world.

However, the focus in this chapter will be on the past decade and how during this time some national security and policing agencies exported various intelligence capacity building programmes. These programmes were often part of broader peacekeeping missions, post-conflict states reconstruction, and/or enhancing security or justice institutions in fragile states. In this chapter, the focus is on fragile or vulnerable states, though many of the issues discussed also apply to post-conflict state contexts, given that a post-conflict state will usually also be a fragile state. But the term seems pretty elastic – what do we mean by a fragile state? For the purposes of this discussion, we will use a definition from the Organisation for Economic Cooperation and Development's (OECD) *Whole of Government Approach to Fragile States Report* which says that: 'State fragility is found in a state's inability or unwillingness to provide physical security, legitimate political institutions, sound economic management and social services for the benefit of its population' (2006: 18).

The growing threat from transnational security actors, particularly transnational crime and terrorism, has prompted Western liberal democratic countries to look more closely at regional vulnerabilities, where a lack of political, economic and security governance could help foster new sources or transit points for transnational threats to fragile states. The Australian government's and the AFP's role in building policing capacity across several countries in the South Pacific in order to deal with offshore threats is an example of one Western donor country's attempt to address regional vulnerabilities.

In the past decade there has been an increasing amount of literature on how to improve policing practice generally in peacekeeping (Oakley *et al.* 1998; Berkow 1999; Bayley 2001) or police reform and capacity building initiatives (Bikales 1997; Rose-Ackerman 2004), however, there is no published research on what donor countries are doing to develop intelligence capacity building, and whether this is effective and sustainable practice. As the global and regional security environment becomes more complex, policy-makers and the community in Western donor countries are increasingly confronted with a range of security governance dilemmas by their vulnerable neighbours. This chapter uses two case studies (the AFP's *Pacific Transnational Crime Network (PTCN)* and the *Extraordinary Chambers in the Courts of Cambodia (ECCC)* to examine how donor countries and agencies have implemented intelligence capacity building initiatives in fragile, post-conflict and vulnerable states or regions. The key aim in this chapter is to examine how effective and sustainable such initiatives have been in their contexts, and the role that evaluation research can play in identifying good intelligence capacity building practice.

The chapter is divided into four sections. The first section will briefly overview the main security governance issues that have prompted donor intervention in fragile and vulnerable states in recent years. The second section will define 'intelligence capacity building', and the third will explore, via the two case studies, how intelligence capacity building has been used in very different contexts. The fourth section draws together the issues raised in each case study to determine how effective and sustainable these initiatives have been and whether they represent good practice. The fourth section will also address how these case studies contribute to our knowledge on how to develop 'democratic' intelligence systems in fragile, post-conflict and vulnerable states. The case studies are drawn partially from interviews of current and former officers involved in each, but also are based on insights from my own involvement in some aspects of the case studies. Before proceeding any further, a note of caution should be added here. Two case studies are what they say they are: 'two studies', and are not of course representative of all the different kinds of intelligence capacity building initiatives that exist globally. Both cases do, however, highlight common issues that require further and more formal evaluation in order to assess their relevance to other locales with fragile states such as in the Middle East, Europe and Africa. The insights from these case studies also illustrate the diversity of intelligence capacity building projects and highlight issues that could be investigated further by researching case studies in other locales.

Security governance and fragile and post-conflict states

Governance is a term with many different definitions. As discussed later in Chapter 5, it is a term which is very relevant to intelligence practice generally, regardless of whether the context is developed or fragile states. However, the focus here is on governance in the capacity building context of fragile states. In the development context there are numerous definitions for governance. The United Nations Development Program (UNDP) defines governance:

> As the exercise of political, economic and administrative authority in the management of a country's affairs at all levels. Governance comprises the complex mechanisms, processes and institutions through which citizens and groups articulate their interests, mediate their differences and exercise their legal rights and obligations.
>
> (UNDP nd)

This generic definition provides some insight into the central role of governance in any state, but it is more focused on the role of political leadership and judicial institutions than on articulating specific types of governance. Although the quality of executive power and parliamentary leadership plays a vital role, governance in fragile or vulnerable states is not only about the effectiveness of political institutions, but also how the state interacts with the private sector and civil society. Security governance is also informed by other political and economic governance issues of the state.

So in this chapter, we define 'security governance' as the effectiveness of processes and institutions of a state that are involved in providing security services to their citizens. Good or high levels of security governance mean that these services are provided efficiently and ethically. Other characteristics of strong security governance include: accountability in decision-making, services provided to protect all people equitably, and the community and the private sector playing important roles in the state's security policy-making and implementation process.

With 'security governance' defined, we can now explore how intelligence capacity building projects in the two cases studies have influenced, or been influenced by, the security governance issues of project recipients. However, before this discussion, it is important first to contextualize issues raised in the case studies by briefly going back to discussions commenced in Chapter 1 about the nature of the evolving security environment. As noted in Chapter 1, the changes in the security environment over the past decade have also required intelligence agencies to adapt to new threats as well as 'old ones', albeit re-packaged in different ways. Strategically and operationally, this has meant that the intelligence priorities many agencies now list are different than what they were at the end of the Cold War. There is now in national security and some (national) policing agencies a greater prioritizing of the many intra-state and international dimensions of this constantly changing security environment. This is clear in both case studies (South Pacific and Cambodia), as the rationale of why donor states sponsor intelligence capacity building projects to support low security governance. From an international and transnational perspective in both the South Pacific and Cambodia, there is a long list of threats to the security governance of each location. Transnational threats such as terrorism, organized crime, environmental crime, illegal fishing, passport fraud, movement of small arms, illegal trade in endangered species and money laundering are of concern. The security environment in the South Pacific also has an intra-state dimension. Threats are generated by political instability such as civil war in Bougainville, instability in the Southern Highlands of Papua New Guinea (PNG), the breakdown of the state in the Solomons and successive coups against elected governments in Fiji (Firth 2005: 91). Low economic growth and the pressures of globalization on vulnerable local industries such as sugar have produced more urbanized populations, with increases in criminality as alienated and unemployed urban youth look to illicit ways to make money. South Pacific nations' security governance is also impacted by natural disasters and disease. For example, HIV/AIDs has become almost an epidemic in parts of PNG. The 29 September 2009 tsunami triggered by an earthquake, which killed 170 Samoans, is a reminder of how natural disasters can impact on these fragile states and their ability to maintain social development and stability (BBC 2009).

Internal threats that produce or worsen existing low security governance levels include situations where police and security institutions are weak in professional standards, training and processes. Corruption, a lack of democratic processes or traditions, and security institutions being a partisan instrument for illegal acts by the state or guerilla movements, also contribute internal threats to security governance. An example of this latter point can be found during 1999 and 2000, where the poorly disciplined Royal Solomon Islands Police Force (RSIP) frequently took sides between the two ethnic militia groups involved in conflict over land (Watson 2005: 404). The net effect of the RSIP actions contributed further to a worsening of security governance and lawlessness in the Solomon Islands. The nature of donor support in both Cambodia and the South Pacific region has also ironically in some instances contributed to lower security governance. For example, in the South Pacific, 'cheque book' diplomacy by some countries in the Asia-Pacific region has also resulted frequently in poorer or uneven economic outcomes. For some fragile states, offers of assistance from Western donors in security areas also raise cultural concerns and can exacerbate existing levels of mistrust local communities have of policing and security agencies. In the Cambodian case, the civil war ended back in 1991, but many of the security governance issues discussed above in the South Pacific context have also played out in this country's pathway towards building more effective institutions of civil society and justice.

What is intelligence capacity building?

Capacity building and governance are related concepts, and arguably an effective capacity building project should deliver enhanced governance within the society concerned. Not surprisingly, the literature shows that capacity building is as contested an idea as governance. For those interested in a brief overview, a peak Canadian non-governmental organization (NGO), Canadian Hunger Foundation (CHF), briefly documents how various historical perspectives have influenced how capacity building has been defined (CHF 2007: 5–10). However, a more comprehensive source is Deborah Eade, a development and humanitarian specialist, who has written extensively on the topic. Eade argues that the term originated in the NGO development literature (1997: 1). Given Eade's background, much of her work sees capacity building from a community-based or NGO perspective rather than from the traditional Western donor view. Eade suggests that many Western donor initiatives implemented throughout the developing world in the 1980s and 1990s, such as the structural adjustment policies, resulted in these countries becoming poorer not richer (Eade 1997: 14; Eade 2007). However, even within the NGO aid sector there is not a unified view on what capacity building is or how best to go about it (Kaplan 2000; Gunnarsson 2001; Low and Davenport 2002).

In addition to the NGO development sector, several ideas about capacity building have also arisen from United Nations' (UN) agencies, particularly the World Bank and the UNDP. The UNDP annually produces its *Human Development Report* that not only examines conventional economic indicators (such as gross national product (GNP) or per capita income), but also assesses other social indicators (such as food security, employment, military expenditure and educational performance). These indicators together produce a composite Human Development Index (HDI) for each country.

In 1997, the UNDP began to define what it called 'capacity development' as:

> Both a means and an end for sustainable human development. It empowers people to realise their potential and better use their capabilities, and assures ownership and sustainability of development programmes.
>
> (UNDP 1997: 12)

In summary, research from NGOs, the UN, government aid authorities and development researchers demonstrates a diverse range of views on capacity building in the broad development context. These include complex issues such as: state vs. community capacity building objectives, sustainability, equity, the social and cultural impacts of intervention, and distinctions such as individual vs. organizational capacity building. All of these issues are also relevant to thinking about intelligence capacity building.

Based on the brief review of the capacity building literature, I have defined intelligence capacity building here as:

> involving the conception, development, implementation and evaluation of a project that involves the transfer of intelligence-related knowledge, processes and technology to an individual, state or region from a locale, where there is weak security governance. The end result of the intervention should be an improvement in the security governance of the recipient.

This definition is intentionally broad for two reasons. First, capacity building can occur on different levels: individual, state, region or a combination of all three. Second, it recognizes the complexity and relativity of the term 'weak security governance'. For example, not all intelligence capacity building will occur at the very fragile or even 'state failure' end of the spectrum. For instance, there are a number of other policing and security intelligence initiatives underway in the Asia-Pacific region and other regions for states that are not at the lowest level in the UNDP human development indices. For example, the regional Jakarta Centre for Law Enforcement Cooperation (JCLEC), partially funded by the Australian Government, has for many years now trained police from the region in specialized subjects such as CT and intelligence. The regional countries which attend these programmes may have specific capacity vulnerabilities, but this does not mean that they have either a low or lack of security governance all together. As noted earlier, at the other end of the scale, however, security governance levels can be so low that the state begins to fail. A good example of this was the Solomon Islands Government's inability to arrest increasing social instability resulting in an Australian-led intervention – the Regional Assistance Mission to Solomon Islands (RAMSI) in 2003. The AFP contingent of RAMSI had to build, virtually from nothing, new policing institutions including the development of rudimentary intelligence capabilities. In summary, a broad enough definition is needed which will allow researchers to evaluate intelligence capacity building projects in different environments along the weak security governance continuum – not just fragile or failing states. The definition proposed above is clearly focused on the developing world context. So I am not referring in this chapter to other 'capacity work' going on around the world *between developed states* to improve intelligence and investigative capabilities, which may occur on a consultancy basis.

What are the uses of intelligence capacity building in states?

The uses of intelligence building capacity building are potentially many. The two case studies below explore two different contexts, i.e. creating a regional intelligence network and developing intelligence capability to support justice and national healing in the case of Cambodia. Both of the case studies show different areas within the intelligence process that have been targeted by capacity building efforts. Depending on the requirements of donors and recipient countries, intelligence capacity building projects could usefully focus on a range of specific issues, such as improved tasking and coordination processes, new doctrinal approaches, training, more effective collection and analysis, enhanced quality products or information management systems. For the tasking and coordination category, it is possible that a donor could sponsor a project offshore aimed at implementing training for intelligence managers or evaluating tasking and coordination processes.

Relating to intelligence doctrine, processes and education training issues, capacity building projects could include implementing an intelligence service model in a government agency, and training staff to work in it. Information management projects could include a wide spectrum of activities, such as funding a new database that can be used by analysts or building one that can be connected to a broader number of departments. Capacity building in the 'intelligence products' category could include training analysts to write effective strategic intelligence products or supervising the development of an effective dissemination process for products.

Finally, a project may take a more macro perspective by seeking to build, almost from scratch, a new intelligence framework in a country or region. The macro approach would include all the key enabling activities, in addition to the core parts of the intelligence cycle, required to support more effective intelligence processes. Chapter 5 will discuss in detail what these key enabling activities and core intelligence processes are, and why they are important to the development of good intelligence frameworks.

Regardless of the nature of a particular project, intelligence capacity building should be about increasing in some way the security governance levels of the recipient. If it does not result in, for example, an offshore policing agency being able to use better collection and analytical methodologies, which result in better informed local and donor decision-makers, then it is not likely to advance the security governance levels of the recipient. However, as shown in the case studies, intelligence capacity building is complex, and unlike the peacekeeping and state building literature, little detailed knowledge is publicly available about the challenges or what donors, intelligence practitioners and academics can learn from their implementation.

I will return to this point later, but it is worth noting based on the case studies below, that intelligence capacity, like any other development strategies, do present broadly similar challenges including different expectations of the project, political, cultural and economic ones. These challenges impact upon how the project is implemented on the ground, and obviously need to be taken into account in the way capacity building projects are designed. For example, the donor and recipient country's expectations may differ from the start or diverge at some point during the project. For the donor, an offshore investment in analytical training or covert collection methodologies might be aimed at containing terrorism or transnational crime far away from its borders. But these donor objectives may clash with local priorities in having, for example, intelligence officers supporting investigations into local threat issues. Monitoring projects effectively to counter the corrupt or inappropriate use of project resources will also be challenges to a lesser or greater degree in some environments.

Case study 3.1 The Pacific Transnational Crime Network (PTCN)

In this case study, we examine briefly the PTCN created incrementally by the AFP since 2002. In the late 1990s, there was a growing concern about the threat posed by transnational crime (particularly drug trafficking) in the Pacific region. Major AFP-instigated regional operations such as 'Operation Logrunner' resulting in the discovery of 357 kgs of heroin in Suva underlined this concern. Other concerns such as political instability in PNG, Bougainville and the regional significance of the 9/11 attacks were also influential in the establishment of the PTCN. Since 2002, the AFP has established Transnational Crime Units (TCUs) in Fiji, Samoa, Tonga, Vanuatu, PNG and Micronesia. In addition, the Network consists of a central coordinating node called the Pacific Transnational Crime Coordination Centre (PTCCC). Its role is to manage and coordinate policing intelligence provided by each TCU, and to exchange intelligence with other stakeholders throughout the wider Asia-Pacific region. The PTCCC was originally established in June 2004 in Suva, but moved to Samoa in November 2007 following the 2006 coup in Fiji. The PTCN is an interesting case of intelligence capacity building at a regional and networked level. It is a unique arrangement in its objectives to promote policing intelligence capacity in a series of interconnected fragile states in the South Pacific rather than just one state. It is not exclusively an example of intelligence capacity building, it also involves strengthening local Pacific policing agencies' ability to investigate transnational crime. The PTCCC does, however, have a number of important intelligence capacity building outcomes. These relate to funding small TCUs and the PTCN to be able to perform a range of intelligence-related tasks at tactical, operational and strategic levels. Supporting the TCUs is aimed at enhancing the investigation of complex transnational criminal cases within the South Pacific that may impact on Australia's or other stakeholders' interests. Other stakeholders and clients of the PTCN include regional institutions such as the Pacific Island Forum, the Pacific Island Chief of Police and other donor countries such as New Zealand, France and the USA, who have either contributed funds to the project or have a close interest in its operations. The PTCCC has traditionally been involved in the selection of policing staff from the PTCN countries, and training them with basic intelligence skills to work in support of transnational crime investigations within TCUs.

The project has involved a range of objectives, including the promotion of policing intelligence skill sets, knowledge and professionalism. Training and mentorship have been an important part of meeting this objective. Another objective of the project is to develop more effective relationships between Pacific policing agencies and other stakeholders in the region. The development of an intelligence IT network has been important in facilitating greater communication and networking between the PTCN members and stakeholders. A third objective has been the development of higher quality intelligence assessments on transnational crime issues that can help set intelligence collection and analytical priorities for the PTCN and its clients and stakeholders. As noted earlier, the central nodal point of all the TCUs is the PTCCC. It has played a coordination role to augment the activities of the various TCUs based in individual Pacific countries. The TCUs are smaller than the PTCCC and may be staffed by only a few investigators who also perform intelligence roles. In contrast, the PTCCC has more staff with a team leader/ manager, and staff are generally more experienced in intelligence compared to those working in the TCUs. TCU staff are normally rotated through the PTCCC to get more experience

The PTCN has had some notable operational successes in recent years such as Operation Logrunner in May 2000, followed quickly by Operations Montego and Hampstead. In June 2004, the seizure of a large methamphetamine laboratory set up by an Asian organized crime syndicate (Operation Deva/Outrigger) in Suva that was capable of producing approximately 500 kgs of methamphetamine a week underscores these successes. Operational outcomes are one indicator that this capacity building project has improved security governance both for Australia and also for the fragile South Pacific states involved. However, it remains difficult to assess confidently how effective and sustainable the PTCN project is, and whether what has been implemented is good practice. It is clear that significant challenges remain for the PTCN. Historically, these have included the tasking and co-ordination of intelligence, training of analysts, managing a diverse array of stakeholder expectations and the ability of the PTCN to move towards a more strategic approach to reducing transnational crime in the future.

Case study 3.2 Intelligence capacity building at the Extraordinary Chambers in the Courts of Cambodia (ECCC)

The ECCC came into practical existence in July 2006 following protracted negotiations between the UN and the Royal Government of Cambodia (RGC) to 'prosecute the Senior Leaders and those Most Responsible for Crimes Committed in Democratic Kampuchea between

17 April 1975 and 7 January 1979'. It is a hybrid tribunal based on the civil law system, modelled on French Civil Law. Cambodia was, until 1954, a French protectorate and has inherited many of the French legal traditions.

Under Civil Law, cases are initially investigated and developed by a prosecutor to whom a crime is reported, either by the police or the complainant themselves. Following this preliminary investigation, the file is forwarded to an investigating magistrate or judge to conduct further investigations. The investigating magistrate or judge is obliged to seek both inculpatory and exculpatory evidence, and acts as a neutral party in the quest for truth. At the completion of the investigation, if there are grounds to commit the suspect for trial, the case file is returned to the prosecutor for presentation before a competent jurisdiction.

The hybrid nature of the ECCC means that there are equal number of International and Cambodian staff in the Office of the Co-Prosecutor (OCP) and Office of the Co-Investigating Judges (OCIJ). International staff are employed to provide transparency and capacity building to the local judicial-legal system. There is generally a lack of confidence in the Cambodian legal system, with reports of corruption and incompetence regularly being reported in the local press. Cambodia lacks the robust judiciary Western liberal democratic countries are accustomed to, and the country has also needed to rebuild entirely its legal system after the downfall of the Khmer Rouge, who utterly destroyed all vestiges of functioning judiciary.

While there are other projects in Cambodia sponsored by the UN and NGOs in capacity building in the local legal system, the scope and nature of war crimes investigations and prosecutions are far more complex than is normally encountered. Typically, the investigation of the deaths of thousands, if not millions, of people becomes the providence of war crimes. Crimes against humanity, genocide and war crimes are the pinnacle of illegal acts committed on the human race. The scope of investigations means that huge amounts of documents, photographs, testimonies and other material are gathered and analysed. The skill sets of persons charged with the analysis needs to be of the highest order due to the complexity of the material, and the laws which relate to the offences. Additionally such complex investigations need to be well resourced.

For example, in previous international investigations of mass genocide and war crimes, such as the International Criminal Tribunal for the

Prosecution of Persons Responsible for Serious Violations of International Humanitarian Law Committed in the Territory of the Former Yugoslavia (ICTY), prosecutors, judges and investigators were groups well supported by intelligence analysts. However, the intelligence support to the ECCC in Cambodia is a much leaner operation.

The OCP contains a small investigation unit, staffed by two international and three Cambodian staff. An information management unit supports the investigation unit and lawyers. The investigation unit provides direct support to legal staff in the OCP with investigatory, research and analytical services. The two international staff members are an historian, who has specialized in Cambodia and in particular the Khmer Rouge, and an intelligence manager, who previously worked on major crime in Australia and on war crimes with the ICTY in The Hague. Combined, these two international staff are able to provide a high level of experience in all aspects of the investigation, not just at a local level but also at a broader international level.

While not a stated outcome in any of the negotiations between the UN and RGC, there also exists a capacity building project to ensure that Cambodian staff are provided with a high level of training in intelligence and investigative skills by the completion of the project. Unlike the South Pacific case study above, the project does not include other 'stakeholders', rather the aim is to pass the knowledge and experience of the international staff on to their Cambodian colleagues, and to ensure world's best practice is being implemented.

Building intelligence and investigative capacity has been hampered by allegations of political interference in the running of the court, and allegations of corruption on the national side. The government has often countered with comments regarding the roles of international staff and counter-allegations of corruption. The RGC has alleged that senior international staff have received instruction from their respective governments as to what and who is to be investigated, along with threats of renewed civil war should more than the initial five persons be indicted.

The Cambodian staff all come from a legal background, which has influenced the way they think and solve problems. Being lawyers, they expect that there will be a degree of completeness in the material they receive rather than viewing any statement from a witness as a start rather than an end point. So the project is partly focused on training to get lawyers to understand avenues of enquiry, and use research and analytical techniques to reach a concluding point in an investigation.

One of the problems faced by international staff, who are trying to build better quality analysis and investigation of Khmer Rouge atrocities, is the strict hierarchical nature of Cambodian society. Deference is always given to those of a higher stature and criticism of such persons is unusual. This presents problems in instructing Cambodian staff regarding the critical assessment of documents, and giving feedback. For example, in the earlier stages of the project, inexperienced investigators in the OCIJ made statements where the explanations of events were often perfunctory or lacking detail. Given investigators are viewed as being of higher stature than an analyst, there was often a reluctance to criticize the statement and request the witness be re-interviewed on specific points. Witnesses have often made a comment which should have been followed up, but this has been ignored by the interviewer. This is often seen as important evidence regarding crimes committed during the regime that has not been obtained. However, due to the hierarchical nature of Cambodian society, for an analyst to return a statement for clarification to a lawyer or investigator for further interview was in the normal course of events a rare occurrence. The loss of face of a person in a higher position would outweigh the necessity of taking such actions.

The training project has started from scratch, and is designed to get the most out of the Cambodian staff. The training of lawyers, analysts and investigators involves attempts to engage the Cambodian staff in left brain/right brain thinking and to develop their capacity to look at issues from both an investigative perspective using deductive logic and from an analytical perspective using inductive logic. Teaching them the methods of brain switching without losing focus has been one of the greatest challenges, according to project staff.

The training project includes basic intelligence theory but with a heavy emphasis on critical thinking and hypothesis development. The practical application of hypothesis development is used by investigators and analysts reviewing statements that have been added to the case file. Analysts are asked to build different hypotheses about cases going before the court, for example, in training they are asked to question whether what the witness is telling them challenges their understanding of aspects of the case, and if so, how? Another focus of training has been on the use of technology, including data storage, mapping and other analytical software. The implementation of computer programs for the efficient storage and exploitation of information is critical to the success of these prosecutions. Unlike a normal domestic prosecution in Cambodia, there is an enormous amount of information gathered during the course of these investigations, ranging from archival material to statements of witnesses and photographs of crime scenes. The use of specific applications that not only categorize information, but also allow value adding has been an essential part of the prosecution process. In all instances, commercially available software has been used as there is little scope for the development of specialized applications due to the budgetary limitations of the organization and of ongoing specialist support for the products.

The applications chosen allow the screening of large amounts of material, drilling down to obtain a common series of facts or entities which can allow for a reasoned judgment or conclusion to be reached. This further allows evidence to be presented before the Trial Chamber in the most effective method possible. The limited number of staff within the OCP has meant that there needs to be the most efficient and effective use of time and resources in order to achieve its ends. Training in information technology is critical to a successful result. The use of search engines that allow for Boolean commands, including wildcard characters, has been an important facet in deriving as complete as possible results.

Case study discussion

The case study material provides the reader with a broad description of some of the key capacity building activities involved in each case study. However, given that both of these intelligence capacity building case studies are still 'works in progress', it is difficult to assess their effectiveness or their longer-term sustainability. Obviously then by extension, it is impossible to determine whether initiatives introduced to date in each case study represent good practice. Further data would first need to be collected from project managers, stakeholders and officers on the ground affected by these capacity building initiatives before more informed answers could be given to questions of effectiveness, sustainability and standards.

However, based on the data available, including from interviews with key people involved in the implementation of both projects, it is possible to identify and summarize what some of the key successes and challenges have been to date in each project. Based on available information in each case study, it seems clear that project successes and challenges are inextricably linked. For example, it is difficult to talk about successes gained in training intelligence officers without also discussing where programmes may have fallen below the mark. In this section, I will summarize four areas of success and challenges from the two case studies including: *training, stakeholder management, focus* and *sustainability* before suggesting ways to address these issues.

Turning to training first, it is clear from the South Pacific PTCN case study that there has been a significant investment made in providing both basic and advanced intelligence training for South Pacific Island police officers. Over the years I have taught many of them. This has been through courses sponsored by the AFP such as the National Strategic Intelligence Course (NSIC) – a two-week intensive course offered by Charles Sturt University in collaboration with the AFP and the ACC. Training has been a big output for the PTCN project, and building human resource capacity in this way demonstrates some success. However, it remains unclear how PTCN intelligence officers have utilized this training, and whether this has resulted in better intelligence products that can influence decision-makers. Further research into how donor or local training is enhancing the ability of officers 'to do the job' or mentor other staff is needed.

As far as the Cambodian case study is concerned, it is clear that international staff involved in it have also been successful in training Cambodian nationals in the OCP, particularly in developing skill bases across a range of areas including investigations, analysis, research, prosecution and the administration of justice. However, the training that has been offered has been given only to a handful of young professionals – although the project leaders hope that those trained will spread the learning they have received to a wider audience. While the few who have been trained well should be counted as a success for the project, it is less clear how this small and targeted investment can provide a catalyst for more widespread training for the broader investigative and judicial sectors of Cambodian society. The challenge is for other donors and UN agencies to pick up on this training and assess how it might be used in creating a more professional, fair and impartial judicial system in that country.

The second success and challenge for both projects is managing stakeholder expectations. It seems that in the Cambodian case this has periodically been an issue, particularly with the international staff dealing with the Cambodian Government. As noted earlier, it has also been challenging getting newly trained analysts to be assertive with investigators due in part to the nature of Cambodian society. Cultural issues over who has 'ultimate' influence or authority are also relevant to the PTCN case study. So managing internal stakeholders involved in a project can be just as challenging as external ones. In the case of the PTCN project, accommodating the expectations of a diverse range of clients and stakeholders has been relatively successful yet also remains a challenge.

As discussed earlier, the PTCN serves the direct interests of the Pacific Island Forum (PIF), the Pacific Island Chiefs of Police and the AFP. A Board of Management (BOM) helps the tasking and coordination of the PTCN's work. However, reconciling the AFP's expectations with local Pacific priorities remains difficult. The interests of other countries, such as New Zealand, France, the USA, China and Japan also intersect across the Pacific and impact potentially on the PTCN's ability to be driven by clear priorities. It's unclear whether the BOM has been able to reconcile all these interests and provide strategic direction for the PTCN. Without a consistent strategic direction, the tasking and coordination of PTCN's intelligence capabilities cannot be optimized.

The third area of 'success and challenge' relates to the focus of each project. The focus of the Cambodian case study is reasonably well defined as the prosecution of those Khmer Rouge leaders who committed atrocities during Pol Pot's regime. However, the question of focus has become more relevant during the implementation of the PTCN project. The project's focus has traditionally been on supporting the development of investigative and intelligence skills among South Pacific Island policing agencies to counter transnational threats to Australia. While the provision of equipment, technology and training to local police has indirectly strengthened their own local capacity, this was not the primary goal of this project. Historically, this created a skills gap between those police officers seconded to the PTCN or TCUs, and their local policing counterparts who in comparison had to rely on more limited local police resources for training and equipment. Most policing agencies in South Pacific countries are also very small, and the secondment of local staff to the PTCN has in some cases placed a strain on local policing intelligence capabilities, which are more important to Pacific countries.

This difference in focus between donor and recipient priorities had created the potential for uneven development in intelligence capabilities of local Pacific police. More recently, however, there has been recognition by the AFP and other donors of this issue. The AFP have now built domestic intelligence units in Tonga, Vanuatu and Samoa to help bridge local investigative capacity alongside the PTCN's transnational focus. While building local domestic intelligence capacity is a good thing, this was never the objective of the original PTCN project. This 'amendment' to the PTCN objectives, though, does raise the question of project mission creep. It is difficult to accurately assess whether the PTCN has suffered mission creep. But it does seem clear that the mandates of individual TCUs within the PTCN have evolved beyond what was conceptualized by the Australian Government a decade ago, which was to build local capacity to deal with transnational issues that might impact on Australia. Further evaluation of the PTCN is required to evaluate how far this project has moved away from its original objectives and whether this matters. Effective project management would suggest that even if there is mission creep, a project can always be renegotiated between donors and recipients. The incremental evolution of the PTCN project and the multi-stakeholder complexity of it require close monitoring and ongoing evaluation to ensure objectives remain focused on meeting donor and recipient objectives.

The last issue that has emerged out of both cases studies relates to sustainability. This is an issue which is common to all development projects, including those involving intelligence capacity building. It is one thing to fund the implementation of a capability, but quite another for it to be effective and sustainable in the longer term. The PTCN has only been in operation for just under a decade, so as noted earlier, it may be too early to make a judgement on its overall effectiveness and sustainability for a few more years. While local police have staffed the network, most of the accommodation, equipment and training have been provided by the

AFP and to a lesser degree other donors such as New Zealand and the USA. So while effectiveness, including doing things well like training and managing stakeholders, is important to overall sustainability, it is likely that, as in all intelligence capacity building projects, ongoing financial support remains a critical factor too. Although the cost of running the PTCN each year is in the hundreds of thousands rather than millions, there will come a time in the future, despite the Pacific region being an ongoing priority for Australia, when the Australian Government may seek to reduce core funding to this project. At the very least, it would be reasonable to expect Canberra to evaluate the current levels of its ongoing investment by requiring more detailed evidence that continuing funding is having a sufficient impact on transnational crime in the Pacific region.

Inevitably in the longer term, based on national sovereignty grounds, it would be desirable for Pacific Island nations to fully fund the PTCN themselves, but this depends on the fiscal ability and willingness of each country to do so. In addition to financial resources, consistent political help from donors and recipients is also an important variable in how sustainable intelligence capacity building projects are. The removal of the PTCCC from Suva, Fiji to Apia, Samoa, after the 2007 military coup in the former country is an example that not just the fiscal, but also the evolving political environment can impact potentially on the longer effectiveness and sustainability of the project.

Similarly in the Cambodian case study, training analysts, lawyers and investigators can be effective in trialling the former leaders of the Khmer Rouge. At some point, however, the ECCC will complete its mandate and the international staff will leave for other postings. The Cambodian staff will return to various government institutions or the private sector. Former OCP Cambodian lawyers may well obtain positions as investigating judges or join the bench. But to what extent will the legacy of the ECCC support the development of an independent judiciary, free from political or other constraints? By demonstrating how a reformed judicial process can hold people accountable for their actions, can this project help bring about a more sustainable change to the country's judicial system that is less corrupt and more accountable? In summary, a single project can be effective, but not sustainable due to a range of factors including financial and political ones. In particular, if local recipient institutions remain weak or there is a lack of political will, the longer-term sustainability without ongoing donor support of projects like these is in question.

Overcoming challenges

On reflecting on the two case studies, there are no easy solutions to the challenges identified in each project. In summary, both projects reveal, to a lesser or greater level in each, a number of problems, including project scope, managing stakeholders' expectations, access to training and training standards, difficulties with how intelligence is tasked and coordinated and the standards of intelligence products. Though discussion of these problems focused on intelligence-related issues, they are similar in many cases to challenges that arise in other non-intelligence capacity building projects as well. A cursory review of capacity building projects sponsored by UN system agencies such as the UNDP or the World Bank identifies a range of similar challenges (such as human resources, leadership, accountability, weak institutions and skills deficiencies) which are also relevant and instructive to the intelligence capacity building context (e.g. UNDP 2002: 10).

UN agencies have also developed a lot of good practice approaches to capacity building, which may help improve the design and implementation of future intelligence capacity building projects. For example, in 2007, based on all the lessons it has learned with capacity building projects, the UNDP published a capacity assessment document, which attempts to examine the significance of these challenges prior to implementing a particular capacity development strategy in-country (UNDP 2007). Much could be learnt about what to avoid or manage better in the intelligence context by reviewing the UN development strategy literature. Additionally, in the case of the PTCN, the AFP's active involvement in other peacekeeping and police building projects in the East Timor and the Solomon Islands also can provide useful practices that donors and police practitioners can adapt to their own situation. The RAMSI mission in the Solomon Islands has resulted in a lot of insights into how military and policing intelligence components can work more closely together and this would have relevance for the PTCN's ongoing development. No doubt the applicability of 'lessons learnt' elsewhere are being considered, but there needs to be a greater desire by those involved in broader policing and security capacity building projects to share these with their intelligence colleagues to improve these project outcomes.

Currently, it seems that there is an ad hoc approach to charting 'lessons learnt' from the field in many Pacific policing programmes sponsored by the AFP. Some projects are evaluated thoroughly while others are subjected more to 'on the run reviews'. The AFPs International Branch and its International Deployment Group are engaging with external researchers to evaluate some projects, but more opportunities need to be made to bring project practitioners, donors, academics and project recipients together to improve project scope and delivery in the intelligence area. In addition to gathering the 'lessons learnt' from other capacity building projects, solutions to specific project scope and implementation problems also lie in donors assessing for any synergies between their projects that may improve effectiveness and sustainability while reducing costs for all. For example, a core deliverable for each of the two case studies and other projects not discussed here is intelligence training. There have been attempts through initiatives such as JCLEC discussed earlier to have a more rationalized and coordinated approach to training between donors and recipients. However, there still remains greater scope for donors to work more collaboratively on training, and other intelligence capacity building projects of mutual interest – particularly in areas such as collection, analytical techniques and strategic intelligence.

Desirability vs. transferability of capacity building projects

While donor governments are learning more about implementing intelligence capacity building projects, further work needs to be done to operationalize the 'lessons learnt' in order to establish whether what is being implemented is 'good practice'. This question of what is good practice is a central theme throughout this book, and it has just as much relevance to how intelligence capabilities are bolstered in areas with low security governance than those with high security governance. In particular, since 9/11, there has been a steady sprouting of new intelligence methodologies particularly in analysis and collection areas. Many donor countries such as Australia and the USA have been particularly keen to fund the transferability of these skills to vulnerable regions, particularly in the context of building stronger intelligence capability within counter-terrorism programmes in the Asia-Pacific region and the Middle East.

However, as the two case studies demonstrate, there is a question of desirability and transferability of Western initiatives, processes and skills underpinning various intelligence capacity building projects. On the desirability side, there are issues relating to the political culture of a recipient country. Does the recipient country's 'intelligence system' exist in a political culture that is sufficiently democratic and accountable for donors to transfer or develop capacity in a sensitive intelligence collection methodology? As will be discussed in Chapter 7, the provenance of intelligence has become an important issue now for Western intelligence agencies, who in recent years have been exposed to criticisms for relying on intelligence collected in third party states, which resulted in abusing human rights or even torture.

Another issue is, how do donors negotiate any corruption in the political, legal or security systems of the recipient country? The extent of corruption in some countries can have a corroding impact on the overall effectiveness and sustainability of the project. Is it possible for donors to 'corruption-proof' their capacity building projects? Leading international anti-corruption network, Transparency International has published some guidance in this area for those working in development projects, such as tackling the supply side of corruption in-country (Transparency International 2007). However, corruption levels simply may make project implementation not viable. But how is a decision made about project viability based on corruption, where greater national security concerns are at stake for the donor country?

The other issue, 'transferability', relates to whether the political, economic and cultural institutions of a recipient country are amenable to the implementation of the capacity building project. Cultural factors can be an important barrier and facilitator to the implementation of an effective intelligence project. For example, in the South Pacific, building effective and sustainable intelligence and investigative processes are challenged by a cultural distrust of 'spying' in some communities and friction between adhering to traditional and common law. In some Polynesian societies, variations between tribal authority and employment status are important considerations when staff are selected to work as intelligence managers. Economic issues also can impact significantly on the transferability of skills and technology to improve local intelligence capability. There is little point, for example, installing complex data mining software if local governments can only afford to provide low-level IT capabilities, or intelligence officers only possess basic computer literacy skills.

The transferability of intelligence capacity building projects from donor to recipients does not necessarily mean the automatic rejection of a project. In some cases, having flexible time frames to deal with local issues, or the acquisition of more user-friendly local solutions to issues such as technology will produce similar results to those originally envisioned by project managers. Some challenges, such as cultural influences, may never be able to be fully addressed or at the very least within the lifespan of the project. However, it may be still desirable to implement the project though taking in consideration that culturally appropriate solutions to some project issues will need to be addressed. Detailed solutions will depend on the specific project's objectives, but a pre-project audit of cultural institutional issues will alert project managers earlier to potential challenges and any solutions.

The role of research

In addition to donors and intelligence capacity building project managers reflecting on the transferability and desirability of a project, as discussed earlier, more needs to be done to evaluate these sorts of projects. There is a role here for researchers who can provide independent evaluations of project effectiveness and sustainability. A close collaborative approach between intelligence practitioners, who are implementing the project, and external researchers should maximize the effective design of evaluations that can assess whether projects are effective, sustainable and therefore represent good practice.

As will be discussed in Chapter 10, empirical research in the intelligence field is still in most areas developmental, but there is an increasingly large body of general and specialized evaluation research methodology literature available (e.g. Pawson and Tilley 1997; Clarke 2000) to help in designing effective evaluations on intelligence capacity projects. Research designs will obviously depend on the research questions requiring an answer. However, in any evaluation of an intelligence project, an early methodological issue to resolve will be whether the approach will be *formative* (focused on identifying strengths and weaknesses of a project or intervention with a view to improve something), or *summative* (focused on determining the overall effectiveness or impact and determining whether or not it should continue to run) (Clarke 2000: 7–8). Research must also be holistic in its approach, given that even small intelligence capacity building projects are likely to impact directly or indirectly on other intelligence processes and structures. Chapter 10 will deal with these broader questions on constructing useful methodologies for intelligence research.

Conclusion

In contrast to the previous two chapters, which focused on how the changing security environment is impacting on traditional and emerging areas of intelligence practice, this chapter has shown how the same security environment exacerbates security governance issues in fragile and post-conflict states. The two case studies and the following discussion survey how some donors have responded to weak governance issues with the implementation of intelligence capacity building projects. The scope of each differs in magnitude and the number of stakeholders involved.

However, just as a decade ago when peacekeeping, practitioners and scholars were first confronted with questions about how effective and sustainable their interventions were, these same questions are now relevant in the intelligence capacity building context. Based on the two case studies, it is likely that project managers and donors are collecting some information about what works or not, but there is little evidence that this information is being shared more collectively so that practitioners can build communities of practice to improve future project implementations. Additionally and similar to other applications of intelligence discussed in Part I, there is also a critical lack of evidence available about what constitutes 'good practice'. Closer collaboration between donors and researchers in designing evaluation strategies should improve this situation and result in better practice and knowledge building about intelligence.

Part II
Understanding structures

4 Intelligence models and frameworks

Introduction

The first three chapters of this book (Part I) focused on how intelligence has been applied in different contexts, including traditional and emerging areas, as well as in the capacity building or development context. However, merely describing applications of intelligence practice in different contexts provides a limited understanding of how intelligence actually works within them. Intelligence provides *services* (usually called 'products' – either orally or written) to decision-makers, and the provision of these services occurs as the result of a dynamic production process. In order to fully understand how intelligence works in different applications and whether it is working effectively, there is also a need to examine both the *structure* of any intelligence system, and how components and processes within the system *function*.

This chapter will focus on five case studies to illustrate how intelligence functions have been conceptualized and structured in some national security and policing environments recently. Given the complexity and dynamism of the security environment, each case study was deliberately chosen to illustrate how 'national security' and 'policing intelligence' are crossing over to deal with threat issues common to both of these areas. More importantly, though, at this point you may be wondering, why devote two entire chapters to intelligence models and frameworks? Some no doubt may be tempted to skip ahead at even the mention of frameworks, which sound dry and perhaps less immediately applicable than other themes and issues discussed in later sections. However, I would argue that this chapter and Chapter 5 (which provides the analysis of the contents of this chapter) are the most important part of the book. In simple terms, there has been insufficient reflection by scholars and practitioners on either the structural or functional components that make up intelligence frameworks. While components of frameworks – collection, analysis or facilitating activity such as technology – are discussed at length generally there is less discussion on how these fit together, and whether they are producing the kind of intelligence support decision-makers can use.

This is not to suggest there has been no discussion on frameworks. The implementation of the UK NIM, coupled with the intelligence-led policing debate, has been influential in shaping views on intelligence frameworks. But there is little other publicly available literature on what makes an effective intelligence framework in different contexts, and how researchers and practitioners can work to build better frameworks that can adapt to the changing security environment. The ever increasing list of 'lessons learnt' from various government inquiries into why intelligence systems failed in many intelligence communities post 9/11 underscores the importance of looking at all the structures and functions that underpin how we do intelligence. It is only by reflecting on what is 'built' and what is contemplated that practitioners and scholars can improve their understanding of all aspects of intelligence. Understanding structures (or frameworks) will not only help identify how to build better frameworks in the future (see Chapter 5), but will also contribute to directing research and theory building efforts (see Chapter 10).

This chapter will reflect on some of the different ways governments and intelligence agencies have been engaging in discussions about intelligence frameworks. The discussion includes how specific agencies or intelligence communities in Australia, Canada, New Zealand, the UK and the USA are designing and implementing new structures in order to adapt to an increasingly complex security environment. Based on interviews of relevant officers from each of the above countries and secondary sources, I will examine five contemporary approaches to intelligence frameworks across policing and national security contexts. The five case studies are:

Case study 4.1 The UK National Intelligence Model (NIM)
Case study 4.2 The Canadian Criminal Intelligence Model (CCIM)
Case study 4.3 US fusion centers – the Los Angeles Joint Regional Intelligence Center (JRIC) and the New Jersey Regional Operations Intelligence Center (ROIC)
Case study 4.4 The New Zealand Police Intelligence Framework
Case study 4.5 The Australian Crime Commission Project Sentinel.

These five cases were selected as they represent a contemporary sample of ideas about intelligence frameworks, which are gaining influence in their respective countries. They were also selected as I was able, in each case, to gain access to practitioners with first-hand knowledge of their design and implementation. Each case study will be discussed using four core areas: *tasking and coordination mechanisms*, *collection*, *analysis* and *intelligence production processes*. Where relevant, discussion of each of these components will also provide an overview of specific collection methodologies, analytical methods and organizational cultural issues relevant to the development of the frameworks. The discussion of each framework is not exhaustive, given it was not possible to access all relevant information. Additionally, in some cases, specific details were not available as aspects of the frameworks are still at developmental stages. But the overviews provided here will show the diversity across contemporary intelligence frameworks, and how their major components are being conceptualized and implemented.

There is a lot that can be learnt by reviewing 'real-life cases', particularly regarding which components of a framework designers and implementers focus more on, and where they see the challenges in implementing their designs. The specific similarities and differences between each of the five frameworks will become clearer shortly. But in summary, some of the similarities and differences between the five frameworks are due to different uses and interpretations of various collection and analytical methodologies and processes. Others are due to different historical, political and legal constructs between the countries which were discussed in Chapter 1.

The similarities and differences between the five case studies discussed here will provide the foundation for a deeper theoretical consideration of the components of intelligence frameworks in Chapter 5. In particular, the case study discussions here will be used to address two central questions in Chapter 5. First, to what extent can these frameworks be exported to different agencies and contexts? Second, how can this greater understanding of intelligence frameworks and components in different contexts be used to build better practice and promote the growth of theorizing in intelligence? In other words, are we simply examining five disparate practice models that currently have no applicability elsewhere? Or, can we generate practice-informed theories about how to build effective intelligence frameworks and functions?

Intelligence frameworks

A cursory review of the case studies below will show that different intelligence 'frameworks' are frequently called different things by their designers. For example, the UK NIM and the CCIM are referred to as 'models'. In contrast, the two US fusion centers discussed, the JRIC in Los Angeles and the ROIC in New Jersey, have more functional names. Again in contrast, the evolving framework in the Australian case study is referred to as a 'project': Project Sentinel.

The term 'model' potentially lacks clarity in the context of all our case studies, so in order to avoid confusion, I will refer to all five case study initiatives simply as examples of 'intelligence frameworks' rather than models or by any other similar terminology. Additionally, there are a number of other 'models of intelligence' discussed elsewhere in the literature, but these are arguably at best models for *components* of intelligence practice rather than a *whole framework*. For example, the acronym 'SARA' or Scan, Analyse, Respond, and Assess, introduced by Eck and Spelman (1987), has been referred to as a model or methodology. While SARA has been useful in getting analysts to focus on crime problems, formulate solutions and then evaluate them, it is really a tool for promoting better analysis rather than a distinct intelligence framework. More recently, there have been other novel models developed such as the fractal intelligence model, which seeks to challenge traditional perspectives about the basic intelligence cycle. The fractal intelligence model represents the intelligence process as a potentially unlimited number of interrelated, overlapping intelligence processes, rather than a set of neat sequential phases as depicted in the intelligence cycle (Hawley and

Marden 2006: 445). The advantage of this model seems to be in tracking operational intelligence progress and processes in more complex criminal investigations. However, it does not show how each step of the process fits into a broader intelligence framework, including other areas of intelligence decision-making such as strategic intelligence.

Other intelligence models such as Ratcliffe's 3-I model, as shown in Figure 4.1, provide a useful functional approach, particularly in helping to explain to new intelligence practitioners how intelligence *functions* and their roles and responsibilities in the intelligence process (Ratcliffe 2008: 109–112). However, as Ratcliffe suggests, the 3-I model is a conceptual one (ibid.: 110), and does not elaborate on the processes underpinning each part of the model.

Our objective in this chapter is to understand how *all* the core components of intelligence (tasking and coordination, collection, analysis and intelligence production) *work together within the broader framework*. In summary, the word framework is sufficiently generic to apply to all the different contexts in our case studies, and its meaning fits with the holistic doctrinal approach taken to intelligence practice in this and the following chapter.

More recently across the national security and policing sector, a number of other concepts and frameworks have emerged. A catalyst for their introduction seems to have been the intelligence failures of key US policing and national security intelligence agencies during and after the events of 9/11. These failures prompted greater reflection on intelligence analysis capability, coordination, sharing and organizational cultural barriers to more effective intelligence practice (McGarrell *et al.* 2007). Some of these initiatives came in the early post-9/11 period and sought to take a wider view of existing intelligence frameworks. These included efforts by some US police commanders in the International Association of Chiefs of Police (IACP) to create the Global Intelligence Working Group (GIWG). The GIWG subsequently created the National Criminal Intelligence Sharing Plan (GIWG 2003). The National Criminal Intelligence Sharing Plan lists a number of

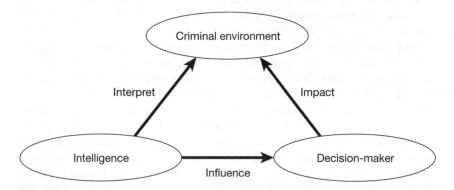

Figure 4.1 Ratcliffe's 3-I model
Source: Ratcliffe (2003).

recommendations, in particular, in training, professional standards, information sharing and building better trusting relations between agencies. It also seeks to promote an intelligence-led policing approach as a more effective framework for policing intelligence in the post-9/11 environment.

While some of the Plan's recommendations are receiving attention, for example, with improvements being made to share information in fusion centers, it is not clear how other recommendations are being progressed across the USA. Hence it is difficult to study them together or see the Plan as a coherent intelligence framework that is being implemented in an ordered manner. Other recommendations such as promoting better trusting relations and professional standards between agencies are still aspirational in many agencies, and it is unclear how US chiefs of police across 18,000 agencies would promote the plan into a more coherent conceptual model that we see in the UK NIM. Some key intelligence managers interviewed for this project were unaware of the Plan, despite its seemingly wide distribution.

Another interesting approach to structuring intelligence modelling and frameworks is conceptualizing these in terms of a *network*. The security network approach takes into consideration the evolving reality that intelligence structures and processes no longer occur neatly (if ever they did) within the confines of state-based bureaucracies. The successful countering of many complex transnational security issues that have global and local manifestations require, as Gill and Phythian (2006: 39–61) suggest, an overlapping and networked reliance of intelligence collection and analysis between the state, corporate and community sectors. The various new counter-terrorism arrangements such as JTAC (in the UK) and the National Counterterrorism Center (NCTC) (in the USA), are recent examples of security networks, which are focused on bringing together security intelligence and related departments to better coordinate intelligence and security assessments on terrorism.

The five intelligence framework case studies

Case study 4.1 The UK National Intelligence Model (NIM)

Chapter 1 provided a preliminary discussion of policing intelligence and the critical role the NIM has played in UK policing intelligence. I will not repeat this discussion nor provide a detailed history or background on the establishment of the NIM in this section. There are plenty of good sources that readers can refer to for such detail, including Flood and Gaspar (2009: 52–64) and Ratcliffe (2008). However, as discussed in Chapter 1, a combination of external political and internal forces within UK policing moved policing agencies in the direction of the NIM.

The pressure from government for police to work smarter, with less resources, combined with the greater uptake and experimentation with proactive policing resulted in the NIM's creation. The creation of the NIM by the then National Criminal Intelligence Service (NCIS) provided a blueprint for how intelligence-led approaches could be applied to national (serious organized), regional and local crime. The NIM was, as Ratcliffe notes, 'a key factor in the development of British intelligence-led policing' (ibid.: 39).

The other important and unique feature of the UK NIM, compared to other frameworks discussed in the other four case studies, was that it was an intelligence framework *mandated* by government. NIM guidelines were issued by the UK Home Secretary under the Police Reform Act 2002. This provided the statutory authority for the implementation of minimal standards of the NIM across all 43 (English and Welsh) police forces. In particular, the expectations of the Home Office regarding the NIM's implementation were articulated in its National Policing Plan published in 2002. The 2002 Plan specified that each UK policing agency was required to be compliant with minimal NIM standards by April 2004 (Maguire and John 2004).

Another important feature of this intelligence framework was that it was designed to help police commanders make better decisions and have more impact on crime reduction. The common intelligence processes adopted by the NIM would also help ensure that a commander, via a suite of tactical, operational and strategic intelligence products, could be given policing, intelligence and enforcement priorities as outputs from the NIM. In other words, intelligence was providing specific support options for the commander. This has also had the effect of making both intelligence staff and decision-makers more accountable. Commanders in particular could be held accountable for how well they delivered against these priorities at the tactical, operational and strategic levels.

The NIM has often been referred to as more like a new 'business model' for policing as a whole rather than more narrowly as an intelligence model. Flood and Gasper, two of its key architects, viewed it in this way. However, they suggest that given UK policing culture in 2000 at the time of the NIM's implementation, describing it in these broader terms may have resulted in its rejection by rank and file police (Flood and Gasper 2009: 53). Regardless of the semantics, the objectives of the NIM's core components, as originally depicted in 2000

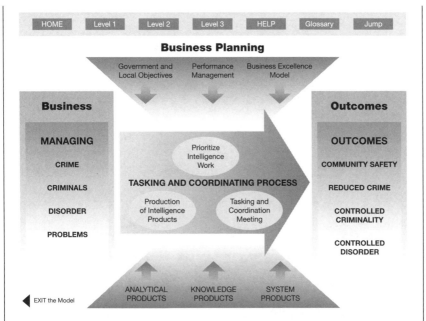

Figure 4.2 The UK NIM 2000 version
Source: NCIS NIM CD 2000.

(see Figure 4.2), were designed to improve intelligence processes *and* through this better overall crime reduction and public safety.

Therefore, it is difficult in the NIM approach to separate the business of improved intelligence practice from better policing. The NIM's focus is on information and how police can use this more efficiently and proactively to respond to rather than merely react to crime or calls from the public. So the NIM represents an integrated information-driven framework that seeks to identify crime patterns and problem-solve more efficiently. Comparing Figures 4.2 and 4.3, it is clear that the model has changed since its original depiction in 2000 and has been revised in recent years. The 2000 version emphasized the business objectives, influences and expected outcomes of the NIM (community safety, reduced crime, controlled criminality and controlled disorder). However, by 2005 the NIM had evolved to place more focus on the Strategic and Tactical Tasking and Coordinating Groups (Figure 4.3).

Although different components within the model have been emphasized in Figures 4.2 and 4.3, the four components of the NIM – tasking and coordination, knowledge products, system products

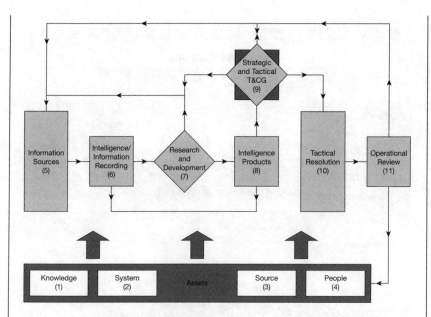

Figure 4.3 The UK NIM 2005 version

Source: NPIA (2008: 14).

and intelligence products – still underpin the model. In both models, though more elaborated in the 2005 version, the NIM's 'assets' are considered the foundations of the NIM process. The terminology for each asset can be a bit confusing on first sight so I will briefly explain each of the key terms. 'Knowledge assets' refer to staff knowing the business of policing, including understanding policy, guidelines and the law. 'System assets' refer to operating in an appropriately secure environment and related issues such as working with secure information exchange protocols. 'Source assets' denote the appropriate procedures and processes for obtaining information from a range of sources including prisoners, victims and CHIS. The last category, 'people assets', details the range of different capabilities required for various intelligence-related positions such as analysts and managers. Figure 4.3 shows that there are a number of other important parts to the model (for example, information sources, research and development and operational review), however, for brevity, I will restrict the remaining discussion to the tasking and coordination, collection, analysis and intelligence production components of the NIM. Together these provide a good overview of the key characteristics of the NIM framework approach, and allow us to draw out differences and similarities which can be compared to the other case studies.

Tasking and coordination

The tasking and coordination groups (T&CGs) (see Figure 4.3), are arguably the most important part of the NIM, because they drive all other components that support strategic and tactical decision-making and the allocation of resources. The NIM has two tasking and coordination groups: one strategic and the other for tactical decision-making. While, in retrospect, the tasking and coordination components of the NIM look to be common sense, in 2000, there were no formally articulated mechanisms in UK policing to align intelligence with decision-makers' priorities. The NIM, and particularly the tasking and coordination components, gave intelligence a 'home to go to', but this also required police managers to be able to use this information to set priorities. Police managers chaired the tasking and coordination groups and the intelligence brought to these meetings helped set 'control strategies' at the strategic level, which included policing, intelligence and enforcement priorities for the police unit or agency concerned. By setting control strategies and then tactical menus of work, the NIM's tasking and coordination component not only established a system for priority and resource allocation, but also one of accountability as police managers became responsible for different outputs from this process.

Collection

The other important output from the tasking and coordination groups was that it identified intelligence requirements or gaps in knowledge that needed to be filled or collected and made someone accountable for them. Since 2000, incremental development of the NIM guidelines has also provided police agencies with more guidance on collection and analytical methodologies. For example, Section 5 of the 2005 NIM guidelines is devoted entirely to information sources and collection processes (NCPE 2005: 46–48). The guidelines stipulate collection processes for different sources and, increasingly since 2000, the NIM has also emphasized the role of community information as an important intelligence source.

The focus of collection efforts depends at which level of the three levels of policing the NIM is operating: local, cross-border or serious and organized crime (usually national and international in scale). In summary, collection has a central role in the NIM, given that this model is under-pinned by an intelligence-led policing approach, which has as its core the proactive collection of intelligence. In many respects, the various collection activities the NIM describes are no different from what exists in the other four case studies. There remain vulnerabilities in police data systems in the UK (see Chapter 5), which still reduce the extent of what can be collected and shared between agencies. However, despite this, the NIM's emphasis on nationally articulated common and minimal standards in collection practice, that are compliant with relevant UK legislation (such as the Data Protection Act and the Human Rights Act 1998), remain important attributes of the NIM approach.

Analysis and intelligence production

In addition to collection guidelines, the NIM implementation team and the NPIA have progressively since 2000 provided similar guidelines on the role of analysts, including various techniques and products they should be aware of when producing strategic and tactical intelligence products. The critical importance of analysis in the NIM is articulated in Section 7.10 of the 2005 NIM guidelines, including an acknowledgement that 'managers often make the fundamental mistake of using analysts' skills inappropriately' (NCPE 2005: 61). The 2005 guidelines also list briefly a range of analytical tools, which are designed to facilitate more effective analysis, including crime pattern analysis, network analysis and criminal business profiles. I will come back to some of these analytical techniques in subsequent chapters. However, briefly, crime pattern analysis is a more general term for a set of techniques that refers to the analysis of where crimes are located. It involves determining whether there is a collection/concentration of criminal activity in one space. Crime pattern analysis is normally associated with geographic information systems (GIS) that support the mapping of crime and iden-tification of crime hotspots, where police can concentrate operational responses. Network analysis involves determining associations and linkages between offenders. Normally analysis of this kind is supported by a range of analytical software. Finally, criminal business analysis is used to assess how criminal businesses and markets operate, to predict new criminal markets and to identify opportunities for early disruption.

In 2008, the NPIA published more detailed guidelines on these and other analytical tools and techniques for analysts across UK policing agencies to either learn new or refresh their existing skills. The 2008 publication, referred to as *Practice Advice on Analysis*, was also significant in that it articulated a series of core skills required for successful intelligence analysis (NPIA 2008: 6). I will return to these issues of analytical skills, competency, professional standards, and other education issues in Chapter 9. Though the standards and skill sets articulated in the NPIA's guidelines and their implementation across UK policing are works in progress, they do represent a good step forward in providing analysts with further guidance on how to promote better practice. This constant development of professional standards across all aspects of the NIM, including intelligence analysis, has no equivalent yet in policing intelligence in Australia, Canada, the USA or New Zealand.

In addition to providing guidance on the analytical process, the NIM also provides clear advice on a suite of intelligence products (e.g. strategic and tactical assessments, target and problem profiles), when to use them and the format in which they should be produced (e.g. NCPE 2005: 63–73; NPIA 2008: 91). Guidance is also provided on the dissemination of intelligence products, which were updated significantly in 2006 following the Bichard Inquiry in 2003.

Strengths and weaknesses

The obvious major strength of the NIM is that it provides a complete set of structures and processes that, if used correctly and consistently, integrate intelligence production into strategic and tactical decision-making. As noted above, the NIM also operates across three levels of policing and this allows flexibility in its application and enhances coordination across local, agency-wide, regional, national or international levels.

Since its establishment in 2000, the NIM has gained wider acceptance by policing agencies. For analysts, it has finally given them a structure to work within, where they can be tasked by managers and commanders to provide intelligence support for meetings and intelligence products. For the commander or manager, it has provided a structure for tasking and coordinating intelligence and other parts of the policing business.

However, since its creation, the implementation of the NIM has been challenging for many UK policing agencies. Maguire and John's evaluation report, which focused on the early implementation of the NIM (2001–2003) in three police forces, reported that progress had been made in some areas; however, it also identified a number of unresolved implementation problems. These included the quality of the new tasking and coordination group meetings and 'missed opportunities by the implementation team to encourage standardization of practices and products' (Maguire and John 2004: 5).

During interviews I conducted in 2008 with key police intelligence officers in the UK, some of the issues raised in Maguire and John's (2004) study were also apparent, including differences in both the pace and overall approach to implementation of the NIM in various policing agencies. One intelligence officer from the Metropolitan Police told me, in his agency, the manner in which the NIM and its standards were implemented often came down to middle-ranking managers' understanding and attitudes towards intelligence. These attitudes are bounded at least partially by the agency's organizational culture, and it was not surprising in the beginning that NIM was going to challenge a broader policing culture that traditionally either did not understand, or was suspicious of, the value of intelligence. Cope's (2004) research on barriers to the integration of volume crime analysis into policing in two UK policing agencies underlined the kinds of organizational cultural barriers existing between analysts and police that have made the effective grafting of the NIM processes difficult in some agencies.

Organizational cultural attitudes aside, other challenges identified during interviews related to how details of the new model were being 'marketed' or communicated to end users in UK policing early in the implementation phase. There were concerns that forces were just presented with guidelines with little further training to explain in simple terms how they worked. One senior UK intelligence analyst from the Metropolitan Police interviewed in 2008 suggested that, 'From the beginning of its implementation, there were communication problems between the NIM implementation team and . . . management. There was not always a clear understanding of what was required.' He added that:

> Trying to embed the NIM was particularly difficult at the mid management and head of command level in . . . agency, as they often had no background in intelligence and no sooner were they trained they were transferred to another area and the new manager needed to be trained from scratch about NIM compliance.
>
> (interview, 29 April 2008)

Another senior intelligence manager, also interviewed in 2008, from a different agency, said that from his perspective: 'The NIM was "over-engineered" – there was too much "machinery" for what it was trying to do.' He added that, 'The NIM raised the profile of intelligence-led policing, but the model is a disservice to policing by being overly complex.' He also felt that, 'There were now increasingly more sceptics in policing about the NIM' (interview, 29 April 2008).

Since implementation, there have also been additional concerns about how UK policing agencies are meant to meet revised or additional guidelines published by the NPIA. For example, unlike the 2005 NIM Guidelines, which articulated minimal standards that must be met, the adoption of the 2008 *Practice Advice on Analysis* is at the discretion of the chief policing officer concerned or the Chief Constable. This suggests that UK policing agencies may be applying analytical capabilities differently, and a less prescriptive attitude to the application of some methodologies and techniques could result in different standards of analytical services provided across UK policing agencies. Comments made by one Metropolitan Police analyst suggested that, at least as far as his agency is concerned, different analytical standards and capabilities have developed since the implementation of the NIM in 2000. He indicated that:

> Even in the one police service there were inconsistencies of analytical practice and products across boroughs and commands, and that the NIM had 'muddied the waters' with its different use of terminology over the years such as crime pattern analysis and criminal intelligence.
>
> (interview, 29 April 2008)

Such comments do not of course, point to any underlining weakness in analytical capabilities in the Metropolitan Police or other UK police agencies. But they do suggest that as intelligence frameworks like the NIM evolve, inconsistent approaches to guidelines (i.e. some mandatory, others voluntary), and ineffective communication of changes in framework terminology and processes can result in a less effective approach to intelligence overall.

In summary, early implementation guidelines demonstrated a rhetoric about NIM minimal standards in various aspects of intelligence that were not always met in practice across UK policing. The question is, does this matter? It depends on the issue, but there seems to be some consensus in UK policing that the NIM is missing its mark in some areas. Currently there is a formal NIM review underway led by the Metropolitan Police and NPIA. This report is expected to examine a range of issues relating to how the NIM is perceived and used in UK policing. In particular, it will be focused on a number of areas, including reducing bureaucracy, organized crime, cross-border issues, neighbourhood policing and citizen focus.

However, despite the existing challenges, the NIM framework has been in existence for nearly a decade, and it has been impressive in its objective to provide a common structure for all UK policing intelligence. The NIM has provided not just for the UK, but other policing agencies in the Australia, Canada, New Zealand and the USA, a framework that covers comprehensively all aspects of the intelligence business in policing.

Case study 4.2 The Canadian Criminal Intelligence Model (CCIM)

In contrast to the UK NIM, the CCIM is still in a developmental phase; however, the concept of a CCIM was endorsed in March 2006 by the CISC National Executive Committee (NEC), representing the Canadian criminal intelligence community. The CCIM is currently being developed by CISC, on behalf of the law enforcement community, and will define how intelligence-led policing could be practised across Canada. Like the NIM, the CCIM will outline how law enforcement activities will interact to lead to informed strategic and tactical decision-making. The CCIM will also articulate common guidelines, standards and strategies to enable Canadian law enforcement to action the model. Application of the model will facilitate greater alignment between intelligence and operations for more effective, consistent and efficient law enforcement in Canada. The model will be applicable to all levels of law enforcement: municipal, provincial and federal.

CCIM's development originated out of a desire expressed by Canada's law enforcement community for more effective intelligence-led policing. It also arose from post-9/11 requirements in Canada for better intelligence-sharing protocols, more comprehensive strategic analysis and the requirement for wider cooperation across agency boundaries and country borders in order to more effectively respond to the global threat environment (whether for national security or criminal threats). In addition, the increased span of policing responsibilities, with limited resources, influenced Canadian policing agencies to explore new approaches that allow for more proactive responses to criminal threats. The CCIM approach is also built on, and connected in part to, Canadian policing agencies' earlier corporate decisions to become intelligence-led policing agencies. For example, in 2001, the RCMP adopted an intelligence-led policing approach, which was influenced by intelligence-led policing models adopted in the UK (Deukmedjian and de Lint 2007: 252). However, despite earlier attempts by Canadian policing agencies to adopt an intelligence-led policing approach, these efforts were never optimal. This was mainly due to the fact that a truly comprehensive intelligence-led policing model with national standards was never achieved. The CCIM is designed to overcome these weaknesses.

Following the March 2006 endorsement by the CISC NEC, for the development of the CCIM, additional 'start-up' processes followed in 2007 and 2008. These included, in March 2007, the NEC unanimously endorsing four recommendations to advance the model's progress following an international best practices survey of global law enforcement practices. The CCIM project team looked at a number of different practice areas across the world, including information-sharing protocols, tasking and coordination, threat assessment production, strategic early warning, training and development for the criminal intelligence.

In 2008, a series of further resolutions were passed by the NEC, and the Canadian Associations of Chiefs of Police (CACP). Following the passing of these resolutions, extensive stakeholder consultation took place during May–November 2008, which led to the identification of key standards and processes required to implement the CCIM. The project team will seek approval and support from the law enforcement community to proceed to the next stage of CCIM development in 2011. While there has been significant endorsement of the CCIM, further development of specific initiatives in the model has taken longer than initially anticipated due to the limited availability of resources required to complete the necessary work. Despite the CCIM being still in the planning phase, significant work required to progress the model can be summarized into four pillars:

1   Intelligence products and services.
2   Information/intelligence storage, retrieval and exchange.
3   Priority setting, monitoring and coordination.
4   Professional development in intelligence-led policing.

More recently, a paper on intelligence-led policing has been developed which underlines the necessity for a CCIM-like model being the foundation for a community-wide and sustainable intelligence-led policing approach.

Tasking and coordination

The CCIM, like the UK NIM, also identifies the central role of tasking and coordination, however, the term 'tasking and coordination' has been replaced by 'priority setting, monitoring and coordination'. Members of the CCIM implementation team believe this term better reflects the context of law enforcement in Canada and what can be achieved collectively through CCIM.

At present, agencies have their own internal processes for how they conduct enforcement action. Individual agencies can practise intelligence-led policing independently, but the goal, as noted above, of CCIM is to achieve intelligence-led policing as a *community*. Other initiatives over recent years, such as the creation of the Canadian Integrated Response to Organized Crime (CIROC), and provincial enforcement coordination committees, have been good attempts to promote more community-wide intelligence-led policing approaches. The CIROC committees provide national and provincial/territorial coordination in intelligence sharing and operational coordination in organized crime. However, the CCIM is seeking a wider, coordinated approach to intelligence sharing across the Canadian policing community – not just in organized crime. A key part of the plan in the CCIM is to build on existing coordinating structures like CIROC to articulate national-level and provincial-level standards for priority setting, monitoring and coordination. In addition, CCIM standards will be developed eventually for local committees in priority setting, monitoring and coordination. Combined, these standards will assist in better aligning intelligence with operations and decision-making.

Though the details are still unclear, the national, provincial and local priority setting, monitoring and coordination standards detailed in the CCIM are similar in some respects to the three levels conceptualized in the UK NIM (local, regional and national). While the existence of well-defined national and provincial committees for sharing policing intelligence will make the tasking and coordination aspects of the new CCIM easier, some agencies will find it more difficult than others to conform to the proposed guidelines on priority setting, monitoring and coordination.

Collection

As noted earlier, the CCIM is an initiative to develop and implement a common model that will allow a community-wide approach to intelligence-led policing in Canada. Given the emphasis placed on collection by intelligence-led policing models, it is not surprising that the CCIM implementation team is currently developing guidelines, standards and strategies that will provide consistent approaches to intelligence collection. One important way the CCIM seeks to improve intelligence collection through the entire policing intelligence community is via the creation of a national database for policing called the Canadian Criminal Intelligence System (CCIS). Based on interviews with key CCIM implementation staff in 2009, the creation of the CCIS arguably will be the most important output of CCIM – pillar 2, information/intelligence storage, retrieval and exchange. Adoption and community-wide use of one national criminal intelligence database will be essential to the CCIM's success. The current national criminal intelligence database – ACIIS – is now considered as ageing infrastructure and not suitable for the CCIM's longer-term objectives.

The new CCIS system is in its early stages of development and is a separate initiative to the CCIM project, but both project teams are in close contact to ensure alignment of their respective deliverables. At the time of writing, discussions are still underway between agencies as to what information/intelligence can be stored and shared, on the proposed CCIS. The underlying philosophy, however, is to have a system, which will dramatically improve the ability to share information and intelligence within and between members of the Canadian law enforcement community. The objective is to create a community-wide intra-net that analysts in all of Canada's agencies could access, except in circumstances where restriction was required, for example, in cases of corruption or where the identity of a source would be revealed. The implementation team also suggested, during discussions in 2009, that the intra-net would also eventually include 'dashboards' with a range of analytical tools and applications for analysts across the community to use, such as sense making, early warning tools, and pattern recognition technologies. There were also suggestions made of including secure *wikis* to help analysts share information in order better identify gaps in knowledge and contribute more effectively to threat assessments produced by CISC.

Analysis and intelligence production

At present, agencies across Canada have different approaches to training intelligence analysts and to developing intelligence products. The CCIM will also implement common guidelines, standards and strategies pertaining to intelligence analysis, which will also be linked to consistent training standards. A working group will be established to examine training requirements for all aspects of CCIM.

Under the CCIM banner, standards and templates for intelligence products such as target profiles and problem profiles will also be developed in collaboration with the law enforcement community. There are already a number of standards in place, for example, the integrated CISC Provincial and National Threat Assessments, but it is expected that a CCIM working group will develop a wider application of standards for various types of intelligence products and reporting. Similarly, the CCIM will also develop and implement standards for the evaluation, validation and classification of information to assist in improved information sharing and management. Canadian policing agencies have some experience collaborating with each other on national intelligence products. For example, CISC's experience with efforts such as the integrated threat assessment process, and the national collection plan will help the CCIM implementation team garner support for standardized intelligence products.

Strengths and challenges

The CCIM represents an improvement on previous efforts, such as the CISC National and Provincial Threat Assessments, Sentinel Strategic Early Warning methodology and the RCMP Sleipnir analytical threat assessment methodology to promote a common intelligence framework for Canada's 400 policing agencies. The main strengths of CCIM are that the initiative builds upon efforts already accomplished, or currently taking place in the law enforcement community, and the implementation team is taking a partnership approach to develop and implement various activities under each of the CCIM's four pillars.

Given the CCIM has not yet been implemented, it is difficult to discuss with much precision the strengths and challenges of the framework. However, a few challenges were identified during interviews with key project personnel. The first involves the culture change required to achieve the CCIM vision of intelligence-led policing as a community. As noted earlier, there are community members who still need to adapt their views towards information sharing from 'need to know' to the 'responsibility to share'. A second challenge for the successful implementation of the CCIM will be further adjustments by the law enforcement community to better align intelligence with operations. This will require all law enforcement personnel to learn and understand their role in intelligence-led policing.

A third challenge will be compliance. Unlike the UK, Canada cannot legislate federally to change policing standards nationally, given policing is the responsibility of the provinces. As noted earlier, CCIM project staff indicated that all policing heads in Canada have approved the concept of the CCIM, but the implementation phase is some time away. Like the NIM, the implementation phase will prove challenging, and compliance with common process and standards cannot be forced upon agencies by the project implementation team housed in the RCMP Headquarters in Ottawa. Communication and marketing, therefore, will be important factors in persuading people of the benefits of the model. The CCIM implementation, will in contrast to the UK NIM, also be on a larger scale with 400 different agencies involved. Given the size of Canada's law enforcement community, there will be challenges in reaching all agencies, and all the right people within these agencies.

In order to overcome this challenge, existing CCIM *champions* as well as the members of the proposed Advisory Board will be used to communicate the value of CCIM, and its implications within their own agencies, among their peers, and outward to governments and other regulatory bodies. Since CCIM is a CISC-led effort, the NEC will need to play a significant role in this area as well. Furthermore, under the project management approach proposed by the CCIM project team, developing each CCIM component will have an embedded communication strategy to ensure the right information gets to the right people at the right time.

As noted earlier, the centralized approach taken in the UK to implement NIM standards is not applicable to the Canadian law enforcement context. Hence, a key requirement of CCIM will be the establishment of an advisory board with representation from various agencies, jurisdictions, functions and levels, under the auspices of the CISC NEC to ensure the principles of partnership and good governance will be practised when implementing standards, guidelines or strategies. The planned advisory board will provide strategic advice to CCIM's governing body, the NEC, and strategic direction to the CCIM pro-gramme. The advisory board will also ensure that the interests of all law enforcement agencies are considered and brought into alignment and that all CCIM activities are carried out by and for the Canadian law enforcement community. Successful implementation of CCIM will rely upon the law enforcement community viewing themselves as partners in CCIM and its success.

Finally, funding is another key challenge to the full development and implementation of the CCIM. Agencies will need to fund initial programme delivery, and also when they adopt specific guidelines, standards, strategies, or training. The CCIM 'roll-out' is intended to take place over time to allow agencies time to absorb the cost and efforts required to implement each component of the project. Nevertheless, it represents a change in approach to law enforcement in Canada requiring a long-term financial commitment by agency members. The next phase of CCIM's development will include research to examine funding options to establish a permanent national programme as well as a pilot test to work with the community in developing standards. As noted earlier, the NEC will decide on whether to implement the CCIM in 2011.

Case study 4.3 US fusion centers

The third type of intelligence framework examined in this chapter is US fusion centers. Although they could be thought of as a network arrangement, they still represent another kind of intelligence framework, which is gaining traction among decision-makers and intelligence managers in the post-9/11 security environment. The US fusion center concept is interesting from two perspectives. First, their structures and processes can be conceptualized as representing a 'nodal point', where an agency's intelligence framework 'plugs' into a broader multi-agency intelligence network. Second, fusion centers become an extension of each agency's own intelligence framework. As noted in Chapter 1, the Bush Administration's creation of the DHS in 2003 impacted on the US federal intelligence arrangements in profound ways that hadn't been seen since the inception of the National Security Act of 1947. The DHS establishment also brought structural change to US policing intelligence at state and local levels. And an important early objective of the new

DHS was the desire to enhance 'connectivity' between all 50 states, emergency services and private security operators in larger cities. The DHS support of fusion centers is part of this mission to enhance connectivity between agencies at federal, state and local level. The term fusion center originates in the US military. In 2006, however, a set of fusion center guidelines were issued by the US Department of Justice in collaboration with the DHS, which defined fusion centers as 'an effective and efficient mechanism to exchange information and intelligence, maximise resources, streamline operations and improve the ability to fight crime and terrorism by analyzing data from a variety of sources' (BJA 2006: 2).

Put more simply, fusion centers are a network approach to intelligence collection, analysis and dissemination. Their objective is to bring together, usually in the same physical space, intelligence assets from a range of different federal, state and local agencies to work on common problems. Theoretically, a networked approach is meant to get around traditional hierarchical boundaries between agencies, promote mutual trust, and share information and other resources. There are of course other non-US 'fusion versions' that have been developed in recent years for counter-terrorism. For example, in addition to the NCTC, there are similar joined-up arrangements in the UK, JTAC, and in Canada, the ITAC, as well as versions in Australia and New Zealand (the National Threat Assessment Centre (NTAC) and the Combined Threat Assessment Group (CTAG) respectively). However, fusion centers are still largely a US approach in practice, and the two overviewed here show some of the different configurations and variations that exist in the 72 fusion centers across the US.

US fusion centers started to appear pre 9/11. One of the earliest versions, the Los Angeles Terrorism Early Warning (TEW) Group, started as early as 1996, and was a multi-agency, multi-disciplinary 'fusion center' for all 88 cities in Los Angeles county (Sullivan and Bauer 2008: 23). The TEW once served as a model for the development of other fusion centers elsewhere in the USA, but its counter-terrorism functions have now been incorporated into the Los Angeles JRIC. Since 2001, the US Department of Justice and the DHS have been building on the common intelligence standards articulated in the National Criminal Intelligence Sharing Plan discussed earlier, by creating further guidelines for state and local authorities on how to establish a fusion center (BJA 2006). The Department of Justice has also issued basic federally identified common capabilities and standards for their operation (BJA 2008). For the DHS, the network of fusion centers has become a major vehicle for it meeting national priorities, including strengthening information sharing and the collaboration of capabilities between local, state and federal agencies. The DHS also provides personnel with operational and intelligence skills to some centers, in addition to indirect funding via a grants scheme. The DHS provided more than $254 million between 2004 and 2007 to state and local governments to support fusion centers (DHS 2008).

As discussed above, this case study will focus briefly on two US metropolitan fusion centers I visited in 2009: the JRIC in Los Angeles, and the ROIC in New Jersey. Not all fusion centers, of course, are in major cities. For example, the one for the state of New York is in Albany – the state capital. Selection of the site for a fusion center is unclear, but in many cases their distance away from major population centers, where threat levels are lower does not appear to be the best use of limited federal, state and local policing resources. The JRIC and ROIC were selected as they show some variations in how two major metropolitan area fusion centers have been established in the USA. Both also demonstrate how different stakeholders and executive influences produce variations on the business and configuration of the fusion center. For example, within the ROIC, the emphasis is an 'all hazards' and threats approach to their function, whereas the JRIC seems to focus on counter-terrorism.

Tasking and coordination

In 2009, the JRIC developed a set of intelligence collection requirements in order to build a better threat picture of domestic and international terrorism in its area of responsibility. This resulted in a survey of all terrorism groups in the area, and has also relied on SAR reports coming in from all JRIC contributing agencies. These reports help focus investigators on which cases they should be looking at (see Case study 6.3 for an explanation of SAR). In the ROIC, intelligence requirements are also driving tasking and coordination and intelligence production. The types of requirements are either customer-focused, event-driven, analyst-driven or scheduled requirements.

The process begins with a 'Request for Information' (RFI) or a 'Request for Proposal' (RFP), if an analyst internal to the ROIC is interested in exploring a topic. Once the RFI/P is approved, the analyst will complete a project proposal, which outlines the aim and objectives of the project, which resources are needed, intelligence gaps and deadlines.

Often a project may not require to be routed through this entire process because many of the ROIC intelligence products are scheduled (i.e. weekly or monthly).

Collection

In both fusion centers, collection is driven by the nature of the task – whether it is a request for information or a more detailed intelligence product. In fusion centers, collection plans can be completed by individual agency members or be combined multi-agency efforts depending on the nature of the task. The storage, sharing and distribution of intelligence follow established protocols set forth by Title 28 Code of Federal Regulations, Part 23 (28CFR23) and respective state intelligence handling guidelines. These guidelines set out parameters for domestic policing agencies in the United States to follow with regard to the collection, storage, dissemination, auditing and purging of criminal intelligence information. The guidelines help to protect against leakage of sensitive information in keeping with safeguarding privacy and civil liberties.

Analysis and production

In the early part of the ROIC's operation, intelligence staff attempted to adopt the product schema of the NIM, however, they quickly learned that it was not suitable for their customers. The diverse range of customers made the standardized smaller number of intelligence product types articulated in the NIM less useful. ROIC intelligence manager, Ray Guidetti said:

> We tried at one time to mimic the four standard products associated with the NIM, but that did not go over well. Our customers come in all shapes and sizes. Some want BOLOs ('Be on the look out for notices'), some want target profiles, some want notifications, some want strategic intelligence assessments. We have also done policy options papers for executive level and policy-makers. Our folks conduct a lot of oral briefings that we also include in our assortment of products.
>
> (interview, 27 February 2010)

JRIC also produces a range of products such as daily and weekly intelligence reports. It also produces a 'Force Multiplier' report which is aimed at local police operating in the field to provide advice on situational awareness. For newsworthy incidents and terrorist attacks in the USA or globally, the JRIC has the capability to produce immediate notification/ bulletins. The JRIC also produces threat assessments that will help agencies understand potential threats they may face during a large event, such as a football game at the Rose Bowl Stadium in Pasadena.

Successes and challenges

The fusion approach to intelligence is still relatively new within the USA though it is clear from discussions with key managers involved in both the JRIC and the ROIC, that their centers have had some success already in connecting local, state and federal agencies – in a way, before 9/11 was for many of these agencies still relatively ad hoc. The ROIC is now identified as the principal fusion center in the state by the New Jersey State Governor and it has developed good relations with their federal counterparts (for example, the FBI and the DHS). Guidetti stated during interviews, that the 'ROIC's staff describe it as an obligation, in support of the *Information Sharing Environment* to "pass-through" federal intelligence products to state and local constituents' (interview, 27 February 2010). The Information Sharing Environment (ISE) is a generic term mentioned in Section 1016 of the Intelligence Reform and Terrorism Prevention Act (IRTPA). This section of the Act calls for an information-sharing environment to be established that would include improvements in current policies, procedures, technologies and people to facilitate better information sharing at all levels of government, including the private sector. The Act also called for the establishment of a Program Manager for ISE, who works within the ODNI and reports to Congress on an annual basis on progress in this area (ODNI 2009a).

However, it is less clear in other fusion centers how they are faring in being the conduit for the exchange of federal and local intelligence to those who need it. In general, fusion centers across the USA seem to be getting better at sharing information with agencies involved in the center, but it is less clear to what extent sharing is going on between all 70 centers across the USA. No doubt a full evaluation of all 70 fusion centers may present some political and logistical hurdles for the DHS, state and local policing across the USA. But it would be a useful exercise to assess whether these fused arrangements, in addition to the two highlighted here, have lived up to their rhetoric of promoting an information-sharing environment and fused intelligence.

From the interviews with key intelligence coordinators both in the JRIC and the ROIC, these fusion centers have produced a range of specific benefits to their stakeholders and clients. For example, one of the key successes of the ROIC has been its ability to generate original intelligence products, which are not just reassembled from other agencies. The ROIC has also been able to also deliver specialized analytical capabilities that do not exist in other policing agencies in New Jersey, such as predictive analysis using the Center's geospatial predictive analytics team. Another success in the ROIC has been an increasing number of clients for its services across New Jersey. Because the number of analysts employed across New Jersey is limited, the ROIC finds itself in a unique position in that it houses the bulk of the analysts working in the state. This situation enables the ROIC to be the primary current and warning intelligence producer for customers in the state.

Providing good intelligence products that service local customers well has also been one of the key successes for the JRIC. JRIC has been able to produce products for its local constituents (local police/fire/public health), that have been seen as relevant to the agencies that dedicate personnel to the JRIC. Another area of success for the JRIC, according to key staff interviewed, was how it has developed highly qualified staff (both analysts and supervisors), who understand the concept of a task force environment and information sharing. Discussions with JRIC staff suggest that a key reason for this success is due to personnel embedded in this fusion center not wearing their agency 'hat'.

However, based on the small number of interviews I completed with fusion staff at both locations, it is difficult to assess with complete accuracy the extent to which these and other centers have created shared normative environments, where previous difficult working relationships, or rivalries between agencies, have been replaced fully with communal or cooperative behaviours. In general, there seems growing evidence of better sharing of information between the FBI and some fusion centers particularly through local JTTFs. However, the

DHS, which has placed great emphasis on fusion centers being vehicles for channelling intelligence from the intelligence community to local police, has not been as good in using the centers to facilitate the retrieval of local intelligence back to Washington, DC. In both cases (JRIC and ROIC), and in other fusion centers not discussed here, there is likely to be a number of challenges still to overcome. In particular, I see challenges relating to different legislation, agency dissemination memorandums of understanding, variation in security clearances and differences between the organizational cultures of agencies. All of these challenges will test just how 'fused' or 'joined up' these centers will be in the future.

There is also the additional and ongoing challenge of financing fusion centers. The operations of both fusion centers discussed here have been impacted by the recent global financial crisis (2009), which resulted in some hiring freezes and reducing the hours that some analysts can work. The fiscal constraint on many public sector agencies in the USA has also resulted in reduced expenditure on technology and training to support analysts.

Many of these issues, and others, such as evaluating the effectiveness of intelligence produced, and the extent to which it influences strategic and operational decision-making fall under the broad remit of 'governance' issues. In both fusion centers, again based on discussions with staff, it appears that governance arrangements are still developing. Little is known publicly about how well different agencies are working together or the impact of individual organizations on the joint effort. But there are likely to be tensions between participating agencies that have similar intelligence capabilities or roles. For example, the DHS and the FBI both have 'domestic intelligence' roles and operational tensions between them may impact on how fusion center members decide on intelligence collection and operational priorities. Further clarification is also needed about whether collectively the tasking coordination, collection and analytical components of fusion centers are good practice. As noted above, the DHS in consultation with state and local partner agencies should consider doing a review of fusion centers, and governance issues would be an important aspect of this process. Effective governance arrangements within fusion centers will help ensure that they become a strong bridge between federal and state sources of intelligence. The DHS, I argue, still needs to take a greater leadership role in concert with local agencies in developing both the intelligence capabilities and mandates of fusion centers across the USA. There also still seems to be a lack of agreement in some quarters of the US federal government and at the local level about what the role and capabilities of fusion centers should be.

Moving forward, a key measure of the success for all fusion centers will be the extent to which they can generate collection and analytical capabilities that have a wider and more efficient impact on their operating environment, beyond what can be achieved by their parent agencies alone. Fusion centers will need to demonstrate that they won't just become a 'mail box' or 'clearinghouse' for intelligence produced elsewhere. In that context, the most effective of them will likely be those that use fused intelligence directly to support multi-operational investigations. I argue, therefore, that fusion centers need to develop greater intelligence collection capabilities than they currently have in order to support fused operational activity. In the end, agencies need to know that they are getting 'bang for their buck' in participating in such arrangements, so it will be important to know whether good practice is being cultivated in these networked environments. Chapter 5 provides a more detailed discussion of this point of what constitutes good intelligence practice in fusion centers and other frameworks discussed in this chapter.

Case study 4.4 The New Zealand Police Intelligence Framework

As discussed in Chapter 1, it wasn't until the early 1970s that 'intelligence' became an integral part of the NZP policing approach. Intelligence was used traditionally for case support, and development was focused mainly on local initiatives, at district and area level. Overall, intelligence *processes* were ad hoc and fragmented. This environment is described well by the National Manager, Intelligence for NZP, Mark Evans, who commented that:

> Management had little (or isolated) knowledge of what intelligence could do for crime and crash reduction. While examples of excellent intelligence *products* did exist, there were no minimum standards and many lacked focus and credibility with police

decision-makers. There was a lack of what intelligence meant or was intended for.

(interview, 10 August 2010)

Many of the problems with the NZP traditional approach to intelligence had also been raised in an earlier study completed by Ratcliffe in 2002 (Ratcliffe 2005). In October 2006, however, the Policing Development Group (PDG) – a national group that had done much to develop the use and focus of intelligence in support of crime and crash reduction – were directed to develop a business case for a national intelligence development project. The business case was approved by the NZP executive, and in September 2007, Mark Evans was appointed (initially on secondment, later permanently) from the Police Service of Northern Ireland to lead the project. A National Intelligence Office (NIO) was quickly established and set out '15 project deliverables', which formed the basis of an initial 12-month action plan. In October 2008, following extensive review and consultation, the Police Executive endorsed one 'NZ Police Intelligence Framework' and approved the creation of a Police National Intelligence Centre at Police National Headquarters (PNHQ) to lead its strategic development.

Tasking and coordination

Prior to the recent reforms, some areas did have deployment meetings which were called 'tasking and coordination meetings', but they were not routinely intelligence-led or consistently based upon a decision-makers' problem solving or preventative model. A new 'National Tasking and Coordination Framework' has been constructed to support the overarching NZP Policing Model. The Framework has been combined with the Ratcliffe 3-I Model (see Figure 4.1), which has been a foundation of NZP intelligence work for several years and is well understood. The Framework is designed to ensure the link between intelligence and operational outcomes is clearly understood at all levels across the organization. Additional steps have been taken in the development of the broader NZP Intelligence Framework to improve tasking and coordination of intelligence at all levels. For example, in July 2009, the Police Executive agreed to nationally mandate a tasking and coordination policy, principles and procedures framework. This framework is still being rolled out (the process is expected to take 24 months to become properly embedded), but key elements of it include:

- District and Area T&CG Meetings, and a National Tasking & Coordination Group (chaired at Deputy Commissioner level) to set and agree national priorities.
- The use of Critical Command Information (CCI) to inform decision-making (CCI is defined as crime and crash priorities, standard intelligence inputs/products, demands for service, performance information and actual strength available for deployment).
- T&CG Meetings that can generate three types of outcomes:

  - Information Only
  - Recommendations for Action
  - Specific, Mandated Taskings

- Problems addressed using a *PIERS Control Strategy* approach. (PIERS stands for priorities set in respect of Prevention, Intelligence, Enforcement, Reassurance and Support activities.)

The emphasis is on greater urgency, problem ownership, local account-ability and follow-up, crime prevention and 'demand reduction' (Evans, interview, 10 August 2010).

The new approach to tasking and coordination has placed a lot of attention on building stronger partnerships with internal stakeholders, Evans notes that:

> There were 'early adopters' to these new tasking and coordination processes, and their successes – together with a coordinated, nationally driven, education and awareness campaign – encouraged other areas. Implementation within the national framework, is the idea being that this will, ultimately, promote greater local ownership – rather than it being seen as 'yet another headquarters priority'.
>
> (ibid.)

NZP have also adopted control strategies to assist in crime and crash management. Evans suggests that control strategies are still developmental. However, in November 2009, the first National Control Strategy was implemented as the chosen NZP response to a whole-of-government initiative to tackle methamphetamine, and more recently national plans have been developed for organized crime and alcohol,

The new T&C Framework is starting to provide greater accountability at all levels and a whole of organization platform for greater inter-agency problem solving. It is encouraging longer-term planning and thinking around future crime problems and trends, and has the potential to drive long-term (and more sustainable) crime prevention measures.

Intelligence collection

An important output for the NZP Intelligence Framework is to put in place robust intelligence collection. Evans reports that the focus for improving intelligence collection processes is 'based on the principle of "collect information once and use it many times"' (ibid.). Another key focus area for improvement is the development of much closer relationships with other government departments – both at a local and national level. The National Intelligence Centre (NIC) is also supporting a new Crime Prevention Partnerships Forum, which is designed to work with key business sectors on mutual problem solving.

Specific improvements in collection articulated in the new Framework include changes to people, processes and products. From the people perspective, an experienced Manager: Intelligence Collections and Requirements has been recruited to oversee a national programme of work. This work includes the establishment of three levels of collectors (Intelligence Collection Coordinators, Field Intelligence Officers and Intelligence Officers). The roles of each of these positions have been clearly articulated in the Framework (ibid.).

In addition to personnel changes, a series of policy, procedures and processes are also being developed to clearly articulate corporate and legislative requirements for all aspects of intelligence collection. For example, Evans reports that significant investment is being made in new policy, processes and procedures to maximize the use of CHIS – including international good practice around risk management and profiling through the establishment of Human Source Management Units. There is also a particular emphasis on a new approach to organized crime. For example, new operational structures have been established (such as a new police-hosted Organized Crime Agency) and the NIC has developed a new Targeting Group to lead a joined-up approach to organized crime intelligence across NZP. The NZP model also is building closer relationships with existing groups like Auckland Metro Crime and Operational Support Group (AMCOS), that have a track record of success with organized crime (ibid.).

Analysis and production

In addition to significant changes to tasking and coordination and collection approaches, identified above, the new framework has resulted in some major changes to the way the NZP assesses and produces intelligence. In 2009, the NZP invested heavily in the recruitment of 14 District Managers: Intelligence (DMIs) (in addition to the 12 Districts, DMIs were also appointed for Auckland Metro and AMCOS) at Inspector level (or police employee equivalent). This has provided, for the first time, a clearly identifiable 'professional head of intelligence' across every district. The DMIs have mostly been selected for their change management and people skills, rather than purely technical intelligence skills. The DMIs are responsible for leading the local development of improved standards in intelligence (including the analysis component).They will also have an important role in 'bedding down' much of the new intelligence doctrine arising out of the new framework. They are supported by a new Manager: Analytical Services position at the NIC that is the de facto Head of Analysis for the organization.

In November 2009, the Police Executive endorsed additional improvements to enhance the analytical capabilities of the NZP under the new framework, including the NZP Professional Development in Intelligence Programme (PDIP). Evans notes that: 'The PDIP is designed to redefine the intelligence workforce (so that it is more visible, flexible, competent, frontline focused and effective)' (ibid.).

Significant resources have been invested in improving intelligence technology to support analytical work. A long-term NIC Technology Plan is being developed and will support the wider NZP 'I&T mobility project'. While there has been good progress in improving the use of the core database that is used to support serious and organized crime investigations, according to Evans, there is much more work to be done to improve tools available to analysts, including effective data mining capabilities (ibid.).

The new NZP Intelligence Framework also includes an intelligence products framework, which defines products and sets out minimum national standards. The framework defines products within the categories of: *core intelligence products, knowledge products, analytical products* and *frontline support products*. According to Evans, this is: 'Similar to the UK NIM though in a way that is perhaps less extensive and therefore less bureaucratic, while every product is supported by guidance notes, a template and advice on how, why, when and by whom individual products should be generated' (ibid.).

Successes and challenges

In only two years since the NZP Intelligence Framework was endorsed by the agency's executive, it is clear that there has been significant gains made in laying down key components of the new framework. In particular, the recruitment of a new cadre of intelligence managers – both locally and nationally – an improved tasking and coordination process and the professional development programme for intelligence professionals are examples of early successes to date. Evans admits that progress has been patchy in some areas and districts, though in others there is already evidence of improvement. In particular, there have been improvements in the production of intelligence products that are resulting in better targeting of more high priority criminals and crime and crash problems. At the national level too, intelligence support to local, national and international organized crime, drug and gang investigations, has also improved since the implementation of the framework.

However, challenges remain in getting the much needed foundations of the new Framework right, at the same time as generating sufficient early evidence along the way that change is having a positive impact. This challenge is not unique to the implementation of the NZP Intelligence Framework. Another challenge for the successful implementation of the Framework will be maintaining the ongoing support of the NZP Executive. As discussed further in Chapter 6, maintaining executive leaders' attention on intelligence reform has been historically challenging. For the NZP Intelligence Framework to be successful, like any other, it will require the focus and investment of the intelligence managers. Executive leaders in turn will be looking for the Framework's ability to impact (strategically and tactically), to be value for money and flexible to cope with future developments in the security environment. Evans, in his interview, summarizes the many challenges ahead for the NZP Intelligence Framework succinctly, as including:

> Overcoming the cultural, organizational and financial obstacles that bedevil most police change programmes. There is also a question of the time needed to embed change. UK experience indicates that the NZ Police intelligence change programme will take at least

5 years – which is a long time for senior management to remain committed in the face of competing demands and pressure to always move on to the 'next big thing'.

(ibid.)

Case study 4.5 The Australian Crime Commission Project Sentinel

As discussed in Chapter 1, the ACC was established in 2003 from three former federal agencies, which had a national criminal intelligence and/or investigative function in countering organized crime. Since the ACC's establishment, the agency has implemented a series of intelligence frameworks, including ones which organizationally resulted in a split between intelligence and investigative functions and later iterations that focused on a thematic approach (i.e. based on classifying crime issues into groups and targets, commodities or methodologies). By 2007, the ACC's Executive had become dissatisfied with both the thematic and bifurcated view of organized crime that the agency held, which had organized the agency into two broad functions: an intelligence arm and an operations arm.

One of the key concerns in 2007 was that both configurations resulted in siloing of intelligence and investigations and Project Sentinel was designed to remove this. Project Sentinel was inspired originally by SOCA's Integrated Lifetime Management Programme (ILM), but was modified significantly as the ACC does not have all the same legislation as that underpinning the SOCA approach. The ethos of Project Sentinel was to make investigations part of the intelligence cycle and to make intelligence part of the investigative cycle.

There were also other catalysts which influenced the development of Project Sentinel, including a gradual shift in the nature of the work the ACC was becoming involved in. The ACC started getting involved in more complex financial investigations involving organized crime (for example, the 'Gordian Money Laundering Taskforce'), that used financial intelligence from the Australian Government's anti-money laundering authority, the Australian Transaction Reports and Analysis Centre (AUSTRAC), and data from the banking sector. The ACC also developed expertise in intelligence collection and analysis in other niche areas, for example, in assessing the nature and extent of organized crime in the private security industry and the aviation sector. These were areas that other federal and state policing agencies were not focusing on and the ACC was able to bring other specialized capabilities such as its coercive powers (see Chapter 6 for an explanation of these powers) to these special intelligence operations.

Around the same time that Project Sentinel was being contemplated, the ACC was also, through its National Criminal Target Report (NCTR) receiving a more informed idea from state policing agencies about the number of high risk targets nationally. The Executive decided that a new approach to intelligence was needed for the agency, which could better integrate the different levels and sources of intelligence it was using. It was decided that Project Sentinel should be a framework that could provide better support for the agency's new focus on complex investigations. These investigations used the large data sets of other agencies (on abnormal patterns in money or trade movements), and combined this data with other specialized operational intelligence capabilities to identify targets and groups involved in illicit transactions showing up in the data. One senior official within the ACC described the new approach as looking for the 'criminal footprints' in the data in order to identify more proactively serious and organized crime. Project Sentinel consists of three phases: collection and analytics (phase 1); target development (phase 2); and intervention and prevention (phase 3). These phases have been progressively established – starting with collection and analytics in October 2009.

The ACC Project Sentinel represents a novel shift in how it will now conduct its intelligence business, but also potentially how the Australian Government addresses organized crime. The Australian Government through its *Organised Crime Strategic Framework,* released in 2009, has given the ACC a central intelligence role in the fight against organized crime (Attorney General's Department 2009).

Although the framework indicates that the ACC will play this central intelligence role, it is brief on details, although its role seems to be in four areas. First, the ACC will be expected to provide a list of harms/threats and up-to-date targets. These targets will be nationally significant high-risk individuals or groups, and the ACC, in the words of one senior manager, 'will put the "who" into the criminal economy by looking particularly at business structures from the Australian Securities Investments Commission (ASIC) and the banking sector'. Second, the ACC will play a fusion role, getting agencies together, into task forces (state and federal). Third, it will be the only agency in Australia that produces strategic intelligence reports for longer-term national criminal intelligence planning, and, fourth, it will play a national criminal intelligence coordinating role through its role as the custodian of the national criminal database, the Australian Criminal Intelligence Database (ACID).

The three phases of Project Sentinel give the ACC the flexibility to run its intelligence business in a way that potentially best contributes to the four areas discussed above, and it is hoped that the new framework will help the agency utilize more efficiently its niche capabilities such as coercive powers and intelligence operations. If Project Sentinel is implemented successfully in the manner its architects hope, it may give the ACC uncontested space to operate particularly well in the complex financial intelligence area of organized crime.

Tasking and coordination

The ACC is governed by a Board, on which sit representatives of all state, territory police and a number of other federal agencies such as ASIO. The ACC Board, in a sense, sets the broad menu of work for the agency. For example, the Board may endorse a multi-jurisdictional intelligence and investigative response (usually referred to as a 'determination'), to a high priority area such as amphetamine-type substances. The establishment of a determination or task force has resource implications for the ACC, and other agencies joining the group.

However, tactical, operational and strategic intelligence tasking and coordination are also the result of a series of other priority setting mechanisms that are both internal and external to the agency. Externally, the agency's work is now being driven by a range of whole of government initiatives, including as discussed, the Australian Government's new *Organised Crime Strategic Framework* and a national criminal intelligence priority setting process, which seeks to articulate priority areas for all territory, state and federal agencies to guide their strategic and operational planning to combat organized crime.

These external processes are largely driven by some key risk and threat assessment processes, which have been developed within the ACC on behalf of the broader Australian policing and law enforcement intelligence community. The ACC produces two seminal risk assessment products that are designed to guide strategic and operational resource allocation. The first product, the Organised Crime Threat Assessment (OCTA) looks at organized crime across crime types, commodities and markets, and has been designated by the Australian Government's

Organised Crime Strategic Framework as the key document to assess organized crime priorities across all government agencies. The other risk/threat tool, the NCTR is entity- and group-based, and surveys Australia to consistently measure the risk and threats posed by various groups. The NCTR and the OCTA assessments are derived from another ACC internal risk and threat assessment process called the Target Risk Assessment Methodology (TRAM), which assesses the threat posed by groups and their impact. The TRAM helps guide Project Sentinel targeting priorities, tasking and coordination decisions within the ACC.

Collection and analysis

Phase 1 of Project Sentinel, *collection and analytics*, is probably the most distinctive part of this new intelligence framework. This is not surprising as Project Sentinel is primarily about developing better collection and analytics capabilities. The vision is to mesh 'top-down' large data sets from relevant government agencies, with the 'bottom-up' flows of intelligence from the more 'traditional' sources of intelligence collection capabilities such as telephone interception and CHIS. The collection and analytics phase, for example, will assess the significance of large flows of money from customs, banking and financial intelligence, and match this with human source or telephone interception. The analytics component is new for the ACC and newer still in most other Australian law enforcement agencies. It involves complex data mining, matching and integration with other criminal intelligence databases. The idea is to use analytics and traditional intelligence methodologies to identify targets that can be further developed by the *target development team*.

As discussed in greater detail in Chapter 8, the development of a specialized analytics capability takes time and involves recruiting statisticians, business managers, analysts and economists. What to collect is determined by the ACC threat and risk assessment methodology. This methodology involves both an assessment of the harm of an activity, for example, the harm to the Australian economy, and the threat of groups/individuals such as the threat of violence. I will return to a broader discussion of risk and threat methodologies in Chapter 6.

From an analysis perspective, as discussed earlier, the new Project Sentinel model places more emphasis on using advanced analytics, and combining this with other operational intelligence data, plus strategic intelligence. Although analytics is not necessarily a new innovation to policing (see Chapter 8), its use in this way in the Australian organized crime context is. Project Sentinel has resulted in an internal re-organization of analysts within the ACC. Analysts are no longer specializing in one crime type or group. Their skills are being deployed across each phase of the model, particularly in the collection and analytics and target and development phases. The plan is to get them working in joint analysts groups on targets in real time. This amounts to a culture change for many in the analytical cadre in the way they work, and presents challenges for the agency in finding analysts who have sufficient skills in advanced analytics. In particular, as mentioned earlier, the analytical focus will be on using operational intelligence and data matching on things like the movement of trade or wealth. From this analysis, the ACC hopes to identify people 'flying below the radar'. In other words, people who may not yet have an established criminal record, but through data matching with other records indicators may suggest they are involved in organized crime activity. In 2010, the ACC received some additional federal funding of $15 million for a criminal intelligence fusion center at its Canberra headquarters. The agency's Project Sentinel approach will provide the operating model for the centre. With additional funding, it is expected that the ACC will build upon its existing expertise in complex financial analysis to assess other areas such as people smuggling, identity crime, and fraud. The increased budgetary allocation will also help build forensic accounting, data integration, geospatial and telecommunication analytical capabilities of analysts working in this centre.

Intelligence production

From an intelligence production perspective, Project Sentinel's objective is to reduce the number of intelligence products currently released from the ACC. At the time of writing, the agency had in excess of 12 different product types across the tactical, operational and strategic spectrum. Interviews with key people involved with Project Sentinel suggest that when the framework is fully operational, the aim is to have 'four flagship products'. These will be *futures products*, *the Illicit Drug Report*, *OCTA* and the *NCTR*. As noted above, the OCTA will be particularly important as it will drive the Commonwealth response on organized crime.

Successes and challenges

Project Sentinel has been rolled out incrementally since 2009, and although all phases have now been implemented, there is still a lot of work to do to 'bed' this new framework down within the ACC. Again, similar to the discussion earlier of other intelligence frameworks, much of the processes which underpin Sentinel are still being implemented, so it is difficult to measure what successes there have been to date. Perhaps, somewhat ironically, one of its key successes so far may be due to 'good timing'. The Project Sentinel framework is being implemented at a time when the government has launched also a major policy statement on organized crime (the *Organised Crime Strategic Framework*), which has given the ACC the central intelligence role in the national effort against organized crime.

The framework not only raised organized crime to the same level as other national security threats, it has given the ACC various distinct and important roles across government, particularly in providing the lead in national intelligence collection, analysis and coordination. It is rare for decision-makers and intelligence executives to be on 'the same page' as far as intelligence reform is concerned, but this has been the case with Project Sentinel. Having decision-makers engaged in and to some extent driving internal reform through has given the new framework a 'good kick start'. The internal reforms of the ACC intelligence capability that Project Sentinel represents have also been implemented at the same time as the agency has become part of a broadened Australian national intelligence community. So while the government's refocus on the ACC, and increased funding for the Project Sentinel arrangements are encouraging, from such political largesse comes expectations, and the new Project Sentinel framework still has a number of challenges ahead of it.

These challenges are both external and internal to the ACC. Internally, Project Sentinel represents a complete break with the past in the processes and structures for delivering intelligence. Therefore, it is likely there will remain challenges for the foreseeable future regarding staffing requirements, governance and how this framework interacts with other agencies in Australia who have a role in looking at organized crime, including federal, state and territory police, and other more traditional national security agencies such as ASIO. From an organizational cultural perspective, investigators in the ACC have been used to 'standing up their own jobs'. The Project Sentinel framework will have them working on targets already identified and partially developed through the first two phases of the new structure. Getting investigators internal to the agency to work in this different way may present a risk to the success of the new model.

Another challenge is, how will the new ACC internal intelligence processes that underpin Project Sentinel – particularly its efforts to join the dots on some complex organized crime groups through its new analytics capability – be coordinated with other approaches used by external agencies? What governance arrangements will be needed to 'hand over' the targets produced by Project Sentinel to other agencies when the resourcing or the remit of another agency requires this? It is clear the ACC's new fusion coordinating function will assist this, but there are questions over how the ACC will hand over newly developed targets to other agencies. Given the rhetoric contained in the *Organised Crime Strategic Framework* about a 'whole of government' approach to organized crime, such governance issues internal and external to Project Sentinel will need careful management.

Additional challenges to the successful implementation of Project Sentinel include the ACC's ability to quickly build sufficient technical capabilities in particular analytics skills, as well as enough programmers and statisticians who can ensure the agency can fuse the data stream in real time, and make sense of what the data mean from the broader intelligence perspective. I will return to this point of the limitations of analytics later in Chapter 8, but a fully functioning analytics capability is a bigger investment than just training a few analysts to exploit data sets. The other challenge will be to retain a focus on strategic intelligence. The Project Sentinel framework thus far appears to place the emphasis on tactical, operational and collection analytics. The system will still need to capture the strategic significance of these data beyond the case being examined. This in turn requires the ability to assess intelligence to identify the threats and risks of groups/crime types to allow a more proactive steered approach to agency collection.

Conclusion

I have briefly outlined five contemporary intelligence frameworks to demonstrate how intelligence frameworks are evolving post 9/11, including identifying some key strengths and weaknesses in each. In each case, I have attempted to capture the outline of five frameworks. The full details of each are not available, and in some cases more information has been available than others. Additionally, some of the frameworks, such as the CCIM, are still in planning mode, so care must be taken in not drawing definitive conclusions on incomplete and dynamic case studies.

However, from the data collected so far on each framework, some obvious similarities and differences are apparent. For example, looking at the main components of each framework, there are some broad similarities with collection and analytical methodologies. Other similarities between frameworks are obvious in the inclusion of various components and their names. For example, some of the UK NIM terminology and components can been seen in the NZP Intelligence Framework and the CCIM. Each framework also demonstrates the blurring between what has been traditionally thought of as 'policing and national security intelligence'. This is clear in the discussion on fusion centers. However, even the single agency-focused frameworks demonstrate a greater emphasis on implementing structures and processes, which support a greater nexus with stakeholders from policing and national security intelligence agencies.

There are also some differences in the scales of complexity between the five case studies. Some frameworks, such as the NZP Intelligence Framework and the ACC's Project Sentinel, are single agency, while others, such as the two fusion centers, the NIM or the CCIM are multi-agency in design. Yet the single agency frameworks still demonstrate, on a range of levels, further integration with other agencies and intelligence communities through various initiatives. Additionally, each framework – both its internal and external dimensions – has been influenced by external bureaucratic politics in each country, which also need to be understood in each case. In Chapter 5, I will focus more deeply on the significance or otherwise of variations between the five case studies discussed here as well as addressing whether these matter to an understanding of intelligence structures more generally. In particular, based on discussion here, Chapter 5 will address two major questions. First, to what extent can these frameworks be exported or replicated to different agencies and contexts? And second (and depending on the answer to the first question), how can we use this greater understanding of intelligence frameworks and components in different contexts to build better practice, and promote the growth of theorizing in intelligence? Is it possible to get beyond merely describing a range of intelligence frameworks to 'test' (evaluate) their applicability in different environments?

5 Building better intelligence frameworks

Introduction

In Chapter 4, I provided overviews of five case studies that illustrate different approaches to intelligence frameworks across Australia, Canada, New Zealand, the UK and the USA. These case studies provide insights into how various agencies and countries are conceptualizing and implementing their intelligence capabilities to deal with a range of threats (including high volume crime, terrorism and organized crime) in the security environment. While I made some brief comparisons between them at the conclusion of Chapter 4, there are more useful observations and questions arising from their discussion, including to what extent they can help practitioners and scholars to understand what makes an effective intelligence framework. In this chapter, I will summarize the issues arising from the case studies in order to explore three critical questions. First, how effective are these intelligence frameworks and do they point towards a more successful way of *doing* intelligence? Second, are these frameworks potentially useful in other intelligence contexts, or are they specific and useful only to the country or communities concerned? Third, based on the answers to the first two questions, what makes a good intelligence framework? Or in other words, how can we improve practitioner knowledge and theory generation about intelligence frameworks?

I argue that these three questions are important as we approach a decade since 9/11. The time seems opportune to take stock of the kind of frameworks that agencies are implementing and governments are funding. The suite of public inquiries into various aspects of the performance of intelligence agencies post 9/11, and the continually politicized context in which these agencies now work, suggest that more focus is required by researchers and practitioners on how to build better frameworks that improve the capabilities of intelligence. As noted in Chapter 4, building better intelligence capabilities rests on improving the performance of a number of core components of the intelligence process (for example, tasking and coordination, collection and analytical techniques). More reflection, however, is required on how these 'parts or components' work in concert together to provide *better frameworks*. Intelligence scholarship has been good at focusing on *parts* of the intelligence process, but less on how these components interact as a *whole* to produce better intelligence. Hence, in this chapter, I move the focus away from a discussion of components to how these work together as an integrated framework.

A focus on intelligence frameworks is a gap in the literature and is due to a number of reasons. First, in all research involving intelligence, access to data is always an issue. It is difficult for researchers to study intelligence systems, frameworks and components. With the partial exception of the UK NIM, which has been studied and discussed widely by researchers, the details of most frameworks remain closely guarded by their agencies. The issue of access, however, has not necessarily stopped researchers examining various parts of the intelligence process. For example, researchers examine the technical components of intelligence, particularly those that cut across the private and public sector, such as data mining. Recently there has also been an increase in research on examining the psychological factors that impact on analysis and how the application of crime mapping techniques can lead to crime reduction. However, there is little research which examines how such specific capabilities impact on and interact within an entire intelligence framework.

Currently, there is little evidence of whether the types of frameworks discussed in Chapter 4 are fit for purpose. Do the 'cogs and wheels' working together in these frameworks support better integration of intelligence into intelligence decision-making and processes? And how can we build more effective intelligence frameworks in the future? These questions may seem to be somewhat arcane or abstract, and not relevant to improving the effectiveness of intelligence in a practical sense. However, I argue that they are critical to improving both the structural and functional aspects of intelligence performance.

In relation to the first question – the effectiveness of the intelligence frameworks – I will address this by exploring some key themes arising out of each case study in Chapter 4, and whether these represent strengths, successes or weaknesses. Assessing the relative strengths and weaknesses in each framework provides an indication, albeit a rough one, of their overall effectiveness. Based on this discussion, I will also draw some conclusions as to whether any of the frameworks underscore better ways of 'doing intelligence' and why this might be the case. The final section of the chapter will address the second key question of whether any of these frameworks are transferable to other contexts.

The five case studies: effective intelligence frameworks?

The UK National Intelligence Model (NIM)

There are a number of strengths to the UK NIM, which have made it a successful and effective way of doing policing intelligence in the UK. As space is limited, I will restrict the discussion to four broad areas of strength. These areas are: *prescribed approach*, *integration*, *defined outputs* and *doctrine*. As noted in Chapter 4, the prescribed approach of the NIM, a framework mandated by the UK Home Secretary under the Police Reform Act 2002, provides a statutory basis for the introduction of NIM minimum standards and its basic principles. The Act provided a political and legal foundation for the NIM's implementation. Having policy-makers engaged in mandating the implementation of the NIM has contributed to its success.

A prescribed or mandatory approach resulted in different agencies having to adhere to similar standards for intelligence processes and products, in addition to promoting a more effective approach to the use of intelligence in strategic and tactical decision-making. In addition to the political and legal underpinnings of the NIM framework, police executives and oversight agencies such as ACPO and (Centrex) NPIA have also been involved from the beginning in ensuring minimum NIM standards have been implemented across all police agencies in England and Wales.

The second strength of the NIM has been its emphasis on integration. The NIM framework offers an integrated set of structures, processes and products for doing intelligence in the broader context of policing. It is not a framework, which involves only some aspects of the intelligence process such as collection or analysis. Rather, it is a holistic approach, as discussed in Chapter 4, for integrating intelligence into the broader policing business rather than a framework which isolates intelligence outputs from the broader organization objectives. It is the four original components of the NIM as designed in 2000, but later elaborated on (tasking and coordination, knowledge products, system products and intelligence products) that give it a systematic and integrated approach to intelligence.

In particular, the tasking and coordination component underpins much of how intelligence, at least in theory, should be tasked at the strategic and tactical levels in UK policing. This component has been important in providing police managers and analysts with guidance on how to task intelligence, but also guidance on how to better integrate intelligence into decision-making, through setting control strategies (for strategic) and tactical menus of work. In summary, it is this integrated approach, ensuring the intelligence framework is embedded into all other aspects of policing that is one of the NIM's strengths. The third area of strength has been the NIM's emphasis on outputs. Intelligence frameworks are vulnerable if they are unable to support the delivery of specific outputs that are valuable to decision-makers. The NIM's focus on outputs particularly at the tactical level, such as prevention, intelligence and enforcement priorities, gives decision-makers 'something' to do with the intelligence. This outputs focus also provides some accountability in the system as intelligence outputs can be tracked to various decision-making points in the framework. Finally, the fourth strength area of the NIM is doctrine. Each of the NIM's four components also provides a foundation upon which a range of other different doctrinal processes and practices have been built. This is important as the framework does not leave it up to individual agencies to design what these doctrinal processes should be. Through the work of the NIM implementation team, and subsequently by ACPO and NPIA, a range of common – even 'corporatized' – standards and guidelines for any number of intelligence processes have been developed which underpin the NIM framework. Some of the specific guidelines were discussed earlier in Chapter 4. Having this doctrine has helped improve standards in intelligence collection and analysis, but also contributed towards building a foundation for professionalizing intelligence in the UK policing context.

The Canadian Criminal Intelligence Model (CCIM)

As noted earlier, in contrast to the UK NIM, the CCIM is still developmental. Hence evaluating the success and effectiveness of this intelligence framework in any definitive sense is premature. Interviews, however, with officers involved in its implementation suggest that already there have been some early 'tentative' successes which may bode well for the future. The two early successes revealed from discussions with implementation team members are *executive patronage*, and the progress that has been made towards more effective *information management*. The establishment of the CCIM has received formal endorsement of all the Canadian Chiefs of Police via the CISC National Executive Committee in March 2006. This endorsement by the heads of all 400 policing agencies in Canada means executive policing is at least supportive of what the CCIM is meant to achieve. Executive championship of the CCIM will also aid implementing various aspects of the new framework in individual policing agencies across the Canadian policing intelligence community. The other area where there has been some early success relates to work under way to develop a CCIS. The CCIS is focused on promoting an improved national database for sharing intelligence to replace the current ageing ACIIS system. While the CCIS is a standalone project, the CCIM implementation team has focused a lot of attention on developing CCIS requirements. This creates synergy between the two projects and will be an important foundation to reinforcing other objectives in the CCIM such as improving intelligence sharing between agencies and enhancing the analytical capabilities of these agencies. At the time of writing, however, not all policing agencies in Canada had signed up for CCIS, and this may impact on the ability of the CCIM implementation teams to progress other work underpinning the framework, in specific areas such as in promoting more standardized approaches to intelligence systems, processes and training.

US fusion centers

Based on discussions with key intelligence staff involved in both the JRIC and the ROIC (see Chapter 4), one important sign of early success seems to be that in each a culture of improved cooperation among agencies participating in them is developing. Given the *raison d'être* of fusion centers is to improve cooperation and collaboration between federal, state and local agencies, one would hope this is so, although it is also clear from discussions that there is still room for improvement in cooperation between some agencies in these centers. Another key strength of both centers has been their ability to service other local policing and public agencies that are not part of the centers, and do not necessarily have the intelligence or investigative capacities to deal with some complex crime areas such as organized crime and counter-terrorism. I would argue that the ability of fusion centers such as the JRIC and the ROIC to effectively use their 'specialized comparative advantages' to help less resourced regional, state and local agencies, is also another measure of their success and relevance. Continuing to support the intelligence requirements of smaller agencies, in addition to enhancing the positive perceptions of the fusion centers, will also be useful to broaden each fusion center's own collection and analytical capabilities.

There are likely to be other more specific successes to report from each fusion center, but it is difficult to speculate on these, given the short time available to collect data at both fusion centers in 2009. Further discussions with not just the key fusion intelligence management staff in each fusion center, but other agency representatives would provide a more accurate assessment of other key strengths and challenges. Additional care must also be taken in assessing 'success' and 'challenges' in any fusion centers when visited in isolation. A sample of only two does not demonstrate necessarily 'effectiveness', 'successes' or the relative strengths of one over the other. Given now there are over 70 across the USA, there is variation in each (despite guidelines issued by the DHS for how they should be structured), depending on location (city, regional or rural), configuration of agencies involved and their functions. Even in the two I visited there was variation between them. As noted earlier, in the JRIC, the focus is more squarely on counter-terrorism intelligence support, whereas the ROIC's mandate is wider, encompassing an 'all hazards' approach. The ROIC also includes both an intelligence analysis function and generating operations within the fusion center directly from this intelligence. A good example of this latter point is the ROIC's supply of intelligence products to local jurisdictions that create a 'common operating picture' for multi-agency and jurisdictional operational initiatives such as the New Jersey Violent Enterprise Source Targeting (VEST) initiative aimed at reducing violent crime and recidivism (Guidetti 2010).

The New Zealand Police Intelligence Framework

The new NZP intelligence framework has been influenced by the UK NIM in some respects for several years. Some of the language, products and decision-making processes reflect aspects of the NIM approach. Additionally, the development of the new framework has also been influenced by the NIM through the appointment in 2007 of Mark Evans to lead much of its development. Evans was formerly in the Police Service of Northern Ireland, which has been using the NIM for the past decade, although is now looking to revise parts of it. Again caution is required in assessing 'successes' in this framework, given much is still to be completed in its implementation. However, it is clear that the new framework represents a significant break with the past for New Zealand policing intelligence and has already shown some tangible benefits. There are three areas where the framework has shown some early success. Again, like the UK NIM and the CCIM, positive 'executive patronage' has been one early area of success. Such patronage has helped the NZP intelligence team implement a series of significant reforms at headquarters, regional and local levels. The second early success of the framework is the development and integration of national and local policing intelligence processes. The establishment of a NIC, perhaps for the first time, gives the agency a central corporate focus for intelligence. The NIC allows the coordination and tasking of intelligence for nationally significant crime, such as organized crime, and an improved ability for the police to lever off the capabilities of other national agencies, both public and private.

At a regional and local level, there has been also been early reform with the establishment in 2009 of district intelligence managers. Their role is to act as change managers for the new framework at the local levels of the agency. While it is still early days, these district managers may become effective facilitators and guardians of standardized processes and doctrine across the entire agency, while still giving district areas the flexibility to manage their intelligence resources as they see fit.

The final area where there has been some early success has been the establishment of a professional development in intelligence programmes to support the development of intelligence analysis within the new framework. There may be some resistance among intelligence staff, who are used to working in familiar ways to different standards, and this will require careful management. But already the articulation and development of improved analytical training, and creating career paths for analysts, demonstrate some early successes for this framework.

The Australian Crime Commission Project Sentinel

Project Sentinel, like the CCIM and NZP intelligence framework, is still being implemented, so again any assessment of its success or strengths must be provisional. But I do think one of Project Sentinel's early strengths is in its design. It seems to be one that is 'fit for purpose' for a small and lean organization, with a highly specialized role in coordinating national intelligence operations and investigations into serious and organized crime. The three-phase (functional) approach of Project Sentinel will also allow the ACC's menu of work to adapt more adeptly as threats change, rather than being constrained by the functions of analytical and investigative teams across all potential areas of work. Another strength of Project Sentinel, as noted in Chapter 4, is that it builds on successes that the ACC has had in adopting specialized intelligence strategies to niche crime areas. The ACC has already for a few years been synthesizing relevant intelligence from large data sets (particularly from banks, the government anti-money laundering agency, AUSTRAC, and the financial regulation agency, ASIC), with other criminal intelligence in support of lengthy financial investigations. Much of this approach underpins the new Project Sentinel framework. Another potential success of Project Sentinel may be that the ACC's investment in advanced analytics could underpin in an effective way more data-driven approaches to intelligence. Given that it is not likely, at least in the foreseeable future, that other policing or law enforcement agencies in Australia will invest as heavily in developing this capability in their intelligence functions, the ACC could develop a distinct comparative advantage in this capability that is recognized by and becomes useful to the entire wider policing intelligence community.

Challenges

The discussion above does suggest that all five frameworks do exhibit both successes and strengths. Though in most cases, with the exception perhaps of the UK NIM, each framework is still being implemented and the CCIM should more accurately be viewed as an initiative still in the planning phase. As each framework develops over the next few years, hopefully other strengths or successes will become apparent. The extent to which these frameworks are implemented successfully, and are effective in delivering good intelligence processes and products will rely on how challenges identified in each framework can be addressed. In the remaining part of this section, before turning our attention to the other two key questions in this chapter, I will provide an overview of the challenges that have been identified in each framework. As space is limited, I will address these challenges together rather than by separate headings for each intelligence framework. It also makes sense to address them together as many frameworks have similar challenges.

An assessment of each framework shows that there are at least three major broad 'challenge areas' common to each. There are very likely to be others, but these came out of the analysis of the data available from each case study. Under each of the three broad challenge areas, there are a number of related issues, but for the ease of analysis, I have summarized them under the three categories: *governance, information communications technology, human resources and capabilities.* Of the three categories, arguably it is the governance issues which present the most difficult challenge to the successful implementation of these intelligence frameworks, and possibly others not discussed here. The analysis of each intelligence framework suggests that governance is a cornerstone of any intelligence framework. In other words, it may be described as the *primary enabler* for the coordination, cooperation and integration of people, processes and products relating to the implementation and sustainability of the framework. It includes not only how the framework and all its components are designed and implemented, but also how these interact with each other internally and externally to the agency concerned.

Other important issues that come under the remit of governance are the development of core components of the intelligence framework, such as effective strategic and tactical tasking and coordination arrangements, and forging effective organizational (cultural) change management to ensure the new framework is implemented successfully. Unsurprisingly, effective governance requires strong executive leadership, both to conceptualize and project manage the suite of changes required to implement the new framework, and then to review and evaluate the doctrine systems and processes that underpin the core components of the framework. In each of the five frameworks, the importance of getting these governance issues 'right' was reflected to varying degrees during interviews with intelligence managers or project implementation team members.

The UK NIM's emphasis on business management processes such as tasking and coordination meetings, the focus on developing doctrinal processes for intelligence collection and analytical activities, have provided a good example of how effective governance can drive the intelligence process. But governance must happen at all levels of management in an agency. The NIM's implementation across all English and Welsh police forces has not been a consistent process. From a policing management perspective in some agencies there was, as discussed in Chapter 4, a lack of understanding, particularly at junior and middle management levels, of what the NIM was meant to achieve. Effective governance must also include processes to integrate inputs and outputs from the intelligence framework to other agencies, stakeholders, networks and geographic areas. In this context, another NIM-related governance issue has been the difficulty of integrating, in some agencies, force-level intelligence with regional and national strategic and operational intelligence activity, and the ability of force-level agencies to capture intelligence support from these higher levels and transform it into actionable local intelligence. The NIM's ability to join up local intelligence outputs with specialized intelligence areas, including the work that SOCA does on organized crime, has also not been optimal, and it may be in the middle area of regional policing where further governance work needs to occur in order to better connect the local NIM outputs to the broader national intelligence frameworks.

The governance issues discussed above in the UK NIM context are also likely to influence how the other four intelligence frameworks develop in the future, though obviously different 'local' conditions will also result in variations in the scale and type of governance issues faced. The CCIM, the fusion centers and Project Sentinel may have more stakeholders, agencies and a wider spread of geographic areas with which to negotiate, but a single agency intelligence framework such as the NZP Intelligence Framework arguably will still need to manage significant complexities in order to build a good framework.

In each framework, however, effective and sustainable leadership in the implementation of these frameworks will be the most crucial governance issue to 'get right'. For example, in the case of the NZP Intelligence Framework, its successful implementation over the next five years will require the development of the efficient nationally focused intelligence processes and products that are relevant to police executives, but also to decision-makers across the whole of government. The recently established NIC will help NZP better integrate and coordinate its intelligence outputs with the rest of government at the national level. Effective governance in this new framework will also require careful monitoring of developments in other parts of the framework, to ensure new arrangements at headquarters can also support local district and area intelligence requirements, which may at times be different to national priorities.

The intelligence frameworks in the five case studies are also being implemented at a time, and this is partly in response to it, when the security environment is becoming more complex. The operating environment for each has become increasingly crowded with new stakeholders to manage, including public and private partners. The evolution of US fusion centers are a good example of new intelligence frameworks developing that will need to adeptly manage more stakeholders than their single member agencies most likely have ever had to do. But the widening of the number of agencies participating in fusion centers directly or indirectly does present challenges for fusion center management to retain focus on key priority areas. Adding value to policy-makers will rely on fusion center leadership being able to clearly articulate mandates, that all stakeholders will agree on, and which describe what kind of intelligence processes and products they ought to be involved in.

The final governance issue I will discuss here relates to organizational cultural issues. During interviews with the key architects or senior intelligence managers associated with each framework, some organizational cultural issues were identified. These issues are not unique and have been raised elsewhere in the book and by other scholars, particularly those working in policing intelligence environments. They include concerns about non-intelligence staff and decision-makers still not understanding or having a negative view about the value of intelligence. Good governance of new intelligence frameworks therefore will require their architects and implementation teams to influence these perceptions of intelligence by creating *value* which is measurable for senior decision-makers. Influential intelligence leadership, however, will remain challenging when political leaders and heads of agencies switch their attention to more other immediate tactical requirements, or when funding limitations result in a recalibration of priorities, rather than investing in a framework which will bring dividends further down the track.

The second category, *information communications technology* includes a number of challenges which will impact on the effective implementation of these frameworks. The two examples of fusion frameworks discussed earlier demonstrate an increasing shift towards networked approaches to intelligence processes and products. Additionally, the CCIM, the NZP Intelligence Framework and Project Sentinel also place an emphasis on how the intelligence efforts of the agencies involved can become more integrated with other agencies' efforts. The CCIM case study underscores the importance of effective information communications technology in supporting other more networked and integrated initiatives planned in the new intelligence framework. For example, the CCIM implementation team's efforts in supporting the introduction of a new CCIS are not only aimed at an improved national database for sharing intelligence among Canada's 400 policing agencies, but also at achieving other specific project objectives, including the planned creation of dashboards for analysts consisting of tools to improve practice. The creation of the CCIS does, however, create challenges for agencies in deciding what they are prepared to share on the system with others. Some of the other planned enhancements for the CCIS, including the creation of a web intra-net environment for analysts, will also be challenging, particularly for small agencies where the integration of the technology is beyond their financial reach.

Project Sentinel's implementation also underscores the ICT challenges. The ACC has inherited a legacy of case management and a number of other databases – none of which has ever been optimal for storing and retrieving intelligence. There are other policing and security agencies in Australia too with similar challenges. The ACC's ability to support the new fusion and analytics capabilities in Project

Sentinel will require further reforms and restructuring of the current ICT architecture. This remains complex, given that any improvements will need to be made in concert and with the consent of all Australian policing agencies. There are also still cultural issues between agencies that need to be resolved to ensure that information is not excessively controlled by its originating agency for no good reason, and that this information is shared in real time between the relevant federal and state agencies. The information architecture and sharing challenges discussed in the five frameworks are also present, to greater or lesser degrees, in the broader intelligence communities in each country. For example, the 2009 report to Congress by the US Program Manager for the ISE initiative lists similar ICT challenges in the broader US intelligence community (ISE 2009: 5–6).

The third set of challenges, *human resources and capabilities*, includes a number of areas that these frameworks need to address if they are to produce effective and sustainable results. The main areas are: training, continual professional development and staff socialization. Starting with the UK NIM (but also clear in the other frameworks), a key strength has been its focus on developing both intelligence and non-intelligence staff to deliver the specific requirements of the new framework. This has involved training programmes to get analysts and others to comply with NIM initiatives. I will come back to a broader discussion of intelligence education and professionalism in Chapter 9. For the NIM, however, one of the key challenges over the past decade has been in investing significantly to get people trained to perform duties in line with new approaches or standards detailed in the framework. Leaving the NIM aside, where it is clear efforts have been made in developing the analytical skills of the police to some standard, in the other four cases studies, strategies to support training and continual professional development will be required in the future.

Intelligence training and professional development initiatives also need to be constantly realigned as additional parts of the framework are implemented. I did note in one of the new frameworks that there was little alignment between the broader reform objectives and the kind of intelligence courses being offered by one agency's education area. This can result obviously in not getting the right kind of trained staff in the correct positions. A lack of synergy between the training curriculum and the broader reform objectives of the framework can also result in poorly trained or disengaged staff, who are not able, or willing, to apply new approaches articulated in the framework. Investing in people development and retaining good staff, particularly specialized staff, is a constant struggle for many agencies. Professional development initiatives are costly and the results of the investment in staff may not be immediately evident. The other issue is *staff socialization*, which in some respects crosses over training and continuing professional development, but is broader and includes issues such as awareness, marketing and team building. In each framework studied in Chapter 4, it was clear from talking to intelligence staff that these issues were also important in determining whether a new framework would be successfully implemented. In large hierarchical policing and security agencies, implementing structural changes is often viewed by staff – somewhat cynically – as 'yet another initiative imposed from headquarters', with perhaps little perceived or actual consultation. While key designers, for example, of the CCIM and NZP Intelligence Framework have indicated the importance of stakeholder management in underpinning the success of their approaches, managing internal and external stakeholders remain challenges in all five frameworks. In particular, there is an ongoing need by framework implementation staff to deliver clear messages to their stakeholders and staff about the need to do intelligence differently. This should include delivering effective awareness and marketing campaigns to demonstrate the benefits of new approaches throughout the implementation stage and beyond. For example, in Project Sentinel, non-intelligence stakeholders such as investigators will need to be sensitized to the benefits of working in an environment where intelligence will more frequently drive their menu of work. Organizational culture is slow to adapt and the intelligence-driven approach that underpins each of these frameworks still needs to be 'sold' to senior managers and non-intelligence staff, who may not be used to doing things differently. To effect cultural change, socialization strategies must be part of the overall enabling efforts of human capabilities in a new framework.

In summary, as noted earlier, accurately assessing the effectiveness of these frameworks is premature given that most frameworks (except the UK NIM) are still being implemented. However, it would be useful to collect more data in each case study in order to provide a more definitive 'interim' assessment of their overall effectiveness. The NIM, which has been in existence for a decade, is now being evaluated by a team led by the Metropolitan Police and the NPIA. The 'lessons learnt' from this review will be useful to other agencies that are implementing new intelligence frameworks, and will also improve general levels of theorizing about frameworks.

Additionally, any assessment of 'effectiveness' must be carefully considered in terms of how the researcher defines and measures 'effectiveness' in their research design. As will be discussed in Chapter 10, there are significant gaps in research and theory building on how to evaluate the effectiveness or 'value' of intelligence processes and products within frameworks. The approach I have taken in examining the five case studies in Chapter 4 was to pose the same semi-structured questions to intelligence managers and other staff with knowledge about each framework. At the start of this project, the research strategy for this part of the book was aimed at making 'analytic generalizations' from a sufficiently large number of case studies (five) in order to develop some theoretical perspectives about 'what makes an effective intelligence framework'. The questions asked of interviewees focused on the core components of intelligence (collection and analysis), and less so on other important enabling activities (for example, governance, human resources and legislation issues). But in retrospect, the collection of additional data on enabling activities would have provided a richer analysis and a greater understanding of what makes intelligence frameworks effective or not. In addition to this reflection about not having asked 'more of the right questions', there were also procedural issues which influenced case study data collection, including limited access to participants and timeframes with participants, who were in many cases senior intelligence officers. I do not want to underplay data access issues, as in most cases, my discussions were with the most appropriate people or key architects of the frameworks being studied. However, all the participants are busy people and, in hindsight, follow-up interviews might have assisted in extracting additional data not collected initially. Another methodological issue that impacts on the ability to 'operationalize' this idea of 'effectiveness' is the variability between case studies. As noted earlier in this book, Australia, Canada, New Zealand, the UK and the USA are all liberal democratic countries with a great deal of similarity between their intelligence practices – particularly in collaborating together historically in dealing with the same threats. Yet it is also clear that all five frameworks described in Chapter 4 are being developed in different countries. Hence, in each case, the frameworks being forged must also be understood as a result of the unique combination of administrative, political, cultural, legislative and geographic variations in each country. There are of course variations within countries, who share intelligence frameworks such as the CCIM, and as noted above, even variations within similar types of structures like the two US fusion centers discussed. This raises questions on the comparability of the structures and functions across each case study. All of these methodological challenges require close attention if researchers and practitioners are to collect data across disparate case studies, and then seek to 'explain' whether the frameworks studied are effective ways to do intelligence. The methodological challenges of accessing sufficient data for all five case studies have resulted, in this study, in a shift away from attempting to explain whether they represent effective frameworks to one where the focus is on understanding how they contribute to our knowledge of what makes an effective intelligence framework.

So in the absence of further data to confirm some of the observations made above about each framework, the better question in the interim may be, what can we take from these case studies, which can help us understand what good practice frameworks might look like? Before addressing this question, however, I want to turn the focus to addressing the second key question in this chapter – to what extent are these frameworks transferable in other intelligence contexts?

Are these frameworks transferable?

This second key question of the chapter represents an important bridge between the first and the third. Although it is not possible to assess fully whether any of the five frameworks are effective, the discussion above does point to how they may be useful in other contexts. But the question is, which frameworks or components and in which other intelligence contexts? Again the answer is not straightforward, yet the issue of transferability of frameworks is important – both in a practical sense, and for those interested in theory-building in intelligence. From a practitioner's perspective, the increasingly complex security environment has resulted in the growth of a number of public and private agencies developing intelligence capabilities. In Chapter 2, I referred to these new capabilities as emerging practice areas, as they do not fit neatly into the traditional practice areas of national security or policing intelligence.

In the public sector, within the past decade, intelligence capabilities have been developed in child and consumer protection, anti-corruption, juvenile justice, transport security, health and the social security sectors. Similarly in the private sector, insurance fraud, forensic accounting, security consultancy companies and even global pharmaceutical companies have established intelligence capabilities. In newer practice contexts, there is a need to quickly identify and implement intelligence frameworks, which can support decision-making in these environments. For intelligence managers, given the responsibility to set up new frameworks in emerging practice areas, there is an obvious interest in examining the adaptability of frameworks used in traditional practice (national security and policing) contexts to their circumstances. However, despite a more networked approach to the security environment, where the interests of public and private sector intelligence capabilities are increasingly intersecting, there is still little sharing of ideas (at least publicly), on how frameworks developed in national security and policing environments may be relevant and transferable to emerging practice areas. On one level, this lack of sharing of ideas about frameworks is not surprising. For many national security and policing agencies, their ingrained 'cultures of secrecy' (discussed in Chapter 1), can prevent them sharing ideas about how their intelligence systems and processes are arranged, out of concern for revealing sensitive methodologies. While in some circumstances, both the culture of secrecy and legislation may prevent a wider sharing of particular processes and structures outside the originating agency, the publication of much of the UK NIM's doctrinal information suggests that useful information can be disseminated to other agencies without compromising sensitive methodologies. In summary, I am referring here to the desirability of exchanging ideas and information about how broad processes are structured, not detailed assessments of how individual intelligence work moves through these frameworks.

Given the importance of sharing information about intelligence frameworks, the more important question is, are these frameworks transferable and relevant in other contexts? There is the obvious list of variables which can either facilitate or inhibit the 'importation' of frameworks or their components to other agencies, contexts and countries. Different legislative, political, geographic variables are obvious ones, but others issues such as the practising context and technical requirements are also relevant. For example, in Chapter 2's discussion of biosecurity, I noted the challenges in linking highly technical areas such as bioforensics with policing intelligence processes. Additionally, when considering the usefulness of these frameworks to other practice contexts, the question of scale also requires consideration. A framework such as the CCIM being developed for an entire intelligence community with 400 members is quite different from one being implemented in the one agency, such as the NZP Intelligence Framework. This question of scale will determine the extent to which broader community frameworks such as the CCIM or those adopted by single agencies will be relevant elsewhere.

So how transferable are these five frameworks to other contexts? A lack of sufficient data and the fact that most of the frameworks are still being implemented make this a difficult question to answer with any confidence. It is difficult to know what exactly we would be mapping across to other practice contexts. But it is still possible to reflect on the overviews of frameworks presented in Chapter 5, and make some general comments about their *applicability* to other contexts, rather than necessarily whether the *specifics* of each framework would work in another environment. There is insufficient space to discuss in detail all five frameworks, so I will concentrate here on the UK NIM, US fusion centers and the ACC Project Sentinel.

Starting with the UK NIM, it is clear that this framework provides a sufficiently broad business model approach to doing intelligence with its emphasis on tasking and coordination processes that integrate intelligence into decision-making processes. As noted earlier, the NIM's focus on setting tactical menus of work and control strategies also promotes greater accountability in tracking how intelligence is used in order to impact on the security environment. Of all the frameworks introduced in Chapter 4, the UK NIM approach has been the most widely applied framework – either partially or in whole – by a number of Commonwealth policing agencies in Australia, Canada and New Zealand. In Australia, different policing agencies have adapted various aspects of the NIM in 2002. For example, Victoria Police adopted the Victoria Police Intelligence Model (VPIM), which was very similar to the NIM framework. Victoria Police is now in the process of reviewing various aspects of the VPIM and it remains uncertain to what extent it will resemble the key components of the NIM in the future. But in the case of Australian policing, while NIM approaches may be transferable, there remain a number of difficulties in many agencies in fully realizing all aspects of the NIM in practice. These challenges are similar to those mentioned earlier in the discussion of the other frameworks. The UK experience with the NIM approach demonstrates that it cannot be implemented overnight. Additionally, some of the Australian attempts to transfer the NIM have not been successful due to a lack of consistent leadership and effective governance of intelligence reform over the past decade in many Australian and other Commonwealth agencies. Other factors have been a lack of interest by relevant federal and state political leaders in either championing or legislating for the implementation of a nation-wide NIM approach in Australia. With the recent (2009) release of the *Organised Crime Strategic Framework*, a greater political appetite may now be developed by the federal government at least for a more national coordinated approach to policing intelligence. The ACC has started to develop a national criminal intelligence model aimed at setting standards for intelligence practice nationally. However, given differences between Australian federal and state governments' policing and security priorities, it is unlikely that such a model will be backed by legislation mandating all states to adopt the one framework to intelligence.

Another major consideration in assessing the NIM's applicability in non-UK policing environments is whether such contexts can be constructed at the three levels seen in this approach: local, regional and national. Some interview partici-pants reported that even after almost a decade of the NIM's implementation, problems remain in integrating local intelligence outputs of the NIM at force level with similar ones at the regional and national level. The legislative and political barriers in some countries, such as Australia and Canada, present challenges to the full implementation of the three geographic levels depicted in the NIM. Beyond the policing context, however, what other intelligence contexts might the UK NIM be adaptable to?

Leaving aside differences in focus, particularly on how different intelligence contexts may identify threats to the security environment, a NIM approach could usefully be implemented in the corrections sector, biosecurity or in some small government compliance agencies, such as a sports anti-doping authority. Using an 'NIM-like framework' in these new emerging practice contexts would require the implementation of all foundational components of the NIM: tasking and coordination, components, knowledge products, system products and intelligence products. But depending on the agency or practice context, there would obviously be variations in NIM processes, particularly doctrine requirements on collection and analytical capabilities to better represent agency requirements. Agencies that are developing a new intelligence capability and wanted to apply the NIM approach broadly would also need to amend the reporting processes and product templates, as different decision-makers and stakeholders would require variations from those designed for UK policing. In such new practice environments, the NIM approach may provide the necessary structure to build key components of an effective integrated intelligence framework. However, in agencies with a small intelligence capability, the adoption of the NIM could become unnecessarily bureaucratic, and like the original UK framework, its success will be measured by the extent intelligence officers and decision-makers understand it and use it.

The second framework which is transferable to other emerging practice areas is fusion centers. As noted earlier, a fusion center with a focus on counter-terrorism was established in the USA in the late 1990s with the TEW being an early example in Los Angeles. Since 9/11, there has been increasing attention paid by governments and heads of intelligence agencies to fusion centers. They seem to have now become 'all the rage', however, as discussed in Chapter 1, such collaborative and coordinated arrangements have been around for decades, particularly in dealing with drug trafficking and organized crime. The High Intensity Drug Trafficking Areas (HIDTAs) established in the USA prior to 9/11, where different agencies worked together in the one area, are a good example of earlier 'fusion arrangements'. In Australian, Canadian, New Zealand, the UK and the US national security and policing, there have always been multi-agency taskforces, where agencies pool their intelligence assets with others to address an issue. But throwing people from different agencies together in the one room does not necessarily result in either fused or improved intelligence. There are now over 70 fusion centers in the USA, and specialized versions for counter-terrorism, high tech and organized crime are being established in the other countries mentioned above. However, the brief overview of the two fusion centers in the USA, in Chapter 4, highlights some of the key challenges in this fused approach to intelligence, which others working in emerging practice contexts need to learn from if they are to adopt them effectively.

There is potentially a long list of serious threat issues, where a case could be made for investing in a fusion center led by agencies working in emerging practice areas of intelligence practice rather than by security or policing agencies. For example, a country's major health, quarantine or biosecurity authorities could establish a fusion center which could fuse intelligence in support of investigations into a range of biosecurity threats including bioterrorism and bio-crimes. In such specialized areas as disease, human, animal or plant health, it makes sense for scientific agencies to drive a fused approach rather than other traditional policing and security intelligence agencies. The scientific community could help traditional intelligence agencies better focus collection and analysis in order to more accurately calibrate the threat of biosecurity issues. Other potential areas that could support a 'fusion center' approach could include critical infrastructure, corruption and environmental crimes. The development of intelligence capacity across a spectrum of security and policing issues in fragile states, such as the South Pacific PTCCC network discussed in Chapter 3, is also another area where the fusion framework might work effectively. Of course a sense of policy urgency may need to develop around these issues, much as it did post 9/11, before a diverse array of public and private agencies see the need to invest resources in a fused intelligence response.

The application of the fusion approach to other emerging threat issues or by emerging practice areas will also face similar challenges identified in Case study 4.3. Governance, including effective leadership, well-articulated doctrine, and clearly stated intelligence priorities will also need careful articulation in emerging practice areas. Additionally a fused approach requires that there is effective legislation, ICT, human resources and capabilities to build fused intelligence, which is supportive and relevant for decision-makers.

An understanding of the organizational cultures of potential agencies and stakeholders that may be involved in the planned fusion center is, as discussed earlier, another important governance issue. There is an external and internal dimension to organizational culture in fusion centers. The importance of both was made apparent during discussions with key stakeholders involved in the two US fusion centers I visited. From an internal perspective, fusion centers, in order to be successful, must forge a common approach to working between the agencies involved and over time there is benefit in this becoming a 'corporatized identity', or an 'organizational culture' shared by all participants in the fusion center. However, regardless of how well agencies fuse and share a common 'organizational' culture, they must also manage disparate and sometimes conflicting worldviews based on the organizational cultures of their parent agencies. The internal and external dimensions of organizational culture may create tensions and impact on views about the way the fusion center should work and what is expected from it. Keeping a diverse number of stakeholders and funders engaged therefore is challenging. While fusion centers might be quite useful approaches in concentrating specialization and technical excellence in one area, strong governance arrangements will be required to ensure a 'corporate identity' is developed. This will in turn be crucial to keep the 'fused mission' clear in order to avoid duplicating what can be done more efficiently elsewhere by single agencies.

The final framework, Project Sentinel, provides potentially another model that could be used in some emerging intelligence practice areas. As noted earlier,

Project Sentinel was inspired originally by SOCA's ILM model. While both agencies operate under different legislation, in some respects, their approach to intelligence is similar in broad terms. Both the ACC and SOCA are relatively small, and focused on nationally significant organized crime operations that lever off other policing agencies regionally and nationally. The three-phased approach to Project Sentinel, described in Case study 4.5, consists of a risk and threat assessment process that helps identify collection and analytics, targeting and intervention priorities. The structure does have potential value for small specialized agencies with limited resources in allowing them to focus on areas where they assess they can have a greater impact. The three-phased approach also allows along the way points of flexibility, where the ACC can choose to reduce or increase its specialized, but limited intelligence and investigative resources based on where its impact can be the biggest. For example, each phase in Project Sentinel allows the ACC to invest intelligence resources in multi-jurisdictional operations or refer the work to another more appropriate agency to deal with.

In particular, Project Sentinel's focus on advanced analytics and current development of an intelligence fusion capability for organized crime will enable the ACC to build on current strengths in linking irregular patterns in complex financial data sets, with other criminal intelligence sources in support of organized crime investigations. The flexible three-phase approach to the development of intelligence processes and products in Project Sentinel may also be suited to some emerging practice contexts, which have specialized niche roles and limited intelligence and investigative resources. In particular, public agencies with special-ized compliance roles such as securities regulation, corruption and environmental protection may find some benefit from a three-stage intelligence process, which gives them other options in addition to using intelligence to support their own operations. For example, a small niche anti-corruption agency with limited bud-getary allocation for in-house intelligence and investigative capabilities might find the three-phase approach in Project Sentinel gives them more options to have an impact beyond just the traditional and expensive intelligence, investigation and prosecution approach. A collection and analytics (phase 1) function could be useful in monitoring a range of potential data sources suggesting financial gain from corruption. Included in this phase, a risk and threat process could provide other options for the agency in moving intelligence into different decision-making processes that do not involve investigations and prosecution. These processes could be legislative reform, strategic intelligence monitoring or public education programmes.

What makes a good intelligence framework?

The answer to this last question, like the former two questions, is not straight-forward. The discussion of both questions above does suggest that examining the strengths, challenges and transferability of these frameworks does provide some indication of which factors make a good intelligence framework. However, each of the five case studies discussed in Chapter 4 is not a completely implemented framework, so it is unwise to overstate any identified 'strengths' in each as representing the 'gold standard'.

Nevertheless, discussion here and in Chapter 4 does suggest at least what we might consider to be on the list of the essential components of a good (effective) intelligence framework. Based on the assessment of these frameworks, there were a few variables, which seem to be common to all frameworks regardless of the specific context in which it is being implemented. If you take back to basics what intelligence is about – it is a set of processes and products to support decision-making about the threats in the security environment – then I argue that any good framework needs to have both effective *core intelligence processes* and *key enabling activities*.

If both terms are used in an engineering context, then the key enabling activities provides the 'structure' on which the 'super-structure' or core intelligence processes rest. The core intelligence processes are what some would describe as the 'intelligence cycle' or the set of essential phases in the production of intelligence. Figure 5.1 describes the core intelligence processes as: tasking and coordination, collection, analysis and production and evaluation. The key enabling activities are the bedrock or foundation on which the essential 'business of

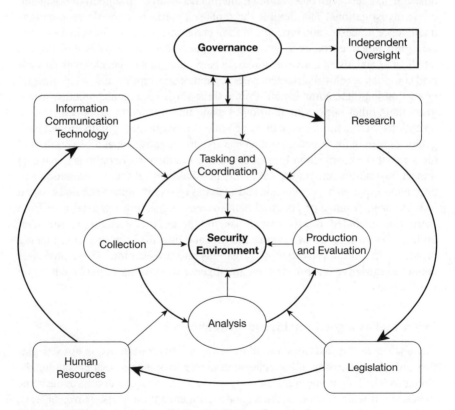

Figure 5.1 Components of an effective intelligence framework

intelligence' takes place. Without these activities being present and operating in an effective and coordinated way, the sustainability of the intelligence framework is questionable. Based on the analysis of the frameworks above, I argue that there are five key activities for an effective intelligence framework: *governance, ICT, human resources, legislation* and *research*. As shown in Figure 5.1, each key enabling activity itself relates to a series of activities and attributes, which describe the specific kind of ways the enabler supports the core intelligence processes in the middle of Figure 5.1. Of all the key enabling activities, I see governance as the most important enabler in building good intelligence frameworks, hence in Figure 5.1 it has been emboldened, and consists of attributes such as strong sustainable leadership, doctrine design, evaluation, effective coordination, cooperation and integration of intelligence processes.

Governance also has an external and internal dimension in any intelligence framework. The external dimension relates to governance issues that impact on the framework from the government or other agencies *outside* of the framework. The internal governance issues are those that are generated by an agency or community's internal management processes. A good example of how a governance issue can cut across both external and internal dimensions is in the setting of intelligence priorities. For example, in Figure 5.1, there is an arrow pointing away from governance towards the tasking and coordination phase and similarly another in the other direction towards the governance circle. This shows that while internal governance arrangements can and do set an agency's intelligence priorities, the government and other external stakeholders also play an important role in articulating priorities. Another example of the external/internal dimensions of governance in Figure 5.1 relates to intelligence oversight mechanisms. From an internal governance perspective, and as will be discussed in Chapter 7, intelligence oversight must be a product of auditing and review measures that occur within agencies and at a political level. However, internal and political oversight is not sufficient to ensure overall effective intelligence oversight governance. In liberal democracies, external and independent oversight must also be present in any effective intelligence framework. In Figure 5.1 the need for a separation between the internal and external (independent) oversight governance processes is distinguished by ensuring 'independent oversight' is depicted diagrammatically as connected to 'governance' but remaining independent of any intelligence framework. In summary, without good governance, the core intelligence components, and the other key enabling activities of the framework cannot function effectively and intelligence failure will soon result.

Another important key enabling activity worth noting (see Figure 5.1) is the role of research in gathering evidence for where improvements can be made in products, processes and other areas of the framework. I argue that research should be included as a key enabling activity to ensure that there is somewhere within a framework where this systematic evidence-driven reflection on practice occurs. Research should not be seen as something that is just external to or considered after the implementation of a framework.

In Figure 5.1, note that the five key enabling activities (governance, information communication technology, human resources, legislation and research), are connected to each other (see the outer circle). The rationale is that each should not operate in isolation, for example, governance influences ICT solutions, and ICT solutions in turn impact on human resources capabilities and the same in reverse. Thus key enabling activities interact with each other and are influenced by each other. However, each key enabling activity also individually plays an important role in the operations of the core intelligence processes.

At the centre of Figure 5.1 and within the four core components of the intelligence framework is the security environment. In considering what makes an effective intelligence framework, I argue the security environment should be placed at the centre of all intelligence activities in the framework as the core components of the intelligence framework can only be constructed around it, not the other way around. In other words, the security environment is the reason the other components exist, and as the security environment changes, so too is there a need to reconfigure or adapt each core component to the new environment. Again as shown in Figure 5.1, in addition to each core component interacting with each other, each phase can separately impact on the security environment. On this point, it should be clear from Figure 5.1 that not all tasking of intelligence processes and products is directed at the tasking and coordination level. In Figure 5.1 there is an arrow going from the 'collection' and 'analysis' components of the framework to the security environment. This underscores how both these critical components can and do operate independently from what is prescribed by the tasking and coordination phase to identify what needs to be collected and how best to assess developments in the security environment based on this collection. The tasking and coordination component has a double-headed arrow denoting that the decision-maker uses intelligence, as Ratcliffe suggests, to make an *impact* on the security environment (see Figure 4.1 Ratcliffe's 3-I Model). But it also denotes that decision-makers in addition to using intelligence products make their own interpretations on what is going on in the security environment, which is often independent of the intelligence support they receive. This issue of policy-driven or 'cherry-picking' intelligence will be discussed further in Chapter 7.

There are obviously a number of different ways to portray this information, and the intention here is not to unnecessarily overcomplicate how intelligence frameworks should be conceptualized. But simple depictions of the intelligence cycle seem to be insufficient in helping to understand or capture what is both a dynamic and, increasingly post 9/11, a more complex process. The point here is that the core intelligence processes, described in each of the five case studies in Chapter 4 also need to be better understood in how they are embedded in even more fundamental enabling processes. Such key enabling activities provide the 'scaffolding' that supports intelligence processes and production for decision-makers. The extent to which the key enabling activities are sound will play a big role in what kind of intelligence product is available to decision-makers in the end. This is not the only way to conceptualize how to improve intelligence frameworks. Each intelligence function, agency, context, network and community will develop their own framework for how their 'cogs and wheels' are meant to turn. The point is that in the future more reflection is required than there has been in the past on how to develop effective frameworks, which are dynamic and adaptive. Part of the answer must be in exploring how to build better key enabling activities, on which the rest of the enterprise of intelligence must rest.

Conclusion

From the discussion of the five frameworks in this chapter and Chapter 4, hopefully it is now clearer how important studying existing intelligence frameworks can be (both for researchers and practitioners) in generating evidence for what makes a good intelligence framework. The answer to this question will always be relative and a bit subjective, but a more systematic evidence-based approach to this question should help build frameworks and components within them that best suit the environment in which they are located. There is most likely not going to be a one-size framework that fits all. However, as argued above and illustrated in Figure 5.1, there are essential structural (key enabling activities) and super-structural components (tasking coordination, collection, analysis and production), which need to considered holistically in any framework, regardless of the context. Additionally, based on the overview of the strengths and challenges of each framework earlier, arguably it is getting the governance issues right in any framework, which is of most consequence. And within the whole series of issues relating to intelligence governance, leadership and the attributes of leaders implementing intelligence frameworks may well be the most important issue. In the final chapter in Part II, I will shift the focus away from the structural and functional aspects of intelligence practice to examine the critical role that leaders and managers must play in creating frameworks which promote 'better value' from intelligence for decision-makers.

6 Intelligence leadership and management

Introduction

In Chapter 5, I argued that both practitioners and academics needed to reflect more on the effectiveness of intelligence frameworks – from the perspective of how core intelligence processes and their key enabling activities can support better decision-making. I also argued that of all 'the moving parts' and the structures that support intelligence frameworks, the overall 'health' of the governance arrangements in a framework is the most important variable in increasing the probability of better intelligence outputs. Within the range of issues that can be categorized as 'intelligence governance issues', high-level leadership capabilities obviously will be the major decider in whether a framework overall is effective and sustainable. In this chapter, I shift the focus away from examining frameworks holistically and their specific components, to exploring the role leaders and managers play specifically in intelligence agencies in promoting better decision-making. How managers and leaders create better 'value' from intelligence for decision-makers will impact significantly on the effectiveness of a number of other issues discussed in the two previous chapters.

A number of developments, particularly in the past decade, have made the role of intelligence leaders and managers even more critical. First, a key factor influencing management activity has been the emergence as in other public sector agencies, of greater 'service delivery cultures' and an enhanced focus on accountability. This change in public sector culture has been incremental, but has had an important impact on the management, operations and performance of intelligence agencies. As noted in Chapter 4, the new public sector management philosophies emerging in the 1990s in the UK were influential in shaping the development of intelligence-led policing, and how UK policing intelligence was managed more broadly. Arguably in the five years after 9/11, this focus on service delivery became even stronger than in the 1990s. In Australia, Canada, New Zealand, the UK and the USA, the series of intelligence failures, subsequent political inquiries and following efforts of reform have focused political and public attention on the effectiveness of intelligence agencies in ways not seen arguably for decades.

The second development which has made leadership and management roles in intelligence agencies more critical relates to the impact of the increasingly complex security environment. While agencies such as the CIA and FBI are undeniably large, hierarchical, bureaucratic organizations, a more fluid, globalized security environment has required such agencies to adapt in more nimble ways to this new environment. The case studies discussed in Chapters 4 and 5 show that for leaders and managers it is now even more critical for them to direct and play a greater role in establishing new frameworks, systems, tools and processes, which will help their agencies adapt to the new security environment. While this seems an obvious point, the ability of leaders and managers of intelligence agencies in the future to manage an uncertain security environment is an open question.

Over the last decade, the contents of a series of official inquiries in the countries we have focused on in this book, such as the 9/11 Commission Report (in the USA), the Butler Report (in the UK) and the Flood Report (in Australia) do show that leaders and managers of intelligence agencies have found it difficult to adapt in an increasingly complex environment.

For example, in the 585 pages of the 9/11 Commission Report, leadership and management challenges were raised and, the report devoted a separate section to 'management issues' (Section 11.4). Section 11.4 described a range of operational and institutional management failures from the ineffective management of information, priority setting and also argued that the Director of Central Intelligence (DCI), George Tenet,

> [Did not] develop a management strategy for a war against Islamist terrorism before 9/11. Such a management strategy would define the capabilities the intelligence community must acquire for such a war – from language training to collection systems to analysts.
>
> (9/11 Commission 2004: 358)

Based on concerns by Commission members about the DCI's ability to develop an effective national management strategy for the US intelligence community leading up to 9/11, they recommended that management of the national intelligence programme be shifted from the DCI to a new national intelligence director (9/11 Commission 2004: 411). The objective was to create a cabinet-level director of national intelligence, who at that level of appointment would have authority to deal with entrenched bureaucratic rivalries and enforce coordination between US intelligence agencies. This all culminated in the Intelligence Reform and Terrorism Prevention Act of December 2004, and the appointment of a Director of National Intelligence (DNI) (John Negroponte) in 2005.

Similarly, another series of high-level inquiries in the USA, Australia and the UK over the accuracy of assessments on the nature of Iraq's WMD programme, revealed other leadership and management issues impacting on the accuracy and quality of intelligence products provided to decision-makers. One of these issues was politicization, which I will return to in Chapter 7. However, reports such as the US SSCI's *Report on the US Intelligence Community's Prewar Intelligence Assessments on Iraq* identified a range of management issues that had also arisen in previous inquiries into US intelligence over several decades.

In the case of the SSCI report, these included insufficient challenging of assessments, within their analytical cadre and by managers, information-sharing problems and unnecessary compartmentalization of information. Significantly, this report concluded that the Director, George Tenet, who was both head of the CIA and the US intelligence community until the creation of the ODNI, was not made aware of alternative views on the questions of WMD in Iraq emanating from other US intelligence agencies other than his own. The SSCI report concluded that this was another serious source of leadership breakdown (SSCI 2004: 24, 27). The UK Butler Report also identified a range of collection and analytical weaknesses, which similarly revealed managerial problems in UK agencies as much as analytical ones. The performance of the FBI leading up to 9/11 and the few years following this event also came under review by a series of inquiries. In addition to the 9/11 Commission Report, others such as Inspector General Glenn Fines' report on the FBI's performance over 9/11 and later the Commission on Iraq's WMD devoted a chapter to the FBI (SSCI 2004). Beyond the official inquiries, concerns have been expressed by academics and the public about FBI shortcomings before and after 9/11 (Hulnick 2004). Criticisms of the FBI's performance had also come from within the agency itself, when FBI officer Coleen Rowley based in the Minnesota field office criticized headquarters for ignoring evidence and intelligence linked to 9/11 co-conspirator Zacarias Moussaoui (Anderson and Fineman 2002). The idea that the intelligence community as a whole (both policing and national security intelligence agencies) was continuing to do a bad job was reinforced from 2003 onwards when it was revealed that the USA had gone to war in Iraq on the basis of 'wrong intelligence' about that nation harboring terrorists and developing WMD.

Outside of the USA, the shooting of Charles de Menezes in the UK also demonstrated that there were other incidents where the poor management of information and intelligence has led to sub-optimal decision-making during investigations. In Australia, the Clarke Inquiry also reported cooperation, coordination and interoperability issues in intelligence and investigations processes between the AFP and other agencies in the investigation of Dr Mohamed Haneef. Haneef was wrongfully arrested and charged on 2 July 2007 for allegedly being linked to terrorist attacks in London and Glasgow that same year. In Canada too, there have been a series of criminal, immigration and counter-terrorism cases, which have highlighted deficiencies in the management of intelligence processes. The 2006 O'Connor Commission, *A New Mechanism for the RCMP's National Security Activities: Commission of Inquiry into the Action of Canadian Officials in Relation to Maher Arar*, is probably the best known. This Inquiry investigated the role Canadian officials (the RCMP and the CSIS) played in the arrest, detention, interrogation and subsequent torture in Syria of the Canadian citizen Maher Arar. Justice O'Connor, who led the Commission, identified many deficiencies in the RCMP and to a lesser extent the CSIS processes. For example, the Commission criticized the RCMP for the inaccuracy of some information it passed onto US authorities and its poor information-sharing policies. The CSIS was also criticized for not having an adequate system to assess the reliability of information that was likely the product of torture by the Syrian Military Intelligence agency (O'Connor 2006: 13–15). Official inquiries such as this show how critical the role of effective leadership and management of intelligence functions are in providing not only valuable, but also ethical and legal intelligence support to decision-makers. I will come back to the ethical and legal dimensions of these cases in Chapter 7.

In addition to several inquiries since 9/11, which have identified various aspects of leadership or managerial deficiencies within intelligence agencies, a number of academics have also focused on these issues. Zegart's work has been cited earlier, but it is one of the more interesting empirical approaches to intelligence failures currently available, and it also does have relevance to understanding how leadership and management issues can play a significant role in intelligence failure. Zegart combines insights from organizational theory and political science to develop a theory of adaptation failure. Her conclusion is that intelligence failure is not so much due to an inability of agencies such as the CIA and FBI to reform, but more that they have been historically unable to adapt to the changing security environment (Zegart 2007: 43). Zegart's conclusion of 'adaptation failure' identifies a range of causes, including political and management failures barriers that have already been identified above as well as in other more general studies (Goodman 2003; Hedley 2005; Hitz and Weiss 2004). The increase in scholarly research into the cause of intelligence failure has also been matched by a plethora of media commentary, films and journalistic accounts speculating on 'what went wrong' with key intelligence agencies leading up to 9/11 and after. Many are more negative about the prospects of reform in key intelligence agencies. Tim Weiner's (2007) *Legacy of Ashes: The History of the CIA* is one example. Weiner seems to be suggesting that these agencies, due to a continual legacy of historical failure, may almost be unfixable (ibid.). While many of these authors provide useful insights into what contributes to failures in intelligence and poor decision-making, I argue we need a more balanced approach to understanding leadership and management failures. Analysis of intelligence failure also needs to be studied in the context of recent improvements in intelligence agencies in order to produce an accurate assessment of the true health of these agencies.

Understanding what is working and why is just as important to evaluating what is broken. It is also important to keep in mind that given the nature of intelligence, which is about trying to estimate the probability of something happening – generally in the absence of all the evidence – some degree of intelligence failure is inevitable. Hence, in any examination of intelligence failure it is important to look beyond single historical cases, or just from one or two (organizational or political) perspectives. As Richard Betts argues in his seminal work on intelligence failure:

> In the best-known cases of intelligence failure, the most crucial mistakes have seldom been made by collectors of raw information, occasionally by professionals who produce finished analyses, but most often by the decision-makers who consume the products of intelligence services. Policy premises constrict

perception, and administrative workloads constrain reflection. Intelligence failure is political and psychological more often than organizational.

(1978: 61)

Beyond suggesting that most failure is political, Betts suggests a more holistic and empirical examination of all factors that contribute to intelligence failure is required, and this is what is missing in many recent commentaries. His approach is also useful in its emphasis on distinguishing between those instances of intelligence failure where leaders and managers have a role and those where they don't. I will return to a further discussion of Betts' work on intelligence failure in Chapter 10. In summary, intelligence failure is complex, and the role of intelligence leaders and managers in intelligence failure may not always be the primary factor. However, it is also clear from Zegart's work that intelligence leaders do have a significant role in providing the right kind of frameworks, which will help their agencies adapt to a changing security environment.

Given the fluidity in the security environment, the management of complex security problems will require intelligence support that is flexible in the short term and adaptable in the longer term. This is particularly the case with national security and policing intelligence where terrorism, organized crime and other transnational crime can no longer be neatly categorized as national security or policing respon-sibilities. Additionally, as discussed in Chapter 2, there are other non-traditional or emerging areas of intelligence practice, such as private industry and the com-munity, that also have a stake in the generation of intelligence that can support safer societies.

In this context of a greater 'blending' with emerging intelligence practice areas, there are questions about how leaders and managers in traditional areas of intel-ligence practice adapt their own 'cultures of secrecy' to link up with these new and broader intelligence networks. Linked to this is how leaders and managers deal both with a recasting of old and the evolution of new threats. For example, are new skills, processes and capabilities required in dealing with old yet evolving threats such as terrorism (where attacks may move from the physical to cyber-space)? What new skills, processes and capabilities are needed to prepare intelligence agencies for new technologically facilitated security problems such as identity cloning? The criminal exploitation of identity cloning involves criminals setting up digital clones of real people with stolen identities in order to conduct a range of global businesses and then disappearing with the funds gained illicitly. Can leaders and managers get ahead of such changes in the operating environment and deal effectively with them so that intelligence has a high value for future decision-makers?

In this chapter, I argue that the days of public and private inquiries into the activities of intelligence agencies and how they are managed are not over. The White House review in December 2009 and a later one in 2010 by the SSCI of an attempt by Umar Farouk Abdulmutallab to detonate an explosive device on board Northwest Airlines Flight 253 en route from Amsterdam to Detroit are more recent US examples of inquiries into the performance of various intelligence agencies

(SSCI 2010). Similarly in the UK, the announcement by the new Coalition Government of a judicial inquiry into MI5 torture allegations provides another example of what I think will be more sustained and regular scrutiny of intelligence agencies. This implies that intelligence leaders and managers will also remain under scrutiny, and their ability to reform and adapt the agencies they lead will be even more crucial. If the dynamic nature of the security environment and increased political scrutiny will require leaders and managers to play an even more critical role in shaping intelligence agencies in the future, then the question is, in what ways? What are the key leadership and management factors that need to be addressed in order to drive reform and adaptation within and across intelligence agencies? How can leaders and managers ensure the value of intelligence is increased and that it becomes more integrated into decision-making?

Leadership and management challenges

Given some of the challenges identified for building better intelligence frameworks earlier and the brief historical overview of recent inquiries, which highlighted leadership deficiencies, we now have a better idea of the areas where leaders need to drive change. The remainder of this chapter will discuss what I see as the six main factors that leaders and managers need to be concerned with: *organizational design*, *ICT*, *human resources*, *risk, threat and prioritization issues, the role of strategic intelligence* and *evaluating performance*. The discussion draws partially on interviews conducted with leaders and managers of intelligence agencies in Australia, Canada, New Zealand, the UK and the USA to better identify what 'for them' are the key issues now. Additionally, through a selection of case studies, based on primary and secondary research, I also illustrate some of the ways that agencies are dealing with leadership and management issues in order to create more 'intelligence value' for decision-makers.

All of these six issues could be classified using the key enabling activity categories and/or the core intelligence processes shown in Figure 5.1. ICT and human resources are self-explanatory. The governance issues in the list would include organizational design, risk and threat prioritization issues and evaluating performance. Strategic intelligence could also be a governance issue, in the sense of a leader deciding that this capability is needed in their framework, as well, of course, as it being an important part of the core intelligence component (analysis). Similarly, risk and threat prioritization in a governance sense 'enables' agency heads and their political masters to determine risk and threat, but it is also a tool used by staff operating in the core intelligence processes of 'collection and analysis' too. This is in line with discussions in Chapter 5 about the dynamic and inter-related nature of enabling activities with core intelligence processes in any intelligence framework.

Organizational design

As noted in the two previous chapters, building better intelligence frameworks that are effective and sustainable, requires getting both the key enabling activities and core intelligence processes 'right' in any framework. This in turn, rests on effective leadership and management of the framework's governance arrangements. Different types of governance challenges will result at varying stages in the implementation of a framework. One of the most important governance issues that leaders and managers will need to constantly deal with is the role of organizational cultural factors in their agencies and intelligence communities. How these issues are managed will continue to have a profound effect on the implementation of effective intelligence frameworks in different practice contexts. Organizational cultural factors is a vague term and can only find a more precise meaning in the specific agency or community context in which it is used. For example, in Chapter 4, it was mentioned that in the early stages of the UK NIM implementation, police leaders and managers did not necessarily understand or 'buy' into this new approach to intelligence, based on a range of reasons, including attitudes about intelligence and perceptions about the new framework being 'over-complicated'. Such organizational culture-bound perceptions by managers at different levels across some policing agencies made it difficult for them initially to drive the necessary cultural changes more widely, and accept a new way of doing intelligence.

Another example of an organizational culture issue is 'reform fatigue', where intelligence leaders in national security and policing agencies find resistance for change among staff. In policing, in particular, a new commissioner often brings with them their own ideas about how their agency should be structured including the intelligence functions. The creation too of the DHS and ODNI and the ongoing 'tinkering' of their structures by senior leaders may result in staff being less willing to change practices, or at the desired pace. The problem of leading or managing intelligence reform in some of the new emerging intelligence practice areas discussed in Chapter 2 is also challenging, for example, in areas such as health, social security and juvenile justice, where intelligence is not considered core business by staff – and there is either a lack of understanding about intelligence or even an underlying suspicion of it. In order to deal with these kinds of organizational cultural issues, obviously the 'right kind of leaders and managers' need to be driving the implementation of the new intelligence framework or approach. For example, in the discussion below of Case study 6.4 on the FBI, it is clear that any success it has in changing the culture of FBI intelligence practice has relied on strong leadership of the Director, Robert Mueller. Obviously, addressing various organizational cultural issues that may impede intelligence reform also requires managers at lower levels in the organization becoming 'project champions' for the new initiatives. The management team at all levels needs to demonstrate through their own behaviour the benefits of change.

In addition to dealing with any organizational cultural differences, leaders and managers of individual agencies must also be able to respond to change that is driven by government across an entire intelligence community. As noted earlier, since 9/11, in addition to the development of an internal reform agenda in many agencies, there is now an external dimension to organizational change. As governments continue to develop different reform measures, single agencies (some more than others) need to change the way they do business. So the leadership and management challenges involved in driving organization reform are not just at the agency level. They also need to be understood at the macro intelligence community level. Post 9/11, there are specific examples in the intelligence communities of Australia, Canada, New Zealand, the UK and the USA of how government-driven macro reform has resulted in some re-engineering in these communities. Some of this re-engineering has been more profound in some countries than others. In Case study 6.1, two examples of community reform – the creation of the ODNI in the USA, and the establishment of the National Security and International Policy Group (NSIP) in the Australian Department of Prime Minister and Cabinet. Both demonstrate leadership and management challenges which arise at the community-wide level, including improving better coordination, standards, strategic planning and priority setting of intelligence. Each case study shows very different solutions to dealing with similar problems of coordination, integration and direction. For example the ODNI's creation by former President George W. Bush was a way to impose cabinet-level direction on a fragmented community. This is in contrast to the former Australian Prime Minister Kevin Rudd's less dramatic approach in establishing the NSIP in the Department of Prime Minister and Cabinet, to enhance already healthy relations between various Australian intelligence agencies.

Getting the right organizational or community design is unlikely to ever be complete, given the constant need to adapt to an ever changing security environment. Inevitably too, intelligence leaders and managers often have to give meaning to vague political prescriptions for reform from above. The creation of the DHS and the ODNI probably fits into this category. Some political actors will opt for more evolutionary change such as in the changes described above to Australian national security arrangements and others, as in the case of the ODNI, will select potentially more revolutionary treatments. While progress is being made in developing the ODNI and the DHS, many in the US intelligence community are still speculating on what their core missions are and where they will seek to add their niche value in the longer term. In the case of the ODNI and the DHS, many longer-standing members of the US intelligence community are not in a hurry to give up their own areas of responsibility just because these other agencies exist.

Case study 6.1 The US Office of the Director of National Intelligence (ODNI) and the Australian Office of National Security

The US ODNI was established following President Bush's signing of the Intelligence Reform and Terrorism Prevention Act on 17 December

2004. The head of that office, the DNI, replaced the DCI as the head of the US intelligence community. The first DNI, John Negroponte, was successfully nominated by the US Senate and was sworn in on 21 April 2005. The ODNI's functions are laid out in Sections 1011 to 1092 of the Act (ODNI 2009a: 146–195). These Sections relate largely to the powers and responsibilities of the DNI in areas such as budget and appropriation for what is now called the 'National Intelligence Program', tasking and information sharing, setting policies and procedures for analytical standards. It is interesting that in Section 102A (g) on intelligence information sharing, the DNI is given 'principal authority to ensure maximum availability of and access to intelligence information within the intelligence community', whereas in Section 102A (c) on budget authorities, the Act states that the DNI 'will provide guidance to heads of agency within the intelligence community for developing the national intelligence program budget pertaining to their agencies'. Providing the DNI with overwhelming authority for information sharing across the community may be showing some improvement (Hulnick 2008: 626), yet equipping the new DNI with no more budgetary power in real terms than the former DCI had will likely lead to conflict and a fractioning of efforts between the ODNI and individual agencies. This is the very thing that the new organization was meant to prevent. Since its establishment in 2005, the ODNI has developed National Intelligence Strategies for the USA, the first was in 2005 and the most recent was released in August 2009 and is current for the next four years. Its aim is to affirm the priorities of the entire intelligence community including the strategic and operational focus during the four-year period. The strategy makes sense, although it is still unclear the extent to which individual agencies will uniformly collaborate on it.

The ability of the DNI to establish more workable community requirements for collection and analysis is also a core function, and it will be interesting to see the extent that improvements in more unified collection and analytic efforts can be made across the US intelligence community. The early absorption by the DNI of two key former analytical functions of the CIA – the *President's Daily Brief* and the production of the more strategic *National Intelligence Estimates* – into the ODNI, may assist in driving more coordinated collection and analytic efforts. In addition to the overarching strategy, the ODNI is assisted by four Deputy-Directors of National Intelligence across planning, policy and requirements, collection, analysis and future capabilities. The ODNI also lends support, what it refers to as 'mission support activities', which include the NCTC and the National Intelligence Council, responsible for providing the National Security Council and now the Homeland Security Council with mid to long strategic analysis (ODNI 2009b: 1–3). The ODNI is in many respects still in its formative stage. Hulnick argues that the ODNI so far has gone through two stages. The first he refers to as 'political', which lasted from April 2005 to January 2007, because the first DNI John Negroponte was a political appointment and this was the period of initial establishment. He sees the second stage of the ODNI's very short history from 2007 to 2009 being one of intelligence reform, starting with the second appointed DNI, Mike McConnell, who embarked on an ambitious 100-day plan to reform the intelligence community. Hulnick considers McConnell's plan as focusing on better management rather than intelligence reform of specific agencies, although I argue in this chapter that you cannot have one without the other. McConnell resigned in January 2009 and the next appointee was former Commander in Chief, Pacific Command, Admiral Dennis Blair. Blair resigned on 21 May 2010 allegedly over the Abdulmuttallab affair in December 2009. Though there were also other incidents during his tenure such as the attack on the military base in Fort Hood and the failed attack on Times Square which reduced confidence by the Obama Administration in Blair. James Clapper, a retired general, succeeded Blair in July 2010, though the appointment of four DNIs in just over six years of the ODNI's existence is not a great track record for the agency. Despite the relatively short tenure of DNIs, in the past five short years, however, the ODNI has made progress in some areas. For example, the August 2009 National Intelligence Strategy (the publicly available version), looks more comprehensive than its 2005 version, and the ODNI is making some progress with improvements in information sharing and intelligence education programmes. However, progress also needs to be assessed against significant challenges that remain for the ODNI. One challenge seems to be the extent to which it is perceived by other intelligence agencies as a valuable addition to the US intelligence community. The sense that I gained from discussions with some former senior intelligence staff in the USA was that the ODNI was viewed as something imposed upon other members of the intelligence community by the Bush Administration and, as discussed earlier, is still in some respects seen as an agency in search of a clear mission. Former DNIs such as Mike McConnell are on public record as saying that much needs to be done to achieve the key objectives of the ODNI, including better collaboration of US intelligence agencies. The issue of intelligence collaboration remains a big challenge for ODNI. There is scope for getting this wrong given the fractured nature of the US intelligence community and clashing with the coordinating efforts of other agencies, particularly the DHS. The demise of Blair's leadership underscores a point made earlier, that the effective governance of intelligence reform has external and internal dimensions which are inter-related. As noted in earlier discussion on Figure 5.1, both of these dimensions of governance need careful managing if an intelligence framework is to be viable in the longer term. From an internal perspective, it is clear that successive DNIs have attempted to articulate specific reform measures across the US intelligence community. Though from an external dimension, such reforms seem to have been out of sync at times with other external political and legislative agendas driven by the White House or other members of the US intelligence community. For example, the period of Blair's tenure as DNI was made difficult by a degree of distance between him and the Obama Administration, which placed a greater focus on intelligence and national security policy generated from within the White House. Blair also did not achieve as the 'head of the US intelligence community' quite the same relations with the White House as the Director of the CIA, Leon Panetta, a former Chief of Staff under the Clinton Administration, has done. The IRTPA which set up the ODNI has also not given its Director the teeth and tools to do the job articulated in the Act. It still remains to be seen whether this political experiment of the Bush Administration will really be able to fix many of the intelligence leadership and management failures identified by several inquiries.

In stark contrast to the USA, the creation of a separate new 'supra-coordinating agency' to fix the problems in their intelligence community by Australian political leaders in 2008 opted for a less dramatic reform of the Australian intelligence community. Different political and social factors were at play in the Australian Government's final decision to build on existing coordination processes rather than create another super-department to make coordination happen. In Australia, there was not the same significant combination of political pressures on the President from Congress, the 9/11 Commission Report members and families who had lost loved ones in 9/11 attacks 'to do something' to fix agencies such as the CIA and the FBI that were considered by many to be broken.

In Australia, the public had been more engaged earlier in expressing their dissatisfaction of the 'failure' of various Australian intelligence communities members after the Bali bombings of 2002, and the publication of the 2004 Flood Report into intelligence assessments provided to government on the issue of WMD in Iraq. But after 2004, most of the Flood Report recommendations had been implemented and the level of public, political and media interest in intelligence reform issues dropped off. However, the new Labor Government had an appetite for further intelligence reform and commissioned Ric Smith, former Secretary of the Defence Department, and Australian Ambassador to China and Indonesia, to report on the best way to improve existing national security arrangements. The Smith Review (2008) into Homeland and Border Security concluded that there were risks in the creation of big departments to fix coordination problems between existing agencies within the intelligence community. He suggested that big departments are at risk of becoming less accountable, less agile, less adaptable and more inward-looking (Smith, cited in Rudd 2008: 33). In 2009, the Deputy National Security Advisor added additional insights to the reasons why the Australian Government had decided against a big super-coordinating agency: 'In Australia we have a deliberately disaggregated homeland security space, because we are dealing with individuals and their rights and the necessary tension between them to sustain democracy' (Campbell 2009).

The Smith Review also concluded that, in contrast to the USA, because Australia had fewer intelligence agencies (six compared to the 17 in the USA), and these were relatively well connected, and had a history of cooperation, that this was a good basis to develop. But Smith did argue that there was scope for increased strategic direction and coordination, and a need for a more interconnected security community with enhanced strategic planning and decision-making arrangements. The Rudd Labor Government adopted the recommendations of the Smith Review and the Prime Minister outlined to the Australian Parliament in his First National Security Statement, in December 2008, a series of new arrangements to promote: 'a new level of leadership, direction and coordination among agencies we already have' (Rudd 2008: 33). The Prime Minister also detailed in his Statement that a new senior executive officer with the title of National Security Advisor would drive all the new national security arrangements planned by the government in the wake of the Smith Review. The National

Security Advisor, currently Duncan Lewis, would also become the single point of focus on national security for the Australian Prime Minister.

In contrast to the appointment of the ODNI by the President on the recommendation of the US Senate, the appointment of the National Security Advisor is made by the Prime Minister. An additional difference between the two positions is that, unlike the US DNI, the Australian National Security Advisor's position is not prescribed in legislation. It is also a role with broader oversight of national security policy matters, not just the Australian intelligence community. The National Security Advisor is driving the intelligence reforms identified by the Smith Review and the government within the NSIP of the Department of Prime Minister and Cabinet. The NSIP has a number of functional areas to drive reform processes. There have been three significant processes for the NSIP that impact on intelligence reform, particularly at the strategic level. First, the National Security Advisor has been appointed to the position of Deputy Chair of the Secretaries Committee on National Security (SCNS), the top inter-departmental committee, which considers national security policy prior to it going to the National Security Committee of the Cabinet. The membership of the SCNS has also been widened to strengthen its capabilities in homeland security and border security areas.

The second significant shift in the governance arrangements of the Australian intelligence community was the establishment of the NICC, chaired by the National Security Advisor. Its role is to ensure the national intelligence effort is fully and effectively integrated. This includes ensuring all foreign, defence, security and transnational law enforcement intelligence is closely aligned to Australia's national security priorities. Another important function of the NICC is to promote a sense of the national security community that is underpinned by a cohesive national security culture, and improved strategic direction and coordination. The creation of the NICC is probably the most important of all the new national security arrangements that have emerged in 2008. It is still early days for the NICC, but it may well become a powerful vehicle to ensure optimal levels of sharing, and leveraging specific capabilities and areas of expertise between each member of the intelligence community. In addition to dealing with core business, such as what the enduring requirements of intelligence are, the NICC provides a good venue for discussion about other leadership and management intelligence issues that have an impact on all agencies in the Australian intelligence community. These common issues include how to improve the efficiency and effectiveness of intelligence supplied to decision-makers, how to ensure intelligence remains an apolitical process, and how the community can advance professional standards across all levels (executive, management, practitioners).

The third important function of the National Security Advisor and the NSIP, outlined in the Prime Minister's Statement, is to ensure, in the Deputy National Security Advisor Angus Campbell's words, that we 'build cultures of effectiveness and efficiency of resources given hard economic times' (Campbell 2009). The fourth function of the National Security Advisor is to build processes which will allow the performance of the intelligence community to be evaluated against broader national security policy priorities set out by the National Security Committee of Cabinet.

Again, it is too soon to assess how effective these new and still evolving national security arrangements are in promoting stronger strategic leadership and coordination across all intelligence agencies within the broader national security policy space of Australia. Much obviously depends on how effective the NICC and its member agencies are in creating 'norms of behaviour' which not only demonstrate enhanced levels of coordination and collaboration, but also underpin their willingness to fully participate in a new national security culture, which is more than just the sum of the individual cultures of intelligence of each agency. The relatively small size of the community, together with little functional duplication between agencies, and a recent solid history of close cooperation on 'whole of government' issues suggest the realization of enhanced coordination and the creation a broader Australian national security culture might be possible in the future.

The two examples of intelligence community reform discussed here both shared a similar desire to improve the central policy coordination of intelligence across two federal governments. But in each case the mechanisms to do this are quite different. They each represent specific leadership and management challenges for those whose role is to drive community-wide intelligence reform and for those leaders inside the agencies concerned who must do things differently.

ICT

The second factor that leaders and managers need to keep on the radar is how to build effective information communications and technology to support intelligence activities in their agencies. As discussed in Chapter 5, ICT is a key enabling activity for effective intelligence practice, and there are significant challenges in these areas. First, there is the perennial question of how do intelligence agencies accurately capture the data they need in real time? This is still a significant problem for many policing agencies, particularly capturing information from disparate legacy data-bases or exploiting new online and digital technologies. Second, how do agencies build reliable data mining systems that allow analysts to 'find the needle in the haystack', given the increasingly unmanageable volumes of information captured by sigint agencies such as the US NSA? The Abdulmutallab attempted bombing on board Northwest Flight 253 demonstrated again the difficulty of not only having systems in place to find the right kind of intelligence, but also an intelligence architecture across government agencies that can present it in a form that will allow intelligence analysts to 'connect the dots'. Third, how do leaders and managers promote the sharing of sensitive information with external, including non-intelligence, agencies, while conforming to all privacy and legislative require-ments? I will come back to all of these questions in subsequent chapters, but I want to pose them here as finding their answers will remain important for leading and managing ongoing intelligence reform.

Human resources

The third area that leaders and managers will need to deal with are those issues related to human capital. All leaders and managers in any sector need to spend a great deal of time recruiting, developing and dealing with a range of human resources-related issues. The 'intelligence industry' is no different. The devel-opment of effective staff obviously must start at the top of an intelligence agency. People at that level in particular have got to be up to the job. What kind of skills and capabilities are needed at that level? These will vary between agencies, and across intelligence contexts, and even countries. But there are likely to be a suite of general and specialized leadership and management skills required in all intel-ligence agencies.

Another issue which is likely to impact on the leadership and management of some intelligence agencies, particularly in the US national security environment, is the retirement of large numbers of the older management generation, who are taking many years of experience with them. This will impact on the strategic leadership and management capabilities of these agencies. On a positive note, however, it will also provide opportunities for them to reflect on what new skills may be required in senior positions in order to adapt more quickly to a security environment that has changed significantly since the Cold War. The current fluid security environment, with its various international, transnational and intra-national threats, undoubtedly requires a new cadre of intelligence and leaders who have a broader world-view, which extends beyond spending one career in a single agency. There is growing evidence in the intelligence communities of Australia, Canada, New Zealand, the UK and the USA that their leaders and managers are starting to spend some time away from their home agencies for their development. Recent discussions with one intelligence executive in Australia suggests that career progression beyond a certain level will be pegged to the time middle-ranking managers spend outside their home agency in other intelligence agencies and even the private sector.

Although some progress is being made to develop future leaders and managers in national security agencies, opportunities for their counterparts in policing are fewer. This is not to say that there are no opportunities or this situation is not improving. In each country, in recent years, courses have developed to train police intelligence managers (rather than executive leaders). The Leadership in Criminal Intelligence Program (LCIP), sponsored by the AFP, a similar new programme in the NZP, and others sponsored by the NPIA, demonstrate efforts to improve intelligence management training in the policing sector. However, in each case, these training programmes are recent creations – generally offered to small numbers of people – and it remains unclear how they equip graduates to become more effective future leaders and managers of intelligence. Some of the courses I have seen still lack clarity in what they are meant to achieve. Is their purpose to train senior analysts in generic management skills or are they for non-intelligence staff to help them understand and better manage intelligence functions with their agency? The answer is, courses are needed that achieve both objectives. The complication, however, in many policing agencies is that intelligence is still generally poorly understood, and limited training resources are often given to improving investigative and technical skills rather than intelligence leadership and management courses. The net result is that the understanding of intelligence is still generally poorer among managers, and this, combined with a tendency for uniformed officers to get revolved in and out of specialized commands such as intelligence, does not help to reinforce good intelligence practice at different levels throughout a policing agency. I will come back to the broader question of intelligence education in Chapter 9.

Risk, threat and prioritization issues

The fourth key area that leaders and management need to address is risk management and prioritization issues. In the intelligence context, risk management is usually thought of in terms of risk and threat. A risk is evaluated based on the 'threat' of something happening and 'the consequences' if it does come to pass, whereas a threat is assessed by its intent and capability. Political leaders and other senior decision-makers arguably are, in the first instance, more focused on the 'consequences' side of the risk formula. After all, they are the ones who have to decide whether and how to treat the risk. For intelligence leaders and managers, measuring the 'consequences' of a threat occurring is important in trying to advise decision-makers what the overall impact might be to society, the economy and so on. However, their focus has been traditionally on assessing the intent and capability of the threat. Over the last decade, this has changed, particularly in policing intelligence, where decision-makers now want to know not only about the threat posed by drug trafficking syndicates, but also how to measure the consequences (or harms) associated with criminal activity. For example, there is now much more interest on the various harms associated with illegal drugs on the financial, social and health resources of the state and on individual victims. In addition to wanting more calibration on the harms caused by organized crime, decision-makers also now want risk and threat models in policing that can better assess the overall size and economic costs of various illicit businesses such as money laundering or people trafficking (Walker 1993; Dubourg and Prichard 2007). In the UK, SOCA issues an annual UK Threat Assessment of Serious Organised Crime, which is based on strategic intelligence work, and is aimed at providing senior policy-makers and political decision-makers with an estimate of the broader harm to society of organized crime groups (SOCA 2009).

In Canada, the RCMP has developed Sleipnir, which measures quantitatively the relative threat posed by different organized criminal groups rather than harms caused by different crime groups. This model has been adopted and modified by other policing agencies in Australia and the UK (for an overview on Sleipnir, see Tusikov and Fahlman 2009: 147–164). For example, in Australia, the ACC has adopted parts of the Sleipnir attributes, though in the past few years the agency has moved in a different direction in developing both its own risk and threat methodologies, which has resulted in a series of intelligence products focused on building better assessments on all aspects of risk associated with serious and organized crime. Specifically, arising out of the ACC risk methodology process comes two major products. The first is the OCTA, which looks at the combined threat assessment of all groups and the harms posed by them (in terms of their involvement in various criminal markets, and the impact on political, social and economic factors). As noted earlier (Chapter 5), the OCTA informs the policy approach adopted in the 2009 Organised Crime Strategic Framework. The Framework notes that 'the OCTA will for the first time ever: provide Australia with a shared picture of the threats and harms arising from organized crime activity, actors and identify intelligence gaps' (Attorney General's Department 2009: 10).

The second product is the NCTR, which is more operationally focused and provides an annual assessment of the risks posed by all organized crime targets in Australia. The NCTR gives decision-makers information about the overall threat posed by a group. And as part of this assessment it includes an impact assessment on the harms caused, including, interestingly, an assessment of any unexplained wealth, which might help decision-makers judge whether they represent a more worthwhile target to go after compared to another. The ACC risk assessment methodology is also showing promise in putting some more precision in areas where there has not been much in the past, particularly in assessing harms. Over the past few years, there has been an increasing effort by policing agencies in the UK, Canada and Australia to share their different perspectives on risk and threat models, which is an encouraging sign that a community of practice in this area of policing intelligence could be emerging.

But despite progress, the models discussed above still lack the necessary rigour to drive confidently the business of intelligence. Many of their architects in SOCA, CISC and the ACC, who were interviewed for this project, freely admit that they are very much still 'works in progress'. Progress is slow due to the limited number of resources dedicated to their development. There are also a number of method-ological issues that need addressing relating to how risk and threat variables are measured and to what extent some of these variables can be measured at all.

In many circumstances it is difficult to assess fully the intent and capability of criminal threats. 'Intent' is a combination of the group's confidence and desire (motivation) to engage in organized crime. We might think that all criminals are motivated by profit, and therefore will commit crimes automatically, but in reality it is more difficult to assess *which criminals* desire to commit *which crime and their confidence levels of doing so*. 'Measuring' the *intent* of different organized crime groups will remain difficult, but in turn relies on the availability of good intelligence that can map spatially both opportunity in terms of time and space, and some assessment of the personalities of the actors involved. It is also chal-lenging to assess accurately across all crime types for their psychological, social, physical and economic consequences. The net result of not being able to accurately define and 'measure' risk and threat terminology continues to conspire against efforts in intelligence agencies to produce reliable threat and risk models. These problems are also enhanced in attempts to articulate either national risk or threat assessments. The utility of national risk assessments can be limited, where there is a reliance on other state and local information (which may itself be poor), or in cases where intelligence staff are not overly familiar with the methodology used to provide input into the assessment.

In contrast to policing intelligence, risk and threat modelling in military and national security intelligence agencies has been more advanced. I have been unable to collect data during this study of how risk and threat modelling works in these environments. This is not surprising given the sensitivities various national security agencies place on this information. But in broad terms, whether it is a threat assessment issued by DHS, or ASIO, there are still similar challenges identified above in the policing context in measuring 'intent' and 'capability' (due to intel-ligence collection gaps), as well as some of the harms associated with terrorist attacks on the community.

Determining how risk and threat models are used in some of the emerging practice areas discussed earlier (Chapter 2) is even more difficult. For public and private agencies, much depends on function and context. In the public sector, two agencies may have a compliance function but different operating contexts. For example, the risk methodology utilized by an anti-corruption agency may be quite different from that used by a security investments authority. It is clear that some public agencies, for example, with regulatory and compliance responsibilities such as taxation or revenue authorities in Australia and New Zealand do utilize specific methodologies. For example, the Australian Taxation Office (ATO) has developed a model, which is a modified version of one used historically in the national security sector. The model is a two-stage process: measuring threat and vulnerability, then assessing risk. In the first stage, the model identifies threats and vulnerabilities, both at the strategic, tactical and operational levels, which drive intelligence requirements across the agency's 12 different business lines. The intelligence requirements are used to identify patterns, methodologies and persons of interest and where gaps in knowledge exist.

The threat/vulnerability part of the model identifies the 'what is going on' side of the equation. Intelligence about threats and vulnerabilities are then fed into a risk assessment process, which assesses the likelihood that the threat will occur and the consequences of it doing so. The ATO has risk analysts, who use the intelligence to make 'impact assessments', on the level of impact posed by the threat or vulnerability. The ATO has a number of impact categories, including compliance, integrity, revenue, workforce and debt. It is the combination of both a threat and an impact assessment process, which provides the ATO with an overall risk assessment.

In addition to threat and risk models developed specifically for emerging practice areas, such as the ATO example provided above, there will also be a need by intelligence leaders and managers to develop models that can be used on topics, which cut across national security, policing and emerging practice areas. A good example of this is the work of agencies such as the DHS where intelligence support for decision-making goes across diverse areas including immigration, customs, terrorism, biosecurity and emergency management. DHS does a Quadrennial Homeland Security Review and an annual Homeland Security Threat Assessment (HSTA). All parts of the agency participate in the creation of the HSTA and provide input and review. In 2008 and 2009, DHS Immigration Customs Enforcement (ICE) also completed a very comprehensive set of risk assessments. They covered every activity that ICE has involvement in or jurisdiction over, such as alien smuggling, introduction into the USA of dangerous materials and commercial trade fraud. The risk assessments defined specific activities, predicted what the effects of the activity would be (including worst-case scenarios) and defined which resources would be needed to combat/mitigate/prevent the activity. However, it is less clear how specific intelligence functions within the DHS, such as the ICE Office of Intelligence really use the HSTA to steer collection, analysis or broader priority setting.

Despite some progress in risk and threat modelling, in general, there is a lack of research currently into how risk and threat assessment is being applied across many emerging areas of intelligence practice such as corrections, immigration, revenue and the environment. So it is uncertain the extent that these areas have developed risk and threat tools and how effective they are in these contexts. The development of intelligence capabilities in emerging practice areas, however, will rely to a great degree on the abilities of leaders and managers to risk manage their environments. So just as with intelligence practice in traditional areas, managers in emerging practice areas will also need to drive the development of better risk and threat methodologies than they have in the past. In both traditional and emerging intelligence practice areas, leaders and managers will need to engineer more accurate risk and threat models, which are based less on 'qualitative hunches' or poor data, and more on the collection of stronger quality evidence. Vander Bekens' (2004) evidence-based approach to measuring the risk of organized crime may suggest one way forward. This approach does not just allocate a group or crime type a rating (high to low), but it also looks at the central processes that drive forms of criminal investment and diversification. While I see it as critical that the next generation of intelligence leaders and managers invest in the development of better risk and threat assessment methodologies, it is also important not to over-emphasize their role in the intelligence process. They are only one tool, but if constructed effectively, they are a powerful tool in helping leaders and managers set priorities and steer intelligence collection.

The role of strategic intelligence

Another important and ongoing issue will be how well intelligence leaders and managers drive their agencies strategically. In leadership and management roles, there are of course, the generic strategic management processes such as business planning that all managers, including those leading intelligence agencies or functions must be adept in. I will not discuss these generic skills here, and readers interested in these can find them discussed in an array of management volumes (Robbins *et al.* 2006; Walsh 2007b). The core issue here is the extent to which intelligence leaders and managers use strategic intelligence to drive the production of their intelligence business, and how these strategic products are used to support better decision-making. Again depending on the particular context (national security, policing, military or emerging areas), strategic intelligence has been seen as either vital to driving better intelligence support for decision-makers or largely irrelevant. The US military has had a long history of using strategic intelligence that included indicator and early warning systems since the 1950s, in the wake of the surprise attacks by the Japanese on Pearl Harbor (Grabo 2005).

In addition to the US military, the development of a strategic intelligence capability has also been considered important in some national security intelligence agencies, particularly the CIA. The influence of Sherman Kent helped establish a fledgling strategic intelligence capability in that agency in the immediate post-war period (Kent 1949). Kent set an agenda for post-1945 US 'strategic intelligence' in the CIA, which has since been passed on to generations of intelligence managers, analysts and academics (see Berkowitz and Goodman 1989). Kent's work on strategic intelligence in the CIA was instrumental in shaping its key intelligence product, the National Intelligence Estimate, which provides a medium- to long-term assessment on a designated subject for the President.

However, Kent's work did not link strategic intelligence in national security to other areas of intelligence practice, and in policing or emerging areas of intelligence there has not been quite the same long tradition or familiarity with strategic intelligence principles as seen in the military or national security sectors. In the policing environment, strategic intelligence has always seemed an 'add-on' to conventional operational or tactical practice that leaders and managers outside of the intelligence function never quite understood. However, this is slowly changing and has to some extent been influenced, at least in Australia, Canada, New Zealand and the UK by the implementation of the UK NIM, and the cross-pollination of former national security intelligence staff moving into these areas with backgrounds in strategic intelligence.

As noted in Chapters 1 and 4, we saw how historically policing intelligence has been focused mainly on supporting and reacting to operational and tactical decision-making. For example, in Australian policing, several agencies over the past few decades have formed, abolished and then reformed strategic intelligence functions. While at certain stages of their development there seems to be a willingness by senior management to invest in strategic intelligence, in reality, these functions are generally resourced by few analytical staff, and management has tended to reduce support to them as the demands for more immediate operational and tactical intelligence support require the reallocation of resources. This issue of 'tactical drag' or strategic resources being pulled away from developing effective strategic intelligence capabilities in policing agencies is not unique to Australia (Walsh 2005).

From my research in the USA, it was also clear that even in large, well-resourced agencies such as the FBI and the New York Police Department (NYPD), any strategic approach with intelligence was more connected with operationally specific priorities. For example, how could a terrorist explosion in some critical infrastructure overseas be replicated in New York or elsewhere in the USA? This is not to suggest that this more 'strategically focused operational intelligence' is not required – it is obviously vital. However, there seems to be a lack of demand from leaders and managers of policing agencies for a more 'over the horizon kind' of strategic intelligence, which assesses the nature of a complex threat in longer time frames of three to five years. This is partly due to the policing culture, which frequently by necessity needs to react and respond to threats in the 'here and now'.

This same culture, as discussed below, also values success that is easily quantifiable (number of arrests or grams of drugs seized) over longer-term strategic and qualitative assessments, the impacts of which are more difficult to determine. But a strong strategic intelligence capability can be a powerful management tool in helping leaders and managers of intelligence agencies get beyond the 'white noise of tactical events' and operational factors to a better understanding of what is driving complex threat issues, and how they can 'warn' decision-makers ahead of time. There are a number of strategic analytical tools that can help with this process (see Chapter 8). While leaders and managers do not necessarily need to be overly familiar with them, it is their responsibility to create the environment, where their analytical staff can use them accurately and effectively to help drive better decision-making.

Additionally and more recently, there have been other attempts by leaders and managers in some policing agencies to enhance the relevance of strategic intelligence to setting the priorities of policing. The focus on building strategic capability in the UK NIM is a good example of this trend. The implementation of strategic tasking and coordination groups and standardized strategic assessments across all UK police forces is still not without its problems, but is a major achievement. As discussed in Chapter 4, it is the strategic tasking and coordination groups in each policing agency that have provided intelligence staff with a structure which feeds their strategic findings into a decision-making process via control strategies. The control strategies provide intelligence staff with a medium in which to integrate strategic analysis into decision-making. The control strategies approach also provides a process, where a police manager is accountable for developing the recommendations from strategic assessments. In recent years, the problems associated with the strategic intelligence aspects of the NIM have related to producing assessments which are distinctly different from operational and tactical assessments. Additionally, police leaders' and managers' attention on the immediate and operational, and differences in capabilities among analysts have produced mixed results in the quality of strategic assessments. This has limited, in some circumstances, the extent to which strategic assessments are able to help set good control strategies or inform operational work. These issues have also limited, according to an officer I interviewed in 2008, the ability to pull together a truly high quality and useful national strategic assessment drawing on those capabilities produced at force level.

In summary, the NIM has represented more standardized approaches to strategic intelligence, but it has not necessarily led to better strategic decision-making within policing agencies or government. Policing leaders and managers are still left with a range of issues within control strategies to choose from. Without reliable risk or threat models to assist them, translating strategic advice into operational and tactical action remains difficult.

The net effect is managers may now have strategic intelligence they can use, but they do not know how to either prioritize the issues presented or transform them into operational or tactical priorities.

Case study 6.2 *Victoria Police Priority Rating System (PRS)*

There are no easy solutions here but the Victoria Police PRS is one new approach that may potentially help leaders and managers better integrate strategic intelligence into prioritizing operational and tactical menus of work. Its designers have developed a range of 'metrics' for existing crime categories, which include assault, property damage, collisions and public order issues (youth crime), against other metrics derived from the Victoria Police Strategic Assessment template (such as long-term and short-term trends, environmental scan). These have then been overlaid by other influences on crimes types (e.g. impact/risk and target ability). These metrics also consider key corporate targets for different crime categories for the entire force.

The PRS uses a combination of 'primary and secondary influences' in order to provide an overall rating for each crime type. The net result of measuring all primary and secondary influences is to produce a list of crime types, each with an overall rating that provides managers with an enhanced decision-making framework for setting strategic priorities and control strategies. Crime types with a high rating are designated as core priorities, while those with lower ratings are assessed as either secondary priorities or are for monitoring only. The basis of the PRS approach is a weighting system of primary and secondary influences used to identify core/secondary priorities. The primary influences are defined as those variables most likely to have the biggest impact on a crime type. Primary influences include five variables: *impact/risk*, *community perceptions*, *proportion of crime* (e.g. the percentage of assaults against all crimes against the person in a region), *long-term trend* (i.e. determines whether a crime type is trending down, static or upwards over a five-year period using a tolerance range of 2.5 per cent above and below the mean to indicate long-term trending) and *target ability*. In the PRS model, target ability is defined and measured by assessing four additional factors: proportion of crimes cleared, opportunity to commit crime, impact of previous operations, and scope for intelligence/ prevention measures.

There are also five secondary influences used to measure the overall priority of a crime type. These are: *projections/emerging trends*, *year to date percentage change*, *short-term trend* (defined as 12 months), *year to date clearance change* and *environmental scan*. The strength of the PRS approach is its use of a combination of quantitative and qualitative measures to more accurately assess the overall priority rating of a crime type. While it measures the impact/risk of a crime type, its mix-method approach seeks to provide more precision as to whether a commander may want to concentrate resources within or across crime types. The overall rating allocated after assessing each of the ten primary or secondary influences may also provide a district or regional commander with better decision-support as to where to allocate resources *within* each strategic priority level (core, secondary and monitor), given there will still be many crime types at each level. The PRS, through a combination of short and longer temporal measures, combined with other novel variables such as 'target ability', offers an evidence-based approach for managers to make decisions about setting control strategies that can more effectively drive operational and tactical decision-making. The PRS has been tested recently using data at the local and regional level within Victoria Police. It has also been presented to the senior executive and received encouraging support for further refinement. However, its overall utility for helping managers set strategic priorities is still uncertain. The PRS has yet to be fully implemented and its architects are reflecting on some of the definitions of certain crime types to ensure they match up with what is being measured.

However, despite some encouraging progress, developing and managing a strong strategic intelligence capability in the policing intelligence context which is integrated into other levels of decision-making (operational and tactical) is still a long way off. The extent to which strategic intelligence is understood and promoted by leaders and managers in emerging practice areas such as corrections, justice or regulatory environments is also still low. The challenge for intelligence leaders and managers will be to try and balance traditional tactical/operational requirements with supporting new strategic capabilities. These capabilities may not reap immediate results for their agencies or decision-makers, but in the longer term they will improve knowledge of the evolving security environment. A sustained investment in strategic intelligence by managers may also allow the more efficient allocation of resources to prevent threats evolving rather than merely reacting to them tactically. But for many leaders and managers, escaping the 'tactical drag' will remain difficult.

Evaluating performance

The final area leaders and managers will need to focus on more in the future is evaluating performance. Figure 5.1 demonstrated how evaluation needed to be an ongoing activity at all levels of any intelligence framework. At the very least, evaluation should occur in three places. First, it should occur at the intelligence production level where products are produced. Second and third, it should be part of the two key enabling activities of 'governance' and 'research' respectively.

Evaluation is obviously important in assessing organizational performance, but it also should be about the extent to which leaders and managers can measure how well their intelligence agencies can learn and adapt to changing operating environments (Walsh 2007a: 31). As with most concepts related to intelligence practice, what it means to 'evaluate intelligence' is not clearly defined in the literature. Formal evaluations of intelligence practice that are also available in the public arena are of course rare, and so for researchers there can be a lack of clarity about what is to be evaluated, and the best way to do it. At the start of any evaluation process, there are some methodological considerations that need to be considered about how we evaluate intelligence frameworks, products and processes, and we will return to this issue during our discussion of intelligence research in Chapter 10. However, at this point it is worth highlighting some of the methodological challenges in evaluating the impact of various intelligence processes and products. For example, to what extent can leaders and managers evaluate the value and impact of strategic intelligence for decision-makers when the threat may not have materialized yet? To what extent does targeting high value targets in one location have an impact on overall crime levels? Similarly, as discussed above in the risk and threat section, at the strategic level, to what extent is it possible to measure the reduction in social and economic harms associated with operational intelligence activity in one or more crime types? There are no definite answers to these questions and attention is largely due to academics and practitioners only recently becoming sufficiently engaged in formally evaluating different aspects of intelligence performance. For many inside national security intelligence and policing agencies, evaluation has traditionally been at best almost an afterthought at the end of the intelligence production process. Historically, one crude evaluation tool has been the 'tick and flick forms' attached to intelligence products disseminated from various agencies. From a macro-perspective, looking at the entire operations of intelligence agencies or even communities, more systemic evaluation processes did take place pre 9/11, but normally *after* some breakdown in an agency's performance. For example, Zegart argues, in the USA 'between the fall of the Soviet Union in 1991 and September 11, 2001, no fewer than 12 major bipartisan commissions, governmental studies, and think tank task forces examined the U.S. Intelligence Community and U.S. counter-terrorism efforts' (2007: 27).

In addition to externally imposed reviews, agencies themselves, such as the CIA, have also completed internal reviews of 'business processes' in the past few decades. However, the daily operational demands of keeping senior decision-makers happy with a constant 'diet' of intelligence products has frequently been the priority over reflecting on whether practices, processes and products are effective. The recent suite of inquiries discussed earlier, all of which address 'intelligence failure' issues, suggest that had more systematic evaluations by leaders and managers taken place earlier, their agencies might have been able to learn from and modify some of weaknesses identified in these reports.

In the policing intelligence context, evaluation has been patchy. On more systemic levels in UK policing, ACPO and the HMIC have played important roles in evaluating the performance of various police forces against various documented standards in the UK NIM. On a micro level, there are some areas where intelligence activity has been evaluated such as COMPSTAT, a process that relies on the delivery of accurate and timely computerized statistics to assess crime problems and police responses (Walsh and Vito 2004). COMPSTAT is supported by analytical techniques such as crime mapping that have been shown in evaluation studies to have a positive impact, at least temporarily, when used to target recidivist offenders (Ratcliffe 2001).

There are also other more advanced analytical techniques, such as interrupted time series analysis, which may be useful for police managers to evaluate the impact of various intelligence-driven crime reduction strategies, however, these evaluation approaches require specialized knowledge that are not found within the analytical cadre of many police agencies (Ratcliffe 2008: 192).

More recently, in the US policing context, there is growing evidence that leaders and managers in some agencies are developing new data-driven approaches to either evaluating parts or all of their intelligence business. In Case studies 6.3 and 6.4, we examine two different evaluation methodologies, yet both with similar objectives of evaluating and improving intelligence performance. Case study 6.3, the nationwide *Suspicious Activity Reporting* (SAR) *initiative,* implemented by the DHS, has two broad objectives. First, the SAR approach aims to collect data to assist managers in identifying a range of potential risks in their operating environment. Second, it also has the function of evaluating various indicators against each risk in order for managers to make operational decisions about resources. In contrast, discussed in the *FBI Strategic Management System (SMS)*, Case study 6.4, is a more holistic performance management system for the FBI.

Case study 6.3 The nationwide Suspicious Activity Reporting (SAR) initiative

The SAR initiative is an idea originally developed five years ago by the National Security Committee, which tasked a NCTC working group to develop a counter-terrorism intelligence monitoring system that could be used at every level of government in the USA. The idea was to achieve a unified approach across the country for assessing behaviour and indicators for counter-terrorism, which local police could use. These indicators could then be pushed up to the state level so that trends could be examined in the context of others seen at regional and national levels. Another objective of the SAR initiative was to help local policing build a reporting system, which could standardize and prioritize information, ensuring it gets to the right people. The DHS argues that this approach is bringing together information that has never been tied together before. Since 2007, the DHS and the US Department of Justice have taken the lead in gradually pushing the SAR approach nation-wide. The SAR initiative has become an important part of the DHS national information-sharing mandate. DHS hopes to promote the collection of SAR data into the 72 fusion centers across the country in order to get a better idea at the national level of the significance of local, and regional, terrorism-related behaviour and activity. The objective is for local police to collect data and evaluate the significance of potentially suspicious activity and feed this through their city or state fusion centers. Once SAR reports are captured in fusion centers, they can be further evaluated by other local police and members of the FBI's JTTFs, generally co-located or near the fusion centers. If the indicators suggest a possible terrorism offence, then the FBI JTTF team would usually take over further development of the intelligence and investigation. However, in other cases, JTTF teams may push back incidents for investigation by state or local police (e.g. a suspicious package), if prosecution would be easier under state rather than federal counter-terrorism laws.

Los Angeles Police Department (LAPD) was one of the earliest driving local policing agencies in the USA to develop a SAR capability. It has been developing a SAR process over the last three years. During interviews in 2009 with senior LAPD counter-terrorism staff, I was advised that at that stage it had developed 1500 SAR reports – 75 of which have resulted in new activity by the JTTF. The SAR initiative consists of a series of 'indicators' that allow local police to report suspicious activity, which may be associated with preparatory acts of terrorism. It might be things like someone taking a picture of a city landmark, or an individual purchasing unusually high volumes of chemical pre-cursors used for bomb making. In the LAPD case, the senior counter-terrorism command has developed a *threatstat analytical model* for terrorism reporting at the local law enforcement level. Compared to other parts of the USA, LAPD has been very engaged in the SAR initiative, and it has caused some major restructuring of the agency. In 2009, LAPD had 125 indicators for terrorism. During interviews, LAPD counter-terrorism command suggested that their SAR model had helped smooth operational responses to data. For example, from a management perspective, it was now easier to know which part of LAPD (e.g. their anti-terrorism intelligence section, organized crime or the conspiracy intelligence section), or whether another agency such as the FBI should take the lead in investigating terrorism or other crime types. During 2009, LAPD were also building sophisticated technologies to support the humint collection of indicators. They had developed 1883 algorithms to support a database that would allow for a more efficient querying across indicators and making connections between them.

Other LAPD and FBI officers working on counter-terrorism issues also commented that a lot of training had gone into getting their investigators to collect counter-terrorism and criminal information based on these SAR codes. In addition to raising internal awareness within LAPD, and the local FBI detachment in Los Angeles, LAPD was also rolling out a public campaign about fusion centers and how the public can help support the SAR approach through an *Iwatch* campaign.

There does seem merit in getting local and state policing agencies to collect data on a range of potentially suspicious behaviour and activity. The 9/11 Commission Report serves as a good reminder that even complex, long and meticulously planned terrorist plots demonstrate local manifestations. The SAR initiative, like the establishment of 72 fusion centers in cities and states across the USA, is another significant plank by the DHS to better risk manage the volumes of data that are coming into local, state and federal intelligence databases and trying to do something with them. However, while it is worth knowing, for example, that 20 people have taken a picture of a nuclear power plant over the last six months, it remains unclear how this system on its own as yet will help leaders and managers better evaluate the *significance* of such information.

The question is, what is being done with the information once it gets tagged by a local policing intelligence cell? Who 'makes the call' on the significance of the information? Are these personnel well trained in analysis? Is this being done by local police, who usually have better insights into the local environment, or federal agencies such as the DHS and FBI, whose staff at regional and local levels tend to rotate fairly frequently? Are all SAR data acted upon in a timely manner or, given the stretched resources of many US local and state police, do they sit in a database and perhaps not get acted on at all? There are also issues relating to accountability. For example, can databases capture how the SAR data were actioned and by whom? In short, it seems doubtful that any SAR indicator can become intelligence without some further analytical and investigative resources being dedicated to it.

There are also a number of questions about how agencies decide what should be on the SAR list of indicators, and how differences are resolved about its contents or priorities – given US agencies with federal jurisdictions may have different interests than local police. How much input is routinely provided by expert analysts about what should be on their SAR lists? Is there a Delphi process, where these analysts can be asked what for them should be on the list and why? Have selections been 'red-teamed' sufficiently by counter-terrorism intelligence and investigators, or are decisions on the list content purely management driven?

There are also a number of potential governance issues with different agencies using SAR data for different ends. From my interviews in Los Angeles, it seemed that the FBI and LAPD have developed good working relations to deal with inevitable differences in jurisdictional interests, but it is unclear how these differences will play out elsewhere across the USA. In simple terms, it remains to be seen the extent to which the SAR approach can help smooth the operational environment for federal, state and local police working on counter-terrorism issues. No doubt in some locales of the USA, there are still significant governance issues to be resolved about how federal and local agencies operationalize SAR data coming into and out of fusion centers.

From my discussions with other key federal, state and city police across the USA, the SAR initiative is viewed by some as something better characterized as a data gathering system rather than an intelligence one. One intelligence manager I interviewed stated plainly that 'SAR was data, not analysis and that his agency had no intentions of doing it'. Another said that this information is only useful 'if it can get into a taskforce where it becomes actionable intelligence'. In 2009, there were also some FBI officers I talked to who were not aware of the SAR approach, so this suggests that the DHS and Department of Justice still has work to do to promote its utility across the broader federal intelligence community. Other FBI officers expressed their concerns that the SAR initiative could produce civil liberty issues. There are also lots of questions about how a pattern of events in one part of the USA can be linked to a series of other incidents in another. Which agencies will be making these links? Will the SAR systems in state and local police be sufficiently linked up to the FBI's e-Guardian systems to allow this to happen? Making the links between local SAR data and federal intelligence will also rely on analysts available with the sufficient training. Well-trained analysts will be required to do the detailed data mining or pattern analysis, while also ensuring 'the dots can be joined', without drowning in a sea of SAR data. In late 2009, a national evaluation of agencies participating in the SAR initiative was completed. The publicly available report, however, does not provide much detail on the lessons learnt so far. The evaluation report listed some things that one might expect, including calling for the need for further SAR training nationwide, and the appointment of a Program Manager to facilitate a more effective national roll out of the initiative. However, the evaluation report suggests that it was difficult to make a full assessment of how well different agencies were able to share SAR reports during the evaluation. Participating agencies were not authorized to share SAR data with each other until they had met the requirements of the National SAR Initiative privacy framework. Meeting these requirements took longer than expected and this left only a few months in which to evaluate how agencies used and shared SAR data (ISE 2010: 5). So the 2009 evaluation report does not demonstrate in any clear measurable way how many SAR reports are being shared and the benefits derived in doing so. Further evaluation of the SAR initiative should occur on an annual basis, particularly after the planned 2010 national roll-out of it is completed. Future evaluations will also need to consider how different agencies use SAR data, including in fusion centers. Are fusion centers just tagging SAR reports and sending them on to their local FBI-run JTTFs or are they also being used inside fusion centers by local and state police to collect further intelligence and mount local operational responses?

Case study 6.4 The FBI Strategic Execution Team (SET) and Strategic Management System (SMS)

As discussed above in addition to the post-9/11 environment, a cocktail of political, media and public pressure coalesced to drive further significant reforms on policing intelligence, particularly at the federal level. The events of 9/11 and the US-led invasion of Iraq led to inquiries – many of which were also scathing about the FBI intelligence performance during these events. In particular, the FBI came under criticism in the 9/11 Commission Report for its poor tracking of some Al Qaeda operatives. However, one of the 9/11 Commission's key recommendations also underscored wider concerns about the FBI's intelligence capabilities. The report recommended that:

A specialized and integrated security workforce should be established at the FBI consisting of agents, analysts, linguists and surveillance specialists, who are recruited, trained, rewarded and retained to ensure the development of an institutional culture imbued with a deep expertise in intelligence and national security.

(2004: 425–426)

In summary, it was clear from the immediate post-9/11 period and particularly after the release of the 9/11 Commission Report, that there was significant political pressure on the FBI to reform its intelligence performance. In the immediate months after 9/11, internal reorganization did start. For example, between 2001 and 2005, the number of analysts rose by 76 per cent to 1800. In April 2003, the new Trilogy network (the FBI's main intelligence database/case management system) was rolled out and involved placing a billion records securely online and making them available to authorized users. The system has some of the data hunting techniques found in the private sector discussed further in Chapter 8 (Cumming and Masse 2004). In October 2003, additional reforms saw the establishment within each of the 56 FBI field offices of a Field Intelligence Group (FIG), consisting of an analyst, surveillance personnel and linguists. The FIGs provided an important foundation for the development of other more recent and significant reforms to the FBI intelligence function, including the SET and the SMS.

Additional reform pressure came from external sources in addition to those internal reforms commissioned by the FBI executive. The White House also applied pressure on the FBI for reform with its passing of the IRTPA, which devoted an entire section (Section 2001) to the improvement of intelligence capabilities of the FBI. In particular, it required the establishment within the FBI of a National Intelligence Workforce and stipulated that every agent hired by the Bureau in the future should have intelligence as well as police training (ODNI 2009a).

Many of the improvements underlined in Section 2001 of the IRTPA were already being actioned by FBI Director Robert Mueller. However, in the autumn of 2007, the development of the SET followed by the SMS became arguably the most important recent intelligence reforms in the FBI and were designed to 'break the back' of the FBI's pre-9/11 largely case-driven culture.

The SET has now become 'the intelligence approach' for the FBI. It had its origins in a headquarters-driven process that involved a team of 100 special agents, intelligence analysts and other staff members, who examined the intelligence activities of all 56 field offices to identify best practice. From this process, a single approach to intelligence was developed, under which all FIGs function across the agency. There are a number of important aspects to the SET approach, which were explained during interviews with senior FBI officers involved in its development.

One factor is that the SET sought to standardize intelligence collection priorities processes, analysis and products across all field offices in the agency. Second, the SET is also aimed at increasing collaboration between the intelligence and operational functions of the Bureau.

In this context, the SET approach is to assess what the nationally significant threats are and then select priorities based on this. Special Advisor (Intelligence) Phillip Mudd described the extent of cultural change desired through the SET approach to the Bureau's intelligence practice using the analogies of a 'starfish' and 'spider's web'. In the past he suggested that the agency may have run an investigation, which resulted in it understanding a single threat and some of its immediate associates at a local level. The subsequent arrest and prosecution of this kind of case, he suggested, were akin to severing one arm of a starfish, but not necessarily resolving the complete threat problem. The intention now in the FBI was to create a culture whereby agents would use intelligence more effectively to take down a more complex network of threats. Using a spider's web analogy, Mudd commented that it was now essential for heads of field offices to collect intelligence more proactively, not just on the 'knowable', or familiar ('starfish') threat networks, but to start probing at the broader complexities of 'known unknown' threats that exist in the broader spider's web. The idea is to use intelligence more proactively to take down the entire 'web'.

Taking down an entire 'spider's web' has meant that FBI managers now needed to place a greater focus on intelligence collection to get a broader understanding of what is going on in their area. In the new SET approach, heads of field officers were expected to rely on their intelligence resources to construct what the FBI refers to as *domains* for each of the 56 field offices across the USA and nationally. The FBI describes the domain as what is known or unknown about different threat types. There is a domain for each crime category – and these are generated by analysts working in FIGs. For example, a field office could have a domain category for counter-intelligence problems. However, rather than immediately building a case to find out if their field office has any active targets involved in, for example, stealing sensitive technology from a government research institute, investigators are taking a more intelligence-led approach under the new SET initiative. This means heads of field offices should now task investigators to collect intelligence from research institutes across their state to assess if there are any vulnerabilities in them, where this kind of theft could occur. If it looks likely that there may be a vulnerability, intelligence and investigators will work together to disrupt and dismantle the case with the view to 'taking not just part of the starfish but the whole spider web'. This is a security and intelligence response rather than an investigation-driven response.

During interviews with senior FBI intelligence managers, who are driving the SET process, the SET's focus was described as a huge shift in the FBI's traditional response to the role of intelligence in the agency. Previously, in the pre-9/11 days, there was a lack of leadership at the executive level with intelligence to drive much of what the SET approach is now trying to achieve. The FBI's Intelligence Directorate, which has now been in existence for three years, is providing the leadership on intelligence at executive level to support field offices in identifying threats, collection planning and pulling together their domains. Intelligence management are also getting out of headquarters to talk more to field offices about their challenges in using intelligence and to explain to investigators what the intelligence programme is trying to achieve.

The other new recent intelligence initiative introduced by the FBI Director in the past two years has been the SMS, which complements the SET objectives and is similar to a COMPSTAT process for intelligence. On one level, the SMS is a manager's accountability mechanism that allows the FBI executive to collect its 'own intelligence' on where there are weaknesses with intelligence collection and analysis, or where gaps in knowledge exist across the agency. During interviews with key FBI officers, the SMS was described as a process where field officers can discuss how they are managing strategic and operational intelligence priorities, and exchange information in a professional way to improve individual and organizational learning. Every 170 days, each head of field office has a face-to-face or video conference with the FBI Director (usually lasting two hours). The manager is asked a number of questions about what is going in their domain (or operating environment). During the SMS meeting, the director will ask local management about what they are doing about specific threats in their domain. During the session, managers need to demonstrate by providing evidence why some issues are being worked on as opposed to others. The SMS, according to senior intelligence managers, has resulted in a big cultural shift for field offices from the pre-9/11 days, where they were used to 'running their own races'. The SMS means that mid-ranking managers in the FBI are now required to account for what their intelligence and investigative assets are doing across all FBI pro-grammes, regardless of whether it is counter-terrorism, counter-intelligence, counter-proliferation or computer crime areas. One senior FBI intelligence manager interviewed suggested that these meetings were beginning to be seen by field officers as useful, although many were still adapting to what was required at the review performance meetings. For example, some managers were still focused on discussing quantitative metrics (i.e. how many intelligence reports were written), rather than more of the qualitative evidence about what might be emerging in their domain, or why some threat picked up in another FBI field office is or isn't relevant to their domain of work. The SMS approach seems to be a very good way for the FBI executive to reinforce a more proactive approach to intelligence underpinned by the agency's new SET approach.

As noted above, the SMS can provide the FBI Director and the executive intelligence management with a good strategic overview of emerging threats and intelligence performance against those threats. So in that sense, it does have the potential to be a useful intelligence evaluation tool. However, it does seem clear from the interviews I conducted that some field officers still don't understand or accept the SMS process and would rather revert back to their familiar practice of case management. The SMS and SET initiatives are asking new things from lower management levels that over the century since the FBI was established they have not been used to doing. As one senior officer suggested, this new approach to intelligence is still not completely part of many agents' DNA. However, the Director and the Intelligence Directorate, which is now the largest division in the FBI, are determined through the SET and the SMS to better link strategic and operational intelligence to driving FBI business. Over the next five years, the extent to which the SET and the SMS become internalized as core parts of FBI culture will also provide a good indication of the extent to which intelligence is seen to be really driving business. As with all intelligence reform, much will also depend on who succeeds Robert Mueller as FBI Director in 2011 and whether this leader can consolidate progress made under the SET and SMS initiatives. At the very least, it is still going to take years for the FBI to move away from being exclusively a case-driven agency to one that can take on a truly national intelligence collection role.

Conclusion

It is clear from our discussion above that the leadership and management of intelligence agencies or functions in the post-9/11 security environment will require a greater ability to deal with uncertainty than even a decade ago. The post-9/11 security environment is still largely evolving and intelligence managers lack the comparative certainty of the old Cold War bi-polar security structure. In contrast to their Cold War counterparts, contemporary leaders and managers have one certainty, and that is the menu of actual and over the horizon threats will require a greater ability to lead agencies that are adaptable in design, but still retain high level capabilities that will deliver 'value' to their customers. There is a long list of issues that leaders and managers will need to deal with in order to promote value for customers – some of these have been discussed above. Key among these perhaps may be the ability of leaders to adapt organizational design. Greater reflection and formalized evaluation of practice will also be important in creating 'learning agencies'. In many agencies, where intelligence is not the sole function of the organization, intelligence leaders and managers may find it especially difficult to convince their sceptical non-intelligence colleagues that intelligence is valuable to decision-making. But even in traditional areas of practice such as national security and policing, organizational reform and change will continue to test leaders and managers working in these environments. From the research conducted for this book in Australia, Canada, New Zealand, the UK and the USA, it is clear that in many agencies leading and managing intelligence change requires transformational leadership qualities. This begs the question of what mix of skills the next generation of leaders and managers require in order to be able to transform their agencies. If the skill base is viewed as a recipe, it may consist of someone who should be: 40 per cent 'intelligence guru', 20 per cent social anthropologist, 25 per cent educator and 15 per cent entrepreneur.

Part III

Developing a discipline

7 Ethics and legislation

Introduction

In Parts I and II, the chapters focused on how intelligence frameworks and processes are being applied and managed in different contexts. In Part III, we turn our attention to three key issues (ethics and legislation, analysis, education and research). These issues will remain important in the future for promoting effective intelligence practice across different contexts. They will also be important factors in deciding whether, at some future point, intelligence can be described as a discipline itself. I will come back to defining what I mean by a discipline in Chapter 9, but, in short, it suggests that intelligence has its own body of ethical, technical, professional and research efforts, which define it from other areas of social-scientific pursuit such as psychology, political science or strategic studies.

In this chapter, I present a summary of recent ethical debates relevant to intelligence collection, analysis, dissemination, in addition to an overview of some of the legislative and accountability structures that have developed recently around intelligence practice. In order to illustrate the critical role of ethics, accountability and legislative reform in developing intelligence practice, examples from agencies in Australia, Canada, New Zealand, the UK and the USA are given. In particular, the focus is on how the evolving security environment has influenced ethical debates and legislative reform on intelligence. I argue that ethics, accountability and legislative reform of intelligence are inextricably linked and are not only vital to maintaining liberal democracies, but that they are also important in promoting better evidence-based intelligence practice in the future.

What is ethics?

Hinman defines ethics simply as:

> the philosophical reflection on moral beliefs and practices. The difference between ethics and morality is similar to the difference between musicology and music. Ethics is a conscious stepping back and reflecting on morality, just as musicology is a conscious reflection on music.
>
> (2003: 380)

If we accept Hinman's definition that ethics is a philosophical reflection on morals, then it follows that intelligence practice also raises moral issues on which individuals and groups may hold varying perspectives.

For many, it remains an anathema to place the words 'intelligence' and 'ethics' or 'morals' in the one sentence and their opinions on the ethical content of intelligence can be summarized by US Judge Richard Posner who recently wrote, 'intelligence is the second oldest profession, only with fewer morals' (Posner 2005: 100). There are also diverse views about ethics within intelligence agencies and the greater community. For example, 'the culture of secrecy' discussed in Chapter 1, which has developed within intelligence agencies, would for many officers working in them preclude intelligence as an ethical pursuit under any circumstances. Additionally, the suite of official reviews post 9/11 – and more recently the release of classified US intelligence by the wikileaks website in late 2010 – have only strengthened many taxpayers in Western liberal democracies' views that the world of intelligence is defined by deception. Some in the media and the public also see practices by intelligence agencies as not fully accountable to the state, rather than them embodying any notion of moral practices for the public good. But even this rather extremist perspective that intelligence is not moral or ethical because it does not promote honesty and transparency is taking a moral standpoint on the question. Others may take an equally absolutist perspective, but at the other end of the spectrum. For them, intelligence is very much a moral issue, given that it seeks to protect the state from those who would harm it. This perspective may recognize that the use of intelligence could result in conflict with the interests of states. Adherents to this view, however, may see intelligence practice as moral, arguing that a global society of nations has not developed the same norms and ethics, and so a state is justified (perhaps if not always morally so), in using intelligence to protect its own people and interests.

In summary, intelligence practice is fundamentally a moral and ethical issue as much as a set of practices or techniques. There are also, of course, several ethical dimensions to intelligence practice across a range of practice contexts. However, space does not allow us to discuss the ethical dimensions of all practice contexts (national security, policing and emerging areas). In some respects, given the increasingly intertwined nature of national security and policing intelligence in dealing with security threats like terrorism, the ethical dilemmas related to collection methodologies, analysis, surveillance, privacy are similar, regardless of whether one is discussing the UK Metropolitan Police or MI5. In order to chart adequately where the key ethical dilemmas have arisen most recently, I will restrict the bulk of discussion to ethical issues arising from national security practice since 9/11. However, in our discussion of accountability mechanisms and legislative reform, I will show how issues under these headings have also resulted in ethical dilemmas for policing intelligence.

Ethics and intelligence practice

As long as intelligence has been around, people have had different ethical perspectives about its practice. Respected British intelligence scholar Michael Herman quotes philosopher Kant, who two hundred years ago condemned 'espionage as intrinsically despicable since it exploits only the dishonesty of others' (Kant, quoted in Herman 2009: 382). However, the reality is that intelligence exists and will continue to do so and any theorizing about ethical intelligence practice must be able to help intelligence practitioners, and their political masters, navigate in practical ways the ethical dilemmas they face. Herman (2009) and Ormand (2009) argue that we are yet to find suitable theoretical frameworks to guide ethical practice in a security environment, which today is defined less by old-fashioned spying between states and more by how states can cooperate to deal with common threats such as terrorism. Ormand notes that it is the contemporary growth in the scale of terrorism that requires greater use of what he calls 'pre-emptive intelligence', which is creating ethical dilemmas about intelligence collection methods and their impact on individual rights (ibid.: 395). By pre-emptive intelligence, Ormand means the extension of a range of human and technical methods and greater cooperation with new partners overseas. Other recent theoretical work on ethical intelligence practice has provided some perspectives on how practitioners might evaluate the ethical impact of their actions, particularly relating to intelligence collection (e.g. Erskine 2004; Gendron 2005). Erskine's work provides a typology of 'realist', 'consequentialist' and 'deontological' approaches to ethical intelligence collection. It is one example of recent attempts to provide better frameworks to describe the different ethical choices intelligence practitioners/ agencies are making and their impact. Erskine's typology is derived partly from broader international relations theory, but is also linked to different ethical perspectives on the rightness or wrongness of actions. I have already introduced the *realist* approach, which implies that acting in the national interest regardless of the consequences is itself complying with a moral principle (Erskine 2004: 364–365).

In contrast, a consequentialist approach to ethical intelligence practice would disagree with the realists and view placing narrow national interests above international norms as immoral. For consequentialists, whether any intelligence activity is 'right' or 'wrong' would depend on their consequences. However, this approach may not provide intelligence practitioners with a great deal more moral guidance than the realist perspective. For example, as discussed later, people have different perspectives on whether torture is morally acceptable depending on whether an 'effective outcome' was achieved or not during interrogations. The consequentialist approach leaves a lot more freedom to the individual making the moral choice to calculate the relative morality of their actions.

Finally, a deontological approach views certain activity as inherently wrong regardless of the consequences. This is a moral absolutist or principled approach. Using our torture example, regardless of whether torturing one terrorist led directly to saving many more lives, the act itself would in all cases still be morally wrong.

It's clear that a deontological approach would also not allow many activities common in intelligence practice such as deception and surveillance.

In 2009, 26 intelligence scholars and practitioners from seven countries met to share their perspectives on what they thought were the key ethical issues confronting intelligence. Discussions ranged from general views on why ethics mattered to more specific initiatives such as establishing a professional code of ethics for practitioners (Andregg 2009: 366–386). There is also now an International Intelligence Ethics Association (IIEA), which holds an annual conference. However, these kinds of symposia are few and far between. More regular and institutionalized exchanges between academics, practitioners and ethicists may help provide better theorizing about ethics in intelligence, as well as further practical guidance for intelligence staff about how to navigate moral uncertainty in an increasingly complex security environment.

While conceptualizing and theorizing about ethics and intelligence are needed, we must also keep in mind the political dimensions impacting on intelligence. The events of 9/11 and the intelligence supplied in support of the US-led Iraq invasion demonstrate that any discussion about ethical intelligence practice also needs to consider how political leaders and other consumers of intelligence choose to use intelligence in their policy-making processes. The extent to which intelligence practice is or isn't 'ethical' also depends on more fundamental perspectives about the way policy-makers view security. One of the most important of these political perspectives is how individual leaders and states construct ideas about what constitutes a 'threat', 'the enemy' and why. The mere identification of 'the enemy' suggests a separation between *us* and *them*. These dual and opposing identities can be constructed at the individual, state and international levels. Modern international relations theory has played a role, particularly in the USA, about how scholars and political leaders view the security environment. For example, many neo-realists or neo-liberalists would not waste too much time looking at social or cultural factors to explain who the enemy is and what is to be done about them. However, others, such as constructivists, argue that power, whether pursued through military competition or via international markets cannot on its own explain national security policy-making, including determining threats and enemies. For them, defining the enemy or threat (the 'us vs. them') is also determined by looking at norms, identity and the political culture of nations and international systems (Katzenstein 1996: 2).

Other scholars using this idea that security policies are socially constructed have also posited that many states have discernible 'strategic cultures' that determine how they use force. Strategic cultures for these theorists are conditioned by historical experiences and historically rooted strategic preferences rather than being determined by changes in the objective strategic environment (Johnston 1995). It remains to be seen whether the strategic culture literature will provide another useful avenue for understanding which longer-term historical and cultural preferences are involved in policy-makers constructing ideas about 'us vs. them'. However, the constructivists' perspective on history, norms and culture does suggest that what states view on balance as morally acceptable in pursuit of security – including how they practise intelligence – is as much socially as materially determined. Others argue that in some countries, a dominant strategic culture also contains a distinct 'intelligence identity' made up of a series of norms and principles. For example, Turner argues that the USA has developed its own 'intelligence identity' (including characteristics such as secrecy, separation of intelligence from law enforcement, ambiguous mandates), which has shaped US policy-makers' preferences regarding intelligence (2004: 48–49). While it is a point for debate whether each country has a distinct strategic culture or 'intelligence identity', there is no doubt that historical events, norms and culture do shape political leaders' perceptions about security. Part of this political perception involves what is considered an 'acceptable role' for intelligence to play in securing the state. However, our discussion below about inquiries in Australia, the UK and the USA and the recent events surrounding wikileaks suggests that the political perception of what is an ethical and effective role for intelligence to play can diverge from that of the public and even from those working in intelligence agencies. Hence the social construction by political leaders of the 'us and them' has an influence both in the way the public views intelligence agencies, but can also have a role in the way these agencies view their role in the policy-making process.

A good example of how political leaders set the policy debate about what their citizens need 'securing from' and the impact this can have on intelligence practice is the Bush Administration's construction of the 'War on Terror' immediately after the events of 9/11. In various speeches to the nation, President Bush started using rhetoric that made it very clear who the enemy was and what needed to be done about them. Al Qaeda and other jihadist groups were frequently referred to in speeches as 'evil doers', who were uncompromising in their radical ideology and objectives. Given the uncompromising nature of the enemy, 'a global war on terrorism' was appropriate, utilizing all military means at the disposal of the USA and its allies. Leaving aside debates about whether it is appropriate to describe global counter-terrorism efforts as a 'war', other speeches by the President suggested that this was a war of epic proportions, which would define a generation much like the allies' struggle against Nazi Germany did in the Second World War. For example, in an address to the nation on the fifth anniversary of 9/11, President Bush said that: 'America had glimpsed "the face of evil" and that the resulting struggle he claimed ought properly to be seen as the "decisive ideological struggle of the 21st century and the calling of our generation"' (Bush, quoted in Mazarr 2007: 3). This rhetoric quickly delineated how foreign policy, defence and intelligence assets were applied to what became a 'total war' on terrorism. The Bush Administration also used language publicly about other regimes in the Middle East (Pakistan, Saudi Arabia) in the early days post 9/11, declaring that they were either with us or against us in this global struggle between good and evil. The subsequent US invasion of Afghanistan and later Iraq – in addition to precipitating more conflict with radical Islamists – also alienated and angered moderate Muslims, whom Washington needed on their side to effectively fight this conflict against violent, radical jihadists.

As Mazarr observed:

> By shaping all of American foreign policy (and a good deal of U.S. constitutional law) to fit a 'global war on terror' that has been nominated as the successor to the Cold War, the United States has adopted an approach seemingly determined to wipe away, over time, the dividing line between the militants and other Islamists. If you are either 'with us or against us,' and no genuine Islamist can morally or otherwise be 'with' the United States, then American policy has declared you to be an enemy before giving an opportunity to choose.
>
> (ibid.: 23)

None of the above is to suggest that the Bush Administration was not 'morally right' to go after violent, radical jihadists responsible for criminal attacks against US interests, but much of its rhetoric was an overly simplistic depiction of 'the enemy'. As Mazarr suggests, the President had an abundant supply of experts on radical Islam who could have influenced the Administration's use of rhetoric to less emotionally and more accurately describe the kind of radical Islamists the 'war' was being waged against. However, as Mazarr argues, 'for whatever reason, these expert views did not find themselves in the Bush Administrations' public characterization of the conflict; and more dangerously, it has not influenced the shape of US strategy and policy for dealing with it' (ibid.: 5).

Whether Mazarr's observations are an over-generalization is again debatable, but there is some evidence to suggest that the Bush Administration's use of simplistic political rhetoric of 'the enemy', did influence US military, intelligence and foreign policy responses in some ways. The question is, to what extent did this rhetoric drive a different moral framework to the one that had guided US intelligence agency's involvement in previous wars? Ethicist and social researcher, Hugh Mackay argues that the Bush Administration's depiction of a 'War on Terror' suggested a different kind of war, where the normal ethical standards enshrined in the Geneva Convention about the treatment of prisoners did not apply. He cites the different treatment of prisoners captured in Afghanistan, for example, those held in Guantánamo Bay without trial, as evidence that the 'War on Terror' was being fought using a different moral framework. Additionally, Mackay suggests that soldiers involved in the invasion of Iraq may have been influenced by the political rhetoric of the 'War on Terror'. This could have resulted in some confusion about whether their prisoners were conventional prisoners of war, subject to the Geneva Convention, or prisoners of the 'War on Terror', with the quite different status that this implied. Mackay argues that this created in some soldiers a sense of moral confusion about the treatment of prisoners, which might help explain abuses by US military personnel of Iraqis held in Abu Ghraib prison in Baghdad (Mackay 2005: 255). It is not possible to accurately assess the extent to which the political rhetoric described above influenced the US intelligence community. However, at the very least the discussion below of 'intelligence collection and torture', and 'the politicization of intelligence', suggests that 'moral confusion' may have also played a role in how some intelligence agencies supported their government's counter-terrorism policy.

In the first year of the Obama Administration, there was a continuation of some of the rhetoric of its predecessor, such as the 'War on Terror' but much less so, and the newly installed president took early steps to shift the discourse in a different direction – one that stressed the commonalities of the US and the Muslim world. Part of this 'new discourse' was also that the 'War on Terror' was clearly not a war on Islam. The President's speech at Cairo University in June 2009, called *A New Beginning*, provides a good example of this shift in rhetoric, which at the time also seemed to be signalling a shift in foreign policy. In that speech, he said:

> I've come here to Cairo to seek a new beginning between the United States and Muslims around the world, one based on mutual interest and mutual respect, and one based upon the truth that America and Islam are not exclusive and need not be in competition. Instead, they overlap, and share common principles – principles of justice and progress; tolerance and the dignity of all human beings.
>
> (Obama 2009a)

In summary, the *Weltanschauung* (world-view) of the political leadership obviously shapes the debate and lays the foundation upon which security policy, both domestic and international, is driven. The political world-view also determines the extent to which ethics plays a role in the prosecution of that policy, including how intelligence supports such a policy.

In addition to any set of strategic/intelligence culture ideas that externalizes who is friend and foe, there are other variables operating *internally* within states such as 'political culture', influencing how intelligence agencies are viewed by citizens, and whether they are considered to be valuable and ethical instruments of state power. Almond and Bingham define political culture as 'the patterns of individual attitudes and orientations towards politics among members of the political system' (quoted in Lovell *et al.* 1995: 395). From this definition, if we count citizens as part of the political system, then their individual and collective attitudes about politicians and the instruments of state power, particularly in Western liberal democracies, do matter. This also informs attitudes about whether the practice of a country's intelligence agencies is considered ethical and legal. As noted in Chapter 1, US citizens have had a long history of suspicion and distrust of their intelligence agencies. To some extent, the abuses of power by certain agencies such as the FBI under J. Edgar Hoover (Jeffreys-Jones 2007: 175–191) have made the public's distrust warranted. But in the USA, there also seems to be a general mistrust by the public of the intelligence community which is not only due to the specific transgressions of agencies, but is symptomatic of greater levels of suspicion of any government authority, reaching back to the post-revolutionary period and the founding of the Union.

Up to this point, I have been discussing some of the theoretical, historical and political cultural factors, which need to be understood in order to discover where the ethical debate about intelligence practice is located. While this theoretical and historical treatment of ethics is interesting, it is more helpful for practitioners and academics to apply these factors to contemporary examples of ethics in intelligence practice. In the remaining section, I will examine three issues: 'intelligence collection and torture', the 'politicization of intelligence' and the 2010 publication of numerous classified Pentagon and State Department documents on the wikileaks organization's website. In recent years, the first two issues have shaped debates profoundly about what is effective and ethical intelligence practice. In some ways, both the issue of 'torture' and 'politicized intelligence' have become as popular discussion points as the 'intelligence failure' debate, and all three are linked. Though it is less clear what the impact of the third issue – wikileaks – will have on our understanding of what is effective and ethical intelligence practice, its consequences arguably will be as profound for government security institutions as the other two issues. The aim here is not to repeat in an exhaustive way all the contributory factors to these complex issues. Readers looking for more detailed background on the first two issues have an ever increasing amount of works to choose from. For the background to how the Bush Administration moved towards supporting coercive interrogation techniques (torture), see, for example, Danner (2004), Mayer (2008) and Suskind (2006). For studies of the politicization of intelligence, particularly leading up to the US-led invasion of Iraq in 2003, see, for example, Treverton (2008), Jervis (2009: 210–212) and Gill and Phythian (2006: 116–119). In addition to summarizing the key ethical dilemmas in each topic, I will also demonstrate how the issues arising from each are relevant to improving the effectiveness of practice overall – particularly through legislative and accountability oversight measures.

Intelligence collection and torture

After 9/11, the Bush Administration launched the 'War on Terror' and the nation's security resources were switched into total war mode. This obviously included enhanced intelligence collection powers for the US intelligence community. One of the Administration's earliest responses (some six weeks after 9/11) was the passing of the US Patriot Act, which granted the FBI and a number of law enforcement agencies specific powers. Earlier attempts to adopt some of the powers in the Patriot Act by the former Clinton Administration, as part of its anti-terrorism legislative approach, had been rejected by Congress. However, the Act, after its passing in 2001, gave agencies more leverage for intelligence gathering and investigating than in the past. For example, under the Act, it became easier to obtain warrants for multiple telephone and communication devices used in many cases by the one terrorist suspect. It also provided agencies with the authority to share information derived from grand juries with intelligence and immigration officers and to confiscate property (Doyle 2002: 1–2). In 2001, the largely bipartisan support for the Act indicated that both the executive and legislative branches of the US government viewed the additional powers it provided to intelligence agencies as appropriate at the time.

However, despite the Act including a 'sunset clause' for its wiretapping and foreign intelligence amendments of 31 December 2005, the legislation continued to concern many Americans for its potential to abuse civil liberties and privacy unintentionally or otherwise. For example, a 2007 finding by the US Justice Department Inspector General indicated that the FBI had improperly used provisions of the Patriot Act to gather telephone, bank and other information about American citizens, which highlighted these concerns, and resulted in less bipartisan political support for the Act (Stout 2007: A1). However, in 2001, the Patriot Act was the first in a line of subsequent shifts by the Administration that would signify a more active approach to intelligence collection efforts in the 'War on Terror', but also one that would continue to raise concerns about whether these enhanced efforts were ethical, legal and effective. And any discussion about the ethical and legal dimensions of intelligence collected from electronic sources would soon pale compared to debates that emerged subsequently around aspects of humint collection which used aggressive interrogation techniques, including torture.

As is widely known now, intelligence collection involving coercive interrogation techniques of terrorist suspects occurred at Guantánamo, and other US military prisons such as Abu Ghraib in Iraq. Additionally, other terrorist suspects were the subject of extraordinary renditions. This is a process whereby individuals were seized from foreign countries and transported to a third country (usually in the Middle East), for coercive interrogation. Interrogation included techniques such as 'water boarding' where the detainee believes they are about to drown. Some have described this renditioning policy as an 'outsourcing of torture' (Mayer 2008). As discussed earlier (Chapter 6), the case of Canadian citizen Maher Arar, who was sent by the USA to Syria, where he was imprisoned and tortured for a year, was an example of renditioning. Arar has never been charged with any terrorism-related offence.

The principal US agencies involved in using or the 'outsourcing' of coercive interrogation techniques were the US Army and the CIA. A key part of the ethical and legal debate that arose from the use of interrogation techniques in the various locations listed above has been the extent to which these coercive techniques constituted torture and therefore human rights abuses and illegal acts. For many senior Bush officials, there were differences of opinion on this issue. In particular, Secretary of Defense Donald Rumsfeld had a different threshold for defining what constituted severe mental and physical pain (or torture) with his authorizing of a series of coercive interrogation techniques that were allowed to be used on detainees in Guantánamo and elsewhere in December 2002. The specific kinds of techniques used have been well documented elsewhere, including in great detail by *Time* magazine in 2005, which published a leaked US military 84-page interrogation log, *Secret ORCON Interrogation Log Detainee 063* (US Military 2002), detailing various tactics used against Mohammed al-Qahtani at Guantánamo. The acronym 'Orcon' stands for 'originator controlled', and it means the material is classified and cannot be distributed without express permission from its source agency. Al-Qahtani was believed to be the twentieth 9/11 hijacker, but he was denied entry to the USA. Over 54 days, al-Qahtani was interrogated on average 18 to 20 hours a day. He was denied anything more than four hours sleep per night, threatened with dogs, stripped naked, humiliated sexually by female interrogators and forced to stand four or more hours at a time.

The coercive interrogation techniques that were used on suspects like al-Qahtani were given approval on 2 December 2002 in a memo signed by Secretary of Defense Donald Rumsfeld, which recommended 15 'counter-resistance techniques' to be used on terrorists held in Guantánamo. These techniques went beyond anything the USA had used in the past and were also used eventually on prisoners in Bagram, Afghanistan, and Abu Ghraib prison in Iraq. In December 2002, just a year after 9/11, senior Bush Administration officials (particularly in the Pentagon and the CIA) were keen to extract whatever information they could from prisoners if it meant preventing other terrorist attacks on the USA. Philippe Sands, international law expert and academic, provides a comprehensive account of how key actors in the Bush Administration redefined US and international charters on prisoners and torture. Sands' work is unique among recent studies about the Bush Administration's use of coercive interrogation techniques in providing documentary evidence, but this is because he was able to interview most of the senior Bush officials involved in their development.

Only two months after 9/11, the White House was referring to prisoners of war as either 'enemy combatants' (i.e. belong to a recognized nation-state) or 'unlawful combatants' (i.e. belong to no state or are international). This change in terminology was followed in early February 2002 by President Bush declaring publicly that coercive interrogation techniques were permissible as detainees in Guantánamo were not protected by the Geneva Convention. Sands maps how these and other policy changes, summarized below, were used to disengage the USA from its commitments to the Geneva Convention, the Convention on Torture, the UN Declaration of Human Rights and previous interrogation rules outlined in the *US Army Field Manual 2-22.3 (FM 34-52)*. Given their different status as 'unlawful combatants' rather than just the standard descriptor as 'prisoners of war', it was now possible to use more coercive interrogation techniques that included torture (Sands 2009).

Sands' book focuses primarily on the al-Qahtani case to test the morality, legality and efficacy of this change in US policy on detention and torture. He mentions a number of key officials by name in the Bush Administration from the President, Secretary of Defense, White House Counsel and later Attorney-General Gonzales, Chairman of the Joint Chiefs of Staff General Richard Myers and several officials within the Justice Department. Special mention is made of John Yoo and Jay Bybee, who drafted the 'legal rationale' behind the new coercive interrogation techniques approved by Secretary Rumsfeld in December 2002. The August 2002 memo argued that the President, as Commander-in-Chief, could order torture without fear of criminal liability, and that existing torture statutes did not prohibit threats of death or severe physical pain as long as the pain was not so severe as to cause organ failure or death (ibid.: 75). Many of the facts described above have also come out from subsequent official hearings held by the US Senate Committee on the Judiciary and the Senate Armed Services Committee in 2008. Some of the official documents sanctioning coercive interrogation techniques discussed at these hearings reveal that top legal counsel for every branch of the US military were concerned that the new tactics might be illegal and FBI personnel testified that such techniques were also ineffective (US Senate Committe on the Judiciary 2008).

In summary, the evidence presented by Sands and subsequent judicial inquiries does suggest that coercive interrogation techniques bordering on and actual torture did occur. These incidents resulted in unethical intelligence activity and violations of domestic (the US Constitution) and international law (Common Article 3 of the Geneva Convention). But immediately after 9/11 and in the first few years of the 'War on Terror' in particular, more practical considerations of extracting as much information as possible from high value detainees such as al-Qahtani reigned rather than any moral concerns about the application of coercive intelligence collection techniques. So using Gendron's typology of classifying ethical intelligence practice discussed earlier, the White House, Pentagon and Justice Department in the Bush years held a realist perspective on these policies.

Leaving aside the important ethical and legal dimensions to this kind of intelligence collection, there are also questions about whether coercive interrogation techniques are effective in collecting reliable intelligence. An increasing body of work is now available that addresses this point. Some of these have been written by former military and CIA interrogators and suggest that there is no evidence that torture is an effective way to collect valuable intelligence (e.g. Rejali 2007; Alexander and Bruning 2008). Alexander led an interrogation team in Iraq that located Abu Masab al-Zarqawi, the then leader of Al Qaeda in Iraq. In their book, Alexander and Bruning suggested coercive tactics were unproductive, and that building rapport through non-coercive questioning was the best way to gain credible intelligence from detainees. These arguments from experienced interrogators were also already enshrined in the FBI rules for interrogation and in the *US Army Field Manual* (FM 34-52) as effective methods of interrogation.

However, despite the release of details about incidents of coercive interrogation in Guantánamo and Iraq, there remains an ongoing debate about the morality, legality and effectiveness of coercive interrogation techniques that either border on or constitute torture. Some scholars and practitioners while admitting that the use of such techniques does violate national and international laws, argue that they may be acceptable in worst case scenarios. These are sometimes referred to as the 'the ticking bomb' defence. For example, if an intelligence agency became aware that a bomb was about to be detonated, and a terrorist suspect in their custody knew its location and time of detonation, would it be morally justifiable and the lesser of the two 'immoral acts' to obtain this information from the suspect using torture in order to save a greater number of innocent people? Well-known advocate of the 'ticking bomb' defence, Harvard lawyer Alan Dershowitz argues that in all probability the intelligence agency would be justified in using torture in this scenario, though he argues that what is needed is better regulation of the use of torture particularly in 'ticking bomb scenarios'. This could be done by officials seeking a 'torture warrant' from a judge in which the intelligence agency would be required to produce evidence that torture is necessary in extreme circumstances. Dershowitz suggests that 'torture warrants' would create more official and judicial accountability and judges and executive officers could be held responsible for any excesses (2002: 152–159). However, it remains unclear how such a system would in practice lessen torture and make those cases where it was used more 'regulated and accountable'. A torture warrant system, like others currently used, for example, in wire-tapping, could be manipulated to get judicial approval to torture suspects, when the evidence is not necessarily strong. Judges faced with a ticking bomb scenario, and not wanting to 'stand in the way of avoiding an alleged catastrophic event', might not want to refuse a warrant, even if the case is of low probability. This approach would also very likely be difficult to administer and review. In addition, as mentioned earlier, as torture is not a reliable way to obtain information, others have argued that Dershowitz's approach remains morally objectionable under any circumstances. Ramsay argues that allowing torture in extreme cases (the ticking bomb scenario) offers a polarized, restrictive and misleading choice between security and individual rights. Ramsay adds that it 'falsely suggests measures to strengthen security necessarily involve the sacrifice of human rights and liberties; and conversely, that in this new kind of war, championing those rights as absolute irresponsibly involves weakening security' (2009: 424).

In contrast to the Bush years, the Obama Administration since taking over the White House in January 2009 has redefined US policy and the ethical debate about coercive interrogation techniques (torture) for the purposes of intelligence collection. The approach so far seems to reflect a more moral absolutist interpretation of the issues compared to Bush's realist approach. In the first three days in office, President Obama ordered a halt to any further legal proceedings against detainees by the US military and signed an executive order (No. 13491), Ensuring Lawful Interrogation, which mandated the closing of the Guantánamo base within a year and revoked President Bush's Executive Order No. 13440 of 20 July 2007, which had suspended Article 3 of the Geneva Convention. Obama's executive order also revoked any additional orders or policies issued by individual intelligence agencies such as those issued by the CIA between 11 September 2001 and 20 January 2009 concerning detention or the interrogation of detained individuals. The first paragraph of Ensuring Lawful Interrogation states that its purpose is:

> [To] improve the effectiveness of human intelligence gathering, to promote the safe, lawful, and humane treatment of individuals in US custody and of United States personnel who are detained in armed conflicts, to ensure compliance with the treaty obligations of the United States, including the Geneva Conventions, and to take care that the laws of the United States are faithfully executed.
>
> (Obama 2009b)

The Ensuring Lawful Interrogation Executive Order also provided guidance on which interrogation techniques were acceptable and these were the 18 listed in Section 8-18 of the *US Army Field Manual 2-22.3* (*FM 34-52*) published in 2006 (US Army 2006). The 18 listed in *FM 2-22.3* include various techniques discussed generally under various interrogation themes including emotional and incentive ones. Each technique is described only in general terms, though various sections also emphasize that any interrogation process must be consistent with US law and the Geneva Convention (e.g. Article 13 of the *FM 2-22.3*). These sections clearly rule out specific techniques that result in emotional, mental and physical pain of the prisoner which have subsequently become public in the leaked al-Qahtani interrogation log and other sources. The Executive Order also called for the establishment of a Special Inter-agency Taskforce on Interrogation and Transfer policies to study whether techniques listed in *Field Manual 2-22.3* provide an appropriate means of acquiring intelligence and whether any additional measures should be adopted.

President Obama's executive order and other public announcements, in addition to representing a significant ethical and policy shift away from the Bush years, signify an attempt by the Administration to demonstrate to the US public and the world that the new approaches to interrogation are much more in sync with enduring American values of democracy, equality, human rights and the rule of law. This rhetoric about the restoration of American values was visible in a few public announcements made by senior officials later appointed by President Obama. For example, prior to being confirmed Director of the CIA, Leon Panetta made the following comment in the media:

> Those who support torture may believe that we can abuse captives in certain select circumstances and still be true to our values. But that is a false compromise. We either believe in the dignity of the individual, the rule of law, and the prohibition of cruel and unusual punishment, or we don't. There is no middle ground. We cannot and we must not use torture under any circumstances. We are better than that.
>
> (Panetta, quoted in *New York Times*, 2010)

President Obama's signing of the executive order on lawful interrogation is not the end of debate on the issue of interrogation and torture for the purposes of intelligence collection. There will remain for quite some time a discussion between intelligence practitioners, government, the media, human rights activists and lawyers about what is the appropriate ethical and policy prescription for this issue. There is still polarity in the debate between moral and legal absolutists such as Phillipe Sands, whose argument is, in the end, one of principle that torture is an affront to human dignity and rights, regardless of whether it is effective or not. Sands also believes that the key Bush architects of the coercive interrogation techniques, people like former Vice President Cheney and Secretary of Defense Rumsfeld and their legal advisers, could be prosecuted outside the US where violations of the Geneva Convention are regarded as international war crimes (Sands 2009: 244).

In contrast, others such as Brian Stewart, while not advocating torture such as water boarding, suggest that we do need to challenge conventional assumptions about some techniques being cruel and unacceptable to come up with methods, which, while not torture, do not in his words, 'allow the terrorists to hold all the cards' (Newbery *et al.* 2009: 643). Stewart's observations underscore still a great deal of divergent views on what constitutes 'torture' and therefore what best defines ethical and legal interrogation techniques. The newly formed Special Inter-agency

Taskforce on Interrogation and Transfer policies provided a report to the President in August 2009, indicating that no further guidance was required on this matter other than agencies should, as required by Executive Order 13491, follow the *US Army Field Manual 2-22.3*. However, of interest to intelligence collection, the Taskforce did suggest the establishment of a scientific research programme for interrogation in order to study the effectiveness of lawful approaches and techniques, including how to improve intelligence interrogation techniques (DOJ 2009b). But there is bound to be divergent views on this point, given that what constitutes 'severe' mental and physical pain may be defined quite differently across practitioners in different agencies.

There are also other practical considerations that intelligence agencies need to work through in pursuing a more ethical approach to interrogation for intelligence collection. Attempts to recast normative attitudes to, and in some cases legal frameworks for, interrogation techniques in many Western liberal democracies also need to consider human intelligence that is sourced from agencies that continue to use 'torture' as part of their interrogation techniques. Obviously, in cases where the Western intelligence agency itself has been involved directly in the collection of the intelligence, personnel may have greater control of the conditions under which information was collected. However, in other cases, determining the 'provenance of the intelligence' might be more difficult when it has not been collected directly from the source.

Humint collection is an expensive, labour-intensive collection methodology. In addition to the painstaking work required to build up access to sources, which may provide useful information, it frequently involves linguistic capabilities in short supply in most Western intelligence agencies. In one sense, one could argue that particularly in the case of national security intelligence agencies in the USA and the UK, they have been confronted with an ethical dilemma partially due to a 'run down' of their own humint collection capability in the Middle East. The knock-on effect of this after 9/11 was that it provided little choice but greater reliance on local intelligence agencies that commonly use coercive interrogation techniques.

Such ethical dilemmas remain and limited resources in Western liberal democracies will require their intelligence agencies to still deal with their counterparts in less democratic regimes, which use collection practices many would consider unethical and illegal. Again assessing the provenance of intelligence from such agencies has now become part of the current post-9/11 reform agenda in many intelligence agencies in Western liberal democracies. For example, as discussed in Chapter 6, provenance of intelligence from countries with questionable human rights records came up in the O'Connor Commission into the actions of Canadian officials surrounding the interrogation and torture of Canadian citizen Maher Arar in Syria. The Commission's Chair, Justice O'Connor made two recommendations (Nos 14 and 15) on this matter, suggesting in recommendation 15 that information from a country with questionable human rights record should be identified as such and 'proper procedures' should be taken to assess its reliability (O'Connor 2006: 368). CSIS officials interviewed for this book indicated that their agency was now much more focused on the issue of provenance. However, it remains unclear what risk management methodologies intelligence agencies can apply to assess the risk of using intelligence from some agencies, where it is likely that torture was involved to collect intelligence

Leaving aside the ethical debate on intelligence collection using torture, it also would seem naïve to think that a ban on the use of torture during interrogations by Western liberal democracies will result in a similar ban by agencies in countries with questionable human rights records. Liberal democratic countries, which eschew torture, may seek to ban the use of some intelligence that in their view may have been the result of torture. However, in practice, it may be difficult in all cases to know with confidence the provenance of all intelligence, particularly if it has passed through a number of agencies. Further, occupational expediency in some parts of the world, such as Pakistan, Afghanistan and Yemen, may require the use of such intelligence in the absence of any other alternative sources. As noted earlier, the limited resources of agencies such as the CIA or MI6 will continue to mean they will need to rely on their counterparts in the Middle East, Africa and Asia for information they are unable to collect themselves.

However, the amount of political and public interest in the issue of torture will continue to place pressure on intelligence agencies to demonstrate as much as possible that they do not use information or are not complicit in its collection where torture has been involved. This will continue to result in a number of ethical and practical issues for Western agencies to resolve relating to the use of human intelligence collected by less democratic regimes. For example, if a CIA operative is present during an interrogation where torture is taking place but does not take part directly, is this ethical and legal? The answer would be a 'no' under the Obama Administration's new approach to this issue. This seems also to be the view being taken by the new UK Coalition Government, who have (in July 2010) commissioned a judicial inquiry into the role of MI5 in interrogations of detainees in Guantánamo Bay and elsewhere. Another point that requires clarification is the ethical issues raised in providing support to intelligence agencies that use coercive interrogation techniques. Is the provision of ongoing financial and technical support for local intelligence agencies that use torture ethical? For example, in December 2009, media reporting suggested that the CIA 'controls' the activities of the two Palestinian security agencies – the Preventive Security Organisation and the General Intelligence Service – and that these agencies have mistreated and tortured Hamas sympathizers (*The Australian*, 2009: 15). These reports also raise additional questions discussed earlier in Chapter 3, about how we can defend our capacity building assistance for local intelligence agencies against 'corruption' and 'torture' so that they too can become more ethical, accountable instruments of the state.

A decade after 9/11, intelligence collection using torture remains an unresolved ethical and practical issue for intelligence agencies of Western liberal democracies such as Australia, Canada, the UK and the USA. Given intelligence collection on terrorism in particular from the Middle East will remain a key objective for Western governments for the foreseeable future, the issues of torture and other human rights abuses are likely to result in ethical and legal dilemmas for Western liberal democratic countries for some time.

The politicization of intelligence

The second area of intelligence practice, which has recently shaped the post-9/11 debate about the role of ethics in intelligence, is the politicization of intelligence. This issue is about the extent to which intelligence agencies (both national security and policing) in Australia, Canada, New Zealand, the UK and the USA have provided full, frank and fearless assessments to their governments – without undue pressure from them to deliver a conclusion that matches existing policy prescriptions.

In recent years, there have been examples in the intelligence communities of Australia, the UK and the USA, where politicization or allegations of it have raised concerns about the ethical practice of intelligence agencies. These concerns relate to whether assessments provided have tried as much as possible to establish the truth of a matter, or embellish or underplay the 'truth' to satisfy the political agendas of policy-makers. The assessments provided to US, UK and Australian decision-makers leading up to the invasion of Iraq in 2003 have all subsequently come under political and judicial review, not only for the way assessment processes were managed in various agencies, but also as we shall discuss here whether there was any undue political interference in these processes by decision-makers.

In the USA, one of the key terms of reference for the SSCI (2004) inquiry into the *US Intelligence Community's Prewar Intelligence Assessments on Iraq*, was to assess whether there had been any political pressure placed on analysts or managers to make their assessments conform to policy conclusions of the Bush Administration. As noted earlier (Chapter 6), the report found significant failures in management, collection and analysis, but no evidence that analysts or managers were pressured to produce conclusions in line with policy direction (SSCI 2004: 272–284). However, several Senators of the Select Committee did express their concerns that they were not able to interview senior policy-makers to get their perspectives on the nature and extent of their interactions with members of the US intelligence community (ibid.: 509). Hence, there was the suggestion in the comments by some Committee members that they could not make a comprehensive ruling on the issue of politicization, given they did not have access to all the facts. While all Senators endorsed the Inquiry findings, several expressed their concerns that the Administration's public announcements painted a more ominous view of Iraq's threat to the USA than was reflected in the intelligence analysis. This may have resulted in intelligence assessments also becoming more negative than previously in line with the Administration's 'drumbeats' that war seemed almost inevitable (ibid.: 503).

In the UK and Australia, a similar suite of official inquiries were launched into the nature of intelligence provided to their governments on WMD in Iraq. In the UK, *Review of Intelligence on WMD* chaired by Lord Butler (the Butler Report), and in Australia, *The Report of the Inquiry into Australian Intelligence Agencies* (the Flood Report) by former Office of National Assessments (ONA) Director both reported their findings in 2004. Similar to the SSCI inquiry, both the Butler and Flood Reports did not find any evidence that intelligence assessments were, to quote a portion of the Butler Report, 'pulled in any particular direction to meet the concerns of senior officials' (Butler 2004: 152). Despite all these inquiries, the nature of intelligence supplied to the UK and US governments in particular and whether it was politicized remain a contentious issue in these countries.

Since the Butler Report, in the UK there has been another recent opportunity to look at the interface between intelligence in the broader context of national security policy-making. The UK Iraq Inquiry, commissioned by the former Gordon Brown Labour Government in June 2009 and chaired by Sir John Chilcot (also a former member of the Butler Review), is probing the decision-making processes across the UK government from July 2001 to July 2009 in relation to the UK's involvement in the Iraq War. The scope of the UK Iraq Inquiry is broader than just the role of intelligence in decision-making. It will also be assessing the 'lessons to be learnt' across all relevant streams of decision-making: intelligence, defence and foreign policy. A full report was expected at the end of 2010 though public hearings have continued into 2011. It remains to be seen if the Inquiry will reveal at least publicly, any evidence of clear cases where political pressure played a role in the intelligence assessments provided to government.

In Australia too, there has been further scrutiny of intelligence assessments produced by the intelligence community's two assessment agencies: the ONA and the DIO. One of the key recommendations of the Flood Report has been to give the independent reviewer of the Australian intelligence community, the Inspector General for Intelligence and Security (IGIS), the power to carry out periodic inspections into the independence and propriety of assessments completed by the ONA and the DIO. The first formal inquiry into the ONA was completed in 2007, and found no evidence of political interference or pressure from policy departments, which resulted in a compromise of its independent assessment status, or the integrity of its assessments (IGIS 2006–2007: 1230).

In summary, the many reviews into the intelligence supplied on the nature and extent of WMDs in Iraq discussed earlier have not only contributed to the reshaping of intelligence accountability mechanisms, they also have caused practitioners and academics to look again at the role intelligence plays in the policy-making process. The intelligence provided to decision-makers prior to the US-led invasion of Iraq prompts us again to ask where is the line between 'intelligence' and 'policy', and what are the consequences of intelligence becoming politicized? As noted earlier, the official reviews in Australia, the UK and the USA did not find any *direct* evidence of senior policy-makers pressuring analysts or managers to change assessments. It remains difficult, however, to assess the true nature of the politicization of intelligence on WMD in Iraq. Despite the many official inquiries and detailed academic studies, much is still not known about the specific roles of key decision-makers, and how they used or 'abused' intelligence in their policy deliberations. However, public announcements, probing questions and other bureaucratic developments leading up to the US-led invasion of Iraq do demonstrate that other kinds of politicization of intelligence, of perhaps more subtle varieties, may have been at work.

For example, one kind of politicization of intelligence may have come from how political leaders selected 'bits' of intelligence in public statements to attract support for invading Iraq. Various announcements were made by senior officials in London and Washington about the imminent threat posed by Saddam Hussein and his WMDs. The net effect of these was to ratchet up the public's attention and justify the need for war. The flurry of public announcements about every single piece of intelligence discovered, whether reliable or not, also hyper-sensitized the intelligence community's analytical processes. While this charged political climate did not, as far as we know, result in politically directed amendments to assessments *per se*, this highly politicized environment gradually resulted in an evolution of analytical judgements that eventually either matched or supported the policy-makers' perceptions of the threat. Jervis (2009) suggests that this evolution in key judgements may have been partly a psychological process, which he describes as 'motivated bias'. According to Jervis, motivated bias is a situation, 'where the analysts seek to avoid the painful value trade-off between pleasing policy-makers, and following professional standards'. In essence, they are motivated in favour of producing assessments that support or at least do not undermine policy (ibid.: 212).

A cursory review of the official inquiries discussed earlier shows that speeches made by the US Bush and UK Blair Administrations did rely on either incorrect assessments, or the selective quoting of them, to build the public support for a policy option of war. It is possible, but speculative, that the frequent announcements about the gravity of the threat by key political leaders might have made it almost an 'act of heresy' for many intelligence analysts to challenge this pre-ordained world-view of a mad Iraqi dictator, with a full suite of WMDs and links to terrorists. For example, prior to the invasion of Iraq in 2003, several public announcements were made by Vice President Cheney and other administration officials about the links between Iraq and Al Qaeda and that Saddam Hussein also had WMDs (e.g. Bumiller and Dao 2002). The CIA consistently denied such links, but senior figures were determined in the Administration, particularly in the Pentagon, to garner evidence about such a link. Such public announcements by Vice President Cheney provide a good example of the politicized environment in which intelligence was being produced and used.

One section of the SSCI report on prewar intelligence assessments on Iraq describes how some analysts, who were asked constant questions and requested to reexamine the issue of Iraq's link to terrorism, thought this was unreasonable pressure on them. Additionally, in the production of an assessment on the link between Iraq and terrorism, some CIA analysts had also complained to the CIA Ombudsman for Politicisation that they felt pressured by the Administration. These allegations, however, were subsequently restated, according to the Ombudsman, as being an issue more about differences of opinions between separate analytical areas of the Agency (SSCI 2004: 360). Similarly, in September 2002, UK Prime Minister Tony Blair made his famous statement that Saddam could deploy chemical weapons within 45 minutes, and implied that they could reach the entire region. This information was included in a public dossier on the Iraqi threat and was based on a JIC assessment. The JIC assessment was inaccurate and unclear in that it implied that Saddam had ballistic (offensive) chemical weapons. The Butler Report speculates that it may well have been left in the public dossier by the government as it was 'eye catching' and would assist in making the desired policy case for the government (Butler 2004: 127). More recently, in February 2011, further evidence of the inaccurate intelligence assessments relied upon by US and UK governments for justifying the invasion of Iraq has emerged. A key source used by London and Washington, Rafid Ahmed Alwan al-Janabi (codenamed 'Curveball'), has publicly admitted that his statement that Iraq had a secret biological weapons programme was a lie (Chulov and Pidd 2011).

The above examples demonstrate a tendency by policy-makers, particularly in times of crisis, to 'cherry-pick' intelligence in the support of policy announcements. Treverton lists other forms of 'politicization', including *direct pressure, maintaining a house line, question asking* and a *shared mindset* for those interested in a more detailed exposition of politicization of intelligence (Treverton 2008: 93). It is of course, the policy-makers' right to use intelligence as they see fit to formulate policy. This is after all the *raison d'être* of intelligence. However, 'cherry-picking' also means that policy-makers exclude other intelligence assessments, which do not conform to their own *Weltanschauung.* The danger in this, as Jervis points out, is that when intelligence is 'used to justify policies to the public, they incorrectly imply the backing of the intelligence community' (Jervis 2009: 210). It is therefore not easy for the public to determine if this is the intelligence community's absolute last word on the subject or if this is the political leaders' spin on a threat whose significance is still being assessed by the intelligence community. Other public announcements, including one leaked from the head of MI6, also give weight to the theory that UK and US intelligence was being manipulated politically to support policy prescriptions. In this case, the contents of a July 2002 Downing Street meeting, including comments made by the head of MI6 reporting back on a visit to Washington, were leaked to the UK *Sunday Times* in 2005. The leaked transcript of the meeting reported the head of MI6 saying that 'the intelligence and facts were being fixed around the policy' (Manning 2005).

In the USA, there were also bureaucratic dimensions to the politicization of intelligence with the creation of the Pentagon Office of Special Plans (OSP), established shortly after 9/11 by Deputy Defense Secretary Paul Wolfowitz. In a series of investigations in May and October 2003, journalist Seymour Hersh interviewed current and former intelligence officers, who were privy to the setting-up of this new unit or had interactions with it from other departments. They reported that the OSP utilized raw intelligence from the field and fed it directly to Secretary of Defense Rumsfeld, Paul Wolfowitz and then to the Vice President's Office in the White House. The information was not filtered or vetted by other member agencies of the intelligence community, who would normally assess its reliability against other sources. Hersh portrays the creation of the OSP as almost a battle between the conventional intelligence community of the CIA and the Defense

Intelligence Agency (DIA) and the Pentagon for control over US foreign policy on the WMD in Iraq issue.

The net result, according to Hersh, was to sideline the CIA, whom Rumsfeld believed was 'unable to perceive the reality of the situation in Iraq' (Hersh 2004: 210). This reality of course being that Saddam Hussein had WMDs and links with terrorism. The OSP relied on information collected by other US intelligence agencies, but also information provided by the Iraqi National Congress, an exiled group headed by Ahmad Chalabi. Much of this information from Iraqi defectors had either already been discarded by the CIA as unreliable, or was subsequently found to be false in later inquiries. The creation of the OSP represented yet another form of politicization of intelligence, where intelligence was 'stove-piped' to the highest ranking officials, while other processed intelligence was blocked or ignored. Hersh interviewed a series of current and former intelligence officials about this issue of 'stove-piping' in 2003. One interviewee, Kenneth Pollack, a former National Security Council expert on Iraq, described this stove-piping process in the following way:

> What the Bush people did was dismantle the existing filtering process that for fifty years had been preventing the policymakers from getting bad information. They created stovepipes to get the information they wanted directly to the top leadership. Their position is that the professional bureaucracy is deliberately and maliciously keeping information from them. They [i.e. the Pentagon] always had information to back up their public claims, but it was often very bad information. They were forcing the intelligence community to defend good information and good analysis so aggressively that the intelligence analyst didn't have the time or the energy to go after the bad information.
>
> (Pollack, quoted in Hersh 2004: 223–224)

What should be clear from the above discussion is that the politicization of intelligence is the result of an increasingly complex set of interactions between intelligence producers and their consumers. The post-Cold War security agenda now dominated by non-state actor issues such as terrorism, illegal immigration and a number of 'homeland security issues' has seen intelligence become a very 'public' policy commodity. Non-state actor security issues have also become intensely political, and as we saw in the case of WMDs in Iraq, politicians are using intelligence now in much more public ways than they did during the Cold War to make their case for policy. There is the possibility that intelligence, particularly around the security issues mentioned above, becomes a 'partisan political football' for politicians wishing to win the policy battle over their opponents. The question of the relationship between intelligence and policy has always been a fragile one, as Sherman Kent noted in his groundbreaking work, *Strategic Intelligence*,

> [The] proper relationship between intelligence producers and consumers is one of the utmost delicacy. Intelligence must be close enough to policy, plans and operations to have the greatest amount of guidance, and must not be so close that it loses its objectivity and integrity of judgment.
>
> (Kent 1949: 180)

The question moving forward will be how to effectively manage this delicate relationship to avoid intelligence becoming too politicized, losing its objectivity and professional integrity. There are no 'off the shelf panaceas' for politicization given the circumstances may be quite different across cases. It can be too simplistic to view every case as the result of pre-meditated or malignant intentions of politicians. Betts' work on 'intelligence failures' also suggests that, in the end, politicization of intelligence may be the result of less pre-meditative or political partisan factors:

> Policy premises constrict perception, and administrative workloads constrain reflection by decision-makers. . . . In a crisis, both data and policy outpace analysis, the ideal process of staffing and consultation falls behind the press of events, and careful estimates cannot be digested in time.
>
> (Betts 1978: 63, 68)

Hence, in the current 24-hour news/policy cycle, the appropriate and inappropriate use of intelligence by decision-makers is likely to continue. However, intelligence managers and analysts can play a role in managing this process in order to mitigate hopefully the worst effects of politicization that would impact on the objectivity of judgements. As discussed earlier, leaders or managers of intelligence must play an important role in more carefully defining the strengths and limitations of products provided to consumers. From an analytical perspective, there still needs to be more precision on probability and estimation terminology used in intelligence products. Intelligence leaders and managers, of course need to be seen to be supporting their analytical cadre's conclusions, particularly in areas where little is known and decision-makers have their own different views on events.

Over the past decade there has been increasing secondment to policy departments by intelligence leaders and managers, which have helped them better understand the role politics plays in setting the policy and intelligence agenda. Managers and analysts must also play a role in anticipating more swiftly policy interests and servicing those in a timely and relevant form. In an increasingly competitive information environment, intelligence is seen by policy-makers, rightly, as only one source of support. To make sure 'the voice of intelligence is heard', there needs to be a greater cooperation between the different strengths of intelligence agencies, rather than a continuation of parochial competition among them. More joined-up or all-source intelligence products whose analysis has been contested from a range of different perspectives will be more beneficial to its consumers. In many national security and policing intelligence contexts, there may also be further scope for describing in intelligence products the source and reliability of the information. Other internal management initiatives should include a formal 'lesson learnt' process, so that agencies can learn not only how to produce better intelligence assessments, but also how to better manage consumers' expectations and perceptions.

Given that politicization of intelligence seems inevitable, it is also important that other processes are in place – external to intelligence agencies – to manage and monitor how policy-makers interact with their intelligence producers and vice versa. It is logical that effective accountability mechanisms that are independent from government should continue to play a central role in detecting, where possible, potential political interference in the intelligence production process. The three reviews mentioned above (the SSCI, Butler and Flood) remind us about the adverse impact some aspects of politicization can have. In particular, the reflection in each on the real or potential political pressure on intelligence raises in the taxpayers' mind questions about the independence and quality of intelligence practice, and whether it is changeable at the whim of the policy-maker. In some quarters, the public's perception and tolerance of 'secret' agencies with the power to intrude on our privacy and civil liberties can only become more negative if they are viewed rightly or wrongly as merely illegitimate extensions of state power. This last point has come sharply into play in 2010 with the bulk release of US classified information by the organization wikileaks.

The wikileaks affair

Wikileaks is a 'whistleblower' website established by Julian Assange in 2006. Assange is an Australian citizen, who just avoided prison after being convicted on 25 charges of computer hacking in 1995. Before the 2010 release of extensive classified information, wikileaks had also published a string of other information on topics of corruption, wars, torture, climate change and suppression of free speech. On Friday, 22 October 2010, the wikileaks organization published a cache of 391,832 classified documents on its website, related to US military forces in Iraq during the period January 2004 to December 2009. This large batch of documents is believed to have been released by Private Bradley Manning, an Army intelligence analyst. Manning has since been charged and is also alleged to have been the source of the bulk release on 25 July 2010 of classified information relating to the war in Afghanistan. A third batch of classified material – some 250,000 US State Department messages (cables) sent by US embassies abroad – was released in November 2010.

Consequences

The wikileaks organization's release of a large cache of classified US documents in late 2010, like the two issues discussed above (coercive interrogation and politicization of intelligence), underlines the ethical tensions of intelligence practice in liberal democracies. As noted earlier, the post-post 9/11 security environment is defined by complex transnational security issues, which, as Ormand describes, require a more 'pre-emptive intelligence approach' (2009: 39) in order to deal with them effectively. The need by the US military and the CIA in particular to use proactive intelligence collection methods (particularly humint) is again highlighted by the nature of the material released on the wikileaks website detailing US intelligence activities in Afghanistan and Iraq. This pre-emptive approach to intelligence collection raises similar fundamental ethical dilemmas described above regarding the earlier two issues. For the public in liberal democracies such as Australia, Canada, New Zealand, the UK and the USA, questions arise about whether intelligence methods that inherently involve secrecy, deception and surveillance are in themselves 'morally wrong' or support 'morally questionable' policies. The wikileaks release also raises in the minds of some of the public and in the media questions about unnecessary invasions of privacy and in some cases abuses of human rights. And like the politicization of intelligence issue discussed earlier, particularly during the preparation of the invasion of Iraq, it also brings again to the public's consciousness whether intelligence is being used in an appropriate legal, accountable and measured way by their elected representatives.

The wikileaks episode therefore heightens rather than resolves ongoing ethical tensions about how intelligence is 'used' and 'abused' in modern liberal democracies. For as long as states continue to use intelligence to prosecute national security policy in peace and war, fundamental questions will remain about what is 'moral' or 'just intelligence practice', and in which ways do democratic societies need to continue to cultivate a 'culture of secrecy' which traditional intelligence collection and analysis relies upon? Additionally, wikileaks serves to heighten, though in ways still too early to assess, how aspects of intelligence practice are becoming again not only 'the partisan political football' of the 9/11 days, but also much more a public policy commodity exchanged between politicians and the public. In summary, it is still difficult to know where the wikileaks releases will take the debate about the extent intelligence practice can be ethical, accountable yet still an effective instrument of state. But the debate so far by the public, media, academics and governments has two important dimensions relevant to this chapter. The first relates to the ethical and legislative nature of wikileaks, and the second point relates to the impact of the release of classified information on effective intelligence practice. Both dimensions will be discussed briefly before moving on to the remaining two sections of the chapter: intelligence legislation and accountability. As the wikileaks episode was still unfolding just prior to this book going to print, the observations below are preliminary remarks on how it may impact on the ethical and effectiveness of intelligence practice.

Ethical and legislative dimensions

The leaking of official sensitive government information, including intelligence, is not a new phenomenon. In the US context, the leaks by Aldrich Ames, a former CIA counter-intelligence officer arrested in 1994 for spying for the former Soviet Union resulted in the death of some CIA agents and the compromise of 30 others (SSCI 1994: 42). Additionally, there is the case of Robert Hanssen, a former FBI agent, who was arrested in 2001 for spying for the Soviet Union and Russia over a 22-year period. Both of these insiders were privy to top secret information. Their motivations came from financial remuneration rather than any ethical or lawful considerations.

In stark contrast to the likes of Ames and Hanson, other leakers of classified material are not motivated by money, fame or ideology. Their motivations may be based on a Kantian or other deontological (duty-based) approach to ethics. In the case of both these approaches, rights and obligations of the individual become important. For deontologists, Hinman suggests that: 'Deontologists see the fundamental question of the moral life to be, "what ought I to do?"' (2003: 221). There is an emphasis on fulfilling duties to respect our and other people's rights. Perhaps the case of Daniel Ellsberg, a US military official, who in 1971 leaked a top secret Pentagon study of the US government's decision-making about the Vietnam War to a *New York Times* reporter, may be an example of someone motivated to leak classified information by moral duty. Ellsberg has said that he was, among other reasons, motivated by patriotism to improve public understanding and better decision-making about the US involvement in the Vietnam War (Ellsberg 2003). But are Julian Assange and the wikileaks organization driven by a similar moral urgency to uphold the public interest and understanding of US national security policy in Iraq, Afghanistan and elsewhere? Max Frankel, a former *New York Times* editor, who oversaw the publication of Ellsberg's Pentagon Papers suggests no. Ellsberg, he claims,

> was not breaching secrecy for its own sake, unlike the WikiLeakers of today; he was looking to defeat a specific government policy. Moreover, he was acutely conscious of the risks of disclosure and did not distribute documents betraying live diplomatic efforts to negotiate an end to the fighting. And it took him years to find a credible medium of distribution, which is now available at the push of a button. The government cried damage and suffered almost none; Ellsberg wanted to hasten peace and failed.
>
> (Frankel 2010)

Second, is wikileaks' motivation to improve policy-makers' understanding of their own decision-making in the way that Ellsberg claimed? Without interviewing Assange directly, it is difficult to get an accurate reading on his motivations or others working in the wikileaks organization. The answers to both questions are also currently clouded by some of the contradictory statements Assange makes, and also the growing partisan political, public and media debate about the merits or otherwise of the wikileaks' release of classified information.

A wide and diverse range of opinions have emerged since late 2010 on whether Assange's and wikileaks' objectives are fuelled by an ethical desire to promote greater public awareness of government policy-making processes and its short-comings, or whether his online version of 'whistleblowing' is merely a self-serving instrument for an egotistical anarchist keen to see government processes fail. There are diverse views on this point, even among journalists about the ethical boundaries of the wikileaks' release of classified information. For example, in Australia, the editors of most but not all major papers signed a letter sent to Prime Minister Gillard opposing prosecution of Assange in Australia or the USA saying 'Wikileaks, an organization that aims to expose official secrets, is doing what the media have always done: bringing to light material that governments would prefer to keep secret' (The Walkley Foundation 2010). In the USA, 19 professors (half the faculty) at Columbia University Graduate School of Journalism also signed a letter to the Obama Administration, arguing that wikileaks engaged in First Amendment (freedom of speech) activity. Some faculty members said that they had different views about his approach and methods, including one professor who did not sign the letter because he felt 'it did not adequately criticize the recklessness – the disregard for the consequences of human lives – of a massive dump of confidential info' (Adler 2011).

The wikileaks website itself is peppered with ethical rhetoric explaining how the organization's activities are based on defending freedom of speech and the declaration of human rights. In one paragraph on the website, wikileaks reports that it has 'combined high end security technology with journalism and ethical principles'. But has wikileaks really used ethical principles in releasing this classified information? Has their interpretation of justifiable means been weighed sufficiently against the actual and potential consequences of their actions? It is a reasonable enough question to ask, given people's careers or lives may end by these revelations. As Caryl notes, 'We do not know and may never know' if deaths occur as a result of these leaks (Caryl 2011: 27). But Assange to date has been unable to address these concerns satisfactorily. In a *Time* magazine interview, he claimed that 'this sort of nonsense about lives being put into jeopardy is trotted out every time a big military or intelligence organization is exposed by the press' (Stengel 2010). Though as Caryl rightly points out, can wikileaks tell us why this was necessary (Caryl 2011: 27)? On the second point raised above of whether wikileaks is motivated to improve US policy-makers' and others' understanding of their decision-making, again it is hard to get an accurate reading on both these questions at present. More time is needed to assess future rhetoric and actions by the wikileaks organization. However, based on media comments and some of his previous writings on conspiracies, it is difficult to believe that wikileaks under the directorship by Assange is motivated by releasing classified material in order to improve policy-making. For example, Assange in media reports has been accused of pursing a vendetta against the United States. In an October 2010 edition of the *New York Times*, one of the mainstream media who have published segments of the wikileaks, Assange was reported to have said: 'America is an increasingly militarized society and a threat to democracy.' Assange added, 'We have been attacked by the United States, so we are forced into a position where we must defend ourselves' (Burns 2010: A1).

Assange's negative view of the USA was also documented in his earlier writings. In a series of essays written in 2006 he describes the USA as an 'authoritarian conspiracy' and highlights the importance of stopping the flow of information that governments rely on which promotes the conspiracy (Assange 2006). This language suggests that it is the author's intention to challenge or disrupt information flows rather than improve them or the decisions they support. Additionally, there are also questions about Assange's and wikileaks' ethical judgement in releasing the Afghan documents without removing the names of Afghan intelligence sources for NATO troops. One *New York Times* article reported that several wikileaks colleagues advised Assange to remove source names but he alone decided to release the documents with them included (Burns 2010: A1).

In summary, the wikileaks episode, like the issues of coercive interrogation and the politicization of intelligence, provides a further example of the moral dilemmas that confront intelligence practice between those who seek to protect it, and others who seek to expose aspects of it for various reasons, including in order to protect the public freedom of information or constitutional rights to free speech. Moral judgements about the motivations and consequences of wikileaks are therefore relativistic, depending on who is making the assessment. In many respects too, the wikileaks release is another important symptom of a broader and growing discord in the post-post-9/11 security environment between governments and the public about what are true secrets, and what information constitutes 'the public good' and therefore what the public should legitimately be expected to know.

More important than Assange himself or the wikileaks organization, however, is the impact this kind of mass 'whistleblower' technique via the internet will have on intelligence practice. Assessments are still being made by the USA and other governments (Australia, Canada, the UK and New Zealand) on the consequence of wikileaks to intelligence practice. The impact of the wikileaks release of classified information will likely change, given, at the time of writing (January 2011), the US Government is still assessing damages to national interests. This assessment will also likely change depending what additional information is released by wikileaks. Not all of the US State Department cables have been released and Assange claims to have an 'insurance file' – a 1.4-gigabyte computer file of additional classified information he would release if something happens to him (Pilger 2011).

From Assange's perspective, his public comments suggest that he sees the release of this secret information as a 'game changer' in the way the USA will be able to transmit classified information and conduct its international policy. Reflecting on the release of diplomatic cables, he declared to many media outlets and blogs that geopolitics will be separated into pre-'Cablegate' and post-'Cablegate' eras. The implication of this comment suggests that the release of several sensitive and sometimes embarrassing cables, which reveal very candid assessments by US diplomats of foreign leaders, will reset fundamentally the way diplomacy is conducted between nations. In the short to medium term, there is little doubt the US Government, particularly its diplomatic officials, are in damage control to rebuild relations with some countries, but in the longer term his comments might be rendered hyperbole.

Based on the cables released to date, the perceived damage to the US national interests may not have been as grave as first perceived by officials in Washington, DC, and their allies in Canberra, London, Ottawa and Wellington. While there have been several official announcements quoted in the media about the potential leaking of the identities of secret sources used by the State Department overseas (e.g. Lakshmanan 2011), and a general condemnation of wikileaks by political leaders in these capitals, there has also been a hosing down of the consequences of the leaks in material from the Pentagon and State Department. No doubt some of the public announcements being made in Washington and elsewhere 'that it's not as bad as we thought' are the rhetoric of political damage control. But senior officials such as Secretary of Defense Gates have expressed views indicating the release of at least some information such as many of the cables has not resulted in any irreversible collapse of US relations with the international community. In a recent media statement, Gates posed the following question: 'Is this embarrassing? Yes. Is it awkward? Yes. Consequences for US foreign policy? I think fairly modest' (Gates and Mullen 2010).

The reality is all country's foreign ministries collect similar candid and sensitive information. It would be naïve to think that nations will cease concealing their views on others in formulating policy. The diplomatic communications system of the US and other governments will continue out of necessity and the national interest. In the same press conference where the above comments were made by Gates, he added that: 'Foreign diplomats speak to the US because they have to, not because they want to or have affinity for Washington' (ibid.). Though given these leaks and the damage that has been done to the US reputation, it is likely that the State Department will tighten standard operating procedures about what information will be permitted to be communicated in cable form, and whether certain material will need to be sent by more secure systems, including secret communications or by secure email and telephone.

Similarly, the first two bulk releases of information on Iraq and Afghanistan by wikileaks were largely dated battlefield reports from soldiers reporting on things encountered on patrol and operational activity, including IED attacks, ambushes, bodies of murdered civilians, friendly fire incidents and traffic accidents. In the main these documents did not contain information collected from sensitive intelligence operations conducted by special forces in collaboration with the CIA, which might have revealed collection methodologies and sources. Though as noted earlier, wikileaks did release the names of some Afghan intelligence sources used by military forces in Afghanistan, which may prove to have serious consequences for some of these sources (Burns 2010).

While the content of classified information may not be *the* game changer in international affairs Assange was hoping for, the wikileaks release might well change the 'rules of the game' in other ways that both facilitate and inhibit good intelligence practice. From a facilitative perspective, one positive fact from the wikileaks release is the opportunity for the US and other governments to review operating procedures for the classification of intelligence documents. The three caches of sensitive information (Iraq, Afghanistan and US State Department cables) were taken from the US government's Secret Internet Protocol Router Network (SIPRNet). This is a network used to distribute classified information marked at the secret level or below. Top Secret and very sensitive information does not travel on SIPRNet. The wikileaks release demonstrates the pervasive culture of over-classification in the US government and other liberal democracies. For example, media reporting suggests that only 204 of the 391,832 documents were classified at the confidential level, while 379,565 of them were classified at the secret level (Stewart 2010).

Given the low-level tactical nature of many of the battlefield reports, this suggests a culture still exists in some US intelligence agencies of over-classification of information beyond that required to protect it. This is not to suggest that information cannot be quite sensitive at the time it is collected, but this changes with time, and there should be more efficient monitoring of processes to downgrade classification of sensitive documents as they become historical. A review of the procedures for classifying and de-classifying intelligence would facilitate better intelligence and information systems by de-clogging already overloaded ICT systems with material that no longer needs to be stored at higher classification levels. This would free up secret systems and above for only the smaller percentage of material that needs high protection and limited access protocols. In summary, the current large bulk of increasingly over-classified information makes it difficult to secure the information that needs securing.

Another area, as a result of wikileaks, which can both facilitate and inhibit effective intelligence relates to a broad suite of interrelated issues of information security, information sharing and privacy. There is always a tension within intelligence agencies or functions between securing sensitive information and sharing it. As noted in earlier chapters, the 'culture of secrecy' of many agencies has been challenged post 9/11 and there are now policy and legislative measures to facilitate sharing within and between agencies in the USA and the other countries discussed in this book. However, a leak in the US SIPRnet system may prompt some agencies to rethink what they upload on this and other networked systems. There is a danger that in the interest of information security that some agencies increasingly stove-pipe their information, which may have a deleterious effect on 'whole of government' collection and analytical capabilities. A knee-jerk response by agencies to silo information again is a contravention of ISE provisions enshrined in the IRTPA and it will be interesting to see if the ODNI can play a leadership role in striking a balance between information security and sharing.

While a return to the compartmentalization of intelligence in the pre-9/11 days is a real concern, the wikileaks episode does point out serious information security issues that also need addressing to avoid as much as possible similar instances in the future. The White House has issued a memo via Jacob Lew, Director of the Office of Management and Budget, setting out requirements and questions relevant agencies need to address to assess their current information security status. These questions will form a broader security review across the US Government and all agencies were expected to complete the survey by 28 January 2011 (Lew 2010). A subsequent Office of Management and Budget memo contains more than 100 questions relating to agency safeguards for ICT systems, management, oversight, counterintelligence, information assurance measures and personnel security (Lew 2011). A key theme in the questions is to get the agencies to reflect on which employees have access to what information. If it is proven that Private Bradley Manning released classified information to wikileaks, his case does raise significant information security questions about why a very junior intelligence analyst needed to have such wide access to information systems such as SIPRNet.

It is likely once the survey results have been completed, the Obama Administration will look to set guidelines for access rights to information, which puts a greater onus on access being relevant to a person's current job. It makes sense to review and limit the feed of intelligence analysts receive. For example, a forward military intelligence analyst working on tactical support issues in the Middle East does not need to have access to all sensitive cables dealing with US efforts in global trade or nuclear proliferation. This may improve information security and prevent leaks in some agencies, but an overly prescriptive or bureaucratic approach could also further unnecessarily compartmentalize information, resulting in slower and poorer analysis.

The 2011 Office of Management and Budget memo places an emphasis on asking agencies about how they measure 'employee trustworthiness'. Agencies have been asked to what extent they 'fuse together' employees' personnel security evaluations with other information security checks such as IT auditing, polygraphing and foreign contact/travel information. The memo suggests that this information, if better fused, would provide security personnel with 'early warning indicators of insider threats'. While assessing employee 'trustworthiness' will be not fully reliable, a better assessment of the above indices of employee security risk may in some cases show those vulnerable to leaking sensitive information. This may facilitate better information security, but if it becomes too invasive and draconian, it would likely have an impact on morale and prove to be an inhibitor to effective intelligence production.

The final area where wikileaks will have an impact on effective intelligence is the extent to which this kind of internet leakage of classified information can be prosecuted and how this is balanced against the public right to know about government decision-making and freedom of information. The US Attorney General and the State Department are investigating whether any prosecution will be undertaken in the connection with the wikileaks disclosure. The difficulty with the wikileaks episode, however, is that the kind of information disclosed comes from State and Defense Departments and there is not one statute that governs the unauthorized disclosure of classified information. Current legislation options differ depending on the nature of the information, the identity of the discloser, those to whom it was disclosed and how it was disclosed. Some of the government information released does not fall under the protection of any statutes. In the case of both Defense and State Department information, there are reports which relate to national defence that could potentially be covered under the 1917 Espionage Act, but this legislation and others do not cover disclosure by persons who are not government employees (Elsea 2010). So a positive outcome of the wikileaks release may be a review and more streamlined approach to legislation and prosecution in such cases where government officials have released sensitive information, regardless of the source agency. Elsea reports that, since the wikileaks episode, additional legislation was introduced in December 2010 in the US Senate. One bill called the Securing Human Intelligence and Enforcing Lawful Dissemination Act ('Shield Act') is designed to prosecute those who release the names of sensitive human sources regardless of where the 'leakers are'. The planned legislation includes information that is both from national security and foreign affairs sources (ibid.: 20).

The difficulty with wikileaks, however, is whether to prosecute those who receive classified information, such as journalists. In the Ellsberg case discussed earlier, it was a crime for a government employee to give the classified material to the *New York Times*, but not for a publisher to publish it. This seems to have been the standard practice in similar cases in the USA since Ellsberg and is in line with

US Constitutional First Amendment provisions. However, if the US Department of Justice can prove that Assange and wikileaks encouraged or facilitated the leaks in some way, he could be prosecuted for espionage. It would not be surprising if further legislative measures are enacted in the USA to define criminal acts where a non-government employee encourages or conspires with a government employee to steal classified information. Such legislation may also usefully criminalize leaking of classified material, which is the result of external threats such as cyber-hackers. But further legislative reform will need to have sufficient safeguard provisions that define further the consequences of leaking classified information at different levels (e.g. potential or actual loss of life and leaking that may threaten defence forces engaged in war) and the burden should be on governments to prove defined damage in legislation is worthy of prosecution. In order to provide appropriate accountability, an independent authority with security clearances could advise the relevant government departments whether the leak of classified information is likely to have moderate to severe consequences for national security. The complication in this, as with all legislation involving crime enabled by technology, is the enforcement of it outside one jurisdiction. Though as in other multi-jurisdictional crimes enabled by technology, such as child abuse, effective joint investigations and harmonious legislation across the globe can make an impact.

Assange and wikileaks are different as this is the first case of the mass release of classified information via the internet. It represents a new method for an old practice, i.e. leaking of government information to influence politics and public opinion. This case shows in a dramatic way the potential damage to the effectiveness of intelligence agencies in liberal democracies by the push of one button on a computer. Moving beyond the personality cult of one person, wikileaks shows what is possible by a small organization run largely by volunteers. The consequences could even be more dire for intelligence operations if the public leaking was being orchestrated by a well-funded and technically capable organization. It challenges the culture of secrecy – the foundation of all intelligence activity – and like the counter-terrorism legislation discussed below underscores the widening gap between official and community attitudes on secrets and intelligence methods.

Intelligence legislation

Any assessment of the ethical and accountability dimensions of contemporary intelligence practice needs also to be understood from their legal perspectives. Legislation in some Western liberal democracies, such as the US and the Netherlands, has defined what their intelligence agencies *do* or are *allowed to do*. However, against the backdrop of 9/11, and a blurring of national security and policing intelligence, there has also been a growing suite of new or amended intelligence and counter-terrorism legislation, which is also changing the way intelligence is being practised. In particular, counter-terrorism efforts since 9/11 in Australia, Canada, New Zealand, the UK and the USA have included the amendment and enacting of new legislation to strengthen the operational, investigative and intelligence capabilities of national security and policing agencies. There has also been in the post-9/11 period a growing pace of legislative drafting in other areas such as organized crime, drugs trafficking and illegal immigration to provide agencies with more proactive intelligence capabilities to address these issues.

This section will provide an overview of some of the major legislative themes that have developed in these countries, which have had an impact on intelligence practice since 9/11. It is not possible, in this chapter, to provide a comprehensive list of all intelligence-related legislation since 9/11. The suite of relevant intelligence-related legislation in Australia, let alone the four other countries discussed in this book, is large and also dynamic. In addition to amendments to the Acts governing the operations of various specific intelligence agencies, there have also been significant legislative drafting and amendments that impact on the intelligence and investigative capabilities of agencies in a range of other related security sectors including: counter-terrorism, aviation, maritime, critical infrastructure, customs and immigration. Instead of trying to cover all legislation across Australia, Canada, New Zealand, the UK and the USA, I will focus here on a selection of intelligence and counter-terrorism Acts in each country. The objective will be to discuss thematically how these Acts have impacted broadly on intelligence practice in each country, rather than providing a detailed analysis of the merits or otherwise of every section in each Act. For each country, I have focused on counter-terrorism-related legislation as this has been where there has been the most profound change in new powers for intelligence collection and investigations since 9/11.

However, before getting into the discussion of specific legislation, it is useful to keep in mind that despite variations in different legislative responses between countries, there are two important questions that arise out of the discussion. They are important, as the answers to both hopefully will drive more effective and ethical intelligence practice in the future. The first is, what is the relationship between new 'powers' enacted in various legislation and effective intelligence practice? The second relates to a range of broader concerns raised about the privacy, human rights, judicial process and the constitutionality of new counter-terrorism and intelligence laws.

Australia, Canada and the USA

Turning to Australian legislation first, the Clarke Inquiry is illustrative of how a combination of factors, including a lack of understanding of new legislative provisions by policing agencies, and deficiencies in legislation, can impact on the quality of intelligence, evidentiary and judicial outcomes of counter-terrorism cases. The Clarke Inquiry into the case of Dr Mohamed Haneef by Justice John Clarke released its report in November 2008 (Clarke 2008). Justice Clarke was appointed in March 2008 by the new Australian (Labor) Government to review the operations of relevant Australian departments and agencies as they related to the arrest, detention, charging and prosecution of Dr Mohamed Haneef and the subsequent cancellation of his Australian visa. Dr Haneef was wrongly charged with providing support to a terrorist organization in the UK. No credible evidence was found to support the charge and the AFP declared he was no longer a person of interest shortly after the Clarke Inquiry commenced. In December 2010, Dr Haneef subsequently received a compensation payout and an apology from the Australian Government for his wrongful arrest and detention.

In his report, Justice Clarke identified deficiencies in the legislation used to charge Dr Haneef, including a lack of clarity within new provisions of the Crimes Act 1914 on the time limit that a suspect can be held in detention without charge. Justice Clarke also called for a review of provisions of Part 1C of the Crimes Act in relation to what constituted a terrorism offence (ibid.: vii). In addition to identi-fying deficiencies in the legislation, Justice Clarke's report was also important in highlighting other weaknesses in the investigation, including disagreement within and between agencies over whether there was sufficient evidence against Dr Haneef to charge him under relevant sections (s.102.7(1) and s.102.7(2)) of the Criminal Code Act 1995. For example, some of the information the ASIO had on Dr Haneef was in conflict with the AFP – the agency driving the investigation. Justice Clarke attributes some of the above weaknesses in the investigation and prosecution to this being the first case ever that some provisions in the legislation, such as Division 2 of Part 1C of the Crimes Act 1914 (which allows for the extended detention without charge of a suspect), had ever been used. Despite training in the new provisions, senior counter-terrorism investigators acknowledged during the inquiry that they still had limited knowledge of their counter-terrorism powers (ibid.: 90).

In Canada, there have been similar cases, where the application of new or amended legislative provisions has resulted in the construction of poor intelligence, evidentiary chains and the wrongful detention or charging of people. Lefebvre provides a good overview of Canada's current legal framework for intelligence, but in this chapter I will restrict discussion to one Act, that has increasingly chal-lenged the effectiveness of the intelligence community and raised concerns about individual rights (Lefebvre 2010). Since the 1980s, the Canadian Government has been using national security certificate provisions within its Immigration and Refugee Protection Act 2001 to detain and deport permanent residents and foreign nationals if they are assessed as having either violated human rights, been a member of an organized crime group, or be perceived to be a threat to national security (Department of Justice, Canada: 2001). Section 34 of the Act lists the grounds for detention and deportation, including engaging in terrorism or being a danger to the security of Canada. Sections 77–85 describe the security certificate process. In brief, the process for approving incarceration under the Act must be given by two ministers (usually the Minister for Public Safety and the Immigration Minister). In particular, Section 81 details the powers the government has to arrest and detain a person named in a security certificate, if the ministers have reasonable grounds to believe a person is a danger to national security, or is unlikely to appear at a proceeding for their deportation. The certificates are prepared by CSIS and reviewed by a Federal Court judge. At no stage is the suspect or their legal team allowed access to any of the information on which the adverse security finding has been made by CSIS.

In recent years, there has been a series of well-publicized cases, where the Canadian Government has used the 'security certificate process' against non-Canadian citizens, who were believed to have links to terrorist organizations. Well-known cases have included Mohamed Harkat (a foreign national) and Adil Charkaoui (a permanent resident), both of which have now been dismissed. In each case the evidence prepared by CSIS was dismissed by Federal Court judges as not credible. The Charkaoui case is broadly similar to the circumstances facing Mohamed Haneef in Australia. Both showed vulnerabilities in the relevant legislation, particularly the circumstances and length of time that someone could be detained without formal charging. These cases also demonstrated the intelligence agencies involved needed to build better evidentiary chains against suspects if the judicial fraternity and the public were going to continue to support the more stringent provisions in both Australian and Canadian legislation.

From the Canadian perspective, the Charkaoui case is particularly significant in understanding Canada's evolving response to counter-terrorism and intelligence legislation. In February 2007, the Supreme Court of Canada ruled that Sections 33 and 77–85 relevant to the issuing of security certificates were unconstitutional, and a violation also of Sections 7, 9 and 10 of the Canadian Charter of Rights and Freedoms. Charkaoui's security certificate was finally declared null and void in October 2009, ending his period of 21 months imprisonment without a trial and his movements being tracked.

The Charkaoui case and the Supreme Court ruling in his favour were also an important catalyst in the government's further amendment of the Act by parliament in February 2008. These amendments now allow the Justice Minister to appoint lawyers to act as a 'special advocate' to review a 'summary' of the evidence against the accused in addition to the assessing judge. These amendments do not mean, however, that the suspect or their legal representative is allowed any access to the material detailing the case against them if it contains sensitive material from intelligence sources. The amendments were not supported by the Canadian Bar Association. In their submission to parliament, they advocated for a full disclosure of all relevant information to the court pertaining to a security certificate, and argued for Canada's intelligence oversight agency – the Security Intelligence Review Committee (SIRC) – to play a role in certifying that all relevant sensitive information has been disclosed to the court (Canadian Bar Association 2007: 14–15). The Canadian Bar Association suggestion does not mean that SIRC, under its own oath of secrecy, would necessarily release any more information than the courts are currently able to do to the suspect. However, their independence from ministerial control may provide more information and assurance of accountability to the suspect, yet not jeopardize the release of sensitive security information.

Other themes and issues arising from new counter-terrorism and intelligence laws, including concerns over privacy, human rights and the judicial process were most starkly revealed during the Bush Administration. As noted earlier, the Bush Administration signified a general shift towards the use of executive powers, where White House legal staff wrote legal memos authorizing coercive interrogation or warrantless wiretaps on domestic and international communications, rather than necessarily relying on pre-existing legal instruments. The existing legal instrument was the FISA 1978, which was enacted, at least in part, to restrain some of the abuses of the Hoover period that resulted in illegal wiretapping of American citizens. It was also designed to provide judicial oversight of intelligence agencies seeking to intercept communications of suspects via a special court, the Foreign Intelligence Surveillance Court (FISC), which would issue warrants based on evidence brought before it by agencies that the interception of communications by these agencies was required. However, the US Patriot Act and subsequent White House legal memos dramatically changed this process. The legality of these memos, and the relevant provisions within the Patriot Act which allowed warrant-less wiretapping and a broader range of materials that could also be seized from an individual, obviously were questioned by some judges and advocacy groups such as the Electronic Privacy Information Center (EPIC) and the American Civil Liberties Union (ACLU). From a judicial perspective, a number of judges were working on the expressed concerns of how the NSA and Justice Department was using warrantless wiretaps.

In particular, during the Bush Administration, there were concerns by judges about the reliability and credibility of information agencies were submitting to the FISC if it was obtained using a warrantless wiretap. In December 2005, Judge James Robertson resigned from the FISC, with the media reporting that it was in protest at the warrantless wiretapping programme (Leonnig and Linzer 2005). Civil liberty activists and legal scholars also contested other mechanisms and legislative frameworks used by the Bush Administration including the use of National Security Letters (NSLs), a provision within the Patriot Act, and the Military Commissions Act (MCA) 2006. In discussions earlier on 'intelligence collection', we saw how in 2007 the US Justice Department Inspector General found that the FBI had improperly used NSL provisions in the Patriot Act to gather information on US citizens.

The Inspector General's first report in 2007 reported misuse of NSL provisions from 2003 to 2005, where the FBI routinely claimed false terrorism emergencies in order to illegally collect the phone records of US citizens. The NSLs allow US intelligence agencies to get information and compliance from private institutions, such as banks and internet service providers, about their customers. However, the FBI was circumventing its own internal guidelines and the requirements of the Electronic Communications Privacy Act (ECPA) by issuing 'exigent letters' or emergency letters to communications companies to secure records without issuing a follow-up NSL as required by the Act. The exigent letter process allows the FBI to collect records when there is a terrorism emergency, but subsequent reviews by the Justice Department Inspector General suggest that from 2003 to 2007 the FBI was using exigent letters when the matter was not necessarily urgent and did not provide the accompanying subpoena or NSL.

In some cases, it was found that the FBI issued NSLs after the fact as an attempt to legitimize the use of exigent letters. The Inspector General has completed three reviews of the FBI's use of exigent letters – the last released in January 2010. In the final review, the Justice Department Inspector General still found practices that violated FBI guidelines, and EPCA statutes, though the agency declared the use of exigent letters had ended in 2007 (Office of the Inspector General 2010: 288).

Another US example where issues of judicial process and human rights have impacted on how intelligence has been practised in recent years was the passage of the MCA. The MCA was designed to authorize trial by military commission for violations of the law of war and for other purposes. Under the MCA, the President, with the approval of Congress, could among other things, indefinitely hold people without charge, and put people on trial based on hearsay evidence. The MCA also authorized trials that can sentence people to death based on testimony derived from torture, and suspend habeas corpus or their constitutional right to be brought before the court to determine whether the government has the right to continue to detain them. On 20 October 2006, the US Government used the MCA to remove detainees from the jurisdiction of the US District Court in Washington, and at the beginning of February 2007 government lawyers confirmed that the MCA applied to US citizens also. Unsurprisingly, there was significant judicial and media opposition to this new Act. At the time of its passing in October 2006, MSNBC political commentator Keith Olbermann issued a brutal attack against the Bush Administration. During his television broadcast, Olbermann said that by accepting this law:

> The nation has accepted that to fight terrorists, the US government must become just a little bit like the terrorists . . . But the ultimate threat to the nation is not terrorists it is George W. Bush himself . . . We have a long and painful history of ignoring the prophecy attributed to Benjamin Franklin that those who would give up essential liberty to purchase a little temporary safety, deserve neither liberty nor safety.
>
> (Olbermann 2006)

In January 2009, the new Obama Administration, as noted above, revoked earlier executive orders and laws relating to interrogation enacted by its predecessor and ordered the closure of Guantánamo Bay. The plan was to close the prison by January 2010 and move detainees to an empty maximum security facility in Thomson, Illinois. But Guantánamo Bay remains open due partly to resistance by some Congress members for them to be transferred to Illinois based on security concerns. There is also a lack of 'meeting of the minds' between the White House and Congress on how to improve legislation to hold suspects without trial. In January 2010, the ACLU released a 'progress report' called *America Unrestored* where it assessed the Obama Administration's efforts in restoring civil liberties across a range of fronts, including in the national security area. The report said, despite the planned closure of Guantánamo Bay, and the introduction of the National Defense Authorisation Act in October 2009, the holding of individuals without charge or trial was continuing, and the Administration still endorsed extraordinary renditions providing that they did not result in torture (ACLU 2010).

The political and operational urgency of countering terrorism has also provided, as seen in the Haneef case discussed above, policing and security agencies with extended powers to question and detain and to restrict the movement of suspects in order to prevent terrorist attacks. Other measures such as questioning without charge have also assisted in providing agencies with greater opportunities to collect intelligence. Yet many of these measures have become enacted in laws that were swiftly drafted (e.g. the Australian Anti-Terrorism Act (No. 1) 2005), and this has created, in some cases, difficulties in their application or political pressures on agencies to use them.

Other identified issues have been a wider definition in many criminal codes of what constitutes a terrorism offence, which may make the collection of intelligence and evidence more difficult rather than easier. For example, in New Zealand, the Terrorism Suppression Act 2002 has been criticized by lawyers and civil liberty groups for defining what constitutes a terrorist offence too broadly, and similar criticisms have arisen in other countries with their legislation. The innate tension between intelligence gathering and evidence preparation for judicial processes has also been underscored with the prosecution of cases using new anti-terrorism laws. Many of the Canadian security certificate cases discussed above have been dismissed due to weak evidence, which in turn has relied on poor or insufficient intelligence. Many of the new counter-terrorism laws also underscore the tension between what is admissible as evidence, and what cannot be revealed publicly in court due to national security considerations. The interaction between intelligence and the judicial process is likely to remain problematic in the future as these anti-terrorism laws are applied.

The Canadian Government's reliance on immigration law in counter-terrorism cases not only raises concerns about adequate and admissible evidence, but also whether such legislation is the most appropriate way to detain people related to counter-terrorism offences. The two cases discussed above demonstrate the risks involved in the interaction of intelligence with legislation and the judicial process. The quashed Harkat and Charkaoui cases show that, as much as is practically possible, both intelligence agencies and the criminal justice system need to work together more collaboratively than in the past to build legislation that can maintain community support and avoid wasting intelligence resources on cases that will never be strong enough.

Some of the issues with the application of new counter-terrorism and intelligence legislation identified above, however, do not mean that problems are endemic with all legislation. It is appropriate for the media, judiciary and human rights groups to raise legitimate concerns about how policing and national security intelligence agencies are using such legislation, particularly where its application leads to the unlawful detention and charging of a suspect. However, a truly informed debate about the legislation must also include discussion about the successes countries are having in using new provisions under the various Acts rather than starting from the premise that such legislation will always be undemocratic or an invasion of human rights.

In Australia, for example, a multi-jurisdictional counter-terrorism operation (Operation Pendennis) used new provisions in the Criminal Code and the Anti-Terrorism Act 2004 to arrest 18 and later convict five men for conspiring to do an act in preparation for a terrorist act. In 2006, new counter-terrorism laws, such as the Prevention of Terrorism Act 2005, helped UK police and security services prevent a trans-Atlantic airplane bombing plot in that country, which would have also involved attacks in the USA and Canada. Similarly, in February 2009, Mohammad Khawaja was the first person convicted under Canada's new Anti-Terrorism Laws (Bill C-36) and provisions of the Criminal Code. The operational sensitivity of these cases prevents the community having a full understanding of the 'successes' that intelligence and policing agencies have had using enhanced legislation provisions since 9/11. If success is publicized, in the counter-terrorism environment this is likely to occur only in a sanitized form, and many details cannot be released even after successful prosecution of offenders. In the absence of intelligence and policing agencies being able to provide detailed comment, it is not surprising, therefore, that this vacuum will be filled by others such as the media, who sometimes inaccurately report on how agencies apply these laws to their operations, rather than educating the community of how they can work effectively. These examples of successful outcomes in such complex investigations demonstrate that legislative measures are required that allow police and national security intelligence agencies to prevent devastating acts of terror before they occur. The broadened definitions of terrorism offences, the control, questioning and detention orders detailed in many of the Acts discussed in this chapter are preventative, while also allowing intelligence to be collected to better understand the threat from terrorism.

The sophistication, secrecy and frequently mutating operational planning of many terrorists' plots require specialized intelligence and investigative provisions supported by effective but accountable legislative instruments. The pre-charge detention of suspects provisions in various Acts has in particular received a lot of public and media attention where they have been enacted. The time period, however, that a suspect can be held without charge has been explicitly prescribed in the counter-terrorism legislation discussed. Additionally, in many new legislative instruments, specific 'sunset clauses' have been included to review these measures as is appropriate in liberal democracies. While control and detention orders in particular, have obvious potential human rights, judicial and privacy concerns, McDonald makes a good point in suggesting that pre-trial detention in general has a much more significant impact than control and detention orders. For instance, in Australia he cites that about 20 per cent of cases in higher courts take more than a year to be completed and 7 per cent take more than two years. Currently 20 per cent of people in Australian prisons are on remand (2007: 114–115). The use of control and detention orders will always need to balance the rights of the accused against the right of the state to protect its citizens against politically motivated violence. These various new enhanced intelligence collection, detention and control powers articulated in counter-terrorism legislation are not innately unlawful in the context of the United Nations International Covenant on Civil and Political Rights, which gives states the rights to defend and protect their existence, values and people.

Though as discussed earlier, in the Haneef case, we can never lose sight of the civil liberty and judicial concerns about this suite of new counter-terrorism legislation. Significant concerns remain about the kind of new and wider offences people can be charged with including the extent to which association with terrorists is an offence. In addition to wider definitions of terrorism, a number of related offences, including those linked to preparatory acts and organizational offences, continue to concern civil liberty, human rights and judicial groups. More broadly, there are concerns within the community about the potential infringement of privacy and human rights of ordinary citizens based on increased surveillance and other powers under such legislation.

The classic case which demonstrates these concerns in the USA has been amendments made under the Bush Administration to the FISA. As noted in earlier discussion, the US Patriot Act, post 9/11, broadened powers of intelligence agencies by amending key provisions of the FISA. This signalled a more proactive approach to intelligence including allowing multi-roving wire-taps (Section 206, Patriot Act), and a wider scope of materials and records that could be seized (Section 215, Patriot Act). During the Bush Administration, the FISC was not always consulted before the FBI used wiretaps and searches in counter-terror cases. Civil rights groups argue information has been collected on innocent US citizens without court approval and that the above enhanced measures undermine Constitutional rights especially the Fourth Amendment. The enhanced measures in the FISA were set to expire in February 2010, and two new bills are currently before Congress: a Senate-sponsored bill to extend current provisions and a House one to amend them.

Added to civil liberty and privacy concerns, there have also been challenges for the security, police and prosecutions in making sufficient links between wider, and in some cases more vague offences, described in new legislation and ensuring effective judicial process and protection of civil liberties. Ensuring intelligence agencies have the appropriate tools provided in part through legislation, but not sacrificing fundamental civil liberties, will continue to be a struggle for governments. Defending human rights, appropriate judicial process and national security, however, should all be pursued as equally important objectives not as a zero-sum game.

From a legislative perspective, what is required is greater accountability and oversight of the newer counter-terrorism and organized crime legislative frameworks that policing and national security and intelligence agencies are now working within. We have seen in each country the willingness of the courts to become more involved in the reviewing of legislation as cases are presented to them. The monitoring and reform of terrorism and intelligence-related legislation, however, cannot be left to the courts alone. Complex organized crime and terrorism cases are long, and a more proactive, independent and ongoing approach to legislative review is required. In the UK, the government has appointed an independent reviewer, Lord Carlile, to provide ongoing monitoring of counter-terrorism legislation (the Terrorism Act 2006 and the Prevention of Terrorism Act 2005).

Reports provided by Lord Carlile have been useful in raising reform of legislation, but his work, rather than being self-generated or linked to broader parliamentary committee requirements, seems to be more driven by the Home Secretary's needs. He would have more independence also if he had statutory authority and adequate resources to investigate concerns about legislation based on his own self-generated taskings. The Australian Government is currently moving in this same direction in appointing an independent judicial reviewer of its counter-terrorism legislation, though at the time of writing no official has been appointed.

Additionally, the IRTPA in the USA also included several new provisions for reviewing both the actions and legislation implemented by the executive and used by intelligence agencies in counter-terrorism. Section 1061 details the establishment of an independent agency, the Privacy and Civil Liberties Oversight Board, which has the right to review laws, regulations and policies of the executive and intelligence agencies to protect the nation against terrorism. A key function of the Board is to ensure civil liberty and privacy is considered in the development of laws and policies. The Board must issue two reports a year to the President and Congress. The Act gives the Board the power to subpoena information or to interview people from intelligence agencies, but this must be done with the agreement of the US Attorney General. This provision seems to be a weakness in this new legislative oversight mechanism (ODNI 2009b: 168–171). Its effectiveness remains uncertain, and at the time of writing, the US Administration still had not appointed members of the Board.

While it seems improvements can be made by some of the new legislative review mechanisms discussed in the last two paragraphs, the responsibility for evaluating how counter-terrorism and organized crime legislation is applied by policing and intelligence agencies should not just be left to the courts or independent judicial review bodies. Overseeing privacy, human rights as well as monitoring the extent that these laws promote effective pro-active intelligence practice must also rest with parliamentary and other specialized intelligence oversight mechanisms which we will discuss in the last section.

Accountability and oversight mechanisms

In this final section, I provide an overview on both national security and policing accountability mechanisms for Australia, Canada, New Zealand, the UK and the USA. It is not possible to list or describe all of them for each country. While the number of national security intelligence agencies in each country is relatively small, the same could not be said for policing agencies. In all these countries, with perhaps the exception of New Zealand and Australia, the number of local, state and national policing agencies would make it impossible to describe comprehensively all their accountability and oversight mechanisms. Additionally, with nearly 18,000 law enforcement agencies in the USA, any discussion of accountability and oversight institutions would be a multi-volume enterprise just for the USA. Hence this discussion is not meant to be all-encompassing, and readers interested in a deeper exposure to the various mechanisms in each country should consult the growing sources on them (e.g. Gill 2007; Johnson 2009: 343–360; Baldino 2010).

Organizational websites are also good sources for links to the accountability mechanisms governing specific agencies. Instead, I have restricted discussion to a thematic treatment of only the key *national* accountability and oversight mechanisms impacting on national security and policing intelligence practice in these countries. For ease of discussion, key accountability and oversight mechanisms will be grouped using the following classifiers: *internal – ministerial* and *parliamentary –* and *external*.

Internal

Effective intelligence practice *within agencies* obviously must come from managerial oversight. This point was underscored in Chapter 6 in comments made in the 9/11 Commission Report about the managerial oversight of the CIA by its director George Tenet leading up to 9/11. In some agencies, internal accountability also includes a designated senior officer responsible for monitoring various activities related to intelligence. For example, within the CIA, an independent Ombudsman has been appointed to deal with complaints about politicization, and in the DHS there is an internal Inspector General to examine all aspects of this department's function including intelligence. These measures can be useful adjuncts to managerial oversight, but full accountability must also include mechanisms that are independent from the agency's internal review processes.

Ministerial

Ministerial or executive oversight is the next obvious level of accountability. Ultimately a minister or similarly appointed cabinet executive is responsible for oversight of the key national policing and national security intelligence agencies in Australia, Canada, New Zealand, the UK and the USA. Ministers are responsible to the parliament for all aspects of their intelligence agencies' activities, including the fiscal and legal aspects of their operations. Ministers also generally have particular legislative responsibilities in authorizing the issuing of warrants to intercept communications, and approve a range of specialized covert activities. But ministerial oversight has also involved setting priorities for intelligence agencies they are responsible for. This kind of oversight can vary widely depending on the agency. It can be informal and general, such as the UK Home Secretary's strategic policing priorities, or formally dictated in the agency's relevant legislation. For example, both Section 37 of the AFP Act 1979, and Section 6 the CSIS Act 1984 set out specific ministerial directions for these agencies.

Another component of ministerial oversight that has developed is the creation of independent executive oversight positions that assist the relevant minister in ensuring ministerial directions and legal requirements are being followed within an agency. These measures enhance ministerial oversight by adding another layer of checks and balances, and can also promote confidence that the 'agency is not being politically misused' (Gill and Phythian 2006: 158). In the USA, the Department of Justice Office of Inspector General has an independent investigative and auditing role for justice portfolio agencies including the FBI, the Drug Enforcement Agency (DEA) and Federal Bureau of Prisons. Similarly in Canada, the Inspector General of CSIS monitors this agency's compliance with operational policies and issues a certificate indicating its degree of satisfaction with the Director of CSIS' annual operational report. The Inspector General of CSIS is an independent internal review body located within the Ministry of Public Safety. The Inspector General issues its report to SIRC, which as noted earlier, is an independent external review body of CSIS reporting to parliament. The Inspector General of CSIS will conduct specific reviews of CSIS activities as directed by SIRC. Similarly in Australia and New Zealand, there are also Inspector Generals of intelligence and security. In Australia, the IGIS plays a role in enhancing ministerial oversight of the six principal Australian intelligence agencies, whereas in New Zealand the Inspector General has oversight just for NZSIS. The NZ Inspector General, unlike their equivalent in Australia, must also have been a judge.

In contrast to SIRC, however, the IGIS Act gives the Inspector General (in Australia), additional powers to initiate independent inquiries directly rather than via an internal intermediary such as the Inspector General of CSIS. Enquiries can be initiated at any time and not necessarily retrospective as is the case with SIRC inquiries.

Parliamentary

Parliamentary oversight of intelligence functions within policing and national security agencies has traditionally been the mainstay of oversight in liberal democratic countries. From one perspective, the range of parliamentary committees provides a wider oversight on crucial issues such as budgeting and operational effectiveness – to the extent that the latter can be revealed to such committees. In some countries such as the USA, parliamentary committees have been powerful counter-weights to executive oversight of the intelligence community. The two US Congressional committees on intelligence (the House Permanent Select Committee and the Senate Select Committee) not only have wider oversight over legislative and the effectiveness of the intelligence community than their counterparts in other countries, they also have the power to authorize the appropriation and distribution of agency budgets.

In contrast, in the UK the Intelligence and Security Committee (ISC) is appointed by and reports to the Prime Minister rather than parliament directly, which raises perceptions in some minds about the independence of the committee from the government. Additionally, the ISC only sees the single intelligence account, hence does not have anywhere near the budgetary oversight of the US congressional committees. In Australia, New Zealand and Canada there are also parliamentary committees for intelligence and/or security, which oversee the operations and expenditure or various intelligence agencies. But they do not have the same oversight authority as their US counterparts, or full access to sensitive information about operational matters. There are also in some countries policing and judicial committees that review the performance of particular agencies such as the Parliamentary Joint Committee on the AFP and ACC in Australia, and in the US congressional judiciary committees, which potentially can oversee aspects of intelligence practice within law enforcement agencies.

External

Under this heading, we could include a range of stand-alone independent organizations and ad hoc commissions which have oversight functions. Some of these have been established in national security and policing agencies of these countries over the past two decades. These statutory independent organizations and ad hoc inquiries have been headed by a mixture of senior judicial, civil servants or retired politicians. For example, the 9/11 Commission was headed by Thomas Kean and Lee Hamilton. Kean was a former governor of New Jersey and Hamilton was a Congressman. The UK Butler Inquiry and the current Iraq Inquiry are chaired by career civil servants. And as discussed earlier, there have been a few well-publicized inquiries into aspects of intelligence practice in policing and national security agencies chaired by current or former members of the judiciary. The O'Connor Commission (Canada), the Clarke Inquiry (Australia) and the Hutton Inquiry (UK) are good examples of ad hoc inquiries run by appointed members of the judiciary.

On a more permanent basis, there are several external accountability and oversight organizations that have developed in each country. Many of these have more specialized roles in that they focus on oversight of only one agency, or of one or two issues or functions across a few agencies. Many also have developed from specific counter-terrorism or intelligence legislation. For example, the Regulation of Investigatory Powers Act 2000 in the UK established two independent commissioners – one responsible for oversight of the interception of communications for the intelligence agencies and the other for a tribunal to examine complaints against these agencies. Similarly, in New Zealand there is a Commissioner of Security Warrants involved in issuing interception warrants. In the UK, a Chief Surveillance Commissioner has been established to oversee all covert surveillance (not telephone interception) of law enforcement and local authority agencies. In Canada, there is also an independent commissioner for overseeing the activities of its sigint agency – the Communications Security Establishment (CSE). All of these posts require that the incumbent commissioner or head has been a senior member of the judiciary.

There is also an extensive range of external independent bodies that deal with aspects of policing practice across Australia, Canada, New Zealand, the USA and the UK. Again there are too many to describe in detail, but they deal with all manner of policing practice, including public complaints, corruption, and professional standards. The increasing complexity of the operational environment in policing will mean that the work some oversight agencies do in monitoring professional standards or privacy will also intersect more frequently with other institutions and mechanisms, which are focused on reviewing intelligence practice such as ombudsmen, inspectors general, warrant and surveillance review bodies. As public concerns grow over the use of more proactive intelligence collection strategies (increasingly now enshrined in counter-terrorism and organized crime legislation), the privacy, professional standards and other specialized intelligence oversight organizations mentioned earlier will need to work more closely to monitor unethical and illegal policing intelligence practices.

In summary, oversight and accountability of intelligence practice in national security and policing contexts occur on a series of levels: internal, ministerial, parliamentary and external. In the liberal democracies that I have been discussing in this book, it is clear that a multi-level response to intelligence accountability has developed. In all these countries, the minister and parliament are seen as the principal overseers of intelligence activity, though additional layers of checks and balances are required, whether they evolved or were implemented by design. The key reason why a multi-level response to accountability is necessary is that ministers and even parliamentary committees have their own agendas, which can impact on the level and quality of scrutiny provided. For example, the US Senate Select Committee and the House Permanent Select Committee on Intelligence have powerful oversight of all aspects of the US intelligence community and are well staffed compared to all other parliamentary committees discussed earlier. Yet despite being so influential, both came in for criticism in the 9/11 Commission Report for poor oversight, and suggestions that improving intelligence oversight has been hampered by partisan bickering (Johnson 2009: 355). Similarly in the UK, Gill has criticized the ISC for being to some extent the captive of the Whitehall political machinery for the management of the security intelligence community rather than its overseer (Gill 2007: 32).

The various inspectors general (e.g. the IGIS and SIRC), particularly those who are independent of the minister, have been effective in identifying deficiencies within agencies including inappropriate application of interception legislation and examining whether agencies assessments have become politicized. However, there are variations between agencies such as IGIS (Australia) and the SIRC, which impact on the kind of reviews they can do and how often. As noted earlier, unlike IGIS, the SIRC can only do retrospective reviews of CSIS, and access to sensitive material is via the Inspector General of CSIS rather than directly via its own channels.

The plethora of specialized external accountability organizations, particularly judicial commissions overseeing interception and surveillance, adds another layer of checks and balances. In addition to their obvious role of ensuring the covert intrusion on people's lives is required and lawful, agencies such as the UK Surveillance Commissioner have taken on important educative roles by publishing standards, guidelines and codes of conduct for policing agencies. This has also assisted in increasing the cases where a trial judge will accept evidence which has been derived by covert surveillance.

The multi-level approach to accountability of intelligence in Australia, Canada, New Zealand, the UK and the USA has ensured no one agency in a democratic system has sole responsibility for overseeing intelligence activities. Such a dispersal of 'authority' is a healthy attribute within democracies. However, the disparate number of actors and agencies involved has also led to a fragmented accountability and oversight of intelligence agencies, particularly in the USA and UK. In the USA, particularly at the executive level, there are too many Inspectors General looking at individual intelligence agencies. As noted earlier, there is an Inspector General for the FBI and another for the DHS. While each agency needs their own oversight area, perhaps an Inspector General for the entire US intelligence community working under the DNI would provide a more coherent review of intelligence activity across the government rather than 'agency snapshots' of good or poor performance. This approach might give the executive a more streamlined and independent review of intelligence agencies; though it is likely that the congressional committees would see it as a new competitor. There is also fragmentation in congressional oversight of intelligence with the intelligence, judiciary and homeland security committees all examining aspects of intelligence practice.

Similarly, in the UK, oversight is fragmented across different commissions, tribunals and legislation. Gill provides a clear example of this fragmentation in some of the judicial oversight functions of intelligence in the UK. Currently judicial commissioners review after the warrants have been issued by ministers for communications interceptions and other covert activity, yet public complaints go to an Investigatory Powers Tribunal unless it relates to a warrant, in which case, it is passed to the commissioner (Gill 2007: 29).

The growth in oversight institutions therefore has not been exclusively by design. Rather, in many cases it would more accurate to describe it as an organic development, as political or legislative reform has resulted in new oversight commissions, tribunals, inspectors general and committees being added as required. This can create barriers and potential duplication between the functions of various oversight agencies. The development of further legislative responses to terrorism and organized crime over the past decade and the increasing complexity of the security environment may result in the creation of further oversight entities rather than a rationalization of what currently exists. We have seen evidence of this possible trend recently with the development of an independent reviewer of counterterrorism legislation in the UK, and a similar function being planned in Australia.

The concern is that adding to current oversight organizations, all of which are generally small resourced outfits, may result in an overly bureaucratic structure that delivers less effective oversight. While it is likely that there will be a need in the future for further ad hoc inquiries into 'intelligence failures', governments should consider reviewing what oversight mechanisms currently exist, and assess whether any rationalizing of current capabilities is possible rather than creating an additional agency. This would simplify the reporting arrangements for intelligence agencies and may result in better-resourced and effective oversight agencies. In Australia, the government is moving in this direction in considering expanding the mandate of the IGIS to conduct certain inquiries into a broader range of federal government agencies as they relate to intelligence and security issues. This could mean that the IGIS in the future will examine the intelligence functions and activities of federal law enforcement agencies such as the AFP and ACC, both of which are part of the current government's expanded view of Australia's national intelligence community. An expansion of the IGIS' mandate, which includes the ability to conduct formal inquiries, would also reduce the need for expensive ad hoc judicial commissions. In summary, while it is difficult to generalize, the accountability mechanisms that exist in Australia, Canada, New Zealand, the UK and the USA are each confronted with similar challenges.

The key challenge is to balance effective oversight while avoiding micro-managing intelligence agencies. The public and political concern about the invasiveness of more proactive intelligence collection methods needs to be addressed effectively, but in a way that does not compromise sensitive operational methodologies or sources. This will not be easy at a time, where intelligence has become much more of a public commodity to be discussed openly like any other public policy area. A second challenge will be for governments to ensure that oversight and accountability mechanisms do not just focus on expenditure and propriety, but also can assist government more proactively in identifying vulner-abilities in certain areas of intelligence practice such as the politicization of intelligence or issues relating to collection and analysis.

The flurry of inquiries post 9/11 and the WMD in Iraq matter should be powerful reminders that accountability mechanisms need not only to be effective, but also more proactive in picking up earlier where support and intervention may be required in our intelligence agencies. Independent oversight agencies such as the IGIS, the SIRC or the ISC are in a good position to develop risk management and early warning systems to support early intervention. Finally, while all publicly funded agencies are at risk of becoming politicized, the various oversight layers discussed above (particularly parliamentary and external agencies), do have a responsibility in promoting a normative culture about the independence of intelli-gence agencies much like the independence of central banks that set monetary policy.

Conclusion

The significant events of 9/11 and the US-led invasion of Iraq have underlined in a way, perhaps more dramatically than ever before, how ethical, legislative and accountability issues both influence and determine the effectiveness of intelligence practice. Intelligence practice is now more than ever just as much a public policy commodity as any other policy in the community, so these questions of what is ethical intelligence practice will continue to become part of the public discourse. Such greater public scrutiny might periodically be uncomfortable for some working in intelligence agencies. For the most part, however, the current discourse of what is ethical, legal and accountable intelligence is useful for both practitioners and academics. For practitioners, in addition to charting the legislative boundaries of practice, it also provides some 'barometric' measure of public consent and trust the community has in those involved in intelligence. Many of the ethical problems discussed in this chapter also provide practitioners with good case studies with which to reflect on their own practice and whether it is ethical.

For academics, the debates in all three areas (ethics, legislation and oversight) help identify research areas that can hopefully assist in the improvement of ethical intelligence practice. As can be seen from earlier discussions, there are no easy answers to what constitutes ethical intelligence practice. We have seen in this chapter that 'legal intelligence practice' does not always equate with 'ethical practice'. The civil liberties, privacy and humane treatment of individuals must be the rights of all human beings. But in the increasingly complex security environment in which intelligence agencies operate, these rights must somehow be reconciled against the even more fundamental human right of individual and nations to collective security. Reconciling these will be difficult, but how this is done will define also how intelligence is viewed as well as contributing to debates about whether intelligence can become a 'discipline of knowledge' in its own right. In the next chapter, I explore further this notion of intelligence being a discipline by focusing on how developments across 'intelligence analysis' can contribute to a broader understanding of what 'an intelligence discipline' may look like.

8 Analytical innovations

Introduction

The preceding chapter provided a thematic overview of some of the current ethical and legislative issues, impacting on how intelligence is being both practised and perceived by the community. The remaining chapters in Part III, 'Analytical innovations', 'Intelligence education and professionalism' and 'Research and theory building', also highlight a number of issues and challenges that require further reflection by academics and practitioners. I argue that together with the need to understand the ethical boundaries of intelligence practice, these other issues will also be critical in defining what a future 'discipline of intelligence' may look like. Arguably nowhere are the challenges more fundamental to progressing a 'discipline of intelligence' than improving the application of analysis and analytical techniques across different contexts and decision-making processes. Much has been said already about the importance of good collection, however, the heart of the intelligence endeavour will always be analysis. Analysis is the set of *methodologies* and *cognitive processes* that 'fuels' everything else in intelligence practice. The extent to which, in the future, intelligence is seen as something of value to decision-makers will depend not only on how analysis is understood, methodologically and in a cognitive sense, but also how scholars and practitioners can identify innovations from within and outside of 'the intelligence field' that develop analytical capabilities further.

In this chapter, I address two central issues. First, I define contemporary analysis in terms of some of the key methodological and cognitive approaches that have underpinned it. I argue that much of what defines current 'analytical approaches' is derived from a range of other fields such as international relations, political science, strategic studies, psychology, social research theories, criminology, business and engineering studies. While this may be stating the obvious, it is the nature of the inter-disciplinary links, between other fields and intelligence, that requires more comprehensive examination and understanding than has been the case to date. If practitioners are to more effectively reap the rewards that other fields bring to intelligence analysis, then more attention and research are required to assess how analytical capabilities are improved by adopting perspectives from other fields (see Chapter 10).

Second, this chapter will examine how the inter-disciplinary nature of intelligence is producing innovative approaches to analysis. On the second point, I will focus on two broad areas: *data mining and analytics* and *sense making and early warning analysis* as examples of recent innovations in analysis. Both areas are interesting as they demonstrate attempts to fuse cognitive and technological approaches to analysis. Each example also demonstrates well the increasing multi-disciplinary public and private collaborative approach to analytical innovation. The chapter concludes with a brief discussion on how both analytical innovations might also be used in non-traditional intelligence practice areas such as those discussed in Chapter 2.

Intelligence analysis: cognitive and methodological dimensions

Before discussing the cognitive and methodological dimensions of analysis, it is logical to step back at this point and ask the obvious question: what is 'analysis' in the intelligence context? Again, there are no straightforward answers to this question. Analysis like intelligence itself is context-driven, based on where it is practised and also what levels of decision-making it supports. What 'crime analysis' in the policing context is clearly results in different decision-making outcomes from the analysis of nuclear proliferation in rogue states in the national security context. Much depends on the kind of data and information being examined – and to some extent what is done with it. For example, in some contexts, the mere collation of a data set might be considered analysis, while in others this would be described as collation of data at best. In the national security context, there is a range of definitions for analysis. Clark has defined it as 'the stage in the intelligence cycle, where information is subjected to systematic examination in order to identify meaning and derive conclusions' (2007: 173). In the policing analysis context, Cope has defined analysis:

> in terms of its techniques and the sort of intelligence products generated from it at different levels of decision-making. At the tactical level analysis aims to maximise the impact of enforcement by reviewing current crime problems and prolific offenders to inform investigations and operations. At the strategic level, analysis identifies longer-term crime problems and future trends to provide management with an understanding of the scope and dimension of criminal activity in order to assist with local policy development and planning.
> (2003: 345)

There is little benefit here endlessly listing different takes on analysis in different contexts. The more relevant point is to state what is commonly meant by analysis regardless of the context or the type of information used. In my view, analysis is both a cognitive and methodological approach to processing and evaluating information – some of which is privileged – in order to produce an assessment for a decision-maker about the security environment. This definition is sufficiently vague that it can be applied in different intelligence contexts. In the following two sections I will discuss the principal cognitive and methodological approaches that have defined contemporary analysis in the policing and national security contexts.

Analysis as a cognitive process

Leaving aside the neurological or neuro-transmission dimensions, analysis is a *cognitive process* and it is this process which gives us the ability to reason. While other animals, such as apes, have intelligence, we are the only animal that can draw conclusions on the basis of observable facts. Reasoning therefore allows us to draw conclusions on the strengths of different reasons, which themselves may be facts, beliefs or observations. The study of reasoning is generally referred to as logic, and its core components – inductive and deductive reasoning, evaluating arguments and inferences – are commonly taught in most introductory intelligence courses. Another quality, which humans possess, is reflection, which means giving deep and focused thought to a problem, and evaluating all the evidence and consequences surrounding a problem or issue. Both critical thinking and problem solving are also core skill sets for intelligence analysts and are examples of reflective thinking (Butterworth and Thwaites 2005: 4–5). There is now a growing number of books available on problem solving and critical thinking, both in a general sense and as applied to intelligence (e.g. Fisher 2001; Butterworth and Thwaites 2005; Moore 2007).

Another important aspect of analysis as a cognitive process is where subconscious biases or mindsets by an individual or group prevent a full reflection of all available possible probabilities and conclusions, which can lead to faulty analysis and assessments. Cognitive biases are mental errors which are a normal part of human reasoning. Psychologists such as Tversky and Kahneman have examined cognitive biases or heuristic biases that impact on how people make judgements in experimental conditions. They concluded that people who were given incomplete or ambiguous information employed heuristic biases (such as representativeness, and anchoring and adjustment) in their thinking, which led to systematic and predictive errors in making judgements under uncertainty. An important aspect of this research is that Tversky and Kahneman also found that people make judgements or predictions on the information provided to them based on the 'favourableness' of the description of the information. And their predictions were insensitive to the reliability of the evidence and to the expected accuracy of the prediction (Tversky and Kahneman 1974: 1126). Such conclusions are relevant also in understanding the cognitive decision-making processes analysts use to estimate the probability of certain potential outcomes, and the impact biases can have on the assessments made.

There are a number of historical cases that have been well documented over the years such as Pearl Harbor, the Cuban Missile Crisis, the Yom Kippur War and Iraq's invasion of Kuwait, where cognitive bias has resulted in less optimal analysis. More recently, as seen in earlier chapters, estimations of WMD in Iraq produced inaccurate assessments partly or fully due to cognitive biases. Many of these historical case studies have now been declassified from the archives, and have subsequently become useful exercises for studies in intelligence classes on how such bias can impact on analysis. While more recently the events leading up to 9/11 and national intelligence estimates about WMD in Iraq may have more currency for analysts, I am still very fond of teaching students about cognitive biases using the Cuban Missile Crisis of 1962. There are still great lessons for analysts to learn from this period, even if they were not born at that time.

The important point about cognitive biases at the individual or agency level is that they cannot of course be surgically removed from the analyst's brain, but rather they need, as Heuer argues, to be made more explicit in the analytical process (Heuer 1999). The point is to manage rather than try to expunge them like some evil spirit from the body. This is a central point made by Richards Heuer, a former senior CIA officer, in his influential work, *Psychology of Intelligence Analysis* (ibid.). Heuer and his colleagues at the CIA also developed and adapted a number of analytical tools called *alternative analysis tools* to help analysts make their biases and cognitive errors more explicit, and to look for other conclusions or possible explanations for events and issues in their analysis. These tools were mainly practised in the CIA's Directorate of Intelligence and at the Sherman Kent School of Analysis. There are several tools now available, including older ones used in earlier contexts such as the military during the Cold War, for example, *red cell analysis* and *devil's advocacy*, and others such as *high impact/low probability* and *competing hypotheses* developed later in the CIA. Heuer (1999) and others (e.g. George 2004; Clark 2004; Heuer and Pherson 2010) have provided explanations of many of these techniques. However, I will briefly explain red cell analysis, competing hypotheses and high impact/low probability.

Red cell analysis involves analysts trying to 'get in the minds of adversaries' to better assess their motivations and the possible scenarios under which they could be planning an attack against our interests. Competing hypotheses is an analytical technique, which is useful in situations where the available intelligence may potentially support different possible explanations for what is happening in the security environment. It provides analysts with a systematic approach to evaluating all the evidence against different hypotheses rather than rushing to the one hypothesis that automatically 'feels right' based on the analyst's predisposed views on the situation. Lastly, high impact/low probability is a tool that can be applied by analysts, who are assessing what the 'signposts' might be for a threat occurring which has a very low probability but would have a catastrophic impact. Or, in Heuer and Pherson's words, the 'focus is not on if something will happen, but to take it as a given that an event could happen that could have a major and unanticipated impact' (2010: 236).

In our discussions of biosecurity in Chapter 2, there is a number of potential scenarios – not just restricted to the classical anthrax scare – where the combination of using an analytical tool such as high impact/low probability and epidemiological modelling can provide more informed assessments. The high impact/low probability tool could help an analyst better understand what 'signposts' might appear, with certain biosecurity threats scenarios (including both bioterrorism and biocrimes). Better analysis in turn could contribute to the prevention, earlier detection or a more evidence-based policy response to a potential threat. In a sense, the use of tools like high impact/low probability also encourages the analyst to think like the threat actor, and using it would no doubt also include some of the thinking processes one needs in red cell analysis.

Most of the analytical tools discussed above have been in existence since the early 1990s, but the number of tools since then has increased, and in 2004 a more encompassing name was found for these and several other techniques called *structured analytical techniques*. Heuer and Pherson describe structured analytical techniques as a 'step by step process that externalises an individual analyst's thinking in a manner that makes it readily apparent to others, thereby enabling it to be shared, built on, and critiqued by others' (ibid.: xvi). There is some overlap between the alternative analysis and structured analytical thinking tools, particularly in some of the tools listed earlier, such as competing hypotheses. But structured analytical techniques is a broader term than alternative analysis as it captures other tools, which until recently have been used only by a few analytical specialities in select parts of the US intelligence community. Heuer and Pherson's recently released practitioner's guide book (*Structured Analytic Techniques for Intelligence Analysis*) lists several structured analytical techniques. The book also includes worked through examples and when they would be most useful to apply to a problem (ibid.: 25).

Another useful tool for analysts to challenge and expand their thinking on a topic is *force field analysis*. Force field analysis can help identify both driving and restraining forces operating on an issue. The tool can be done in table format or graphically (for worked through examples of force field analysis, see Heuer and Pherson (ibid.: 281) and Quarmby (2009: 177). The objective of force field analysis is not just to identify driving forces that are either facilitating or constraining an issue, but also to assess drivers where decision-makers can have the greatest impact over time. Force field analysis, like high impact/low probability, is useful in strategic intelligence, where you are trying to assess how drivers are changing and diagnose those where there is an ability to intervene effectively.

Our understanding of the psychological dimensions of analysis must also go beyond the individual cognitive capabilities of analysts and how we can improve their analytical judgements. Psychological theory can also provide an additional methodological approach to profile the motivations, beliefs and interests of threat actors or offenders, and assist in target development in an operational intelligence context. Psychological profiling of offenders has been in existence since the late 1970s – becoming popular in the USA first in the FBI's Behavioral Science Unit and then later in some policing agencies in the UK. The FBI approach developed typologies of offenders in sexual assaults and homicides (Ainsworth 2001). David Canter, a pioneer in profiling in the UK, has, however, questioned the usefulness and accuracy of the typologies approach. In its place, he argued for a more evidence-based approach to profiling by applying psychological theory to the analysis of crime data (Alison and Canter 1999). The debate is ongoing about the value of different psychological profiling approaches, though at the very least, it is clear that these techniques have informed how some policing analysts have developed target profiles and tactical assessments in support of investigations.

The complexity of many transnational crime actors, including terrorists, may provide another opportunity for mapping their psychological motivations. This psychological 'mapping' of terrorist offenders, when combined with other collection capabilities at the analysts' disposal, could increase our understandings of particular criminal behaviour and offender patterns. For example, the role of specific motivations and psychological stress and their contribution to the radicalization of youth to commit terrorism or other acts of violence are not well understood. Yet further research into the psychological motivations for violence and radicalization of youth would be beneficial for operational intelligence officers trying to evaluate indicators showing that individuals may be heading in this direction. As noted in Chapter 2, the psychological dimensions to radicalization will also be increasingly important for analysts working in the corrections sector. Social psychology, which examines group dynamics, group thinking and identities, can be usefully applied to counter-terrorism investigations, but also allows intelligence analysts to look for intervention and disruption points in terrorist groups (Roberts in press).

Moving away from the use of psychology in understanding the motivations of threat actors, the other important psychological dimension impacting on analysis is not just how the analysts' cognitive processes allow them to make the leap from reasons to inferences or conclusions about the security environment, but also how the decision-makers' cognitive processes influence or bias the receipt of intelligence assessments. There seem to be many unanswered questions around what motivates decision-makers to use or discard intelligence assessments provided to them. As discussed in Chapter 7, decision-makers obviously have different views on the value of intelligence – some informed by evidence, others not. In an increasingly competitive information environment, where senior decision-makers have other sources for decision support, how can intelligence managers better influence the perception, uptake and use of analytical products by decision-makers? Research which draws on decision-making theory from other fields such as psychology and sociology may be useful in exploring under what circumstances leaders were motivated to alter their own judgements on policy matters based on intelligence assessments. Again using the empirical analysis of cognitive biases by psychologists Tversky and Kahneman discussed earlier, may also be helpful in understanding how such biases in decision-makers impact on the judgements they form about the value of intelligence. Recent research on the policing critical incidents context, where a number of heuristics were found to influence decision-making under uncertainty and time constraints, may also be useful in evaluating how decision-makers are influenced by intelligence assessments (Almond *et al.* 2008). As noted in Chapter 6, decision-makers like analysts also use psychological processes that are underpinned by world-views or their own values. It is these values, as Marrin points out, that also 'drive their mindsets and in turn drive decision-making processes rather than data or expertise based on that data' from the analyst (2009: 142).

In summary, it should be clear that intelligence analysis needs first to be understood as a cognitive exercise. However, like any other complex thinking, analysis also needs to be defined in terms of the overall strategies, approaches and tools that are used to synthesize raw data and information into some kind of refined assessment which a decision-maker can digest. So understanding contemporary analysis also requires reflection on some of the key methods applied to facilitate effective analysis in the national security and policing contexts. In the next section I have grouped the discussion on strategies, approaches and tools which have shaped the development of analysis under broad disciplinary themes. The objective is not to provide an endless list of strategies, approaches and tools, but to show how methodologies from other disciplines in intelligence analysis have had a significant influence on the development of intelligence analysis. The aim is also to highlight areas where promising future areas of research and theory building will occur, based on this inter-disciplinary nature of intelligence. I use the term 'methodologies' here quite broadly. For the purposes of this chapter, 'methodologies' include the 'frameworks or paradigmatic assumptions that are used to conduct research on intelligence analysis, plus the techniques and tools for collecting data for this kind of research' (O'Leary 2007: 85).

Analytical methodologies

There are a number of methodologies that could be discussed here, which have influenced analysis, but due to space constrictions I will limit discussions to eight 'discipline areas'. I argue that each area has shaped intelligence analysis in a number of different ways, particularly in influencing the development of intelligence analytical frameworks, or providing techniques and tools to better interpret the security environment. These discipline areas in addition to psychology discussed above, include *international relations, political science and history, sociology, criminology, business* and *management.* The intention here is not to reproduce an exhaustive list of how each discipline has influenced innovations in analysis in the past several decades. You could fill an entire book trying to do this. Instead, I merely provide some examples of methodologies and theories from key discipline areas that have influenced intelligence analysis in national security and policing contexts. For ease of discussion, 'like disciplines', such as international relations, political science and history, are discussed as one 'discipline area' even though in reality of course they are three separate fields.

Looking at international relations first, Chapter 7 provided some detail about how different theories on international relations – realism, neo-realism, liberalism and others – have helped shaped analysts' understanding of the security environment from the Cold War to the present. In particular, the long period of the Cold War – defined largely by a bipolar power system between the two great powers (the Soviet Union and the United States) – became the prism through which the Australian, Canadian, NZ, UK and US national security agencies interpreted threats of any kind. Realism and neo-realism were the dominant international relations theories supporting national security policy setting during the Cold War, though others became more popular with the growth in the inter-dependence of states in the global economy. International political economy and regime theories were two examples that recognized how states' relations could be modified by political and economic collaborative arrangements. Both these theories began to gain some traction as early as the 1970s, and became even more entrenched in scholarly thinking at the end of the Cold War.

International political economy theorists are focused on how national and international distribution of power impacts on the global economic system (Gilpin 1988). And in the 1980s and at the end of the Cold War, theorizing on regimes also became popular among international relations scholars in order to understand how states interact and cooperate with each other in multi-lateral forums and the impact of regimes on security (e.g. Keohane 1984; Krasner 1983). Regime theorizing became important to liberal democracies such as the USA and Australia at the end of the Cold War in how they 'invested' in new global and regional security institutions such as the Asia-Pacific Economic Cooperation (APEC) or the ASEAN Regional Forum (ARF). This shift in the policy environment in turn influenced how national security intelligence agencies identified collection and analytical priorities on a range of issues. International relations scholars are still locked in debates about how best to understand the global distribution of power between states, but the current post-9/11 security environment is a much more fluid multipolar structure. This fluidity and particularly the role of a number of non-state actors are making the delineation and assessment of many threats more challenging for analysts. Such theoretical debates about what kind of framework best describes the security environment, and even more fundamental ones about what constitutes 'security', will continue to impact how analysts and policy-makers understand the security environment and the threats within them.

Political science and history have also provided theoretical frameworks that have impacted on the way national security intelligence agencies have understood threats in the security environment. Political science, particularly theoretical works on political culture and bureaucratic politics, became important in the 1960s and up to the 1980s in US policy discourse circles. They also provided insights to analysts in agencies such as the CIA into understanding how political actors were likely to behave. Political culture theory represents a diverse set of perspectives which cannot be faithfully described here. However, in general, it became a popular aspect of political science in the 1960s by theorists interested in how national culture, values and 'culturally learned behaviour' impact on political power (Pye and Verba 1965). Similarly, bureaucratic politics became popular among political scientists during the same period. Its focus is on explaining how bureaucratic systems within governments generate a country's foreign policy. Critics of this approach, however, suggested that just focusing on the bureaucracy and not other dimensions of domestic and international politics will not lead to a comprehensive understanding of foreign policy generation. The classic in the bureaucratic politics field is Graham Allison's work on the Cuban Missile Crisis, which provided analysts with different models for understanding how Soviet leaders were making decisions during the crisis. The three models comprised a rational actor model, an organizational process model and a bureaucratic politics model (Allison 1971). However, care needs to be exercised in relying on theories such as rational actor explanations for foreign policy decisions, given it is difficult to view states as unitary actors like individuals. Foreign policy decision-making is generally the result of a complex and ever changing suite of decision-making processes and a decision-maker's preference for action may be quite different from what a foreign intelligence officer would select or view as 'rational' under the circumstances. In the political science context, US analysts spent a lot of time during the Cold War assessing how foreign leaders would respond to issues based on rational actor approaches. The history of intelligence failures such as the Cuban Missile Crisis, shows, however, that this kind of 'mirror imaging', or *leader x would behave this way – as this is what we in country y would do*, has not always been a helpful aid to analysis.

Other political science approaches include a blending with other disciplines such as cognitive psychology. Some of these apply the psychology of decision-making work of psychologists, such as Tversky and Kahneman, discussed earlier, to studying international political behaviour. Robert Jervis' work, *Perception and Misperception in International Politics*, is a good example of this 'inter-disciplinary approach'. Jervis rejects a purely rational actor approach to understanding how foreign leaders make policy decisions. Instead he argues that rationality is impaired by a complex and highly ambiguous decision-making environment, where decision-makers hold different perceptions and misperceptions of the world based on beliefs, attitudes, and values, which are not necessarily bounded in a rational view of reality (Jervis 1976: 35).

Methodological perspectives from history have also complemented those used by analysts for the political analysis of leaders and foreign policy decision-making processes. History has been useful in the development of historical case studies, or analogies that allow analysts to study how threats that have developed in one context may manifest in another in the future. History as a discipline has also shaped, in a more general sense, the development of approaches to intelligence analysis in the CIA since its establishment in 1947. For example, Sherman Kent, viewed by many as the 'founding father' of intelligence analysis in the US, taught history at Yale University. Kent saw intelligence as the pursuit of a 'certain kind of knowledge' and took an academic researcher and historian's approach to his view of how intelligence should be practised. In his early seminal work, *Strategic Intelligence for American World Policy*, he saw intelligence activity as being at least in part the result of research activity in order: 'to establish meaningful patterns out of what was observed in the past and attempts to get meaning out of what appears to be going on now' (Kent 1949: 4).

The third discipline area that has been influential in the development of intelligence analysis has been sociology. A key sociological methodology which has been applied in the past two decades in policing and national security intelligence is social network analysis (SNA) (e.g. Sparrow 1991; Koschade 2006). The pioneers of SNA came from sociology and social psychology, but it has become increasingly an inter-disciplinary methodology, drawing on approaches in mathematics and anthropology (Wasserman and Faust 1994: 10). SNA involves, in the first instance, examining and charting associations between people, activity and places. In the intelligence context, this process results in a link chart, which can be published as part of a tactical intelligence product. However, SNA goes beyond the simple charting of the relationship between entities. It seeks to measure 'empirically' the value of these networks in order to understand patterns between nodes (or individuals) and their relationships to links. In addition to identifying patterns, associations and degrees of influence between nodes and links, SNA also seeks to predict the behaviour of members in the network. In complex networks where there are many nodes and links, network analysis software is available to measure mathematically variables such as the distance between nodes and the significance of relationships between nodes. SNA is becoming more popular in both national security and policing intelligence, particularly in attempting to identify and assess how networks of individuals are involved in complex transnational offences such as drug trafficking and counter-terrorism (Sparrow 1991; Koschade 2006).

SNA is particularly helpful for analysts in mapping complex transnational crime syndicates, by identifying vulnerabilities in networks, such as individuals, who are key enablers or facilitators of criminal activity for the group. It has also been used by national security intelligence agencies seeking to understand the relationships between political leaders in countries and predicting their behaviour and decision-making. An NSA and National Air Intelligence Centre-commissioned SNA of the Iranian Government in 2001 is a good example of this application (Renfro and Deckro 2001). SNA does have its limitations. The two key ones being the dynamic changing nature of networks, and insufficient intelligence collection can reduce the currency and accuracy of the network analysis.

In the context of sociology, a range of social research methodologies have also provided intelligence analysts with structured approaches to their research and analysis on various issues relevant to decision-makers such as political behaviour, illicit drug markets, economics, social value systems of individuals and groups and so on. Research methodologies, not just across sociology, but other social sciences mentioned in this section, are providing analysts with ways to frame and test hypotheses, and develop systematic data collection and analytical approaches that can improve the validity and reliability of intelligence products. The extent, however, to which one can 'measure' data in the intelligence context depends on what is being measured and how that is operationalized at the research design stage. This raises the broader question of whether we can really *measure* variables and *know things* as a result in the intelligence context – a question I will return to in Chapter 10. Leaving this epistemological and ontological question aside, there is, however, at least a growing recognition in the literature that analysts should be more conversant in a range of quantitative and qualitative methodologies used in the social sciences, and that their application can produce better intelligence analysis (Clauser 2008; Prunckun 2010). From my experience of teaching intelligence, there is a need to improve the general research literacy of analysts – particularly in basic quantitative techniques used in policing intelligence contexts.

The fifth discipline area, criminology and within it policing studies, has obviously been influential in shaping the development of policing intelligence analysis. As discussed in Chapter 2, policing models such as problem-orientated policing and intelligence-led policing have promoted a more problem solving and data-driven analysis of crime. But these policing models were themselves driven by broader criminological research on offender patterns. For example, landmark research such as the Cambridge Study in Delinquent Development, which interviewed a series of boys in the 1960s as they progressed through their teens, twenties and thirties found that one-third of the group by their 25th birthday had been convicted of a notifiable offence. This study and similar ones conducted in the USA were important in understanding the careers of criminals, and from an intelligence perspective it made sense to identify and target these prolific and recidivist offenders as early as possible (Ratcliffe 2008: 55). In summary, an understanding of recidivism has had particular resonance in the development of intelligence-led policing, which has sought to apply a more evidence-based approach to analysis – particularly at the tactical and operational policing context. Environmental criminology has also been influential in the development of other evidence-driven analytical techniques such as crime mapping. Crime mapping, 'hot-spotting' and GIS have been used proactively by operational policing and have led to crime reduction in some cases. Ratcliffe (ibid.: 186–211) provides a comprehensive evaluation of these techniques in the context of their influence on crime reduction.

In this brief overview of the influence of criminological approaches to policing intelligence analysis, it is of course important to remember that the nature and extent of their adoption in Australia, Canada, New Zealand, the UK and the USA have been different in each country. Furthermore, the different application of criminological and policing approaches to analysis also very often resulted in the creation of different kinds of policing analysts such as 'crime analysts' or 'criminal intelligence analysts', which continues to cause confusion in many of these countries about what analysts are and should be doing.

The final discipline area I will discuss here is 'management', which has also played an important role in the development of various intelligence analytic methodologies. A host of simple analytical tools, such as Gantt charting, brainstorming, Political, Economic, Social, Technological, Environmental, Legislative and Organizational (PESTELO) analysis and Strengths, Weaknesses, Opportunities and Threats (SWOT) analysis, have long been used by management in business planning and project management. These tools have also been adapted to national security and policing intelligence contexts, and there are now numerous guides for analysts on how to use them (e.g. Heldon 2009; Prunckun 2010). Other examples of qualitative tools now increasingly used by analysts that originated partly or wholly in business and engineering fields include force field analysis, scenario generation, indicators and warning. These tools help analysts develop their judgements, identify drivers for issues and estimate possible future alternatives. Though as discussed earlier, in the discussion of structured analytic techniques, some of these tools have also been developed further in national security agencies and/or have a pedigree (e.g. indications and early warning tools) in US defence intelligence.

Contemporary analytical innovations

Analytics

Although it may be accurate to describe analytics as 'contemporary' in many national security and policing intelligence contexts, it is not new in and of itself. Analytics is defined by Davenport and Harris as: 'the extensive use of data, statistical and quantitative analysis, explanatory and predictive models and fact-based management to drive decisions and actions' (2007: 7). Davenport and Harris have academic backgrounds in information technology and management and add to this definition by suggesting that: 'analytics is a subset of what has now become "business intelligence"' (ibid.). In addition to this definition being very business focused, it is broad and does not pin down analytics as a single unique methodology or technique. Perhaps what Davenport and Harris are implying is, if all processes and methodologies described in their definition are combined, they present a more unique systematic data-driven approach to support decision-making in the business context. It is also not clear, however, from this definition whether analytics as it is understood in the business and management context can be viewed in the same way in the national security and policing intelligence worlds. It also remains to be seen, as will be discussed below, whether policing and national security intelligence agencies can use analytics effectively for predictive modelling or fact-based management of threat issues.

Before discussing how analytics is being applied in the national security and policing intelligence context, it is useful to distinguish the difference between analytics and data mining. In some of the literature these terms are used interchangeably without much of an attempt to distinguish between them. While both seem to involve similar processes and seek to achieve the production of actionable information, there does appear to be differences between them. Data mining is the older of the two terms, and is more restricted to the process of retrieving and analysing data, whereas analytics, according to the website of a major, analytics software company, SAS, is a broader term that also encapsulates data mining and other techniques (including time series forecasting, operational research and text analysis) for the collection of data and then using these sources to test a hypothesis or be predictive about future events (SAS 2009: 2).

As noted above, analytics has been practised in the private sector for decades, particularly in the financial sector such as banks and credit card companies. Financial companies have been motivated to identify ways to not only increase profit margins against competitors, but also reduce threats to business such as financial fraud. More recently, analytics has moved from simple manipulations of data to advanced 'competitive analytics approaches', which are designed to be used strategically to protect and grow market share from rival companies. Competitive analytics is now seen by many large companies as essential in providing a 'deeper understanding' of their customers so that they can sell more goods and services than their rivals. Companies that have advanced analytic capabilities use it to drive decision-making at all levels rather than it being just another 'back office' tool used by some in a company. The objective for a company with a fully integrated competitive analytics capability is to have a data-driven approach to operational and strategic decision-making in the company. In the USA, there are now a number of large companies such as Proctor & Gamble, FedEx, Google and Amazon.com, that are using analytics in this way, and Davenport and Harris refer to them as analytic competitors (Davenport and Harris 2007: 7). In the retail sector, a good example of how analytics has helped a company gain more advantage over its peers is the UK supermarket chain Tesco. Since 1995 when Tesco introduced a loyalty card – the 'Clubcard' – it has been able, with the assistance of marketing data specialist company Dunhumby, to capture data from its customers about what they buy. Using this data, Tesco has built up profiles of different shoppers that allow it to better tailor marketing campaigns to specific groups. For Tesco, this data-driven approach has provided more informed decision-making about what customers are interested in. In 2007, Tesco's data-driven approach resulted in it commanding a 31.3 per cent share against its rival, Sainsbury's which held 16.5 per cent of the supermarket sector profits (Davis 2007).

The number of companies, however, even large ones, that use advanced analytics or have become, in Davenport's words, 'analytical competitors' is still small. In a global survey of 371 medium to large firms conducted in 2005, Davenport and Harris found that only 10 per cent of participants stated that analytical capability was a key element in their strategy for the business. Additionally, the study found that only half of the firms who reported using analytics as a key element in their business had the full characteristics of what the researchers describe as required for a 'full-bore analytical competitor' approach (Davenport and Harris 2007: 23–24). Further research is required to get a better understanding of how analytics is being used in the private sector, and this can assist the development of similar business intelligence methodologies in traditional and emerging intelligence practice areas.

The current status of data mining and analytics in national security and policing intelligence is difficult to assess. Historically, it is well known that major sigint agencies such as the NSA in the USA for decades have had impressive data mining capabilities to help with guiding and managing the collection of massive amounts of communications data. In the sigint agencies, such as NSA and the Defence Signals Directorate (DSD) (in Australia), analytics is predominantly used on electronic communications of all types, including email, text messages, voice and other data traffic. There are a number of analytics techniques used in the sigint context, including neural networks, clustering and decision trees. Neural networks are predictors built on technologies which function like the neurons in the brain. Computer scientists have been able to replicate some aspects of neural processing through developing neural network algorithms. The networks seek to detect anomalies based on input data and how these data are replicated in other hidden layers of data. The net result of a neural network is a computer-weighted sum of inputs, which produce output values indicating a prediction of relationships and associations between data and targets (Skillicorn 2009: 101). Clustering involves using algorithms which group cases based on similarities between them. Clustering is also used in the policing intelligence context. Decision trees are another example of a predictive analytics approach, where the objective is to make a prediction of an outcome. An example might be the likelihood of data patterns suggesting individuals may be involved in planning a terrorist attack. A single attribute value is given to a specific piece of data located at the 'base of the tree' which is then tested. Based on the results of the test, additional values are applied to alternative sub-trees or branches. The objective is to find the target attributes out in the far parts of the 'tree' – the 'leaves – and these become the prediction for this particular case. The decision tree helps make predictions about cause and effect, but not with any indication of confidence in its prediction (ibid.: 85). Though in contrast to sigint collection agencies, other national security agencies, including those with humint or assessment functions, have had relatively less experience with data mining and analytics capabilities. The events of 9/11, however, have placed a greater emphasis across a wider number of national security agencies to increase their use of data mining and analytics. As noted earlier, the 9/11 Commission Report, identified information sharing and technological deficiencies contributing to analysts not being able connect the 'dots'. The post-9/11 environment has been marked by greater legislative, policy and research responses aimed at improving data mining and analytics capabilities more broadly across the US intelligence community – not just in defence and the NSA. From a research perspective, an ODNI report from its Office of Science and Technology Intelligence Advanced Research Project Activity (IARPA), provides insight into the range of research projects the US intelligence agencies are focusing on in order to improve data mining and analytics (ODNI 2008). A lot of the projects listed in the report are designed to develop capabilities to help the analyst look through large volumes of data to uncover relevant information quicker. The report lists a number of projects, which include the development of technologies referred to as 'knowledge discovery and dissemination' (KDD). KDD is a generic term for technologies that are meant to help harness data mining and analytics technology to better coordinate the access and exploitation of multiple data sources across the fragmented US intelligence community. Other research projects listed are more aspirational and include data mining and analytics technologies that may eventually provide analysts with enhanced surveillance and early warning capabilities. This technology could assist analysts to better assess incoming information against patterns of known criminal or terrorist behaviour to reveal changes in the likelihood of a known individual becoming a threat (ibid.).

In contrast to the national security community, the use of data mining and analytics in the policing intelligence context has been slower to develop. I am not suggesting here that police have not developed any capabilities in this area over the past decade, but in general data mining and particularly analytics are still relatively new to many policing agencies. Police have always had large databases, containing a range of different data sources, such as computer-aided dispatch (CAD) systems, intelligence reports, call charge records and case management databases. With this data – depending on the specific capabilities of a specific agency – police intelligence analysts have been able to make links between individuals, places and transactions that have improved operational outcomes. There are also some examples of more sophisticated approaches to data mining and analytics. For example, NYPD has been expanding its analytics capabilities over a number of years through its Real Time Crime Center (RTCC), which connects the agency's databases containing over five million New York city criminal records, parole and probation files. The RTCC provides investigators in the field with information about crime scenes, potential suspects and other leads. The RTCC uses analytics-based technology that connects data with GIS and a pattern management system.

But for many policing agencies, the ability to exploit data mining and analytics techniques to their maximum with the data available to them has been constrained by a number of factors. For example, both the costs associated with deploying data mining and analytics technology, and training analysts in its use, have been prohibitive for many policing agencies. Additionally, while for many agencies, data may be abundant, their quality and accessibility have not been good. And the events of 9/11 also highlighted for policing intelligence, as much as in the national security context, the problem of legacy databases, where extracting data from many databases within one agency, let alone across an entire policing community, is extremely difficult. However, this is changing and since 9/11, the IRTPA of 2004 (which introduced the term ISE), has provided the basis for other legislative and policy measures to support further development in data mining and analytics. The ISE underlined a 'need to share philosophy', and resulted in a series of policy initiatives to develop technology to connect disparate data sets across local, state and federal policing agencies with that of national security agencies. Westphal provides a good summary of the key policies, laws, reports and technologies that have sought to promote the ISE approach (2009: 371–405). In the USA, the new SAR approach for terrorism, discussed in Chapter 6, is also a recent example of renewed efforts to both share information between agencies, and 'connect the dots' using advanced data mining and analytics capabilities. The DHS and FBI coordination of 'CyberStorm' which tests critical infrastructure protection for cyber attacks is another information sharing example between US 'policing intelligence' and their 'national security intelligence' counterparts, and is focused on establishing common approaches to data mining and analytics across the entire 'intelligence community' in this area. The CyberStorm initiative is also run across national security intelligence agencies in Australia, Canada, New Zealand and the UK.

Outside of the USA, the post-9/11 environment has also seen a growing sense of urgency among other national security and policing agencies in Australia, Canada, New Zealand and the UK to get better at 'connecting the dots' by investing in data mining and analytics. In general, though, as far as policing intelligence is concerned, it seems as though capabilities vary from simple data extraction, to more comprehensive knowledge discovery systems that can extract, analyse and even 'predict' the activities/behaviour of threat actors using technology with complex algorithms (McCue 2007). In Australia, the ACC has started to build an analytics capability for organized crime as part of its new intelligence model (Project Sentinel, see Chapter 4), though generally in other state policing or law enforcement agencies, the capability is still low. The recent establishment in the ACC, however, of a national criminal intelligence fusion center may encourage state policing agencies to develop capabilities in data mining and analytics in order to benefit further from a national approach to the fusion of large data sets and criminal intelligence. Another recent example of the implementation of more sophisticated data mining and analytics in the policing intelligence context is the Vancouver Police Department's (VPD) Consolidated Records Intelligence Mining Environment (CRIME) system. In interviews in 2009, Ryan Prox, the Analytic Services Coordinator for VPD, explained how CRIME provides the technological infrastructure which allows the integration of all the Department's databases in one place. This is now allowing a more proactive intelligence-led approach to operational policing. For example, the technology being used is enabling GIS to be integrated with other offender data in real time, which is improving the time analysts spend identifying trends. CRIME is also providing the medium for strategic data mining to identify police performance much like a Compstat approach. The CRIME system is also at the centre driving the VPD's new approach to intelligence called the Strategic Targeting and Resource Selection (STARS) (Prox, interview, 9 September 2009; Brewer 2008).

Turning to the use of data mining and analytics in the national security contexts of Australia, Canada, New Zealand and the UK, much of this work is classified, so it is difficult to assess both the level of sophistication and the extent to which these techniques have been operationalized across the intelligence communities in these countries. What is known, though, is that in the national security context of Australia, Canada, New Zealand and the UK, like the USA, significant efforts are being made to increase information sharing across 'traditional members' of their national security communities, and to better integrate these efforts with those under way in their broader policing communities. While in most cases, the national security intelligence agencies within these countries have long had classified intranets to share information, the reality is that not all information is shared through such networks. To a large extent, individual defence and national security agencies historically have developed their own ICT systems to suit their particular needs, and this has created silos – reducing information sharing and the development of common architectures for analysis and data mining. The challenge for national security agencies in this decade will be how they consolidate their separate intelligence databases in order to allow a single fused data mining and analytics capability on 'whole of government' national security issues such as terrorism. Each intelligence community is now working towards the policy, legislative and technological solutions to this challenge.

The potential value in both data mining and an analytics approach to intelligence analysis is in helping the analysts extract knowledge from the ever increasing volumes of data policing agencies collect. There is now a growing amount of work in some agencies, where analysts and investigators have been able to connect increasingly complex sets of names, addresses, phone numbers, identity documents and financial transactions and make some determination of whether the patterns or relations between the data suggest a criminal offence such as fraud or money laundering. Perhaps in the future it will be possible for highly trained analysts to 'diagnose' data patterns more quickly and assess what kind of criminal footprints (e.g. terrorists, money laundering) they are looking at. With an increased uptake of analytics technology and well-trained staff, it may be possible in the future to assess a pattern as most likely the result of global drug trafficking or terrorism. However, it is important not to over-exaggerate the actual or potential successes of these approaches. Care is required in interpreting the results from advanced data mining and analytics. Results need to be weighed up against any potential vulnerabilities in these technologies. As Skillicorn suggests: 'One of the most subtle and surprising features of existing knowledge-discovery technology is how fragile it is in the face of actions taken by those who want to conceal themselves and their actions' (2009: xvii). Conclusions will always need to be 'triangulated' by the analyst using other traditional intelligence databases, which store offender history and profiles, and match that with other available forensic data where relevant. Analysts will also still need to rely heavily on surveillance and humint to validate other data sources about a target's intentions.

In summary, despite the potential of data mining and analytics, both are methodologies which cannot be developed in isolation of other intelligence systems and processes in agencies. The complexities of advanced data mining and analytics suggest that if both are going to be utilized properly, they need to be built into a fully effective intelligence framework for an agency. And in the context of a fully integrated analytics function, it will be the totality of intelligence available from all sources that should drive the intelligence priorities and tasking of this function, not the other way around. A fully developed analytics capability also requires the appropriate level of support in non-intelligence areas to make it function effectively, including statisticians, data mining people, business unit managers and of course the analysts. This may sound like common sense, but in general these technical support specialists are in short supply in many policing agencies.

While advanced knowledge discovery technologies such as data mining and analytics may be showing benefits, the expense in developing this capability – both in additional ICT and analytical training – suggests that it may remain beyond some agencies' financial and human capabilities. Under these circumstances, it may be better in smaller agencies that only a few personnel are 'analytics literate'. These agencies could 'outsource' this function to larger national counterparts through some kind of fusion arrangement. There are signs that this is already occurring in the USA. In addition to all the above constraints on agencies using analytics, there are the other standard intelligence information architecture issues that still present ongoing challenges to this methodology being fully realized in national security and policing intelligence contexts. These were outlined earlier in Chapter 5, but to summarize again they include: a lack of connectivity between some legacy systems, inaccurate or incomplete data entry, multi-jurisdictional databases, organizational cultural issues and privacy and legislative restrictions.

Sense-making and early warning analysis technology

As suggested above, it may be too soon to really judge the value analytics will have for many national security and policing agencies. There are two key questions though which will ultimately determine its value. First, to what extent does it improve the ability of intelligence analysts to make links between potential threat actors operationally in real time? Second, to what extent can data mining and analytics help predict the indicators or 'footprints' of complex criminal and security issues such as identifying if irregular money flows are indicative of corporate fraud, global drug trafficking or terrorism? In addition to data mining and analytic techniques, there may be other technological innovations which can improve intelligence outputs particularly in the strategic or early warning context of intelligence analysis.

A key theme running through all chapters in this book is that intelligence analysis, wherever it is practised (national security, policing or some of the emerging areas in Chapter 2), is rapidly being tested by an increasingly complex security environment. While it may be difficult to define or characterize this new environment, it is clear that many contemporary threats are manifesting themselves at international, national and intra-national levels. And while the growth in ICT allows intelligence agencies to collect more information about potential threats at all these levels, the irony is that this has not necessarily translated into a better ability to operationally and strategically assess the significance of this information. As noted in Chapter 6, this message is one of the key outcomes from reviews completed by the White House and Congress over Umar Farouk Abdulmutallab's attempt to detonate an explosive on board Northwest Airlines Flight 253 in December 2009. Both reviews concluded that the failure to gain *warning* of this impending attack had less to do with agencies not sharing information, and more with analysts not being able to 'connect the dots' with the information that they had in a timely way (ISE 2010: 3).

Analytics may help make the extraction and identification of patterns easier but in many threat areas, such as counter-terrorism, WMD proliferation and cyber attacks, there is a lot more to be done before such technology can help analysts validate the 'data footprints' of such potential future threats. The issue is not just to validate current operational indicators of an impending execution of a threat, but also to build in an analytical model a capability to assist with anticipating future threats. In this last section we focus on technological systems that are seeking to give early warning of possible strategic threats so that proactive policy or other disruptive measures can be taken. While it is still currently difficult to use analytics and data mining to extract patterns from databases, the ability of analysts to use these patterns to assess the significance of emerging indicators is currently another analytical innovative area being explored.

It is not possible to comprehensively describe here the boundaries (and functions) of all the available or emerging technology that may support analysts to better anticipate indicators, outliers or weak noise that suggest a strategic change in the security environment. Instead I will provide one example, the Risk

Assessment and Horizon Scanning Programme (RAHS), to illustrate the kind of sense-making analytics currently being explored in intelligence communities.

The RAHS in recent years has generated some attention at international conferences such as the Global Futures Forum and the European Futurists Conference. It began in July 2005 as a collaboration between the Government of Singapore, the Arlington Institute (in the USA) and a UK company called Cognitive Edge (RAHS 2007). The key focus is to provide a coordinated whole of government horizon scanning (out to 2–5 years) capability. The RAHS describes the capability as a series of different processes including: 'modelling, data collection, detecting emerging trends and matching those against models and collaborating with other analysts in an online secure environment' (ibid.: 2).

The RAHS staff emphasize that they are not trying to establish an automated early warning system, rather the objective is to develop enabling technology that will help intelligence analysts discover patterns in data sets and compare these with new incoming data to provide an enhanced human-driven early warning system. Since its establishment in 2005, the RAHS has been a major collaborative project between Singapore's National Security Coordination Centre (providing policy direction and resourcing), the newly established Horizon Scanning Centre (responsible for coordinating the information sharing within agencies networked in the RAHS), the RAHS Experimentation Centre (driving the technology research and development efforts) and the Centre for Excellence for National Security (responsible for researching new concepts, methods and techniques) (ibid.: 3). Since 2007, the RAHS has broadened the number of security issues the model is now working on.

Conclusion

The cognitive, methodological and technological issues discussed above highlight a number of exciting innovations in analysis in recent years. The broad challenge, however, moving forward is to generate more *evidence* of how various methodological approaches allow intelligence analysts to better interpret the security environment and add greater value to the decision-making process. In Chapter 10, we will explore this question using some of the key analytical innovations discussed above. For example, to what extent can data-driven technological approaches like analytics help analysts interpret the security environment, and where are their limitations both operationally and strategically? And to what extent do simple qualitative structured analytic techniques result in more systematic and less biased assessments? As discussed further in Chapter 10, posing such questions is often easier than operationalizing them in a research-driven process. However difficult the questions are, governments will continue to both scrutinize and insist on more efficient and effective intelligence practice. So practitioners and academics are left with no choice but to provide evidence for the effectiveness of various analytical innovations to policy-makers. Intelligence scholars need to get beyond just describing these techniques and start evaluating if they actually work. These questions also need exploring if we are to generate a more research- and theory-driven approach to intelligence practice. A research- and theory-driven approach to intelligence practice in turn will be important to many in the academy and in agencies, who aspire one day to transform a largely uncoordinated set of theories and practices into a discipline.

While it is difficult to currently assess how a disparate set of developments in analysis contributes to defining a 'discipline of intelligence' in any coherent way, on a positive note, the discussion above at least provides educators with more informed views about what analysts need to be equipped with to deal with the security environment in the future. How we equip the next generation of analysts with the skills they need in this increasingly complex operating environment is the subject of the next chapter (Chapter 9). Additionally in Chapter 9, I argue that while research and innovation are critical in helping to define a discipline of knowledge so too are teaching, education and professional development.

9 Intelligence education and professionalism

Introduction

In the previous chapter, I highlighted a number of analytical innovations and techniques available to analysts and other intelligence workers from a range of disciplines. It is clear that the development of a future discipline of intelligence will continue to rely on such developments being implemented in the workplace. However, arguably more significant to the development of any 'intelligence discipline' will be the quality of *human resources* available which can exploit adeptly such techniques. In this chapter, I survey some of the key developments in intelligence *education* and *professionalism* post 9/11. It is not easy to delineate the discussion of each separately, as there are many overlaps between the two. For example, you cannot have an effective education approach, without this being embedded in a professional environment and vice versa. However, some issues are more relevant to each, and they are best discussed separately for clarity.

In the area of intelligence education, for example, there has been a dramatic increase in universities offering intelligence courses across Australia, Canada, New Zealand, the UK and the USA. This has also been accompanied by an expansion of short training courses offered within intelligence agencies and by external private contractors. In this chapter, I argue that much of the increase in the number of education offerings for analysts is welcome and services a growing demand for training by governments, agencies, managers and the analysts themselves. However, the rush to meet this demand has not been without problems, and I will identify where key challenges remain in providing quality and industry-relevant education for intelligence professionals, and what can be done to address them.

The second focus of this chapter is to define intelligence in the context as a *profession.* There are increasing discussions among intelligence officers, managers, academics and intelligence professional bodies as to whether intelligence is a profession – similar to the way most would view medicine or law. In the second part of the chapter, I identify the main threads of this debate across Australia, Canada, New Zealand, the UK and the USA, before providing my own view on this question. This chapter concludes by arguing that while the answer to the 'intelligence as a profession' question is interesting, it may be more useful to ask slightly different questions. For example, what characterizes professionalism in the intelligence context? And, second, what are some of the current challenges to building intelligence professionalism, and how can academics, governments, private industry and intelligence agencies collaborate more effectively to enhance intelligence professionalism?

Developments in intelligence education

The limited space available does not allow a detailed analysis of all developments in intelligence education across Australia, Canada, New Zealand, the UK and the USA. Instead discussion will be general and thematic, drawing on examples from research conducted in each of these countries as well as secondary sources where relevant. Discussion will be limited also to trends in national security and policing intelligence education; however, this is not to suggest that education developments are not taking place in some of the emerging practice areas, such as immigration, taxation, social security, as from my own experience I know they plainly are.

So what have been the major trends in intelligence education since 9/11? In simple terms the answer is that in general, there has been both an increase in the *number* and *diversity* of intelligence education courses since 9/11. But what major environmental factors are behind this increased growth and diversity in intelligence education courses, training and providers? As discussed in Chapter 2, the post-9/11 security environment resulted in changes in the structures, processes and products of many policing and national security intelligence agencies. The forging of a new security environment – one marked increasingly by transnational security and complex and serious organized crime issues – has had a significant impact on the number of intelligence analysts being employed both in specialist and general roles in national security and policing agencies. Responding to these threats has, over the past decade, also resulted in more reflection by agency heads on what kind of educational and professional requirements analysts need to work within these complex, non-state threat areas.

In addition to reflections internally, by agency heads and intelligence managers responding to the new security environment, there have also been external drivers influencing changes to intelligence education. The suite of parliamentary, judiciary and independent reviews into the performance of intelligence agencies in the wake of 9/11 and the WMD in Iraq matter have provided further reflection on skills, capabilities and education standards. In the USA, but also in other countries such as Australia and the UK, seminal reviews, discussed in earlier chapters, also identified weaknesses in analytical standards and training as contributing to the intelligence failure involved in both cases. For example, the authors of the 9/11 Commission Report included a number of comments relevant to analytical skills and education standards and what should be done about them. Earlier in the 9/11 Commission Report, reference was made to the 'declining attention to the craft of strategic analysis'. And one of its key recommendations in the context of arguing for the need for a new national intelligence director also suggested that an important function of this new position would be: to 'establish standards for education and training across the intelligence community' (9/11 Commission 2004: 109, 414). Similar observations about US analytical standards, competencies and training were also mentioned in the Senate Select Committee's *Report on the US Intelligence Community's Prewar Intelligence Assessments on Iraq* (SSCI 2004). In Australia, the Flood Report commissioned by the government to inquire into Australian intelligence agencies mentioned a lack of contestability in analysis within Australia's national security assessment agency, the ONA, and also suggested that there was little focus by management on staff's training needs (Flood 2004: 82, 112).

Given these background issues, which have contributed to the increased attention on intelligence education since 9/11, what have been the trends which have typified changes in this area? Perhaps the first identifiable trend would be to describe changes we will be describing here in national security and policing intelligence education as 'evolutionary' rather than 'revolutionary'. The events of 9/11 clearly had an impact on perceptions within many agencies about how well trained their intelligence staff are and which gaps existed in skills and capabilities. But in many respects, the key trends presented here show an 'adding on' of educational providers and programmes, rather than in every instance a completely new approach to intelligence education across the national security and policing intelligence sectors. For example, analyst training at the CIA including its Career Analyst Program (CAP) pre-dates more recent developments in education approaches, including the reorganization of the directorates of intelligence and operations, which resulted in the establishment of the Sherman Kent School of Intelligence in 1999. Post-9/11 developments have not necessarily seen the recasting, rationalizing or removal of such older approaches to intelligence education. Rather it seems now in the USA, anyway, there is an increasing number of intelligence education opportunities for analysts across the entire US intelligence community.

National security intelligence education

What have been the trends in national security intelligence education? Trends vary a bit across Australia, Canada, New Zealand, the UK and the USA due to a number of factors. These include different policy responses to the new post-9/11 security environment, funding and individual agency responses to assessing priorities in education programmes. As stated earlier, a key mission in the IRTPA of 2004 (see for example, subtitle D 'Improvement of education for the intelligence community, additional education and training requirements'), which created the ODNI, was to ensure the future DNI would have a greater oversight role of education requirements across the US intelligence agencies (ODNI 2009b: 164–166). In contrast to the USA, governments in Australia, Canada and the UK, have sponsored less formal and non-legislated approaches. The objective instead has been to encourage intelligence agencies to promote better intelligence education and standards by funding various education initiatives – allowing different agencies across their intelligence communities to participate in new or revised education programmes.

While it is difficult to generalize about education developments in Australia, Canada, New Zealand, the UK and the USA, there have been some discernible similarities between them since 9/11. Of course, many of the trends discussed here were already in existence at the time of 9/11. However, they received a 'kick along' by the policy responses of governments to 9/11 and subsequent events, such as the inquiries into the intelligence assessments on WMD in Iraq. The first trend, starting before 9/11, has been an increase in the number of internal analytical specific courses in national security agencies that went beyond induction programmes for new staff. Over the past decade, specific agencies within intelligence communities have developed courses on sigint, geo-spatial and alternative analysis, which have been offered to other agencies in the community as well as their own staff. However, the number of different courses offered by agencies across their intelligence communities clearly increased after the post-9/11 reform agenda began in earnest in these communities. This was particularly the case in the USA, which is not surprising, given the size of its intelligence community. In 2009, during discussion with one DHS intelligence manager I was shown a list of courses available to intelligence officers right across the community; including courses run by DHS, the FBI and ODNI. While I did not count the number on the list, the DHS manager suggested that course offerings were now in the hundreds across the community. The second trend in intelligence education has been increased focus on reforming intelligence frameworks (see Chapter 5) which has resulted in further resources being allocated to intelligence agencies to develop a suite of intelligence education programmes, which are pegged to professional development pathways for intelligence officers. A good example of this trend was the creation at the FBI Academy of the School of Intelligence, at Quantico, Virginia, in October 2008.

Another important outcome of the broader post-9/11 intelligence reform agenda has been, in some countries, a greater centralized oversight, coordination and development of intelligence education across the intelligence community. In particular, in the USA, the ODNI has tried to play a coordinating role in education. Additionally, in Canada, the Privy Council has also played a role in developing intelligence courses that provide a common approach to analytical education across its intelligence community.

A third trend emerging since 9/11 has also been a greater preparedness by national security agencies to engage external contractors, whether they be universities, vocational training institutes or private training consultants. In each country, there has been the development of university intelligence programmes at undergraduate and post-graduate levels. In Australia, a number of intelligence specific programmes are offered in select universities, including Charles Sturt University, Macquarie, Queensland University of Technology and the newly established College of National Security at the Australian National University. Carleton University, New Brunswick, Toronto and York Universities are examples of intelligence education providers in Canada. In the USA, there seems to be an increasing number of programmes, but the mainstays have been the American

University, University of Georgia, Georgetown University and Mercyhurst College. In the UK, Cambridge, Salford, Brunel, University College London, and in New Zealand the University of Victoria Wellington, offer some intelligence subjects. While it is clear that some governments see value in universities being involved in intelligence education, there is not one model for how tertiary institutions deliver programmes. Most of the universities listed above have stand-alone programmes that intelligence staff from national security community can enrol in along with any other student who wishes to study intelligence. In other ways, the intelligence community's relationship with the tertiary provider is formalized, and the intelligence community has a greater direct involvement over who can enrol, curriculum design, oversight, assessment and teaching. The National Intelligence University (NIU) concept in the USA has been one approach to tertiary-level intelligence education, where the idea is to have it run under the auspices of the US intelligence community. The NIU concept is meant to be similar to a National Defense University. Although efforts have been made to develop the NIU, it seems more virtual than reality currently. It has had four different chancellors over the last four or five years, and it will need more consistent and stronger leadership and will need to buy in from agency heads if it is still to gain traction across the intelligence community. A similar intelligence community/ university collaborative effort is currently being developed in Australia with a College of National Security. The College officially opened its premises in 2010 within an existing public university, the Australian National University in Canberra. However, despite as described above the increased number of courses being offered by agencies across the intelligence community, in general, most civilian analysts compared to their military counterparts spend very little time focusing on professional development activities (George and Bruce 2008: 297). In addition, more needs to be done to promote a 'one community' approach to national security intelligence education.

Policing intelligence education

In some respects, the trends in intelligence education in the policing context follow those discussed above. For example, the challenges posed by terrorism and organized crime in the policing context have resulted in police leaders reflecting on intelligence education and other professionalism issues. Similar to intelligence education trends in the national security context, there has also been an increased involvement in external education providers, including again tertiary, vocational and private contractors delivering training for intelligence officers. There has also been an increased specialization in many policing intelligence courses within agencies, and those offered by external providers; such as tactical, operational and strategic courses.

But there are other themes, more unique to policing, such as the new public management models and intelligence-led policing approaches, discussed in earlier chapters, which have also driven internal reflection on police intelligence education requirements. For example, in 2000, the development of the UK NIM, which is underpinned by an intelligence-led policing approach to intelligence, also provided a catalyst for a number of intelligence education and training strategies developed through the NPIA. These training programmes were aimed at providing similar standards to practise across all English and Welsh police forces. Such attempts at developing common training standards were also nurtured internally by senior analysts and managers. In Australia, Canada, New Zealand and the USA, there have also been recent attempts within agencies to develop education programmes that promote a more effective and proactive use of intelligence in policing agencies. A recent example of this is in Canada, where the RCMP has been doing its own intelligence training since 1991, but is currently developing a much more extensive approach to training than what has been offered in the past. The RCMP has been developing the Criminal Intelligence Understudy Training programme (for analysts, intelligence officers and information officers), which will be implemented in 2011. This programme will offer intensive two-year training courses in each sector. This initiative is to provide for more extensive training to meet current needs and establish career paths for these three key sectors within the RCMP Criminal Intelligence programme.

However, in contrast to the UK, education developments in Australia, Canada, New Zealand and the USA have been generally more *agency-focused* rather than *nationally driven*, and standards have not as yet been as formally articulated or clarified to the same extent as they have been through the NPIA's involvement in the educational and professional aspects of the NIM. Across the USA, despite the role of professional bodies such as the International Association for Law Enforcement Intelligence Analysts (IALEIA) and the International Association of Crime Analysts (IACA), in attempting to address analytical training needs, a lot of training is fixated on technical skills – rather than providing a broader *education* that supports a more proactive and strategic use of intelligence analysis (Ratcliffe 2008: 230–231). Across Australia, Canada, New Zealand, the UK and the USA, there is also still a significant lack in training opportunities available to end users of intelligence, particularly mid-ranking officers. This is concerning, as if it is not rectified, it may result in managers not being able to use effectively intelligence in operational and strategic planning. This in turn could renew concerns in some agencies about the utility of intelligence in operational decision-making.

Key challenges and solutions

The discussion of trends above provides a sketch only of which influences have steered the directions of intelligence education post 9/11. What is more important, though, is to understand how these influences have generated real challenges to the promotion of sound intelligence education programmes across these countries, and what can be done to overcome these difficulties. The challenges faced by both national security and policing agencies are similar in some respects, but there are also variations in these which will be discussed below.

The political cultures of liberal democracies such as Australia, Canada, New Zealand, the UK and the USA have generally in each country (with the partial exception of the USA), resulted in the creation of national security intelligence communities consisting of a small number of agencies. In contrast, in policing, the same political systems resulted in multiple agencies at national, state and local level. The large number of policing agencies operating at a range of jurisdictional levels resulted in more fragmented and localized approaches to intelligence than the closed, *national* and more integrated systems of national security intelligence communities. Unsurprisingly, the localized approach to policing has resulted in localized approaches to intelligence education.

Another important historical distinction between national security and policing agencies has been the *role of intelligence* in national security and policing agencies. Traditionally, the focus of intelligence has been quite different in national security and policing agencies. In most policing agencies, intelligence has always been viewed as a supportive function to the 'main game of policing', which is to investigate and prosecute specific crime cases. In contrast, in the national security context, intelligence has always played a central role in detecting and disrupting threats, and prosecution has been a lower priority. However, care must be exercised in making such generalizations about the role of intelligence in policing. For example, Brodeur has made the distinction between 'high' and 'low' policing to describe the different ways police can be involved in intelligence. High policing, he generally equates with security intelligence work. In other words, intelligence is used to protect the state, and there is 'a greater tendency to absorb intelligence translating it into action only when there are no more justifiable alternatives' (Brodeur 2008: 27). Low policing work, he equates with criminal intelligence, which is case-driven and uses intelligence as noted above, as a means to an end. Brodeur's distinction is helpful to a point, but the reality is there is now an increasing blurring between what is considered national security and policing intelligence, particularly in complex threat areas such as terrorism and organized crime. Additionally, a lot of the intelligence approaches used in 'high policing' issues, such as informants, surveillance and GIS also underpin intelligence-led policing models being adopted at 'low policing' levels. Nevertheless, despite these different views of the role of intelligence in policing, historically there have been differences in the size of these two communities (national security and policing). There also have been different views about where intelligence 'fits' between the police and the 'spies', and these differences have resulted in some unique challenges in intelligence education in policing and national security contexts.

In particular, in the case of the policing communities, given the size of most of them, it has been difficult to articulate common standards to intelligence education programmes – particularly in the USA with over 18,000 agencies. However, despite the historical fragmentation and different emphasis placed on intelligence in national policing communities, progress is being made in some countries to articulate common standards to designing internal intelligence training and accredit teachers/instructors. Examples of this progress in Australia include accreditation of intelligence training through national vocational bodies such as the Australasian Police Professional Standards Council (APPSC), and the Australian Qualifications Training Framework (AQTF). Similarly, in the UK, the National Vocational Qualification (NVQ) provides a vehicle for nationally accrediting intelligence training courses, along with ACPO and the NPIA. However, despite the articulation of national intelligence training standards, there is still a lot of variation in the content and quality of training delivered nationally in these countries. These issues of content and quality are made more difficult given generally the fragmented and multi-level approach to policing intelligence in Australia, Canada, the UK and the USA. It has meant that policing agencies have developed historically different training and education requirements for analysts. This means that in a local policing area, the skills and capabilities of an analyst may be quite different from what would be required from someone working in an analyst role in a major city or national police agency. Similarly, another key challenge for the development of effective intelligence education in policing agencies relates to the priority attached to intelligence and therefore education. Even in large well-resourced policing agencies in the USA such as LAPD and NYPD, the approach to internal intelligence analysts' education has been ad hoc in recent years. There has been in these agencies some focus on counter-terrorism intelligence training but less on other areas of intelligence practice. Additionally, in my experience in teaching intelligence, in many policing agencies, there remains, albeit at an unconscious level, a 'cultural bias' towards providing adequate training to investigators – who are viewed often as the priority resource for training if training budgets are tight, rather than analysts.

In contrast to a more fragmented approach to policing intelligence education, it may be reasonable to expect, given the smaller number of agencies in each national security intelligence community that greater synergies and more uniform approaches to intelligence education might have emerged historically in these communities. There is no doubt since the Second World War intelligence analysts in each country have participated in courses and training offered by other members of their communities. Most countries have offered analytical training organized by their defence and assessment agencies, and these have generally been available to analysts working outside the agencies offering them. However, in general, individual agencies historically developed training for their own staff requirements rather than reflecting on how their training could be better coordinated with others to improve skills across the entire community. Obviously this is no longer the case, and by the 1990s, and more recently post 9/11, there has been a growth in the number of analysts courses offered by different agencies. This trend has also been marked by a greater desire to develop training, which has not just single agency but community-wide relevance. Despite some general variations in how intelligence education has developed in the national security and policing sectors, it is clear regardless of the context, both sectors face common challenges almost a decade on from 9/11. In the remaining part of this chapter, I will examine these challenges and identify where the solutions to them may be found.

Common challenges

Sustained focus by agency leadership

The first common challenge shared both by national security and policing agencies to building effective intelligence education programmes is achieving a sustained focus by executive leaders on this issue. This is not to suggest that heads of these agencies have not sponsored the implementation of education programmes in their agencies. The discussion above suggests otherwise. The CIA has had training in intelligence analysis for decades. Other intelligence agencies such as MI5 in the UK and ASIO in Australia, have also long had intelligence analysis training, though in many cases this training has been part of a broader 'intelligence officers' training programme. From the policing perspective, commissioners and chiefs have also been 'patrons' of all kinds of education including intelligence programmes. For example, the AFP and the RCMP have run intelligence courses since the early 1990s.

However, the development of intelligence education for many policing agencies has been inconsistent to some extent due to varying levels of executive attention paid to it. For example, in the Australian policing context, both at the federal and the state level, the executive attention to intelligence and intelligence education has waxed and waned depending on whether the leader has had a negative, positive or indifferent attitude to it. In Australia, this is changing dramatically now – particularly at the federal level. For example, in early 2009, the AFP executive commissioned a training needs analysis, aimed at assisting the agency's learning and development section to better identify what various managers and analysts need to learn in different intelligence roles across the agency. There are also efforts in other state policing agencies, such as Victoria Police, to develop and manage intelligence training as part of a broader education strategy. However, despite encouraging progress in many other policing agencies in Australia and in the other countries discussed in this chapter, intelligence education has not received the sustained executive attention that it deserves. Intelligence education programme development has traditionally been left to one or two senior staff members to deal with. These officers may make a positive impact, but if they are operational police officers, their 'tour of duty' in an education role can be short-lived. I have talked to police officers in different Australian agencies over the years who have told me that they liked being educators, but were unable to stay in these roles. In addition to the regular rotation that occurs in senior policing staff in most Australian policing agencies, staff also need to move out of education and intelligence functions if they are seeking further promotion. Additionally in Australia, while intelligence education opportunities have been provided, these have been constrained frequently by tight budgets for learning and teaching areas. In the interviews I conducted in UK, Canadian and US policing agencies, similar challenges relating to intelligence education, including sustained executive leadership, exist. All of these factors just discussed have contributed to the development and delivery of education programmes, where relevance, quality and sustainability have been affected.

There can be no 'one size fits all' approach to building sustainable executive leadership for developing intelligence education in either national security or policing agencies. Each agency and intelligence community across Australia, Canada, New Zealand, the UK and the USA will develop their own pathways to improving intelligence education over the next decade. However, the complexity of the security environment, and the need to respond to real or apparent intelligence failures, will increasingly demand sustained attention by heads of agencies on education. A sustained leadership approach to education in the national security and policing context will be one where the head of agency and the senior management team view education as equal to the other outputs coming out of intelligence areas, such as assessments and operational support. A sustained rather than a sporadic or haphazard approach to intelligence education, in addition to obviously being funded appropriately, also requires the development of a *strategy* to ensure education outputs remain aligned to organizational requirements.

Education strategy

A brief survey of some national security and policing agencies across Australia, Canada, New Zealand, the UK and the USA, since 9/11, shows that education strategies are now being developed in some agencies. Prior to 9/11, there were some earlier attempts made by some agencies to adopt a more strategic approach to education, but in general these tended to be ad hoc and did not become part of the 'corporate DNA'. For example, since the 1990s the CIA attempted to plan education requirements around the kinds of knowledge/skills/abilities required by their analysts (Marrin, interview, 8 May 2010). More recently, however, in the post-9/11 era, there has been a growing focus in agencies to take a more strategic view on intelligence education requirements. In the Australian intelligence community, some agencies, such as ASIO, have articulated a learning and development strategy which informs training and course development in intelligence analysis, and other practice areas (ASIO 2009). Though, as noted earlier, in some agencies, the role of 'analyst' is not necessarily defined using that word, and training is provided for a more generic role such as 'intelligence officer'. Agencies such as MI5, ASIO and CSIS have intelligence officers who may have an analytical role in one position, but then move on to a different operational role in another area of the agency. These agencies often augment internal analytical training with programmes offered in other parts of the intelligence community. For example, CSIS sends staff to analytical tradecraft courses provided by the Privy Council Office. DHS has also shown leadership in developing an MA programme in security studies open to middle and senior ranking federal, state and local homeland security agencies across the USA. The programme is delivered by the Center for Homeland Defense and Security, located at the Naval Postgraduate School in Monterey, California. This programme is not an analysts' programme but it does include a range of national security intelligence-related topics. The Office of Intelligence and Analysis in DHS could do more though with the ODNI to build a national intelligence analysis education strategy that is aimed at the analytical cadre level at federal, state and local level.

However, in my experience of teaching intelligence in the policing and national security environments in Australia and overseas, the adoption of comprehensive education strategies in many settings remains work in progress. For many agencies, not much thought has gone into which principles, resourcing and performance indicators should be included in an education strategy. In place of a fully developed strategy, often the approach has been a case of getting a course funded and running quickly to demonstrate that 'things are being done' in this area – even if the course will not serve the agency in the longer term. Reflecting on my experience in the Australian context, intelligence training and education of analysts have frequently been an ad hoc combination of internal and external programmes without too much deliberate strategizing about what an agency requires out of these programmes. However, this is changing as agencies respond, as noted above, to an increasingly complex security environment and identify in more systematic ways, where improvements need to be made in analytical capabilities and other areas of intelligence practice.

This more reflective approach to education planning has also been driven by increased levels of recruitment over the past decade. For example, staff numbers in ASIO have almost doubled between 2005 and 2009 from 900 to 1800 officers. This increase has resulted in significant reflection internally on what kind of graduates ASIO wishes to attract, and what other internal and external training programmes staff should attend in addition to the usual entry foundational pro-grammes – in order to more effectively function in an increasingly complex work environment. Similarly, in Australian policing, there is further evidence in some agencies of strategizing at a corporate level on intelligence education and training requirements for their analysts. The AFP's training needs analysis mentioned earlier has resulted in that agency creating an education strategy that will define a career path for their analysts. The strategy has since resulted in the implementation of a six-course or phased approach to intelligence training – starting with an induction to the intelligence management phase. The programme also includes extensive practicum and mentoring in the workplace after formal class contact time. In addition to Australia's national police, one of its state agencies, Victoria Police, has also over the past four years completed extensive reviews and development of intelligence courses aimed at developing analysts and providing them with career pathways in the agency. Though in this case, a further mapping of education outputs to career progression still needs to occur. In Canada, one of the key objectives of the CCIM discussed in Chapter 4 is also to develop an education strategy that can support standardized approaches to intelligence practice across all 380 agencies. However, it is clear from my visit to the Canadian Police College that further work will need to be done on intelligence programmes offered there to map them with the implementation of CCIM initiatives. Similarly, in October 2008, the FBI established a School of Intelligence for its analysts and those doing humint training at their Academy in Quantico, Virginia. The Head of the School of Intelligence indicated during our interview that the FBI had now developed a five-year plan for intelligence education, and was also focusing on identifying gaps between courses. This suggests that there is now corporate intent within the FBI to invest in strategically planning education requirements for analysts. The FBI's analyst cadre has increased significantly from pre 9/11 of around 260 analysts to over 2600 in 2009. All new recruits will need to be offered basic and additional advanced training which can be pegged to promotion. In the UK, there is no formally articulated national education strategy for intelligence officers at the national level, though the NPIA regularly publishes on behalf of ACPO a series of practice advices that underpin training and professional development requirements. In the past, practice advices have included topics on analysis, resource and people assets in the NIM approach and an introduction to intelligence-led policing (NPIA 2007, 2008). The NPIA also delivers national training and articulates competencies across different analytical roles, but it is less clear what role it or any other agency plays in forging a national intelligence education strategy across UK policing agencies. It is not certain at this point if the current review of the NIM will identify the need for a national intelligence education strategy, which can look at all aspects of education and training.

Designing and implementing an education strategy for intelligence analysts working in either national security or policing involve more than listing a string of programmes for staff to attend. While some academics have started to articulate what types of skills, knowledge and capabilities analysts may need (e.g. Moore *et al.* 2005), there is still no agreement in the academy or among practitioners which skills, competencies and knowledge are required of analysts. What is still missing in many agencies is any deep analysis of what intelligence staff need to know, learn and be proficient in. Many agencies, particularly larger ones, or those with a national responsibility, no longer employ analysts just with generic skills. There is greater specialization within the analytical role and so a mixture of basic and more complex skills and capabilities needs to be identified in certain positions, and relevant education strategies built around it.

There are foundational skills and capabilities that every analyst should demonstrate proficiency in, including critical thinking, research skills, good use of information technology and analytical software and excellent written expression. More senior or specialized analysts may require additional skills in particular content or methodological areas, for example, Middle Eastern politics, WMD technology, language skills (Arabic and Chinese) or adeptness in particular methodologies, such as estimative intelligence tools or manipulating financial intelligence databases and analytics. It is clear, for example, that some specialized analytical skills, such as being a WMD analyst, may be less 'transportable' between agencies, but there need to be education strategies developed within and between intelligence agencies that can at least articulate what are the basic standards and skills required to work as an analyst in specialized and general functions.

Establishing common education standards across national security and policing communities would facilitate better performance and career mobility for analysts within and between agencies. Given the changing nature of the security environment, an important step in any education strategy would be to have identified skills, competencies and proficiencies which remain under periodic review. Another important part in developing effective intelligence education strategies is to identify particular vulnerabilities, where additional resources may need to be allocated to build certain capabilities. In the policing context, strategic intelligence remains an obvious area where policing analysts in many agencies remain weak. Based on my own teaching experience, this is not for the want of analysts wanting to develop these skills, but there has frequently not been the demand – or an organizational culture where strategic intelligence has been viewed as a valuable tool in decision-making. An effective education strategy also needs to consider the appropriate mix for delivery of programmes: internal, vocational, tertiary, private consultant, contractor or a mixture of these.

An education strategy should articulate which kinds of intelligence programmes (graduate or postgraduate) analysts should participate in and how they relate to other programmes offered. There are lots of different configurations for how universities and other training providers could be involved in delivering the key outcomes of an agency's education strategy. For example, the intelligence programme I coordinate at Charles Sturt University in Australia consist of a core postgraduate programme, plus a number of short intensive courses, which are delivered in direct collaboration with the policing agency. The best-known of these is the National Strategic Intelligence Course, which is run by the university in collaboration with the AFP and ACC. This course has been in existence for ten years, and is a good example of how tertiary and policing agencies can collaborate in the delivery of a strategic intelligence course (Walsh and Ratcliffe 2005).

An education strategy also needs to help those responsible for intelligence analysts' professional development to risk and project manage the planning and delivery of education programs. While skills, competencies and graduate attributes need to be articulated clearly in the delivery of each programme, quality and cost control also require monitoring. Since 9/11 there seems to have been a burgeoning number of education providers, big and small, offering their services to national security and policing agencies, and there are likely to be a few 'snake oil charmers' out there offering all and under-delivering. So the articulation of a quality assurance framework will be an important component within an agency's education strategy.

The final point to developing effective intelligence strategies is to ensure agency strategies are informed by and implement common professional standards that are now evolving in the broader context of whole intelligence communities. For example, as noted in Chapter 4, in UK policing, common analytical standards that support the more effective application of the NIM principles have resulted in the NPIA producing several practice guidelines which articulate good practice for the entire UK policing sector. In contrast, in Canadian policing, the development of professional standards has been largely left up to each policing agency historically, though it is expected the new CCIM (discussed in Chapter 4) will eventually bring a lot more standardized approaches across agencies to education approaches and standards. In Australia too, the ACC is currently mapping analyst training content and standards to better support new analytical roles for its analysts under its new Project Sentinel.

On the national security front, various senior government intelligence coordinating fora could also take on, as part of their responsibilities, a community-wide leadership role to articulate common standards that better inform agency education strategies. In Australia, the newly established NICC (see Chapter 6) could, for example, establish a sub-committee to take on this role. In the USA, the ODNI has established an Office of Analytic Integrity and Standards (AIS) to promote better analytic standards across the US intelligence community. The Office has been led mostly by academics, and under the tenure of different assistant deputy directors the AIS has made some progress in developing analytic standards that can also be used to guide the development of education programmes. Historian Richard Immerman held the positions of Assistant Deputy Director of National Intelligence for AIS and Analytic Ombudsman for the ODNI from September 2007 to December 2008. During this time, he set up processes for the review of products written up by all members of the intelligence community, resulting in the review of between 1200 to 1500 products annually. Products were evaluated for good tradecraft, timeliness, political influence and related criteria. His review processes produced other important key outcomes, including distilling 'lessons learnt' for analysts and identifying best practices for analysts' writing products. The AIS also deployed some outreach teams that periodically visited US intelligence agencies to discuss key evaluation findings with relevant managers, but also to develop training capacities within agencies to improve tradecraft.

In respect to developing common training standards, Immerman noted that AIS developed a course 'Analysis 101', which was periodically revised during his tenure and is now offered to all incoming analysts across the US intelligence community, run by the DIA. This work, however, has been achieved largely by a small team (around a dozen) of officers within AIS, with the advice of a limited number of senior analysts from across the intelligence community. Limited resources obviously make it difficult for the ODNI to push proactively the agenda on standards and informing education strategies across the US intelligence community. Despite some progress in this area, rivalries between agencies still exist, and some member agencies continue to drive largely their own current training requirements. There seems to be a reluctance in some of them to sign up completely for an ODNI-driven approach to training or the common analytic standards reflected in such training (Immerman, interview, 3 May 2010). As a result, there is still no nationally artic-ulated training strategy for the entire US intelligence community, nor despite some progress recently at ODNI, has there been a comprehensive training needs assess-ment of what agencies require separately and collectively (Breckenridge 2010: 309).

Promoting effective teaching and learning in intelligence

The third challenge to the promotion of effective intelligence education pro-grammes relates to how intelligence is taught, and the way analysts learn its theoretical and practical components. The promotion of effective teaching and learning, as noted above, is a critical component of any education strategy. The strategy needs to include measurables that allow an agency to assess teaching approaches, and whether new skills are being incorporated to improve practice. Although effective teaching and learning are a core component of any education strategy, I have included it as a separate and third challenge. This is to underline that in the past, what constitutes effective teaching and learning in intelligence education has not necessarily been a conscious or an elaborate component in the intelligence education programmes in many national security and policing agencies. At first glance, this may seem like a statement of heresy for all those educators of intelligence analysts reading this book. Both experienced senior intelligence officers and seasoned academics may view themselves as excellent teachers, and their end-of-course student feedback proves the point! But reflecting on my own transition from seasoned intelligence officer to university teacher, there is clearly a difference between having good content knowledge, and being able to ensure it is linked to appropriate learning outcomes – and identifying the most appropriate teaching strategies. The importance for the 'academic/content specialist' promoting effective teaching and learning in intelligence as in any field is well encapsulated by higher education academic, Paul Ramsden:

> The professional authority of the academic-as-scholar rests on a body of knowledge; the professional authority of the academic-as-teacher should rest on a body of didactic knowledge. This comprises knowledge of how the subject he or she professes is best learnt and taught.
>
> (1992: 9)

Breckenridge (2010) recently raised a range of learning and teaching issues relevant to intelligence education in the US context, in particular how can educators promote better learning environments and assessment in intelligence education? Put in other words, further pedagogical reflection on the teaching and learning of intelligence studies is long overdue. For example, what are the best ways to teach good practice analysis at tactical and strategic levels in different delivery modes, such as distance learning and classroom-based learning? Anyone can feasibly stand in front of a class and show a few PowerPoint slides on how, for instance, to improve critical thinking. But the teaching challenge is how to engage students on both the theoretical and practical aspects of intelligence so they leave the class thinking; in this case, critical thinking is as important as you think it is. Additionally, the central role of assessment must be given more deliberation, and wherever possible best match which skills, competencies or knowledge need to be learnt. Preferably assessment strategies that promote deep rather than surface learning should be considered in the overall teaching approach. The terms 'surface' and 'deep' learning originated with Swedish academics Marton and Saljo in the 1970s, who conducted a series of research projects on how students learnt. In simple terms, surface learning is engaging in only superficial content of a subject, while deep learning is about trying to understand the meaning of a problem. In other words, they are approaches to learning which 'describe the way students relate to a teaching/learning environment: they are not fixed characteristics of students' (Biggs 2003: 17). Surface and deep learning can be promoted from both the teacher's and the student's perspective. For example, considering the surface approach first, from the teacher's perspective, he or she may find it simpler (and less time-consuming) to set a multiple choice test to recall facts rather than an essay. An essay would require the student to engage more deeply with a problem that may have no clear-cut answer. From the student's perspective, a multiple short answer quiz may be preferable as they only want to recall enough facts to pass the subject and/or they have high anxiety over writing essay papers, which require them to demonstrate the ability for deeper analysis. However, in many subject areas relating to intelligence, it may be preferable to design assessment items which promote a deeper learning outcome. For example, the teacher could set a question for research by the student, which requires them to investigate and analyse it rather than just commit facts to memory. This approach helps reinforce other student learning in areas such as critical thinking, research skills and analysis – all important attributes you want to develop in someone who aspires to be an analyst. From the student's perspective, and again depending on the nature of the assessment item, a deeper learning approach may instil in them a desire to work conceptually on a problem – with curiosity rather than just wanting to get the assessment over with. Both of these concepts are useful to considering how intelligence educators may find ways to improve teaching (ibid.: 12–17). Effective teaching in the intelligence context therefore must try to increase the opportunities that students will use a deep approach to learning. Effective teaching, like any other skill, involves trial and error. Critical reflection on one's teaching therefore is very important in assessing what works and what doesn't, and this will also be an important quality for those involved in intelligence education to develop in themselves and their colleagues.

Teaching and learning are, as suggested above, inevitably linked, and while there needs to be more critical reflection by intelligence educators about their teaching approach, arguably what is most important in this relationship (between teaching and learning) is how can we gain a better understanding of how analysts learn. Research into how analysts assimilate learning provided in various education programmes, particularly back in the workplace is non-existent. For example, in the National Strategic Intelligence Course mentioned earlier, there is now a decade of alumni of analysts who have completed this two-week intensive course in Australia. While the focus of the course does a good job of mixing theory with practice, there is little evidence available to assess how students are or are not assimilating strategic analytical skills back in their workplace, and why. Anecdotally we know from assessment of course feedback that students do get something out of attending, but feedback forms are a pretty blunt instrument. We also know that in many policing environments in Australia, the ability of students to incorporate strategic intelligence skills into their daily practice is constrained for a range of organizational cultural and other reasons. It is clear then that a more conscious and formalized approach to research that informs such pedagogical issues is essential. How, for instance, do we most effectively teach intelligence students to be better researchers, problem solvers or do threat assessments on different threat groups? Arguably these are essential professional attributes to becoming effective analysts. This raises related questions of how much can be learnt in the classroom, and what kind of things?

It seems clear enough that students need to be exposed, for instance, to a range of research methodological approaches and the theory of logics and argumentation, but these skills need to be adapted in the real world of intelligence practice. This is where the real learning will happen but I would argue as 'intelligence educators', we are often not very good at providing teaching and learning strategies that allow students to continue lifelong learning beyond the classroom. Students also need to understand how various topics taught in the classroom (such as research methodologies), are not simple linear activities that once neatly applied to a problem will in textbook fashion reveal in all cases the truth or resolve the problem. The 'real world' of an analyst, of course, is one where there are often very few absolute truths, and – although frequently the expectation by some decision-makers is for analysts to approach the problem with the same social scientific rigour of an economist or political scientist – the results of intelligence analysis will frequently not neatly support one overwhelming hypothesis. A research-enhanced teaching approach may reveal better ways to teach such important attributes and skills to analysts about how they apply the theory on research and assessing problems to work through real problems. Alternatively to get around using classified material, researchers could give analysts sanitized material to work with or design scenario or mock problems for them to research and solve (Brew 2006: 15). The results of this research can be used to better inform teaching in these areas and promote more student- rather than teacher-focused strategies to learning. In addition to this kind of pedagogical research, other theory- or practice-based research within intelligence may not only improve practice, but also better inform the teaching of this practice. So the link between teaching and research in the intelligence context needs to be considered more than it has so far.

Professionalism

The second component of this chapter deals with a number of issues that can be bundled loosely under the heading 'professionalism'. As noted earlier, the development of effective intelligence education strategies and programmes should be at the core of professionalism in the intelligence context. But it should be clear to most that professionalism has wider scope than education, and includes other important factors such as codes of behaviour, mentoring, continuing professional development, career progression, recruitment and attrition and collegial association. All these factors arguably may be attributable to an 'intelligence discipline', and I will discuss them all in this context. But first it is important to step back from this discussion and ask ourselves, is it appropriate to be talking about intelligence being a discipline? And if it is a discipline, then do the above factors or additional ones accurately describe it?

Depending on who you talk to, the answer to the above question may be a definitive yes, no or maybe. The current debate requires reflection first on what are meant by the words 'discipline' and the related term 'profession', as they tend to get used interchangeably. For many, a profession usually refers to a specific vocation one chooses, which requires the mastery of a related body of knowledge.

While clearly related in terms of accomplishing a branch of learning, with discipline the focus is more on the rules, training, behaviour or conduct required to accomplish that branch of learning. Fisher and Johnston, who have examined professionalism in the intelligence context also (cited in George and Bruce 2008: 55–68), prefer to use the term 'discipline' and describe it as a type of profession, but one where rules, both voluntary and mandatory, serve to guide, inform and ensure the highest possible quality of professional conduct and activity (ibid.: 55). Interestingly, Fisher and Johnston also emphasize the importance in the generation of knowledge production and sharing as being important in developing disciplines (ibid.: 65). Marrin has also provided a good overview of the growth of 'intelligence professionalism' in the USA. He suggests that intelligence analysis has developed aspects of professionalism, but there is still a way to go – particularly, he argues, in the production of consistent performance standards and turning disparate intelligence analysis disciplines (in national security, intelligence and business sectors) into a coherent whole profession (Marrin and Clemente 2006).

I do not wish to dwell on these definitional issues of whether intelligence analysis or more broadly intelligence is either a discipline or a profession. But based on the discussion above about the attributes of professions and disciplines, I would argue the field of intelligence and intelligence analysis, more narrowly, is neither a profession nor a single discipline. Intelligence analysis is an evolving set of skills, practices, theories and issues that in most cases are still developing attributes identified above necessary for classification as a discipline. Given this evolving state of intelligence analysis practice, the more relevant question is then, how do we engender greater *professionalism* within intelligence practice so that at some undefined time in the future it is possible to more confidently answer this question of whether intelligence is a profession or not? More relevant questions, then, are what are the current challenges and barriers to greater professionalism within intelligence in the national security, policing and other contexts and what can be done about them?

There are many attributes of professionalism that we could discuss here but there are five major ones, which define the current challenges and barriers to greater professionalism within national security and policing intelligence analysis. These are: *education, continuing professional development, career structure, professional association* and *community engagement* and *research*. I have discussed education in detail above so there is no need to repeat much of this. It is important to keep in mind, however, that enhancing intelligence professionalism will require that education strategies not only reflect good teaching programmes, but also these programmes are clearly linked to common and agreed professional standards, skill sets and graduate attributes. In my teaching experience, what is missing is a greater focus on what analysts need to *know* in particular roles and to what standard. The development of common standards within and across agencies obviously would promote increased levels of confidence in standards and competencies, and engender a greater sense of professionalism. Intelligence agencies, governments and academics should play a greater role in the future in articulating common standards in education that ensure analysts both in generalist and specialist roles receive appropriate training. Training received in one agency, particularly at the generalist analytical level, should also allow some uniformity and transferability of skill sets across national security and policing intelligence communities. As noted earlier, over the past decade, in some sectors of the policing intelligence communities in Australia, Canada, New Zealand, the UK and the USA, there have been attempts by governments and heads of agencies to articulate common skills, competencies required at different levels and analytical roles.

However, these efforts and specifically linking standards to education pro-grammes (with perhaps the exception of UK policing), have often not been formally implemented or consistently applied. There are likely to be a number of reasons for this – some of which have been discussed earlier in the chapter. But no doubt one major factor has been a failure to agree at a corporate level within and across intelligence agencies what analysts need to know. Without this agreement, it is not surprising that common skills, competencies and standards have not been articulated. For example, in the Australian national policing environment efforts were made a decade ago to articulate common standards for analytical skills required by analysts working in federal agencies, but these were never adopted formally by the agencies involved. A number of policy initiatives which are cur-rently under way as a result of the release of the 2009 Organised Crime Strategic Framework, and work being done by the ACC to develop analytical standards and competencies may complete work started a decade ago.

Similarly, in the history of many agencies in the national security intelligence communities of Australia, Canada, New Zealand, the UK and the USA, any reflec-tion by governments and agency heads on analytical standards, and mapping those to education programmes have been organic or ad hoc rather than a strategically driven processes. There have been exceptions of course. The CIA, as noted earlier, had attempted to develop education requirements that were matched against spe-cific analytical skills and capabilities in the 1990s. Though for other agencies, there was no mapping of standards to training. Indeed, beyond general intelligence officer training provided during induction of new staff, not much thought went into specifically what analysts needed to know and at what levels of proficiency. I once heard a former senior MI5 officer saying that in the days of the Cold War, as a new recruit, his training consisted of little more than a more senior intelligence officer pointing to where the files where located. Little thought was given to what agencies wanted from people in analyst roles, and training was viewed as very much about 'learning on the job'. Over the past decade, there are now signs that this ad hoc approach to analysts' training and setting standards is becoming more strategic. For example, in the USA, the Deputy DNI Analysis did articulate analytical standards for the intelligence community in 2007. The *Intelligence Community Directive Number 203* listed eight standards such as objectivity, independence from political influence, distinguishing between underlying intelligence and analysts' assumptions and judgements (ODNI 2007). The last standard was to make accurate judgements and assessments. These standards, however, have been criticized by some former intelligence officers I interviewed, who believe that they have a mechanistic or process-driven feel about them. One former US intelligence officer commented that 'You can get an analyst to go through all these steps, and still not come up with an accurate judgment or assessment.' To some extent, this seems a reasonable comment. While effective analysis can be improved by articulating important standards and these can be taught, at its fundamental level, analysis always goes back to thinking. There is a limit to how much you can teach someone to think and, as noted in Chapter 8, there is always plenty of scope for 'analytical thinking' to go wrong. It is unclear at this stage, the extent to which these eight ODNI standards are being used to conduct evaluations of intelligence products, or are linked to training programmes within individual agencies in the US intelligence community. I suspect, based on discussions with some former senior intelligence officers in the USA, that there is still some resistance across the intelligence community to follow to the letter directives given by the ODNI, and it is not clear what, if anything, the DNI can do to get agencies to comply with standards or the regular evaluation of these.

The context in which the ODNI works is likely to remain a highly politicized and sensitive bureaucratic environment and achieving common (consensus-driven) community-wide standards that are reviewed regularly by individual intelligence agencies and the ODNI will remain difficult. In the end, ODNI does not control the budgets of US intelligence agencies and so any monitoring and evaluation of standards are not likely to be enforceable. ODNI also does not have sufficient staff to adequately evaluate analytical standards and their adoption in education programmes across all US intelligence agencies. Added to this is that after half a decade in existence, I would argue that the ODNI still has a credibility gap with some members of the US intelligence community, so this too constrains its influence across the community on this and other issues. This raises the question as to whether other institutions may be better placed to articulate and monitor analytical standards and other related professional matters. I will come back to this question in the section below on *professional association*.

Further evidence is required on what other national security intelligence communities, apart from the USA, are now doing to promote education programmes that are underpinned by clearly articulated standards for analysts. The various post-9/11 reviews of intelligence agencies pointed to further training needs of analysts in different communities, particularly in the UK and Australia, so one would expect that more thought is now going into articulating analytical standards for practice and training in these communities. In the UK, after the Butler Report's criticism of analytical performance, a professional head of intelligence analysis was established in that country, though this position has now been subsumed within the Chair of the JIC. It is not clear now how analytical performance and standards are being articulated and monitored.

In Australia, there is currently no formalized national focus on intelligence analysis training and standards. The recently established NICC, chaired by the Australian National Security Advisor, would seem the appropriate body to examine these issues. The NICC could develop a sub-committee to examine education, training and professional issues related to intelligence analysts. This sub-committee should include appointed academics who teach and research in intelligence, and who could advise the intelligence community on the setting and reviewing of standards and advising on curriculum issues. In Canada, the Intelligence Assessments Committee – a group of eight heads of assessment from the country's security intelligence community – in 2008 approved eight 'best practices' that are used as the core of training. The practices include things like *reflecting on a problem*, *critical evaluation* and interestingly a focus on using *structured analytic techniques.* The Canadian approach seems less formalized and prescriptive than what the ODNI is trying to achieve in the USA. For example, the Canadian intelligence community has not adopted specific mechanisms for formal review, and the ethos is to encourage practices rather than articulating minimal standards that must be achieved.

From the policing perspective, I have already discussed in Chapters 4 and 5 some specific initiatives that individual agencies and policing communities are adopting to promote common perspectives on analytical skills and education more broadly. In Australia, in the policing context, there is the potential for ACC to articulate analytical standards on behalf of all Australian policing agencies, though this will require greater focus and assent by federal and state policing heads than has been the case in the past. In the UK, the NPIA has played an important role in identifying common analytical standards but it is less clear how it plays a role in evaluating them at police force level. Perhaps, though, this evaluation role is more appropriately the function of the HMIC. In Canada, an important part of the planned CCIM is the generation of common standards and approaches to training, though it is still not clear if the model will be implemented. In the US policing intelligence sector there exist some professional bodies such as the IALEIA and the Society of Certified Criminal Analysts (SCCA) that offer some credentializing of analytical standards, though it is doubtful if these agencies have the mandate of all US police chiefs to promote a common standardized approach to analysts' training or standards. In New Zealand, the situation, in contrast to the USA, may be a lot easier, given there is only one police agency in that country – NZP. As noted in Chapter 4, NZP are making progress in articulating common analytical standards mapped across to training programmes, though this is still a work in progress

The second challenge, *continuing professional development*, is another issue that needs to be addressed as part of any education strategy within an agency. An important characteristic of professionalism is a conscious and ongoing commitment to practitioner improvement. As noted in the above examples of the legal and medical professions (e.g. the Federation of Law Societies of Canada and the Royal College of Surgeons), in both cases, practitioners are expected to, and provided with, opportunities for ongoing professional development after graduating with qualifying degrees and completing relevant internships. In the colleges of medicine and the law societies of Australia, Canada, New Zealand, the UK and the USA, there is a suite of programmes practitioners can complete to remain current, but also to assist in further specialization and promotion. While there are always exceptions, the general trend, until recently, in the intelligence context, has been the opposite. It has only been in the past few years since 9/11, that a conscious and strategic effort has been made in many agencies to provide continuing professional development pathways for analysts. This is not to suggest that elements of a continuing professional development initiative have not existed; quite the contrary. Both national security and policing agencies are increasingly offering analysts a range of internal and external development opportunities to attend workshops, seminars, conferences and exchange sessions with colleagues in other agencies. But a more formalized approach to continuing professional development is needed that connects this to the broader education strategy of the agency, and it also needs to be linked to performance pay and promotion. While there may be some broad similarities in areas of continuing professional development across agencies and even countries, for example, in sending analysts off to complete various IT software courses, the focus of any plan might be quite agency-specific in many areas depending on the function of intelligence within that agency. For example, an analyst joining a financial intelligence unit in a national policing agency is likely to benefit from additional training opportunities in banking and forensic accounting, whereas an analyst working in a national security agency on WMD issues in the Middle East is likely to benefit from further language training in Arabic and Farsi.

Given that in many agencies analytical staff are considered mobile resources, it is also important to have a more strategic approach to continuing professional development so that analysts can, wherever possible, be made ready for other roles across the agency. It is not possible or fiscally wise of course to offer professional development opportunities in every potential area to all staff. Not all analytical staff would have an interest, aptitude or require, for example, specialized skills in forensic accounting or tracking sophisticated illegal arms transfers between countries. But there are a number of continuing professional development opportunities that heads of agencies should consider offering to most of their analytical cadre to improve overall capability. The list is endless, but could include things like improving critical thinking, peer review, alternative analysis and structured analytical thinking, understanding relevant ethics and legislative frameworks, GIS and the causes of radicalization. Other important areas that need to be considered under a strategic approach to continuing professional development are the role of mentoring for staff (interns, junior and more senior staff), and how to more effectively link internal programmes with those offered by universities, professional bodies and training providers.

The third challenge, *career structure*, is closely linked to the first (education) and the second (continuing professional development). While the first two challenges are critical in promoting better professionalism, what is absent in many agencies, particularly policing agencies, is a career structure that can take an analyst to a more senior position in an agency once they gain some experience, and complete all the education and continuing professional development opportunities provided. In the key US intelligence agencies that employ the most analysts, for example, the CIA, and in other agencies such as ASIO, CSIS and MI5, there are career structures in place for intelligence analysts. Analysts have somewhere to go beyond their current position, although in the latter examples, most senior intelligence positions are not designated as senior analysts' roles necessarily. In many of these organizations once an analyst moves to middle ranking management level, the emphasis becomes less on analysis or writing products, and more on generic management functions of coordinating an analytical team, unit or branch. As a senior analyst becomes a manager, they frequently also need to gain additional skills other than analytical ones, and rotation through different functions within the agency is seen as important to being eligible for senior executive appointment – and increasingly now periods of time outside one's agency. While ensuring the best and brightest get the opportunity of 'knowing all parts of the business', this approach can impact on retaining expertise in critical areas as people are moved on to focus on another intelligence priority. For example, a middle section manager may be in charge of a geographic region for a few years and then moved on to human resources or the training area. As a general rule, the CIA has tended to move analysts, particularly those with linguistic skills, around to different posts, while in other parts of the intelligence community such as the Bureau of Intelligence and Research (INR) in the State Department, analysts stay in the same area longer.

This issue of how you create a career path for analysts to senior management calls for a balance between strategies. An agency obviously needs to create experienced generalists, but also must retain specialists who have technical skills (that frequently involve years of experience), but who may not want to take on management roles. Developing an appropriate mix between generalist and specialist career options for analysts, senior analysts and beyond is complicated further by the retirement of a number of baby boomer intelligence officers in agencies like the CIA, who leave with a great deal of technical and general experience. In the CIA, the analytical workforce is the youngest it has been since 1947, and across the US intelligence community 30 per cent of analysts have less than three years experience.

In contrast to national security agencies, in many policing agencies there has not been until the past decade formalized career structures for analysts. The discussion in Chapter 4 of new evolving intelligence models in Australia, Canada and New Zealand policing shows that career development is an important by-product of intelligence reform in these agencies. Though in many of these agencies, and others examined during this project such as NYPD and the FBI, the development of career pathways is still work in progress. There are a few variables operating in some policing agencies, which are constraining attempts to create viable career pathways for analysts. One important variable, mentioned a few times already, relates to vestigial organizational cultural attitudes to intelligence within some policing agencies. This can be summed up as either a negative, neutral or an indifferent attitude to intelligence analysts, who are seen as support staff, not specialists in their own right as investigators would be viewed. Whether a negative or neutral view held consciously or unconsciously by those who hold financial delegation authority, this translates frequently to a diminished *value* for what analysts do, and therefore operates as a constraint on the creation of a career structure that would ironically improve their professionalism and create more value for those who question it. This is not to suggest that *all* policing agencies do not place any value in analysts and will not create career paths for them. As noted in earlier chapters, starting with the UK NIM, but more recently with new intelligence frameworks in the policing communities of Canada, Australia and New Zealand, efforts are being made to create career pathways for analysts. But for some, despite a greater urgency in needing to understand a complex security environment, there has not yet been a sufficient 'mental shift' in their view of what intelligence can provide, let alone a view on a career path for their analysts.

An examination of recent attempts in some Australian and UK policing agencies to provide career pathways shows that even where career pathways are established, they can come under threat due to financial constraints, questions again of value for money (from other non-intelligence managers) and lack of sustained leadership on whether to retain higher analyst career positions. For example, in the UK, a major by-product of the UK NIM was the creation within UK policing agencies of an analyst career pathway, with the establishment of roles such as senior analysts, principal analysts and higher analysts. In particular, the role of higher analysts came into being in some UK policing agencies partly to recognize experienced analytical staff with greater remuneration, but also to provide a coach or mentor role to junior analysts (NPIA 2007: 44). However, in some UK policing agencies, questions are being asked by non-intelligence managers whether 'higher analysts' represent an 'essential' role.

In the policing context, the ability of agencies to create career paths that will allow experienced analysts to move up to management position, and/or others to receive higher remuneration for specialized roles, will be important in promoting greater professionalism within the analytical cadre. It will also be important for agencies in attracting new staff and keeping well-qualified analysts.

The fourth challenge to promoting professionalism in national security and policing intelligence contexts is *professional association and community engagement*. An important component to an established profession is having professional bodies that promote the profession, and provide a gateway to who can belong to the profession via coordinating education, accreditation and registration of practitioners. Many professional bodies also have lobbying and workplace conditions (union) roles that protect their members' interest in the policy-making process. In the intelligence context, there is still no equivalent of, for example, the American Medical Association in the USA, the Australian Medical Association, the Royal College of Surgeons in the UK or the Federation of Law Societies of Canada. All of these examples have been in existence for extended periods. For example, the Royal College of Surgeons can trace its lineage back to 1540 during the reign of Henry VIII. Most of them also have well-established services for their members, which include accreditation, continuing professional development and advocacy.

In intelligence, there are a number of professional bodies that analysts could belong to, particularly in areas such as international affairs, but there are also specific intelligence professional associations such as the Australian Institute of Professional Intelligence Officers (AIPIO), the Canadian Association for Security Intelligence Studies (CASIS), the New Zealand Institute of Intelligence Professionals (NZIIP) and the IALEIA in the USA. There is no national security intelligence analytical society equivalent in the USA for serving intelligence officers. In general, the professional associations listed above have only been in existence for a short time, but have tried to promote professionalism for their members, who generally are intelligence officers, academics or industry partners, who have links to intelligence agencies. In each case, the range of services provided to members varies widely, but could include accreditation, training, publications, conferences, professional advocacy and lobbying with government and relevant industry partners. There is insufficient room to provide a detailed description of the particular services provided and the problems/challenges each of these professional bodies faces in representing the intelligence practitioners in their country.

While all have aspirations of representing 'the intelligence profession', the reality is that for the most part they represent *their members*, who in most of these agencies, with the exception of IALEIA, number hundreds rather than thousands. There are many reasons why membership size of these associations has been historically small. One important constraint on membership numbers relates to the historical legacy of the 'culture of secrecy' discussed in Chapter 1 – many intelligence officers have not felt comfortable freely associating in these ways in the past. In particular, the 'culture of secrecy' means for some intelligence officers, particularly those involved in sensitive operational work, they may want to become members, but are reluctant to identify themselves or their agency.

The small size of these associations, compared to professional medical and legal bodies, means their mandates to represent the 'intelligence profession' remain aspirational. Small membership size also means that income from membership fees does not allow a full suite of services (for example, established continuing professional development programmes, accreditation), or even a CEO or administrative staff to support basic membership services. Rather than any paid positions, these bodies are usually run by a Board, who are either retired intelligence professionals or still active in various services but commit to these organizations on a volunteer basis. What membership services that are provided mainly focus on a regular newsletter, journal and an annual conference rather than investment in other more costly and time-intensive activities, such as accreditation of analysts, the provision of education programmes or well-developed lobbying programmes to government on behalf of members.

Given the small membership base, low income and volunteer basis of these professional bodies, it is difficult to assess, in some cases, their ongoing viability, let alone their ability to speak for the profession. In summary, for many of the professional agencies listed above, there are still significant challenges to overcome before they can be seen to represent their members' interests, let alone those of the entire profession. Not all existing professional bodies, of course, will want to position themselves as representing the profession, though others will see this as their mission. But in the next decade, it is in the interest of intelligence professionalism that associations develop the ability to provide high quality membership services including professional accreditation and representing the profession to government, the media and the community as an honest broker for a wider spectrum of 'the profession'. Looking back over the past decade, if there had been effective professional intelligence associations in each country, they could have represented their members in various senate and parliamentary inquiries which investigated a range of issues relating to analytical performance, particularly the 9/11 Commission and the US SSCI report into WMD in Iraq. It is likely that in the future some of the current professional intelligence associations will wither for the reasons described earlier, while others may develop the capacity in the longer term to meet the broader professional accreditation and continuing professional development needs of their members. Marrin argues that the creation of a single association modelled on the American Medical Association – called perhaps the *American Intelligence Analysis Association* – might help advance common standards for the entire analytical discipline regardless of whether these practitioners were from national security, policing or the business sector (Marrin and Clemente 2006: 656). There is merit in this idea, particularly in trying to unite the fragmented strands of a number of different analytical disciplines. AIPIO in Australia does represent all analysts, regardless of where they practise, so this is one approach which may be useful to adopt elsewhere. An independent non-political professional body that unites analysts of whatever persuasion is attractive, yet for them to offer the important services required of a mature professional body, such as accreditation of members, then governments, individual agencies and analysts themselves need to invest in these professional bodies to ensure they have viable secretariats that do not just rely on the goodwill of a few volunteers. If the government is serious about recognizing such agencies, then they also need to confirm on them chartered rights to bestow accreditations on individuals' practice as analysts.

Linked to professional association is *community engagement*. While it seems appropriate for professional associations to engage with the broader community about the 'intelligence profession', intelligence agencies themselves need to engage more strategically with the media and general community about issues that cut across their interests. This, of course, like any other government agency, must be done with the consent of appropriate political decision-makers. Most national security and larger policing agencies have their own media and public relations teams to do this work already. The events of 9/11 and the WMD in Iraq issue, however, piqued public and media interest in the operations of intelligence agencies, arguably like no other period in their existence. While heads of agencies are expected to 'take the heat' for real or apparent failures, there is now a growing commodification of a 'profession' that was until recently rarely on the front page of newspapers or on television. This growing public and media interest obviously for the agencies themselves is not entirely welcome. But there may also be some opportunities for agencies in promoting a more positive understanding of their work to the community. However, more thought will also be needed on how agencies can proactively engage in debates about intelligence, while balancing fundamental needs to protect information that could jeopardize national security.

The objective of any strategic approach to community engagement is to promote the interest and perceptions of intelligence officers' professionalism in order to raise greater understanding and tolerance for their activities in the community. This will continually be important in the future as public opinions about the effectiveness and even requirement for intelligence services are again challenged by future events that will rightly or wrongly be labelled 'intelligence failures'. Promotion both of generic details of what an analyst does and of a positive image of this role from within intelligence agencies will also assist in recruitment. There is already evidence of this in Australia, the USA and the UK in how intelligence agencies have begun increasing community engagement since 9/11. For example, many national security intelligence agencies or communities have developed open source material explaining generally their broad roles and functions. The former DNI, Admiral Blair, also published a number of publicly available information booklets including the National Intelligence Strategy that identify the national intelligence priorities for the USA (see Chapter 6). In contrast, major policing agencies have been slower to release public information on how intelligence is applied to their work, though perhaps publicly available material such as the national threat assessment on organized crime by SOCA in the UK, and the organized crime reports by the ACC in Australia and CISC in Canada demonstrate this is changing.

The fifth and final challenge to building greater professionalism within intelligence relates to *research*. I will not spend time on this issue here as the relationship between research and professionalism will be discussed more fully in Chapter 10. However, it is clear that an important characteristic of any profession is the development of new knowledge that can improve practice. Research plays a key role therefore in improving practice. Arguably up until recently, while research has always occurred in science and technological aspects of intelligence, particularly in the military and national security context, there has been less focus on improving analysis.

As noted earlier in Chapter 8, 'intelligence analysis' is a vague and multi-faceted term, and could include a range of discipline areas, where research may be useful in improving analysis. There are issues relating to cognitive psychology and how analysts and decision-makers process information. There are questions relating to knowledge management and how analysts work with disparate information sets, and there are also issues on how analysts calibrate threat and risk. In addition to some of these generic analytical skills, there are also a range of issues about how analysts interpret complex specific global threats and events relating to terrorism, criminal exploitation of digital technology, or whether a country will seek to develop a nuclear weapon capability. The identification of an appropriate research agenda, one that can look at the technological, but also the human, side of analysis will be important in advancing professionalism.

In conclusion, since 9/11, there has been an expansion in the education opportunities available for analysts inside their agencies and outside. The sheer increase in recruitment in analysts, particularly in larger national security and policing organizations, has required a greater focus on training requirements. The number of inquiries into the intelligence assessments provided to governments leading up to 9/11, and the WMD issue in Iraq has also caused agencies to reflect on training needs and professional standards. At the same time, increases in recruitment of analysts have resulted in the growth of education providers, though questions remain whether some programmes are fit for purpose. It is clear that within agencies, there will need to be sustained corporate attention on intelligence education and professionalism to articulate in a more strategic way what current and future skills are required. Agencies should also consider inviting some external education providers to regularly participate in the development of education strategies. For example, I am a member of the AFP's Law Enforcement Intelligence Training Consultative Committee, which is a very useful forum to bring academics and industry partners together to talk about intelligence education and training. The second part of this chapter dealt with the issue of professionalism. While I do not think that intelligence is a profession in the same way that one would think of the medical or legal profession, the debate should be shifted away from the unhelpful dichotomous framework it currently occupies. A more constructive and realistic question is, how do we engender a stronger sense of professionalism across the different practice contexts that make up intelligence? I mentioned five challenges to developing professionalism in this field, the last of which was research. The next chapter will explore how the development of a research agenda can inform better practice and help bind a disparate set of discipline activities more tightly together.

10 Research and theory building

Introduction

The preceding chapters have focused on examining different contemporary intelligence practice issues across the three broad themes of the book: *applying intelligence, understanding structures* and *developing a discipline*. In this last chapter, we focus on how research and theory building can help to define a discipline of intelligence in the future. Starting with research, I discuss the implications of doing research in the intelligence context before drawing on key themes raised earlier to develop an *intelligence research strategy* for intelligence. The research strategy section will list some priority research objectives and related tasks in order to provide a strategic framework (see Table 10.1 on p. 289) for generating further discussions on specific research projects, methodological considerations and how practitioners and academics might collaborate on various projects. The final section of the chapter will describe current theoretical developments in the intelligence field, and explore to what extent they are linked to research, or informed from other fields such as cognitive and social psychology, management and criminology.

The chapter argues that better research and theorizing in the field have been hampered by a number of factors. One of the key ones has been disagreements over what intelligence is meant to do. For example, is intelligence a tool to explain (a scientific approach) or understand (an interpretative approach) the security environment? Finally, the chapter will explore the extent to which research and theory are being successfully integrated into education and continuing professional development.

Intelligence research

Before discussing the research strategy in Table 10.1, it is useful to take a step back to reflect on whether intelligence and research belong in the same sentence. Is it possible to do research on aspects of intelligence practice? I think the answer is 'yes', given that fundamentally research is about generating knowledge, but it is important first to recognize the challenges in doing intelligence research in order to address these issues more effectively. As noted earlier in Chapter 5, the culture of secrecy, and in many cases specific legislative barriers, have prevented researchers external to national security and policing agencies from engaging in some sensitive areas of research. The sensitive nature of some intelligence methodologies, particularly in collection and defence-related technologies preclude external researchers' involvement. This kind of research tends to be done 'in-house' by appropriately cleared staff. Though having said this, there are a lot of technologically-based areas where intelligence agencies are interested in sponsoring research, such as biometrics, forensics and more generally information communication technology and where external (university-based) researchers can collaborate with intelligence agencies.

While there may be topic areas where external researchers, working in universities, cannot contribute due to their sensitivities, there are a range of others where the opposite case is possible. We will come back to these in the discussion below on the proposed research strategy. Other challenges in doing research with intelligence agencies relate to *trust* and *relevance*. Again, intelligence research particularly relies on researchers being able to develop trusting relations with practitioners and stakeholders. All researchers need to do this of course with 'industry partners', regardless of the research area, but gaining the trust of members of the intelligence community is even more critical. The relevance of research for intelligence agencies sounds like an obvious point, but in my experience there can be a mismatch between what the researchers and industry partners think is important. I will come back to the issues of trust and relevance in the next section.

The challenges in doing intelligence research, however, are even more fundamental to those just described. The most fundamental challenge is a philosophical one. It is really a question of what intelligence *is* and what it *does*. This is one of the three central question raised in the book. In Chapter 8, I provided my definition of intelligence analysis as being:

> Both a cognitive and methodological approach to processing and evaluating information – some of which is privileged – in order to produce an assessment for a decision-maker about the security environment.

Though we know there are countless other definitions of intelligence, it is these diverse views and the disparate and fragmented nature of the 'intelligence field', which have created different perspectives on what is 'knowable' from doing research in this area. In other words, the nature of theory building and research on intelligence issues depends where you stand on some basic epistemological and ontological questions relating to intelligence. From an epistemological perspective, there is the broader question about the grounds by which knowledge about intelligence can be gained and assessed. From an ontological perspective, there is for some an even more fundamental question of what exists in the first place in the 'intelligence world' that can be studied. Moving away from these philosophical underpinnings, and assuming that there is intelligence knowledge, the next question is, what methods can we use to best understand it?

Broadly, in social sciences, there are two methodological frameworks under-pinning intelligence research: a positivist and a post-positivist approach. The positivist approach argues that all true knowledge is scientific and can be gained using scientific methods, which include developing theories based on observations (O'Leary 2007: 10). This approach is also sometimes referred to as empirical as it is believed that collecting data to explain a hypothesis or problem is the only way to generate theories. The post-positivist approach also believes that the world that is 'knowable' through research, but that scientific positivist approaches have their limitations. Post-positivists identify two key limitations to the empirical or positivist perspective. First, they argue that positivist approaches cannot be completely objective as the researcher brings their own theories, background and values to what is observed, which results in bias. Second, the post-positivists dispute the positivists' argument that there is only one social reality able to be revealed to the researcher. The post-positivists believe there is a social reality, but the researcher can only know it partially because of the researcher's own limitations (Robson 2002: 27). Post-positivist approaches are sometimes referred to as relativistic or interpretive as the researcher's reality constricts the kind of things we can know and understand about the world.

Debates between researchers on the merits of positivist and post-positivist approaches have gone on for decades and the above is a very condensed perspective on them. These debates are more nuanced than the summary here suggests, but what is important is how they shape researchers' views about investigating problems and questions in the intelligence field. Those adopting a positivist/empirical perspective believe that intelligence itself can be used to *explain* events, issues and the behaviour of threat actors in the security environment. And by extension, the ways in which intelligence can help explain events and threat behaviour can themselves be explained and tested using positivist research designs. Positivists would also argue that it is possible to extrapolate observations and patterns seen in one research project to others, which can alert us to similar patterns developing in another context in the future. In contrast, post-positivists would say the knowledge generated by intelligence leads us only to a greater *understanding* or *interpretation* of the security environment. The implication of this is that a post-positivist research approach should be directed to generating a greater understanding of what is going on in the security environment. The goal for post-positivist intelligence researchers, then, is not to explain or predict the significance of events, issues and behaviour in the security environment.

Deciding what intelligence is and what it is for therefore influences how we conceptualize intelligence research. If one decides that intelligence can only help understand the security environment, this constricts the kind of theory building that is possible. Adopting a purely interpretive approach to intelligence knowledge suggests that we can know things but not necessarily explain or predict them. This is a bit worrying, given, as noted earlier in Chapter 1, the ability to predict and provide warning should be a core function of intelligence. If intelligence cannot provide warning or improve our ability to do this, then there is little reason to invest in it.

The lack of a common agreement on the purpose of 'intelligence knowledge' has not only produced different methodological perspectives to intelligence research, but it has also resulted in a partial vacuum in the field in terms of its ability to generate its own coherent approach to research. This vacuum has been filled partially by intelligence scholars using research approaches from a range of other fields. To some extent, as noted in Chapter 8, this is not surprising, nor necessarily a bad thing given the inter-disciplinary nature of intelligence. A good example, of knowledge (theory) generation from outside the 'field' is Phythian's discussion of international relations theory – structural realism in the intelligence context. Phythian suggests that structural realism is an approach that can be used to explain the role and performance of intelligence and how intelligence secures the advantage over other states (Phythian 2009: 57). This is an example of an empirically-based approach to intelligence research, as it is based on a theory that behaviour between states, and by extension the role of intelligence in their security policies, can be explained.

It is not of course the only approach for understanding the role of intelligence in contemporary security policy. As discussed in Chapter 1, the growth in the significance of non-state actor threats in the security environment suggests that purely realist (or neo-realist) approaches – focused only on inter-state behaviour – constrain the generation of knowledge of how intelligence can respond in this increasingly complex security environment. An example of a post-positivist research approach in intelligence is the current focus on why intelligence failures have occurred using historical case studies. The objective is to understand what went wrong in that specific case rather than extrapolate to others.

Equally, though, intelligence research can use both interpretative and empirical approaches. Again using the last example, researchers can try understanding individual case studies for factors that contribute to intelligence failure, but then extrapolate from them to develop an empirical understanding of how intelligence agencies fail (Betts 1978). The inter-disciplinary nature of intelligence studies also adds another dimension to how we conceptualize intelligence research. For example, what is intelligence research and what is sociological, political or criminological research applied to an intelligence issue? I will come back to this in the theory building section below.

What is clear is that thinking about intelligence research in the same way we would think about historical, psychological or criminological research still feels a bit anomalous. The international relations and history examples given above are connected to more defined bodies of knowledge and developed research methodological approaches than are currently seen originating from the 'intelligence field'. It is important not to overstate by implication that other non-intelligence fields have 'arrived' complete with well-defined research agendas, theories and paradigms. Obviously in these and other branches of the humanities and social sciences, there is much conjecture still about what is knowable and in what ways research in these fields can illuminate this. Any quick review of the social sciences research literature shows diverse views on these broad questions of epistemology, ontology and what constitutes a legitimate approach for research enquiry.

In one sense, then, intelligence research reflects a similar set of challenges present in the broader social sciences, perhaps with the critical difference being that conceptualizing research in the intelligence context is still comparatively recent, compared to other fields such as international relations, history, political science, sociology and criminology. Over the last couple of decades, scholars trained in these fields have been interested in researching aspects of intelligence practice, but it is probably only since the 1990s, in the USA and UK that scholars have started to specialize in intelligence itself. The greater access to archives, and an increasing number of publicly available reports about the performance of national security and policing agencies, have facilitated the growth in more intelligence-focused scholarship. In particular, policing intelligence research probably started to come more into focus in 2000, in the wake of a number of UK police reform initiatives, and the development of new terminology and models such as intelligence-led policing (Sheptycki 2000: 9).

In summary, given a lack of agreement among researchers and practitioners on what intelligence knowledge is and does, debates will remain about the best way to research or investigate problems associated with it. These debates are important, but in the interim there are issues in intelligence practice that research should address. It is better to get on with research that can improve intelligence practice, however one chooses to define its role. Whatever the approach – positivist, post-positivist or a methodology that seeks to bridge both – I argue that simply *doing* more intelligence research in the end will generate more knowledge, which in turn will further clarify what intelligence does and how to improve it. I also argue that in addition to the physical scientific applications of intelligence, those related to issues, events or behaviour demonstrate that intelligence might also be considered a social science. This notion of intelligence being a 'social science' is not new and may have first been taken up by Sherman Kent who described 'the social sciences as very largely constituting the subject matter of strategic intelligence' (Kent 1949: 156). The boundaries of intelligence as a social science may be unclear, but the core activity of any intelligence activity is to make clearer the behaviour of threat actors and prevent or disrupt their activities, so in that respect intelligence has the characteristics of a social science. Some may argue, however, that the enterprise of intelligence itself can frequently only gather 'shards' of information about an issue – much like an archaeologist might do. Others would also argue that in many circumstances, researchers are not in a position to even access this fragmented 'data', which in turn makes it difficult for them to reliably conceptualize or design intelligence research methodologies using an empirical hypothesis testing approach. Additionally, no doubt some social scientists may criticize intelligence scholars for trying through research to explain or understand the intentions of threat actors, which are not knowable – yet in many respects this is what other fields of social science are also trying to do. In the end, just as in the classic research methodological debates in other social sciences, much depends in intelligence on what needs investigating. Relying on a purely empirical or an interpretivist approach does not give researchers the flexibility to design the best research approach around the particular problem and available data. As will be discussed in the next section, the wide disparate set of what we may potentially call 'intelligence research' suggests a multi- or mixed method approach to research is required.

Developing a research strategy for intelligence

The aim in drafting a research strategy in this chapter is to encourage more discourse about intelligence research and to identify ways both researchers and their intelligence agency partners can work together to strategically develop suites of research projects, which will have an impact on intelligence practice and more broadly on the security environment. Much has been said already in earlier chapters about the fragmentation across the intelligence field. It is true that in the past decade, mostly due to counter-terrorism, we are seeing a greater fusing of intelligence practice, processes and frameworks particularly with national security and policing intelligence. It may be that in some of these transnational security areas, where there is a fusing of national security and policing intelligence responses, the labels 'national security' and 'policing intelligence' are looking less clear-cut. But our discussions in Chapters 4 and 5 suggest that there are still significant challenges in achieving more fused or networked approaches across national security and policing intelligence. The field is even more fragmented if you look at other areas of intelligence practice, both in the public and private sector. So to some extent it is not surprising given this fragmentation of the 'field' that articulating a strategic approach for intelligence research has been difficult.

A discipline of intelligence cannot develop unless research can be generated in a coherent way that has impacts applicable to 'industry partners'. I will come back to this point in the final section on theory building. But arguably most important to intelligence practitioners, managers and stakeholders is having access to research that can improve practice. A more strategic approach to intelligence research across the field will help address both these two issues: developing the discipline and improving practice. A good place to start in articulating a strategic approach to intelligence research is for both parties to collaborate on drafting a research strategy that will best meet the demands of practitioners. There is little doubt that the creation of research strategies across the intelligence field in Australia, Canada, New Zealand, the UK and the USA will become critical as the security environment becomes more complex. Governments will need to plan ahead to anticipate what research they may need to commission on intelligence-related issues in order to try to keep ahead of the changing threat environment. The recent Global Financial Crisis is underpinning the need in many governments in Australia, Canada, New Zealand, the UK and the USA, to reduce running costs across the public sector. This seems to be the ethos of the Coalition Government in the UK, and public sector 'efficiency dividends' are part of a review under way there (the Strategic Defence and Security Review), which is seeking to provide a revised strategic and policy baseline for the country's intelligence defence and other security agencies. In this era of greater fiscal restraint, research will become important to identify efficient, effective and cost-effective ways to do intelligence work.

The challenge, however, is to decide what should be included in any research strategy given the fragmented and inter-disciplinary nature of intelligence. Rather than attempt to articulate a research strategy for a specific practice context of intelligence; for example national security or policing intelligence, I will use Figure 5.1 on p. 148 instead as the basis for addressing what a broad research strategy for intelligence could look like.

As explained earlier in Chapter 5, an effective intelligence framework is the product of an equally effective set of core intelligence components, and key enabling activities, which support these components. The framework depicted in Figure 5.1, therefore, allows a holistic approach to developing a research strategy, which is not bogged down in a specific intelligence context or at a research project level. It can be used by researchers and practitioners in different contexts to identify broad research priorities at the strategic then the individual project level.

As shown in Table 10.1, I have used the key headings from Figure 5.1 to inform the broad objectives of the research agenda. The framework provides a strategic approach to intelligence research regardless of area of practice (national security, policing, compliance or the private sector) under consideration. As depicted in Table 10.1, the focus for research can be on individual issues relating to the core processes of intelligence (e.g. collection, analysis or production), or on the enabling activities detailed earlier in Chapter 5 (e.g. governance, ICT and human resources). Table 10.1 reflects this by 'splitting up' research priority objective areas into 'Part I: Core Intelligence Processes' and 'Part II: Effective Enabling Activities'. This of course is a fairly arbitrary distinction. There is a lot of overlap between the

Table 10.1 An intelligence research strategy

Part I: Core intelligence processes

Research objective A: Effective tasking and coordination of intelligence

A1: Improve risk and threat modelling

- research projects for better modelling of biosecurity threats and risks
- research projects for better modelling of the consequences of a range of threat activity, e.g. organized crime, terrorism, financial crime

A2: Improve priority-setting processes

- evaluate existing coordination of priority-setting processes across and between government agencies
- examine the role of intelligence failures historically on priority-setting processes
- explore the role of politicization on intelligence priority-setting processes

A3: Improve integration of intelligence products into decision-making

- evaluation and auditing of how strategic and tactical intelligence products have influenced specific identified priority targets and issues within the security environment

Table 10.1 continued

Research objective B: Effective intelligence collection

B1: Develop and evaluate new technologies to improve the collection of new or emerging intelligence sources

- evaluate current use and integration of forensic data, biometrics, health, corrections and private sector information into traditional intelligence practice areas (national security and policing)
- develop new technologies to better integrate new or under-exploited information sources into intelligence practice

B2: Develop surveillance capabilities across intelligence field

- identify or enhance surveillance techniques such as analytics, early warning systems, border security detection systems and biosensory equipment

Research objective C: Effective analysis

C1: Improve evaluation of existing analytical methodologies and tools

- evaluation research on the effectiveness of existing COMPSTAT, crime mapping, SNA and qualitative tools such as structured analytical techniques

C2: Develop new analytical methodologies

- evaluation research on effectiveness of data mining, advanced analytics and other knowledge discovery techniques to different intelligence contexts, including identifying patterns and predicting capabilities
- identify new technologies used in non-intelligence areas from the private sector and assess their applicability for intelligence analysis

C3: Develop a greater understanding of the psychological influences on intelligence analysis

- evaluation of how cognitive processes, including bias, impact on what analysts view as important in their assessments
- evaluation of how analysts feel influenced by decision-makers' bias or attempts to 'satisfice' outcomes in line with decision-makers' expectations

C4: Improve analytical standards

- evaluation of analytical processes, argumentation and presentation of key judgements
- develop enhanced agency and inter-agency capabilities for promoting analytical standards

Research objective D: Effective production and evaluation

D1: Improve technological capabilities for the production and dissemination of different intelligence products

- identify appropriate new technology to facilitate both the production and dissemination of intelligence products in different environments, including the ability to provide flexible yet secure delivery modes to different clients in real time

D2: Improve security capabilities for the production and dissemination of different intelligence products

- identify security vulnerabilities for the production and dissemination of different intelligence products across diverse contexts, including assessing future counter-intelligence vulnerabilities to systems and processes using emerging communications technologies

Part II: Effective enabling activities

Research objective E: Effective intelligence governance

E1: Develop better decision support systems between intelligence agencies and contexts

- develop knowledge to improve decision-making systems within and between disparate agencies that use intelligence, including how to improve governance arrangements between single agencies and fusion centers, between traditional practice areas such as policing and national security and emerging practice areas such as biosecurity, corrections and compliance
- develop knowledge to improve frequently ad hoc decision-making systems between national security, policing intelligence providers and private sector agencies

E2: Evaluate intelligence capacity building projects in fragile states and regions

- evaluate current programmes implemented by country, regional and multi-lateral donors focused on intelligence capacity building in fragile countries for their effectiveness and sustainability

E3: Contribute to the evidence base on what constitutes effective intelligence frameworks

- evaluate existing intelligence models; how they impact on core intelligence activities and enabling activities
- investigate new models from non-intelligence agencies, such as the business and engineering sector, for examples of good practice governance arrangements applicable to intelligence frameworks
- examine historical cases studies (official reports, reviews) for factors resulting in intelligence failure within agencies

E4: Identify factors to improve intelligence leadership and management decision-making

- evaluate historical case studies for intelligence failures involving poor decision-making by intelligence leaders and use evidence to develop communities of practice for how to make better decisions and build more effective decision-making support
- evaluate current barriers to effective leadership and management decision-making within intelligence agencies
- identify best practice leadership theory and skill attributes from the private sector and evaluate applicability in intelligence environments

Research objective F: Effective information communications and technology

F1: Identify current barriers to the effective application of ICT in the intelligence context

- identify appropriate new technology to facilitate both the production and dissemination of intelligence products in different environments

Table 10.1 continued

- assess evidence for key barriers for effective ICT application across different intelligence agencies and contexts and identify solutions for better support or best practice based on existing systems

F2: Develop new ICT systems to capture, integrate and analyse information from multiple sources

- develop new technological capabilities for the real-time analysis and fusion of information from multiple sources of intelligence, particularly linking policing and national security intelligence with emerging practice areas (biosecurity, forensics, corrections, compliance and private sector)
- develop new technologies for the development of intelligence to evidence assessment

Research objective G: Effective human resource capabilities

G1: Develop national and international standards for best practice intelligence education

- contribute to the development of nationally and internationally identified standards in education programme strategies and design for all intelligence officers
- identify specific education requirements of specialised intelligence roles
- evaluate existing education programmes in collaboration with external providers such as universities

G2: Develop effective career pathways for intelligence officers

- develop and map continuing professional development programmes and training pegged to existing job descriptions
- develop training programmes for raising awareness about intelligence practice and the appropriate use of relevant legislation
- enhance on-the-job support through more effective mentoring and staff rotation in and outside the agency
- increase understanding of the psycho-social stress involved in the intelligence profession and factors involved in the successful recruitment and attrition of intelligence officers
- improve performance management process of intelligence staff

G3: Evaluate the effectiveness of intelligence doctrinal processes, guidelines and policies

- contribute to the evidence base underlying the design of various doctrinal processes, guidelines and policies related to all aspects of intelligence practice (e.g. tasking and coordination, collection, analysis and production)
- develop best practice doctrinal standards and promote a community of practice on standards

Research objective H: Effective legislation and oversight

H1: Contribute to the effective drafting of intelligence legislation that is proportionate to requirements, privacy and civil liberty concerns

- contribute to the review of existing and planned legislation related to intelligence
- improve the independent, statutory, judicial and legislative intelligence oversight mechanisms
- improve understandings about ethical intelligence practice

Research objective I: Effective research

I1: Promote a research culture in the intelligence field

- investigate processes, policies and procedures in other contexts which could promote research cultures in intelligence contexts

I2: Develop research agendas at agency, community, national and international level

I3: Promote peer review of intelligence research and communities of practice

---

two parts. This is partly deliberate given the design of a research strategy should list projects that include issues that relate to core intelligence processes and effective enabling activities.

Looking at the research design again in Table 10.1, the idea is to first to generate further discussion on how specific research projects from all *nine priority objective areas* and *research tasks* could be identified. It is also designed to illustrate and encourage researchers and practitioners to shift their focus from thinking beyond one research project in isolation. A good research strategy should help the design of projects, which can look for broader impacts beyond their primary scope. The objective should be to implement research projects, which can also have an impact on other areas across intelligence practice, including projects which can lead to improvements in one or more of the enabling activities. For example, rather than just design a research project aimed at identifying technology that can more quickly assemble data from different government sources, a secondary phase of the project could use the outcomes of this to evaluate potential impacts on a series of key enabling activities such as governance and legislation before recommendations were made to research sponsors. The idea of producing a research strategy focused on both intelligence components and enabling activities is therefore to encourage inter-disciplinary research projects, which may have benefits for more than one intelligence framework or practice context. Using this philosophy to underpin a research strategy, it is possible that we can generate a lot more knowledge about a range of intelligence related issues than research directed only on one aspect of intelligence.

The research strategy shown in Table 10.1 is also not an exhaustive list of all potential broad objectives or key research tasks that would meet everyone's objectives. It is not the intention to produce an endless 'wish list' for researchers, and I am conscious what is one researcher's 'must do' is someone else's 'why do?' Gaining significant agreement from a diverse array of researchers working on aspects of intelligence practice on what the priority task areas should be is unlikely. Rather, the research strategy seen here focuses on those broad areas identified in earlier chapters, or topics that have been raised as priority areas elsewhere in the literature or by discussions with key practitioners across Australia, Canada, New Zealand, the UK and the USA. In the end, they may not represent an appropriate list in order of priority for all researchers, but they are nevertheless important areas which require attention from the research community.

Finally, you will note that the number of research tasks listed under each priority objective area is also small. This is deliberate for two main reasons. First, I argue it is important for researchers to focus on fewer strategic research areas over the short (one to two years) to medium term (three to eight years), rather than provide an over-ambitious programme of work that is open-ended and not deliverable. Each of the listed research tasks in Table 10.1 of course could result in a larger number of research projects depending on the number of researchers and intelligence agencies involved. This will require careful management by an appropriate board of management consisting of senior researchers and intelligence agency representatives. Second, the strategic list must translate into a menu of work that keeps stakeholders engaged. Beyond an eight-year period, except in some areas of defence and national security, it may be difficult to retain industry partner focus and funding due to the political, policy and funding cycles in different countries.

Due to limited space, I will not discuss here all of the research tasks listed in Table 10.1 as most are self-explanatory. However, there are three points which should be made to help the reader understand the approach taken in the strategy. First, it should be clear that many listed in Part I are similar to or overlap in some respects those listed in Part II. As indicated earlier, this underlines not only the multi-disciplinary nature of intelligence research, but the essential synergies that exist between core intelligence components and key enabling activities explained in Chapter 5. So the development of a research strategy for an intelligence agency should consider how different research tasks can lever off each other to have the most impact in the longer term. For example, an agency might want to do some research on *developing new analytical methodologies (C2)*, but this research would be even more effective if it was completed simultaneously with research that was also looking more broadly at *identifying current barriers to the effective application of ICT (F1)*. A strategically focused research strategy may want to make these synergies more explicit by putting them together in their plan, but in Table 10.1 I have kept them separate. This is to illustrate that while some are different, research at Part I and Part II levels are still focused on different aspects of the intelligence process.

Second, there are also a number of research tasks which have been discussed in earlier chapters, for example, *risk and threat methodologies (A1)* and *improving the evaluation of analytical methodologies (C1)* such as COMPSTAT and crime mapping, where research has been under way for decades. I am not trying to imply in the research strategy that no research has been done on many of these areas, in fact, looking through all the tasks you could argue the opposite. But for the most part, research in these areas, as it is applied to intelligence problems, still has a way to go in resolving them or producing the evidence that they have the desired impact in different intelligence practice contexts. The objective, therefore, in drafting this research strategy, is to list research tasks that are general enough so that researchers and their industry partners can design projects for those aspects where the most work is yet to be completed.

Finally, another important thing to keep in mind is while an intelligence agency or community may collaborate with external researchers in designing a research strategy, for all the reasons mentioned earlier, this does not mean that collaborating parties will be able to design research projects around all tasks. Some research tasks will remain 'off limits' to all but a few external researchers. Other tasks will allow a more collaborative arrangement, while there will be others where the research task can be completely out-sourced to an external research body. But arguably a strategic articulation of research priorities for an intelligence agency or community will be richer if at the broadest levels (such as those detailed in Table 10.1), it can be drafted in collaboration with the research community.

Theory building and developing a discipline

In this last section, I want to connect the discussion above about intelligence research to how research informs theory building and how in turn theory can contribute further to developing a discipline for intelligence. As noted above, there are difficulties in conceptualizing what intelligence is meant to do and therefore what is 'knowable' from the intelligence enterprise. Can we explain events, trends and behaviour or can we only interpret/understand these from the security environment? The answer to this question influences the researcher's perspective on methodology and determines what kind of knowledge generation and theory building is possible. Additionally, as noted earlier, the inter-disciplinary nature of intelligence studies also raises questions about what counts as 'intelligence research'. For example, is a research project on the psychology of analyst decision-making psychological or intelligence research? Despite these questions, my view, as stated earlier, is that intelligence is a kind of social research, and that there are things that are knowable about the security environment. This also means that if there are things knowable, we use these to build theories.

But what kind of theories can be built? In the remaining section I will address briefly what kind of theories have developed in intelligence, how they have been linked to intelligence research, and what areas across the field may generate more useful theorizing about intelligence in the future. Over the last few decades, there have been a growing number of examples of theoretical perspectives developed, particularly in the USA. There is insufficient space to list them all here, and a more thorough discussion can be found in the Gill, Marrin and Phythian edited collection, *Intelligence Theory* (2009). However, some of the more dominant theoretical streams seem to be theorizing on intelligence failures, or the role of intelligence in questions of national security in its narrowest sense, and have come from historians, international relations and political scientists applying their theoretical perspectives from these disciplines to intelligence-related issues (e.g. Betts 1978; Kahn 2001; Scott and Jackson 2004). More recently, other political scientists have developed theoretical perspectives about the causes of intelligence failure, which adopt political and organizational theory to explain the causes. Zegart's work, mentioned in previous chapters, is an example of this approach. Since 9/11, however, there seems to have been a greater emphasis by scholars to 'dissect the entrails' of publicly available reports into the blunders of intelligence agencies, and less focus on what processes and frameworks might make intelligence agencies more effective. In other words, there seems to be less theorizing on explaining or understanding what effective intelligence reform looks like.

Other theoretical perspectives have developed as suggested earlier, from psychology and how cognitive processes influence analytical bias (Heuer 1999). More recently too, Hatlebrekke and Smith have also emphasized the cognitive rather than technical processes for intelligence failures, arguing that a cognitive closure/ discourse failure model may be useful 'in providing a wider theoretical understanding in which to appreciate the notion of intelligence failures' (2010: 171). They define cognitive closure as a 'human defence mechanism' to impose order, structure and stability as a counterweight to uncertainty. Cognitive closure is experienced by both analysts and decision-makers looking for a definitive answer – any answer rather than confusion and ambiguity in information. This rush to limited cognitive decision-making (or cognitive closure) increases 'discourse failure'. Discourse failure in turn decreases 'the adequate understanding and perception of both information of possible intelligence value, as well as the finished intelligence product'. Hatlebrekke and Smith argue that critical rationalism where everything is open to question and debate will reduce discourse failure and ultimately intelligence failure (ibid.: 149–182).

Hatlebrekke and Smith's cognitive approach to intelligence failure provides a useful way to explain the relationship between cognitive processes and discourse failure between analysts and decision-makers. But it is less clear how their theorizing particularly on critical rationalism can be applied to 'real-life' intelligence processes. In the area of cognitive psychology, intelligence analysis and decision-making, there is still limited theorizing, beyond the role of alternative analysis, on what measures if any might reduce the impact of these biases. The growing literature on alternative analysis and structured analytical thinking is welcomed, but again there is little to no evidence to suggest how these techniques reduce cognitive biases in analysis. More recently, since the 1990s and into the new millennium, the intelligence field has also been influenced increasingly by theoretical perspectives from sociologists, criminologists and scholars working in policing studies. As noted earlier, the development of intelligence-led policing approaches in the UK has resulted in an increased research output about policing intelligence and its role in security more generally (Ratcliffe 2008). Additionally, the development of the human security perspectives discussed in Chapter 1 have helped broaden out a body of theoretical perspectives dominated by historians and international relations scholars, who were focused on a narrow view of national security as being between states rather than featuring other security actors: non-state actors such as individuals and communities (Sheptycki 2000). Other scholars working in the intelligence field have developed theoretical perspectives around one core concept. Gill and Phythian use *surveillance* which they define as the relationship between power and knowledge as a useful way to study intelligence. They also argue that surveillance can be assessed at different levels of intelligence activity: individual, group, organizational, societal and trans-societal. This approach produces a more networked approach to intelligence – one no longer dominated by the arbitrary distinctions of foreign, military and domestic intelligence. Using these principles, against temporal and spatial dimension Gill and Phythian have produced a map for theorizing and researching intelligence (2006: 37).

In all the theoretical perspectives listed above, there is plenty of scope for more reflection, and the collection of further evidence to support or deny their utility in understanding the role of intelligence and improving it in a 'real-world' sense. The intelligence strategic plan in Table 10.1 suggests there are broadly a number of areas across intelligence practice and processes, where further research may also improve theorizing. But to name just a few specific examples, which may profit from further theorizing, they would include: intelligence failure, intelligence reform, strategic intelligence and decision-making. Current intelligence failure theorizing would benefit not just from looking at aspects of the intelligence cycle, but also from examining how agencies and communities fail in key enabling activities such as governance, outlined in Chapter 5. Betts is correct in saying that there is a need for transforming 'lessons learnt' from studying intelligence failures into intelligence reform and adaptation. Additionally, perhaps other inter-disciplinary research, which examines organizational adaptation and learning in the business sector, might also be of assistance in theorizing about intelligence failure. Intelligence theorizing has not been good at looking at theoretical developments in other fields for relevant implications that could be imported into practice. Theorizing has also not been good at capturing 'communities of good practice' that can be fed back into real policy deliberations on intelligence reform measures *before* political leaders make often quick and profound changes to intelligence communities such as the establishment of the ODNI and DHS.

As discussed in Chapter 7, there is also a need for the development of theoretical perspectives on how to improve intelligence oversight and accountability. Additionally, as mentioned in Chapter 8, further theorizing on how to improve early warning and strategic intelligence practice and to what extent automated analytical systems can help this is also required. In the context of the rapid uptake of data mining and analytics technology now under way in national security and policing intelligence, further theorizing on to what extent these improve the quality and speed of analytical outcomes is required. It is still unclear how effective some data mining and 'surveillance technology' are in different contexts. For example, there are challenges with biosurveillance systems, which are used to identify unusual clusters of symptoms or diseases and, problems with correlating physical surveillance and surveillance activities on the internet. Further research into these technologies and how they apply to intelligence work will help validate their effectiveness and generate theories about which data mining and analytics approaches should be more widely used by intelligence communities. Finally, as noted in Chapter 8, further theorizing on which factors influence decision-makers' use of intelligence may reduce ambiguities, and help intelligence officers better anticipate or work around cognitive barriers and misperceptions by decision-makers.

Problems in theory building

In the short time (roughly two decades) that scholars have been involved in what might loosely be called intelligence theorizing, it is clear some areas, such as intelligence failure and the role of intelligence in supporting state power, have received a lot of attention. But research output is not the same as developing theories or contributing to existing ones. Much of what has been proposed to date which is labelled intelligence theory is at best what Davies describes as 'loosely associated assumptions, premises, and conventional wisdoms, that do not typically involve the kind of effort at comprehensive logical consistency that the use of the term theory normally implies' (2009: 188). In the strictest positivist sense of a 'scientific theory', it is less clear how many of the theories I have outlined above are actually 'testable'. Some areas of intelligence practice for reasons described earlier will never fall into the category of 'testable' and that is not necessarily a bad thing. Given the lack of clarity on what intelligence is, and what knowledge it produces, it is doubtful we will see in intelligence the development of a grand theory explaining all of intelligence. Nor will we see the development of theories that will result in paradigm shifts that mark the progression in physical sciences much as when Newtonian physics was replaced by that of Einstein. What theory will emerge is likely to be smaller in scale and incremental.

But these incremental improvements will not be possible if scholars are not able to shift their sights wider than the currently narrow and US-dominated approaches, focusing on an equally narrow view of national security. Each country will have its own issues which need to be examined not only through a US-dominated scholarly prism. The USA, in turn, can learn a great deal more from looking further afield than their own scholarship. Theorizing and research also need to cast the net wider to other practice contexts, including the emerging practice areas mentioned earlier. Theory building, like research, in addition to being multi-disciplinary, must also go beyond looking at the intelligence cycle to examine how enabling activities interact with these components within the dynamic security environment.

Conclusion

Research and theory building can help define a discipline of intelligence for the future but there are clear limitations in both. In this chapter I have provided an overview of what some of these limitations are. A very real and ongoing challenge is the lack in precision among researchers on what intelligence is and what kind of research and theorizing is possible. However, I have argued that in research and theory building, we should start from the premise that some things are knowable and get on with it. Some things may be testable, others can be understood. As this debate about what intelligence is and what knowledge it produces becomes more sophisticated, we may gain a better idea of which category (i.e. explain vs. understand) an issue will fall into. The best way to inform this debate is for scholars to *do* research that industry partners can apply to improve intelligence practice.

11 Conclusion

This book has sought to explore three major questions relating to intelligence:

What is intelligence?
What makes intelligence practice effective?
Is there a discipline of intelligence?

Based on discussions in previous chapters, I argue that there simply is not a definitive answer to these three questions. In Chapter 8, I defined intelligence analysis as both a cognitive and methodological approach to processing and evaluating information – some of which is privileged – in order to produce an assessment for a decision-maker about the security environment. But it is clear that there is an endless supply of other definitions for intelligence and intelligence analysis. Given the lack of unity among academics and practitioners on what intelligence *is* and what it *does*, it may be fair to ask at this point whether the answer to question 1 really matters that much. Perhaps intelligence is a bit like air or electricity – we can observe its effect by what it *does* rather than being able to define it easily in the moment. While there is no definitive answer to what intelligence is, I argue that defining and continual redefining of what is meant by intelligence are important, particularly in addressing the other two questions raised. As noted in Chapter 10, one of the reasons why there is no discernible body of research or theories about intelligence is because there remains a lack of clarity across the field as to what intelligence is and what kind of knowledge is generated by it.

Despite still some fundamental lack of agreement about what intelligence is, nevertheless I argue in the discussions in all three Parts of the book that getting clearer insights – if not answers – to each of the three questions above is possible. And if intelligence is like electricity, then the chapters in Part I demonstrate where intelligence has come from (Chapter 1), where it might be going (Chapters 2 and 3) and the impact it is having in these different environments. Discussions in each chapter underline therefore a basic axiom that the meaning of intelligence will remain context-driven. This point was made early in Chapter 1, where I argued that the evolution of traditional intelligence practice resulted in a set of characteristics, which I called an 'intelligence tradition' (security environment, secrecy and surveillance). Articulating an 'intelligence tradition' for national security and policing agencies, however narrowly or widely one wishes to define it, does help put parameters around what is intelligence – and therefore its uniqueness compared to any other similar discipline such as research, data collection or information management. In summary, understanding how this intelligence tradition has evolved in traditional practice contexts has helped historically to narrow down what we think of as intelligence as opposed to other activities.

Our discussion of emerging practice areas in Chapter 2, however, highlights that intelligence is now becoming a much 'broader church'. This is the result of a combination of factors discussed earlier, including a greater focus on integrated, fused or 'whole of government' policy responses to complex security issues which increasingly include 'non-traditional intelligence players' as part of the solution. However, it is now some of the emerging practice areas, including immigration, corrections, social security, biosecurity, private security and corporate intelligence which are also challenging traditional perspectives on what intelligence is and how it can be applied in different ways. I argue that many scholars and practitioners are playing catch-up with how emerging practice areas are not only redefining what intelligence is, but also with taking better advantage of their capabilities. There are a number of broad emerging intelligence practice areas, where still little is known by scholars, and more importantly other intelligence officers in traditional intelligence areas. It is hoped that the two case studies in Chapter 3 provide a spark for further reflection on how intelligence is being applied in emerging areas, how they can be mutually beneficial to both contexts and how further knowledge can improve practice and reduce some of the fragmentation across the intelligence field. As discussed above, Chapter 3 shows intelligence can also be understood in the context of how liberal democracies deliver intelligence capacity building projects in fragile states. But this chapter provides a good link between Part I and Part II in its focus on what is good and sustainable practice in these intelligence capacity building situations. This question has broader applicability and goes to the heart of the second central question in the book – what makes intelligence practice effective?

Chapters 4 and 5 focus on this important question, by examining the five frameworks. As explained earlier, in each of the frameworks presented there was at least some evidence of good practice, but with perhaps the exception of the NIM, the other four are works in progress. So it makes little sense, without further evidence, to hold all of them in their entirety up as examples of good practice for all to follow. Nevertheless, the analysis of the five frameworks underpins the need for further reflection by scholars and practitioners on intelligence frameworks more generally in the future. The analysis of the frameworks in Chapter 5 also suggests that intelligence needs to be understood as a series of functions going on within a broader structure. The key to being more confident in the future about what is good intelligence practice, therefore, is to investigate the effectiveness of core intelligence processes (functions) and how they are facilitated by key enabling activities (structure). There is no need to over-complicate this point, but Figure 5.1 provides a way to conceptualize the interactions of the functions and the structure and also underlines a more holistic and integrated study of intelligence, regardless of whether the framework is for one agency or an entire intelligence community. Another important outcome of discussions in Chapter 5 is that the most important key enabling activity that researchers and practitioners will need to focus on over the next decade is 'governance'. The group of issues related to intelligence governance can be thought of as the 'lynch-pin' on which much else will depend in building effective intelligence frameworks. In all the intelligence communities discussed in this book in Australia, Canada, New Zealand, the UK and the USA, 'intelligence governance' will remain an important challenge in designing better intelligence communities and agencies within those communities. Governance includes the strong development of mandates, coordinating intelligence reform in the other key enabling activities and core intelligence processes identified in Figure 5.1. Effective intelligence governance also means developing frameworks within and across agencies in intelligence communities that can result in holistic and fused intelligence products for decision makers.

As noted in Chapter 6, the role of strong leadership and management will be critical in developing sustainable and effective intelligence governance across intelligence frameworks and communities. Each intelligence community in Australia, Canada, New Zealand, the UK and the USA will be confronted with similar governance issues – although the complexity of them may be quite different in each case. Perhaps in the US intelligence community, the ability of intelligence leaders and managers to build effective governance relations with each other may present the most significant challenge. The establishment of the ODNI and DHS may have complicated US efforts for a 'whole of government' approach to intelligence rather than simplifying it. There are also significant governance issues that still need to be resolved about the relations between the ODNI, DHS and the FBI. All of these agencies, particularly the latter two, have overlapping mandates relating to domestic intelligence, yet it remains unclear the extent that they are able to provide a nationally coherent perspective on domestic intelligence collection and analytical priorities. Additionally, in other non-US intelligence communities, there are similar governance issues to be resolved regarding how to increase connectivity between different intelligence contexts: military, foreign, domestic, policing, emerging practice areas and the private sector. The issues raised in Chapter 7, particularly those related to the balance between effective intelligence and oversight, will also be important in addressing the second question in the longer term. Intelligence can only be effective if the community on balance trust that it remains primarily to serve their public safety, not the narrow needs of its elected political leaders. Yet, as argued earlier, intelligence must also be able to retain much of its culture of secrecy if it is to serve the public effectively. The chapters in Part III which explore several aspects relating to the question of whether there is a discipline of intelligence are also important in addressing the second question of the book: what makes intelligence practice effective? The development of analytical innovations, professionalism and a research agenda for the field over time ought to provide more evidence for what constitutes effective practice.

Finally, turning to the last question: is there a discipline of intelligence? The discussion in Chapter 9 argued that this question is more appropriate rather than asking if intelligence was a profession. The word 'profession' usually conjures up a *specific* vocation one chooses, which requires the mastery of some related body of knowledge. While intelligence loosely has a body of knowledge to draw on, it is doubtful that it represents a 'specific' vocation such as law or medicine with a prescribed body of knowledge just for it. The field is too diffuse and the boundaries unclear. Hence describing intelligence as a discipline may be more appropriate. As argued in Chapter 9, a discipline suggests something with less clear boundaries, yet still with branches of learning, training, behaviour and conduct required to accomplish that branch of learning. Intelligence and intelligence analysis may more accurately be thought of currently as like an 'apprenticeship' – though unlike studying to be a mechanic or plumber, progression through it is achieved with less structure, and professional rules are not entirely mandatory.

Though a definitional debate of what constitutes an intelligence discipline is interesting, this discussion needs to shift to how practice contexts are developing the attributes identified in Chapter 9 as being necessary for a discipline. And the question for intelligence leaders, researchers and educators is how to overcome some significant challenges to greater professionalism and build a discipline for intelligence. There are still major issues that need addressing in areas such as: education, continuing professional development, career structure, professional association, community engagement and research.

It is clear too, as discussed in Chapter 10, that if in the next decade both researchers and scholars can develop a more strategic and collaborative approach to setting research priorities, then this will help develop the discipline of intelligence to a point where we may be able to start referring to it as something recognizable and explicable to outsiders. Perhaps a key weakness to date of much intelligence researching and theorizing has been that it has been an agenda set by scholars from other fields (international relations, sociology and psychology). However, in the future, perhaps ironically, the inter-disciplinary nature of intelligence may end up being a key strength, if those who now call themselves intelligence scholars (many who have been practitioners) are more proactive in steering the research agenda. Intelligence scholars and practitioners need to start having more frequent, useful and strategic conversations about what the research priorities are than has ever been the case before. There will be ways to deal with the innate sensitivities involved in doing intelligence research, but developing trust between researchers and 'industry', and designing applied research projects, which result in positive improvement in intelligence practice, should remain the key objective. If we get this right, then we are also in a better place to really address all three questions posed in this book.

Bibliography

9/11 Commission (2004) *The 9/11 Commission Report: Final Report of the National Commission on Terrorist Attacks upon the United States*. Washington, DC: 9/11 Commission.

ACLU (2010) *America Unrestored: An Assessment of the Obama Administration's Fulfillment of ACLU Recommendations. "Actions for Restoring America"*. New York: American Civil Liberties Union.

ACPO (1975) *Report of the ACPO Subcommittee on Criminal Intelligence (Baumber Report)*. London: Association of Chief Police Officers.

ACPO (1978) *Report of the ACPO Working Party on a Structure of Criminal Intelligence Officers (Pearce Report)*. London: Association of Chief Police Officers.

ACPO (1986) *Report of the ACPO Working Party on Operational Criminal Intelligence Officers (Ratcliffe Report)*. London: Association of Chief Police Officers.

Adler, B. (2011) 'Why journalists aren't standing up for WikiLeaks', *Newsweek*, 4 January. Available at: http://www.newsweek.com/2011/01/04/why-journalists-aren-t-defending-julian-assange.html (accessed 19 January 2010).

Ainsworth, P. (2001) *Offender Profiling and Crime Analysis*. Cullompton: Willan Publishing.

Alexander, M. and Bruning, J. (2008) *How to Break a Terrorist*. New York: Free Press.

Alibek, K. (1999) *Biohazards: The Chilling True Story of the Largest Covert Biological Weapons Program in the World – Told from the Inside by the Man Who Ran It*. New York: Random House.

Alison, L. and Canter, D. (1999) *Profiling in Policy and Practice*. Aldershot: Ashgate.

Allison, G. (1971) *Essence of Decision: Explaining the Cuban Missile Crisis*. Boston: Little, Brown and Co.

Almond, L., Alison, L., Eyre, M., Crego, J. and Goodwill, A. (2008) 'Heuristics and biases in decision-making', in L. Alison and J. Crego (eds) *Policing Critical Incidents*. Cullompton: Willan Publishing.

Anderson, N. and Fineman, N. (2002) 'Someone had to say it, so Coleen Rowley did', *Los Angeles Times*, 26 May. Available at: http://articles.latimes.com/2002/may/26/nation/na-rowley26 (accessed 1 May 2010).

Andregg, M. (2009) 'A symposium on intelligence ethics', *Intelligence and National Security*, 24(3): 366–386.

Andrew, C. (2009) *The Defence of the Realm: The Authorised History of MI5*. London: Allen Lane.

Andrew, C., Aldrich, R. and Wark, W. (eds) (2009) *Secret Intelligence*. New York: Routledge.

ASIO (2009) *ASIO Annual Report 2008–09*. Canberra: Australian Security Intelligence Organisation.

Assange, J. (2006) 'State and terrorist conspiracies', (November 10). Available at: http://cryptome.org/0002/ja-conspiracies.pdf (accessed 19 January 2011).

Attorney General's Department (2009) *Organised Crime Strategic Framework*. Canberra: Commonwealth of Australia.

Audit Commission (1993) *Helping with Enquiries: Tackling Crime Effectively*. London: Audit Commission.

Australian, The (2009) 'Americans "supervise" Palestinian agencies: CIA link to torture of Hamas', *The Australian*, 19–20 December, p. 15.

Baker, K. (2009) 'The meaning and practice of biosecurity', *International Journal of Risk Assessment and Management*, 12(2/3/4): 121–146.

Baldino, D. (ed.) (2010) *Democratic Oversight of Intelligence Services*. Sydney: Federation Press.

Bayley, D. (2001) *Democratizing the Police Abroad: What to Do and How to Do it*. Washington, DC: National Institute of Justice – US Department of Justice.

Bazan, E. (2007) *The FISA Act: An Overview of the Statutory Framework and the US Foreign Intelligence Surveillance Court and US Foreign Surveillance Court of Review Decisions*. Washington, DC: Congressional Research Service (No. RL30465).

BBC (2009) 'Deadly tsunami strikes in Pacific', *BBC News Online*. Available at: http://news.bbc.co.uk/2/hi/8281616.stm (accessed 5 September 2010).

Beale, T. (2008) *One Biosecurity: A Working Partnership*. Canberra: Commonwealth of Australia.

Berkow, M. (1999) 'Practical issues in providing policing assistance abroad', in J. Burack, W. Lewis and E. Marks (eds) *Civilian Police and Multinational Peacekeeping: A Workshop Series: A Role for Democratic Policing*. Washington, DC: National Institute of Justice.

Berkowitz, B. and Goodman, M. (1989) *Strategic Intelligence for American National Security*. Princeton, NJ: Princeton University Press.

Betts, R. (1978) 'Analysis, war, and decision: why intelligence failures are inevitable', *World Politics*, 31(1): 61–89.

Biggs, J. (2003) *Teaching for Quality Learning at University*. Maidenhead: Open University Press.

Bikales, W. (ed.) (1997) *Capacity Building in a Transition Country: Lessons from Mongolia*. Cambridge, MA: Harvard University Press.

BJA (2006) *Fusion Center Guidelines: Developing and Sharing Information and Intelligence in a New Era*. Washington, DC: Bureau of Justice Administration in collaboration with US Department of Justice's Global Justice Information Sharing Initiative and the US Department of Homeland Security.

BJA (2008) *Baseline Capabilities for State and Major Urban Area Fusion Centers: A Supplement to the Fusion Center Guidelines*. Washington, DC: Bureau of Justice Administration in collaboration with US Department of Justice's Global Justice Information Sharing Initiative and the US Department of Homeland Security.

Breckenridge, J. (2010) 'Designing effective teaching and learning environments for a new generation of analysts', *International Journal of Intelligence and Counterintelligence*, 23(2): 307–323.

Brew, A. (2006) *Research and Teaching Beyond the Divide*. Basingstoke: Palgrave Macmillan.

Brewer, B. (2008) 'C.R.I.M.E fights crime with intelligence led policing', *Public Safety IT*. Hendon Publishing.

Broad, W. (1998) 'Sowing death: a special report: how Japan germ terror alerted world', *The New York Times*, 28 May. Available at: http://www.nytimes.com/1998/05/26/world/ sowing-death-a-special-report-how-japan-germ-terror-alerted-world.html (accessed 15 August 2010).

Brodeur, J. (2008) 'High and low policing in the post-9/11 times', *Policing*: 25–37.

Brower, J. and Chalk, P. (2003) *The Global Threat of New and Reemerging Infectious Diseases: Reconciling US National Security and Public Health Policy*. Santa Monica, CA: RAND Corporation.

Bumiller, E. and Dao, J. (2002) 'Eyes on Iraq: Cheney says peril of a nuclear Iraq justifies attack', *The New York Times*, 27 August.

Buring, L., Pack, D. and Shroeder, P. (2007) 'Corrections business intelligence: safety in numbers', *Corrections Today*, June: 46–49.

Burns, J. (2010) 'WikiLeaks founder on the run, trailed by notoriety', *The New York Times*, 24 October. Available at: http://community.nytimes.com/comments/www.nytimes.com/ 2010/10/24/world/24assange.html?sort=recommended (accessed 19 January 2010).

Butler, R. (2004) *Review of Intelligence on Weapons of Mass Destruction: Report of a Committee of Privy Counsellors, UK Government*. London: The Stationery Office.

Butterworth, J. and Thwaites, G. (2005) *Thinking Skills*. Cambridge: Cambridge University Press.

Buzan, B. (ed.) (1991) *People, States and Fear*. Hemel Hempstead: Harvester Wheatsheaf.

Cabinet Office (2003) *Dealing with Disaster*. London: Cabinet Office UK.

Campbell, A. (2009) 'Evolving intelligence communities: leading change to face today's national security dynamic'. Paper presented at AIPIO Intelligence Conference, 2009. Canberra.

Canadian Bar Association (2007) *Submission on Bill C-3 Immigration and Refugee Protection Act Amendments (Certificates and Special Advocates)*. Ottawa: Canadian Bar Association.

Carlson, R. (2003) 'The pace and proliferation of biological technologies', *Biosecurity and Bioterrorism: Biodefense Strategy, Practice, and Science*, 1(3): 203–214.

Carter, D. (2004) *Law Enforcement Intelligence: A Guide for State, Local and Tribal Enforcement Agencies*. Washington, DC: Office of Community Oriented Policing Services.

Caryl, C. (2011) 'Why WikiLeaks changes everything', *The New York Review of Books*, (13 January–8 February), pp. 27–28.

Cavadino, M. and Dignan, J. (eds) (2006) *Penal Systems: A Comparative Approach*. Thousand Oaks, CA: Sage Publications.

CDC (2009) *Biosafety in Microbiological and Biomedical Laboratories*, 5th edn. Atlanta, GA: Centers for Disease Control.

CHF (2007) *The CHF Capacity Building Approach*. Ottawa: The Canadian Hunger Foundation.

Christopher, G., Cieslak, T., Pavlin, J. and Eitzen, E. (1997) 'Biological warfare: a historical perspective', *The Journal of the American Medical Association*, 278(5): 412–417.

Chulov, M. and Pidd, H. (2011) 'Curveball: how US was duped by Iraqi fantasist looking to topple Saddam', 15 February. Available at: http://www.guardian.co.uk/world/2011/ feb/15/defector-admits-wmd-lies-iraq-war (accessed 5 March 2011).

CISC (2009) *Annual Report on Organised Crime in Canada*. Ottawa: Criminal Intelligence Service Canada.

Clark, J.R. (2007) *Intelligence and National Security*. Westport, CT: Praeger Security International.

Clark, R. (2004) *Intelligence Analysis: A Target-Centric Approach*. Washington, DC: CQ Press.

Clarke, A. (2000) *Evaluation Research*. London: Sage Publications.

Clarke, J. (2008) *Clarke Inquiry into the Case of Dr Mohamed Haneef*. Canberra: Attorney General's Department.

Clauser, J. (2008) *An Introduction to Intelligence Research and Analysis*. Lanham, MD: The Scarecrow Press, Inc.

CLER (1984) *Report of the Review of Commonwealth Law Enforcement Arrangements*. Canberra: Commonwealth of Australia.

Clough, C. (2004) 'Quid pro quo: the challenges of international strategic intelligence cooperation', *International Journal of Intelligence and Counterintelligence*, 17: 601–613.

Cope, N. (2003) 'Crime analysis: principles and practice', in T. Newburn (ed.) *Handbook of Policing*. Cullompton: Willan Publishing.

Cope, N. (2004) 'Intelligence-led policing or policing-led intelligence?: Integrating volume crime analysis into policing', *British Journal of Criminology*, 44(2): 188–203.

Costigan, F. (1984) *Royal Commission on the Activities of the Federated Ship Painters and Dockers Union (Final Report)*. Canberra: Government Printing Office.

CSC (2008) *CSC Annual Report 2008–09*. Ottawa: Correctional Service Canada.

CSC (2009) *CSC Research Plan*. Ottawa: Correctional Service Canada.

Cumming, A. and Masse, T. (2004) *FBI Intelligence Reform since September 11, 2001: Issues and Options for Congress*. Washington, DC: Congressional Research Service.

Danner, M. (2004) 'Torture and truth: America, Abu Ghraib, and the war on terror,' *The New York Review of Books*, 10 June.

Davenport, T. and Harris, J. (2007) *Competing on Analytics*. Boston: Harvard Business School Press.

Davies, P. (2009) 'Theories of intelligence: where are we, where should we go and how we might proceed?' in P. Gill, S. Marrin and M. Phythian (eds) *Intelligence Theory*. New York: Routledge.

Davis, G. (2007) 'How Tesco became Britain's top supermarket', *Money Week*. Available at: http://www.moneyweek.com/news-and-charts/how-tesco-became-britains-top-super market (accessed 30 May 2009).

Department of Health and Ageing (2009) *Health and Ageing Annual Report 2008/09*. Canberra: Department of Health and Ageing.

Department of Justice, Canada (2001) *Immigration and Refugee Protection Act*. Available at: http://laws.justice.gc.ca/PDF/Statute/I/I-2.5.pdf (accessed 24 August 2010).

Department of Prime Minister and Cabinet (2010) *Counter-Terrorism White Paper: Securing Australia – Protecting our Community*. Canberra: Department of Prime Minister and Cabinet.

Dershowitz, A. (2002) *Why Terrorism Works: Understanding the Threat, Responding to the Challenge*. New Haven, CT: Yale University Press.

Deukmedjian, J. (2006) 'Executive realignment of RCMP mission', *Canadian Journal of Criminology and Criminal Justice*, 48(4): 523–542.

Deukmedjian, J. and De Lint, W. (2007) 'Community into intelligence: resolving information uptake in the RCMP', *Policing and Society*, 17(3): 239–256.

Deutsche Welle (2009) 'Deutsche Bank: spying scandal widens', 28 May, Deutsche Welle News Service Website. Available at: http://www.dw-world.de/dw/article/0,,4287967,00. html (accessed 6 August 2010).

DHS (2002) *Homeland Security Presidential Directive (HSPD 4-unclassified version)*

National Strategy to Combat Weapons of Mass Destruction. Washington, DC: Department of Homeland Security.

DHS (2004a) *Homeland Security Presidential Directive (HSPD 9) Defense of United States Agriculture and Food.* Washington, DC: Department of Homeland Security.

DHS (2004b) *Homeland Security Presidential Directive (HSPD 10) Biodefense for the 21st Century.* Washington, DC: Department of Homeland Security.

DHS (2007) *Homeland Security Presidential Directive (HSPD 21) Public Health and Medical Preparedness.* Washington, DC: Department of Homeland Security.

DHS (2008) *Fiscal Year 2009: Homeland Security Grant Program Guidance and Application Kit.* Washington, DC: Department of Homeland Security.

Diamond, D. and Kim, M. (2010) 'A public health model for WMD threat assessment: connecting the bioterrorism dots on the local level', in P. Katona, J. Sullivan and M. Intriligator (eds) *Global Biosecurity: Threats and Responses.* London: Routledge.

DOJ (2006) *Fusion Center Guidelines: Developing and Sharing Information and Intelligence in a New Era.* Washington, DC: US Department of Justice, in collaboration with the Department of Homeland Security.

DOJ (2009a) *Baseline Capabilities for State and Major Urban Area Fusion Centers.* Washington, DC: Department of Justice and Homeland Security.

DOJ (2009b) 'Special Task Force on Interrogation and Transfer Policies Issues makes its recommendations to the President' (Press Release), 21 July 2009. Washington, DC: Department of Justice and Homeland Security.

Dorril, S. (2001) *MI6: Fifty Years of Special Operations.* London: Fourth Estate.

Doyle, C. (2002) *The USA PATRIOT Act: A Legal Analysis.* Washington, DC: Congressional Research Service.

Draper, T.H. (1997) 'Is the CIA necessary?' *The New York Review of Books*, 14 August, p. 18.

Dubourg, R. and Prichard, S. (2007) 'Organised crime: revenues, economic and social costs, and criminal assets available for seizure', Home Office Online Report 14/07. London: Home Office.

Eade, D. (1997) *Capacity Building: An Approach to People Centered Development.* Oxford: Oxfam.

Eade, D. (2007) 'Capacity building: who builds whose capacity?' *Development in Practice*, 17(4–5): 630–639.

Eck, J.E. and Spelman, W. (1987) *Problem Solving: Problem-Orientated Policing in Newport News.* Washington, DC: Police Executive Research Forum.

Ellsberg, D. (2003) *Secrets: A Memoir of Vietnam and the Pentagon Papers.* New York: Viking Press.

Elsea, J. (2010) *Criminal Prohibition on the Publication of Classified Defense Information.* Washington, DC: Congressional Research Service (No. R41404).

Enemark, C. (2007) *Disease and Security.* London: Routledge.

Erskine, T. (2004) 'As rays of light to the human soul? Moral agents and intelligence gathering', *Intelligence and National Security*, 19(2): 359–381.

Evans, M. (2009) 'Influencing decision-makers with intelligence and analytical products', in J.H. Ratcliffe (ed.) *Strategic Thinking in Criminal Intelligence*, 2nd edn. Sydney: Federation Press.

FAS (1995) 'PDD35 Intelligence Requirements', in *Presidential Directives and Executive Orders.* Washington, DC: Federation of American Scientists.

Feris, S. (2003) 'Netcentric warfare, C4ISR and information operations: towards a revolution in military intelligence?' *Intelligence and National Security*, 19(2): 199–225.

Finnane, M. (1994) *Police and Government: Histories of Policing in Australia*. Oxford: Oxford University Press.

Firth, S. (2005) 'A new era in security', in J. Henderson and G. Watson (eds) *Securing a Peaceful Pacific*. Christchurch: University of Canterbury Press.

Fisher, A. (2001) *Critical Thinking: An Introduction*. Cambridge: Cambridge University Press.

Flood, B. and Gasper, R. (2009) 'Strategic aspects of the UK National Intelligence Model', in J.H. Ratcliffe (ed.) *Strategic Thinking in Criminal Intelligence*, 2nd edn. Sydney: Federation Press.

Flood, P. (2004) *Report of the Inquiry into Australian Intelligence Agencies*. Canberra: Government Printing Office.

Frankel, M. (2010) 'Secrets shared with millions are not secret', *Guardian*, 1 December. Available at: http://www.guardian.co.uk/commentisfree/cifamerica/2010/nov/30/wiki leaks-secrets-pentagon-papers (accessed 19 January 2011).

Garzarelli, L. (2004) 'Correctional administrator's attitudes: making a difference in correctional intelligence gathering and sharing', *Corrections Today*: 119–121.

Gates, R. and Mullen, M. (2010) 'US Department of Defense news transcript', US Department of Defense, The Pentagon, 30 November 2010. Available at: http://www. defense.gov/transcripts/transcript.aspx?transcriptid=4728 (accessed 19 January 2011).

Gendron, A. (2005) 'Just war, just intelligence; an ethical approach for foreign espionage', *International Journal of Intelligence and Counterintelligence*, 18(3): 398–435.

George, R. (2004) 'Fixing the problem of analytical mind-sets: alternative analysis', *International Journal of Intelligence and Counterintelligence*, 17(3): 385–405.

George, R. and Bruce, J. (2008) *Analysing Intelligence, Origins, Obstacles, and Innovations*. Washington, DC: Georgetown University Press.

Gill, P. (1996a) 'Sack the spooks: do we need an internal security apparatus?' *The Socialist Register*, 32: 1–23.

Gill, P. (1996b) 'Reasserting control: recent changes in the oversight of the UK intelligence community', *Intelligence and National Security*, 11(2): 313–331.

Gill, P. (2000) *Rounding up the Usual Suspects? Developments in Contemporary Law Enforcement Intelligence*. Aldershot: Ashgate.

Gill, P. (2007) 'Evaluating intelligence oversight committees', *Intelligence and National Security*, 22(1): 14–37.

Gill, P. and Phythian, M. (2006) *Intelligence in an Insecure World*. Cambridge: Polity Press.

Gill, P., Marrin, S. and Phythian, M. (eds) (2009) *Intelligence Theory: Key Questions and Debates*. New York: Routledge.

Gilpin, R. (1988) *The Political Economy of International Relations*. Princeton, NJ: Princeton University Press.

GIWG (2003) *The National Criminal Intelligence Sharing Plan*. Washington, DC: Department of Justice (Global Intelligence Working Group). Available at: http://.iir.com/ global/products/NCISP_Plan.pdf (accessed 1 August 2010).

GIWG (2005) *The National Criminal Intelligence Sharing Plan* (revised June 2005). Washington, DC: Department of Justice (Global Intelligence Working Group).

Goodman, M. (2003) '9/11: the failure of strategic intelligence', *Intelligence and National Security*, 18(4): 59–71.

Grabo, C. (2005) *Anticipating Surprise: Analysis for Strategic Warning*. Washington, DC: University Press of America.

Grieve, J. (2009) 'Developments in UK criminal intelligence', in J.H Ratcliffe (ed.) *Strategic Thinking in Criminal Intelligence*, 2nd edn. Sydney: Federation Press.

Gronvall, G., Bouri, N., Rambia, K., Franco, C. and Watson, M. (2009) 'Prevention of biothreats: a look ahead', *Biosecurity and Bioterrorism*, 7(4): 433–441.

Guidetti, R. (2010) 'Rethinking the purpose of fusion centers', *The Police Chief*. Alexandria: International Association of Police Chiefs. Available at: http://policechiefmagazine.org/magazine/index.cfm?fuseaction=display_arch&article_id=2017&issue_id=22010 (accessed 3 September 2010).

Gunnarsson, C. (2001) *Capacity Building, Institutional Crisis and the Issue of Recurrent Cost: Synthesis Report*. Stockholm: Almkvist and Wiksell International.

Gursky, E., Inglesby, T. and O' Toole, T. (2003) 'Anthrax 2001: observations on the medical and public health response', *Biosecurity and Bioterrorism*, 1: 97–110.

Hamilton, D. (2006) *Inside Canadian Intelligence*. Toronto: Dundurn Press.

Hamm, M. (2009) 'Prison Islam in the age of sacred terror', *British Journal of Criminology*, 49: 667–685.

Hammond, E. (ed.) (2006) 'Synthetic Biology Working Group Presentation', at the Meeting of the National Science Advisory Board for Biosecurity (NSABB), Bethesda, MD.

Hampson, F.O., Daudelin, J., Hay, J.B., Reid, H. and Marting, T. (2002) *Madness in the Multitude: Human Security and World Disorder*. Toronto: Oxford University Press.

Hatlebrekke, K. and Smith, M. (2010) 'Towards a new theory of intelligence failure? The impact of cognitive closure and discourse failure', *Intelligence and National Security*, 25(2): 147–182.

Hawley, M. and Marden, B. (2006) 'FIM: a business information system for intelligence', *International Journal of Intelligence and Counterintelligence*, 19(3): 443–456.

Health Canada (2003) *Learning from SARS: Renewal of Public Health in Canada*. Ottawa: Health Canada.

Hedley, J. (2005) 'Learning from intelligence failures', *International Journal of Intelligence and Counterintelligence*, 18(3): 435–450.

Heldon, C. (2009) 'Exploratory intelligence tools', in J.H. Ratcliffe (ed.) *Strategic Thinking in Criminal Intelligence*, 2nd edn. Sydney: Federation Press.

Henderson, J. and Watson, G. (eds) (2005) *A New Era in Security*. Christchurch: Canterbury University Press.

Herman, M. (1996) *Intelligence Power in Peace and War*. Cambridge: Cambridge University Press.

Herman, M. (2009) 'Ethics and intelligence after September 2001', in C. Andrew, R. Aldrich and W. Wark (eds) *Secret Intelligence*. London: Routledge.

Hersh, S. (2003) 'Selective intelligence', *The New Yorker*, 12 May, pp. 1–8.

Hersh, S. (2004) *Chain of Command*. London: Penguin Books.

Heuer, R. (1999) *Psychology of Intelligence Analysis*. Washington, DC: Center for the Study of Intelligence, Government Printing Office.

Heuer, R. and Pherson, R. (2010) *Structured Analytic Techniques*. Washington, DC: CQ Press.

Hinman, L. (2003) *Ethics*. Belmont, CA: Thomson.

Hitchcock, P., Chamberlain, A., Van Wagoner, M., Inglesby, T. and O'Toole, T. (2007) 'Challenges to global surveillance and response to infectious disease outbreaks of international importance', *Biosecurity and Bioterrorism*, 5(3): 206–227.

Hitz, F. and Weiss, B. (2004) 'Helping the CIA and FBI connect the dots in the war on terror', *International Journal of Intelligence and Counterintelligence*, 17(1): 1–42.

HMIC (1997) *Policing with Intelligence*. London: Her Majesty's Inspectorate of Constabulary.

HMIC (2000) *Calling Time on Crime*. London: Her Majesty's Inspectorate of Constabulary.

HMIC (2005) *Closing the Gap: A Review of the 'Fitness for Purpose' of the Current Structures of Policing in England and Wales*. London: Home Office.

HMIC (2008) *The Role of Her Majesty's Inspectorate of Constabulary*. London: Home Office.

Home Office (2002) *The National Policing Plan*. London: Home Office.

Hope, R. (1979) *Protective Security Review*. Canberra: Australian Government Publishing Service.

Horton, M. and Airs, S. (2009) 'Border agencies working together', *MAF Biosecurity NZ*. Wellington, New Zealand: MAF Biosecurity NZ.

HSC (2005) *The Human Security Centre: Human Security Report*. Oxford: Oxford University Press.

Hulnick, A. (2004) *Keeping Us Safe: Secret Intelligence and Homeland Security*. Westport, CT: Praeger.

Hulnick, A. (2008) 'Intelligence reform 2008: where to from here?' *International Journal of Intelligence and Counterintelligence*, 21(4): 621–635.

IGIS (2007) *IGIS Annual Report 2006–2007*. Canberra: Commonwealth of Australia.

Innes, M. and Sheptycki, J. (2004) 'From detection to disruption: intelligence and the changing logic of police crime control in the UK', *International Criminal Justice Review*, 14: 1–24.

IPCC (2007) *Independent Police Complaints Commission (Stockwell) Investigation into the Shooting of Jean Charles de Menezes on 22 July 2005*. London: Independent Police Complaints Commission.

ISCR (2010) *Prisons and Terrorism: Radicalisation and De-radicalisation in 15 Countries*. London: International Centre for the Study of Radicalisation and Political Violence, Kings College.

ISE (2009) *ISE Progress and Plans Annual Report to the Congress, Prepared by the Program Manager, Information Sharing Environment (June)*. Washington, DC: Information Sharing Environment.

ISE (2010) *Nationwide Suspicious Activity Reporting Initiative Status Report – February*. Washington, DC: Program Manager, Information Sharing Environment.

Jeffreys-Jones, R. (2007) *The FBI*. New York: Yale University Press.

Jervis, R. (1976) *Perception and Misperception in International Politics*. Princeton, NJ: Princeton University Press.

Jervis, R. (2009) 'Reports, politics, and intelligence failures', in C. Andrew, R. Aldrich and W. Wark (eds) *Secret Intelligence*. London: Routledge.

Johnson, L. (ed.) (2009) *Handbook of Intelligence Studies*. New York: Routledge.

Johnston, A. (1995) 'Cultural realism: strategic culture and grand strategy in Chinese history', in P. Katzenstein (ed.) *Culture of National Security*. Princeton, NJ: Princeton University Press.

Jones, D. (2005) 'Structures of bio-terrorism preparedness in the UK and the US: responses to 9/11 and the anthrax attacks', *British Journal of Politics and International Relations*, 7: 340–352.

Kahn, D. (1996) *The Codebreakers: The Story of Secret Writing*. New York: Scribner.

Kahn, D. (2001) 'A historical theory of intelligence', *Intelligence and National Security*, 16(3): 79–92.

Kaplan, D. (2000) 'Capacity building: shifting the paradigms of practice', *Development in Practice*, 10(3–4): 517–526.

Katona, P., Sullivan, J.A. and Intriligator, M. (eds) (2010) *Global Security*. London: Routledge.

Katzenstein, P. (ed.) (1996) *The Culture of National Security.* New York: Columbia University Press.

Kelling, G. and Wycoff, M. (2002) *Evolving Strategy of Policing: Case Studies of Strategic Change.* Washington, DC: National Institute of Justice.

Kent, S. (1949) *Strategic Intelligence for American World Policy.* Princeton, NJ: Princeton University Press.

Keohane, R. (1984) *After Hegemony: Cooperation and Discord in the World Political Economy.* Princeton, NJ: Princeton University Press.

Koblentz, G. (2009) *Living Weapons: Biological Warfare and International Security.* Ithaca, NY: Cornell University Press.

Koschade, S. (2006) 'A social network analysis of Jemaah Islamiyah: the applications to counterterrorism and intelligence', *Studies in Conflict and Terrorism,* 29: 559–575.

Kovacs, A. (1997) 'The nonuse of intelligence', *International Journal of Intelligence and Counterintelligence,* 10(4): 383–417.

Krasner, S. (ed.) (1983) *International Regimes.* Ithaca, NY: Cornell University Press.

Lakshmanan, I. (2011) 'US helping secret sources put at risk by WikiLeaks cables', 8 January, *Bloomberg.* Available at: http://www.bloomberg.com/news/2011-01-07/u-s-helping-secret-sources-put-at-risk-by-wikileaks-cables.html (accessed 19 January 2011).

Lefebvre, S. (2010) 'Canada's legal framework for intelligence', *International Journal of Intelligence and Counterintelligence,* 23(2): 247–295.

Leonnig, C. and Linzer, D. (2005) 'Judges on surveillance court to be briefed on spy program', *The Washington Post,* 22 December.

Lew, J. (2010) 'Memorandum for the heads of executive departments and agencies. WikiLeaks: mishandling of classified information', *Office of Management and Budget.* Available at: http://www.whitehouse.gov/sites/default/files/omb/memoranda/2010/m11-06.pdf (accessed 19 January 2011).

Lew, J. (2011) 'Memorandum for the heads of executive departments and agencies. Initial assessment of safeguarding and counter-intelligence postures for classified national security information in automated systems', *Office of Management and Budget.* Available at: http://www.whitehouse.gov/sites/default/files/omb/memoranda/2011/m11-08.pdf (accessed 19 January 2011).

Los Angeles Times, The (2002) 'Sharp note from a whistleblower', *The Los Angeles Times,* 28 May.

Lovell, D., McCallister, I., Maley, M. and Kukathas, C. (1995) *The Australian Political System.* Melbourne: Longman.

Low, W. and Davenport, E. (2002) 'NGO capacity building and sustainability in the Pacific', *Asia Pacific View Point,* 43(3): 367–379.

McCue, C. (2007) *Data Mining and Predictive Analysis.* Burlington, MA: Butterworth-Heinemann.

McDonald, D. (1981a) *Commission of Enquiry Concerning Certain Activities of the RCMP.* Ottawa: Minister of Supply and Services.

McDonald, D. (1981b) *Commission of Inquiry Concerning Certain Activities of the Royal Canadian Mounted Police (McDonald Inquiry), Second Report, Freedom and Security Under the Law.* Ottawa: Minister of Supply and Services.

McDonald, G. (2007) 'Control orders and preventative detention: why alarm is misguided', in A. Lynch, E. McDonald and G. William (eds) *Law and Liberty in the War on Terror.* Sydney: Federation Press.

McGarrell, E.F., Freilich, J.D. and Chermak, S. (2007) 'Intelligence-led policing as a framework for responding to terrorism', *Journal of Contemporary Criminal Justice*, 23(2): 142–158.

Mackay, H. (2005) *Right and Wrong*. Sydney: Hodder.

Mackenzie, D. (2009) 'Revealed: scientific evidence for the 2001 anthrax attacks', *New Scientist*, No. 2697.

Maguire, M. and John, T. (2004) 'The National Intelligence Model: early implementation experience in three police forces', Home Office Online Report, 30/04. London: Home Office.

Manning, D. (2005) 'The secret Downing St memo', *The Sunday Times*, 1 May.

Markle Foundation (2003) *Creating a Trusted Information Network for Homeland Security*. New York: Markle Foundation Task Force.

Marks, R. (1978) *Report to the Minister for Administrative Services on the Organisation of Police Resources in the Commonwealth Area and Related Matters*. Canberra: Government Printing Office.

Marrin, S. (2009) 'Intelligence analysis and decision-making: methodological challenges', in P. Gill, S. Marrin, and M. Phythian (eds) *Intelligence Theory*. London: Routledge.

Marrin, S. and Clemente, J. (2006) 'Modelling an intelligence analysis profession on medicine', *International Journal of Intelligence and Counterintelligence*, 19(4): 642–665.

Mayer, J. (2008) *The Dark Side: The Inside Story of How the War on Terror Turned into a War on American Ideals*. New York: Doubleday.

Mazarr, M. (2007) *Unmodern Men in the Modern World*. New York: Cambridge University Press.

Mickolus, E. (2002) 'How do we know we're winning the war against terrorists? Issues in measurement', *Studies in Conflict and Terrorism*, 25: 151–160.

Moore, D. (2007) *Critical Thinking and Intelligence Analysis*, National Defense Intelligence College Occasional Paper. Washington, DC: National Defense Intelligence College.

Moore, D., Krizan, L. and Moore, J. (2005) 'Evaluating intelligence: a competency based model', *International Journal of Intelligence and Counterintelligence*, 18(2): 204–220.

NCPE (2005) *Guidance on the National Intelligence Model*. Wyboston, UK: National Centre for Policing Excellence on Behalf of ACPO.

NCPE (2006) *Guidance on the Management of Police Information*. Wyboston, UK: National Centre for Policing Excellence on Behalf of ACPO.

Newbery, S., Brecher, B., Sands, P. and Stewart, B. (2009) 'Interrogation, intelligence and the issue of human rights', *Intelligence and National Security*, 24(5): 631–643.

New York Times, The (2010) 'The New Team', *The New York Times*, 1 August. Available at: http://projects.nytimes.com/44th_president/new_team/show/leon-panetta (accessed 25 August 2010).

New Zealand Biosecurity Council (2003) *Tiakina Aotearoa: Protect New Zealand: Biosecurity Strategy for New Zealand*. Wellington: Biosecurity Council.

Norton-Taylor, R. (1995) *Truth Is a Difficult Concept: Inside the Scott Inquiry*. London: Fourth Estate.

NPIA (2007) *Practice Advice on the Resources and the People Assets of the National Intelligence Model*. Wyboston, UK: National Policing Improvement Agency on Behalf of ACPO.

NPIA (2008) *Practice Advice on Analysis*. Wyboston, UK: National Policing Improvement Agency.

Nuzzo, J. (2009) 'Developing a national biosurveillance program', *Biosecurity and Bioterrorism*, 7(1): 37–38.

Oakley, R., Dziedzic, M. and Goldberg, E. (eds) (1998) *Policing the New World. Disorder:*

Peace Operations and Public Security. Washington, DC: National Defense University Press.

Obama, B. (2009a) *Remarks by the President on a New Beginning*, Cairo University, Cairo, Egypt. Available at: http://www.whitehouse.gov/the_press_office/Remarks-by-the-President-at-Cairo-University-6-04-09/ (accessed 24 August 2010).

Obama, B. (2009b) *Executive Order No. 13491: Ensuring Lawful Interrogation* (74 FEA REG.4893 January 22, 2009). Washington, DC: White House.

O'Connor, D. (2006) *A New Mechanism for the RCMP's National Security Activities: Commission of Inquiry into the Actions of Canadian Officials in Relation to Maher Arar*. Ottawa: Public Works and Government Services Canada. Available at: http://www.sirc-csars.gc.ca/pdfs/cm_arar_rcmpgrc-eng.pdf (accessed 4 August 2010).

ODNI (2007) *Intelligence Community Directive Number 203: Analytic Standards (Effective 21 June 2007)*. Washington, DC: Office of the Director, National Intelligence.

ODNI (2008) *Data Mining Report*. Washington, DC: Office of the Director, National Intelligence.

ODNI (2009a) *National Intelligence Strategy*. Washington, DC: Office of the Director, National Intelligence.

ODNI (2009b) *ODNI Intelligence Community Legal Reference Book*. Washington, DC: Office of the Director, National Intelligence.

OECD (2006) *Whole of Government Approach to Fragile States Report*. Paris: OECD.

Office of the Inspector General (2010) *A Review of the FBI's Use of Exigent Letters and Other Informal Requests for Telephone Records* (January). Washington, DC: Office of the Inspector General, Department of Justice.

Olbermann, K. (2006) *Olbermann and MCA: The Beginning of the End of America*, 19 October (transcript of television program). Available at: http://www.historycommons.org/entity.jsp?entity=keith_olbermann_1 (accessed 24 August 2010).

O'Leary, Z. (2007) *The Essential Guide to Doing Research*. London: Sage Publications.

Ormand, D. (2009) 'Ethical guidelines in using secret intelligence for public security,' in C. Andrew, R. Aldrich and W. Wark (eds) *Secret Intelligence*. London: Routledge.

O'Sullivan, M. (2009) 'Stern Hu "Thrown to the Wolves"', *Sydney Morning Herald*, 11 July.

O'Toole, T. and Inglesby, T. (2003) 'Toward biosecurity', *Biosecurity and Bioterrorism*, 1(1): 1–3.

O'Toole, T. and Inglesby, T. (2009) 'Strategic priorities for U.S biosecurity', *Biosecurity and Bioterrorism*, 7(1): 25–28.

Pawson, R. and Tilley, N. (1997) *Realistic Evaluation*. London: Sage.

PDD35 (1995) *Presidential Decision Directive 35*. Federation of American Scientists (Intelligence Resources Program). Available at: http://www.fas.org/irp/offdocs/pdd35.htm (accessed 4 August 2010).

Peterson, M. (2005) *Intelligence-led Policing: The New Intelligence Architecture*. Washington, DC: Bureau of Justice Administration.

Phythian, M. (2009) 'Intelligence theory and theories of international relations,' in P. Gill, S. Marrin, and M. Phythian (eds) *Intelligence Theory*. London: Routledge.

Pilger, J. (2011) 'Exclusive interview: Julian Assange on Murdoch, Manning and the threat from China', *New Statesman*, 12 January. Available at: http://www.newstatesman.com/blogs/the-staggers/2011/01/china-wikileaks-assange (accessed 19 January 2011).

Posner, R. (2005) *Preventing Surprise Attack: Intelligence Reform in the Wake of 9/11*, Lanham, MD: Rowman and Littlefield.

Prowse, S., Perkins, N. and Field, H. (2009) 'Strategies for enhancing Australia's capacity to respond to emerging infectious diseases', *Veterinaria Italiana*, 45(1): 67–78.

Prunckun, H. (2010) *Handbook of Scientific Methods of Inquiry for Intelligence Analysis*. Lanham, MD: Scarecrow Press, Inc.

Pye, L. and Verba, S. (eds) (1965) *Political Culture and Political Development*. Princeton, NJ: Princeton University Press.

Quarmby, N. (2009) 'Futures work in strategic criminal intelligence', in J.H. Ratcliffe (ed.) *Strategic Thinking in Criminal Intelligence*, 2nd edn. Sydney: Federation Press.

RAHS (2007) *Risk Assessment and Horizon Scanning*. Singapore: National Security Coordination Centre.

Ramsay, M. (2009) 'Can the torture of terrorist suspects be justified?' in C. Andrew, R. Aldrich and W. Wark (eds) *Secret Intelligence*. London: Routledge.

Ramsden, P. (1992) *Learning to Teach in Higher Education*. London: Routledge.

RAND (2008) *Radicalisation or Rehabilitation: Understanding the Challenge of Extremist and Radicalised Prisoners*. Washington, DC: RAND Corporation.

Ratcliffe, J.H. (2001) 'Policing urban burglary', *Trends and Issues in Crime and Criminal Justice*, 213: 1–6.

Ratcliffe, J.H. (2002) 'Intelligence-led policing and the problems of turning rhetoric into practice', *Policing and Society*, 12(1): 53–66.

Ratcliffe, J.H. (2003) 'Intelligence-led policing', *Trends and Issues in Crime and Criminal Justice*, Australian Institute of Criminology, paper 248.

Ratcliffe, J.H. (ed.) (2004) *Strategic Thinking in Criminal Intelligence*. Sydney: Federation Press.

Ratcliffe, J.H. (2005) 'The effectiveness of police intelligence management: a New Zealand case study', *Police Practice and Research*, 6(2): 435–451.

Ratcliffe, J.H. (2008) *Intelligence-Led Policing*. Cullompton: Willan Publishing.

Ratcliffe, J.H. (ed.) (2009) *Strategic Thinking in Criminal Intelligence*, 2nd edn. Sydney: Federation Press.

Rejali, D. (2007) *Torture and Democracy*. Princeton, NJ: Princeton University Press.

Renfro, R. and Deckro, R. (2001) *A Social Network Analysis of the Iranian Government*. Washington, DC: National Security Agency and National Air Intelligence Center, 69th MORS Symposium, 12–14 June.

Rieber, S. (2004) 'Intelligence analysis and judgmental calibration', *International Journal of Intelligence and Counterintelligence*, 17(1): 97–112.

Robbins, S., Bergman, R., Stags, I.A. and Coulter, M. (2006) *Management*. Englewood Cliffs, NJ: Prentice-Hall.

Roberts, K. (in press) 'Social psychology and terrorism investigations', in J. Pearse (ed.) *Investigating Terrorism*. Chichester: John Wiley & Sons,.

Robson, C. (2002) *Real World Research*. Oxford: Blackwell Publishing.

Rogers, K. (2009) 'Developments in Australian strategic criminal intelligence,' in J.H. Ratcliffe (ed.) *Strategic Thinking in Criminal Intelligence*, 2nd edn. Sydney: Federation Press.

Rose-Ackerman, S. (ed.) (2004) *Establishing the Rule of Law*. Princeton, NJ: Princeton University Press.

Rovner, J. and Long, A. (2005) 'Intelligence failure and reform: evaluating the 9/11 Commission Report', *Breakthroughs*, 14(1): 10–21.

Royal Society (2009) *An Integrated Approach to Infectious Diseases in the UK*, RS Policy Document 2/09. London: The Royal Society.

Rudd, K. (2008) *The First National Security Statement to the Australian Parliament. Address by the Prime Minister of Australia, the Hon. Kevin Rudd MP*. 4 December.

Rudner, M. (2006) 'Protecting North America's energy infrastructure against terrorism', *International Journal of Intelligence and Counterintelligence*, 19(3): 424–442.

Ryan, J. and Glarum, J. (2008) *Biosecurity and Bioterrorism*. Burlington, MA: Elsevier.

Sands, P. (2009) *Torture Team: Rumsfeld's Memo and the Betrayal of American Values*. New York: Palgrave Macmillan.

SAS (2009) 'SAS for homeland security', 1–4. Available at: http://www.sas.com/resources/ brochure/homeland-security-brochure.pdf (accessed 6 March 2011).

Scott, L. and Jackson, P. (eds) (2004) *Understanding Intelligence in the Twenty-First Century*. London: Routledge.

Seifert, J. (2004) *Data Mining: An Overview*. Washington, DC: Congressional Research Service.

Sheptycki, J. (2000) 'Introduction', in J. Sheptycki (ed.) *Issues in Transnational Policing*. London: Routledge.

Shoham, S., Beck, O. and Kett, M. (eds) (2007) *International Handbook of Penology and Criminal Justice*. Boca Raton, FL: CRC Press.

Sims, J. and Burton, G. (eds) (2005) *Transforming US Intelligence*. Washington, DC: Georgetown University Press.

Skillicorn, D. (2009) *Knowledge Discovery for Counterterrorism and Law Enforcement*. Boca Raton, FL: CRC Press.

Skogan, W.G. (2006) 'The promise of community policing', in D. Weisburd and A. Braga (eds) *Policing Innovation: Contrasting Perspectives*. New York: Cambridge University Press.

SOCA (2009) *The UK Threat Assessment of Organised Crime 2009/10*. London: Serious Organised Crime Agency.

Spalek, B. and El Hassan, S. (2007) 'Muslim converts in prison', *The Howard Journal*, 46(2): 99–114.

Sparrow, M. (1991) 'Network vulnerabilities and strategic intelligence in law enforcement', *International Journal of Intelligence and Counterintelligence*, 5(3): 255–274.

SSCI (1994) *An Assessment of the Aldrich H. Ames Espionage Case and its Implications for US Intelligence*. Washington, DC: Government Printing Office.

SSCI (2004) *Report on the US Intelligence Community's Prewar Intelligence Assessments on Iraq*. Washington, DC: Government Printing Office.

SSCI (2010) *Attempted Terrorist Attack on Northwest Airlines Flight 253. Report on the Senate Committee on Intelligence United States Senate Together with Additional Views* (111th Congress, 2nd Session). Washington, DC: Government Printing Office.

SSCI and House Permanent Select Committee on Intelligence (2002) *Joint Inquiry into Intelligence Community Activities Before and After the Terrorist Attacks of September 11, 2001* (107th Congress, 2nd Session). Washington, DC: Government Printing Office.

Stengel, R. (2010) 'TIME's Julian Assange interview: full transcript/audio', *Time*, 1 December. Available at: http://www.time.com/time/world/article/0,8599,2034040,00. html (accessed 6 March 2011).

Stewart, S. (2010) 'WikiLeaks and the wacky world of classified information', 1 November. Available at: http://www.thecuttingedgenews.com/index.php?article=21731&pageid= 20&pagename=Security (accessed 19 January 2011).

Stout, D. (2007) 'FBI head admits mistakes in use of Security Act', *The New York Times*, 10 March, p. A1.

Sullivan, J. and Bauer, A. (2008) *Terrorism Early Warning: Ten Years of Achievement in Fighting Terrorism and Crime*. Los Angeles: Los Angeles County Sheriff's Department.

Sun Tzu (2002) *The Art of War*. New York: Dover Publications.

Suskind, R. (2006) *The One-Percent Doctrine: Deep Inside America's Pursuit of Its Enemies Since 9/11*. New York: Simon and Schuster.

Taylor, S. and Goldman, D. (2004) 'Intelligence reform: will more agencies, money, and personnel help?' *Intelligence and National Security*, 19(3): 416–435.

Tenet, G. (2002) *Written Statement for the Record of DCI before the Joint Inquiry Committee*, 17 October. Available at: www.fas.org./irp/congress/2002_hr/101702tenet.html (accessed 6 September 2010).

Tenet, G. (2007) *At the Center of the Storm: My Years at the CIA*. New York: HarperCollins.

Transparency International (2007) *Policy Paper Number 1/2007*. Berlin: Transparency International.

Travers, R. (1997) 'The coming intelligence failure', *Studies in Intelligence*, 1: 35–43.

Treverton, G. (2008) 'Intelligence analysis: between "politicisation" and irrelevance', in R. George and J. Bruce (eds) *Analysing Intelligence: Origins, Obstacles, and Innovations*. Washington, DC: George Washington University Press.

Tumin, Z. (2007) *Closing the Information Gap in Biosecurity Readiness*, Working Paper 011.007. Cambridge, MA: John F. Kennedy School of Government, Harvard University.

Turner, M. (2004) 'A distinctive U.S. intelligence identity', *International Journal of Intelligence and Counterintelligence*, 17: 42–61.

Tusikov, N. and Fahlman, R. (2009) 'Threat and risk assessments', in J.H. Ratcliffe (ed.) *Strategic Thinking in Criminal Intelligence*, 2nd edn. Sydney: Federation Press.

Tversky, A. and Kahneman, D. (1974) 'Judgment under uncertainty heuristics and biases', *Science*, 185: 1124–1131.

UNDP (nd) *Governance for Sustainable Human Development*. A UNDP policy document (executive summary). Available at: http://www.mirror.undp.org/magnet/policy/summary. htm (accessed 4 March 2011).

UNDP (1997) *Capacity Development: Technical Advisory Paper 2*. New York: United Nations Development Program. Available at: http://www.mirror.undp.org/magnet/Docs/ cap/Capdeven.pdf (accessed 4 March 2011).

UNDP (2002) *National Program for Strengthening Good Governance for Poverty Reduction in Rwanda*. New York: United Nations Development Program.

UNDP (2007) *Capacity Assessment Methodology: User's Guide (May 2007)*. Geneva: United Nations Development Program.

US Army (2006) *Field Manual 2-22.3 (FM 34-52)*. Washington, DC: Department of the Army.

US Military (2002) 'Secret ORCON interrogation log detainee 063'. Published in *Time*, 12 June 2005.

US Senate Committee on the Judiciary (2008) *Senate Committee on the Judiciary Concerning Detainee Interrogation Techniques: Do They Work, Are They Reliable and What Did the FBI Know About Them?* Washington, DC: Senate Committee on the Judiciary. Available at: http://judiciary.senate.gov/hearings/hearing.cfm?id=3399 (accessed 24 August 2010).

Vander Beken, T. (2004) 'Risky business: a risk based methodology to measure organised crime', *Crime Law and Social Change*, 41: 471–516.

Vito, G.F., Walsh, W.F.A. and Kunselman, J. (2005) 'Compstat: the manager's perspective', *International Journal of Police Science and Management*, 7(3): 187–196.

Walker, J. (1993) 'How big is global money laundering?' *Journal of Money Laundering Control*, 3(1): 25–37.

Walkley Foundation, The (2010) 'Australian media's finest defends WikiLeaks', *The Walkley Foundation*, 13 December. Available at: http://www.walkleys.com/news/1076/ (accessed 18 January 2010).

Walsh, P. (2005) 'Intelligence-led policing: evolving Australian perspectives', paper presented at International Forum on Intelligence-Led Policing, Hangzhou, China.

Walsh, P. (2007a) 'Knowledge from evaluating intelligence', *AIPIO Journal*, 15(3): 31–49.

Walsh, P. (2007b) 'Managing intelligence: innovation and implications for management', in M. Mitchell and J. Casey (eds) *Police Leadership and Management*. Sydney: Federation Press.

Walsh, P. and Ratcliffe, J.H. (2005) 'Strategic criminal intelligence education: a collaborative approach', *IALEIA Journal*, 16: 152–166.

Walsh, W.A. and Vito, G. (2004) 'The meaning of COMPSTAT', *Journal of Contemporary Criminal Justice*, 20(1): 51–69.

Walsh, W.F. (2001) 'Compstat: an analysis of an emerging police managerial paradigm', *Policing: An International Journal of Police Strategies and Management*, 24(3): 347–362.

Wasserman, S. and Faust, K. (1994) *Social Network Analysis: Methods and Applications*. Cambridge: Cambridge University Press.

Watson, G. (2005) 'Conflict overview', in J. Henderson and G. Watson (eds) *Securing a Peaceful Pacific*. Christchurch: Canterbury University Press.

Weiner, T. (2007) *Legacy of Ashes: The History of the CIA*. New York: Doubleday.

Weiss, R. and South, N. (eds) (1998) *Comparing Prison Systems: Towards a Comparative International Penology*. Amsterdam: Gordon and Breach.

Westphal, C. (2009) *Data Mining for Intelligence, Fraud, and Criminal Detection*. Boca Raton, FL: CRC Press.

Wood, J. (1997) *Final Report of the Royal Commission into the NSW Police Service*: Vol. 2: *Reform*. Sydney: RCNSWPS.

Wood, J. and Adler, J. (2001) 'Gang activity in English prisons: the staff perspective', *Psychology, Crime and Law*, 7(1): 167–192.

Woolsey, J. (n.d.) 'R. James Woolsey: uncompromising defender', *The Center for the Study of Intelligence*, CIA. Available at: https://www.cia.gov/library/center-for-the-study-of-intelligence/csi-publications/books-and-monographs/directors-of-central-intelligence-as-leaders-of-the-u-s-intelligence-community/chapter_12.htm#_ftn1 (accessed 4 August 2010).

Zegart, A. (2007) *Spying Blind*, Princeton, NJ: Princeton University Press.

Index